Fortress-Churches of Languedoc traces the changing relationship between military and religious realms as expressed in the architecture of medieval Europe. The scholarship of medieval architecture has traditionally imposed a division between military and ecclesiastical structures. Often, however, medieval churches were provided with fortified enclosures, crenellations, iron-barred doors, and other elements of defense. In her study of fortress-churches, Sheila Bonde focuses on three twelfth-century monuments located in southern France—Maguelone, Agde, and Saint-Pons-de-Thomière, which are among the earliest examples of the type. She provides new surveyed plans of these structures, as well as a reexamination of their documentation, which is here presented both in the original Latin and in new English translations. *Fortress-Churches of Languedoc* also explores the larger context of fortification and authority in twelfth-century Languedoc and examines the dynamics of architectural exchange and innovation in the Mediterranean at a moment of critical historical importance.

FORTRESS-CHURCHES OF LANGUEDOC

Architecture, Religion, and Conflict in the High Middle Ages

FORTRESS-CHURCHES OF LANGUEDOC

Architecture, Religion, and Conflict in the High Middle Ages

Sheila Bonde

Brown University

CAMBRIDGE UNIVERSITY PRESS

Published by the Press Syndicate of the University of Cambridge
The Pitt Building, Trumpington Street, Cambridge CB2 1RP
40 West 20th Street, New York, NY 10011–4211, USA
10 Stamford Road, Oakleigh, Victoria 3166, Australia

First published 1994

Printed in the United States of America

Library of Congress Cataloging–in –Publication Data

Bonde, Sheila.
    Fortress-churches of Languedoc : architecture, religion, and
conflict in the High Middle Ages / Sheila Bonde.
        p.   cm.
    Includes bibliographical references and index.
    ISBN 0-521-45084-5
        1. Church architecture—France—Languedoc.   2. Architecture,
Gothic—France—Languedoc.   I. Title.
    NA5549   L35B66   1994
    726' .5' 094480902—dc20   93-31741
                                                                 CIP

A catalog record for this book is available from the British Library

ISBN 0–521–45084–5 hardback

For my family

CONTENTS

LIST OF
ILLUSTRATIONS

ACKNOWLEDGMENTS

This book developed out of my curiosity about the apparent paradox of fortified churches. I first became aware of these buildings during work on my doctoral dissertation, which treated architecture at the time of the Norman Conquest. Following the model of the good historian of medieval architecture that I aspired to become, I began by amassing information exclusively on church buildings. I kept bumping into castles, however, seemingly at every turn. These castles were too big to be ignored and (I noticed with increasing annoyance) were too integrally connected with the construction histories of "my" churches to allow me to omit them from my analysis. When my attention had finally been diverted to their study, I began to see not only common patrons and design elements linking the building of castles and churches but also a number of frankly military aspects in many Anglo-Saxon and Anglo-Norman church towers. I was especially struck by the anomalous west façade of Lincoln Cathedral with its mural passages and machicolated arches. With the help of Peter Kidson and Richard Gem, I identified parallels for the Lincoln machicolations in the fortified churches of Languedoc. Thus began my decade-long fascination with the combination of military and religious elements that characterizes these buildings.

I was surprised to discover that these intriguing fortress-churches had attracted only a modest bibliography. Only three main sources exist: a chapter on fortified churches in the Zodiaque volume, *Languedoc Roman* (1985); survey articles in the 1950 *Congrès archéologique*; and Raymond Rey's *Les Vieilles Eglises Fortifiées du Midi de la France*, published in 1925, which provides an initial cataloguing of the monuments. Despite inevitable changes in scholarship since its publication over fifty years ago, Rey's book remains the standard in the field, and I am greatly indebted to it. The present study focuses on the three earliest machicolated fortress-churches and attempts to provide a wider architectural and historical context for them.

Throughout the past ten years of research I have incurred a number of debts that it is my pleasure to acknowledge here. My dissertation advisers, James Ackerman and Oleg Grabar, supported and encouraged my early interest in this not-very-mainstream material. I presented a short paper on the relationships between castle and church building in Anglo-Norman England (originally a chapter of my dissertation) at the University of Minnesota and published a version of those results in the Minnesota Medieval Series in 1986. Kay Reyerson, an editor of that volume, and the late Stephen Gardner, a participant in my session, both contributed to the development of my ideas on the subject of religious fortification.

A Henry Merritt Wriston fellowship from Brown University allowed me to spend the fall semester of 1987 in the south of France. A full year of research, 1989–90, was funded by sabbatical leave from Brown and by a Fulbright fellowship. I am grateful for these generous subventions, which gave me the time necessary to travel, look, measure, read, and, most importantly, to think.

In Montpellier, the staffs of the Direction des Antiquités, the Archives Départementales, and the Bibliothèque Municipale aided my research. At Agde, M. l'Archiprêtre Joseph Terré permitted access to the church. At Maguelone, the staff of the Association des Compagnons de Maguelone also permitted me access to the grounds and surviving structures. In Saint-Pons, I must acknowledge the kindness of many people: M. l'Archiprêtre Michel Quatrefages; Claire Granier of the Archives de Saint-Pons-de-Thomières; Jean-Paul Kherif and Jean Benoît of the Parc Naturel Régional du Haut-Languedoc, and the staff of the Service de l'Equipement.

During the period of research and writing, I benefited from discussion with a number of colleagues. The late Robert Saint-Jean discussed the buildings with me several times. Jean-Claude Richard shared the results of his excavations at Maguelone and his observations on that building. Marcel Durliat graciously answered questions on his work on Saint-Pons, as well as other issues. Janice Mann discussed her work on Loarre and enhanced my understanding of the fortification of religious sites in Spain. Fredric Cheyette shared his thoughts on systems of fortification in the Midi. Thomas N. Bisson kindly offered guidance for my study of the Peace of God in twelfth-century Languedoc, and suggested that I examine the struggles of Aldebert of Mende as a valuable textual parallel for the physical fortification of the Languedoc churches. William Clark, Vivian Paul, Amy G. Remensnyder, and Richard Sundt read and commented very helpfully on portions of the manuscript.

I have presented aspects of this research at conferences and in invited lectures: at Wellesley College in 1988, at the University of Minnesota in 1990, at the Rhode Island Medieval Circle in 1991, and in the ICMA-sponsored sessions on "The Representations and Concepts of War and Peace" organized by Carol Pendergast in Kalamazoo in 1992.

All of the plans, sections, and elevations for Maguelone, Agde, and Saint-Pons were measured and drawn by me in the the autumn of 1987, the summer of 1988, and the year of 1989–90. Many of the other plans in the book are also my own. Several Brown University students helped at various times, among whom I must mention Arabella Berkenbilt, Elizabeth Baer, and Mark Wilson. The translations found in the Appendixes are also my own, but here I am happy to acknowledge the very substantial help rendered by Michael Gleason.

In the physical production of the manuscript, I am pleased to acknowledge the help of Janice Prifty, Monica Bessette, Brooke Hammerle, and the staff of the Interlibrary Loan Office of Brown University. A grant from the Faculty Development Fund at Brown helped to defray the cost of photographic reproduction. Beatrice Rehl, fine arts editor at Cambridge University Press, and David Lott, managing editor at G&H SOHO, provided support and direction in the final stages.

Finally, I owe the greatest thanks to two people: Clark Maines, who helped immeasurably with ideas and photographs and with a critical reading of the manuscript, and my daughter Emma, who spent much of her first two years playing patiently in and around fortress-churches.

INTRODUCTION

The records of church councils bear witness to the presence of *ecclesiae incastellatae* across the medieval landscape. The relatively common medieval practice of fortifying churches may appear paradoxical to our modern sensibilities, which tend to regard castles as secular, functional creations of feudalism, and churches as more symbolic expressions of medieval spirituality. Indeed, castles and churches are seldom considered together in the literature on medieval architecture and are normally examined by different scholars. Contrary to the rather arbitrary division of modern scholarship, however, the two sets of monuments were often closely related, sharing common patrons, technological innovations, and designs. Evidence of this association is readily available in contemporary texts as well as in surviving buildings. Patrons responsible for the construction of both military and ecclesiastical buildings can be identified from documentary sources. Gundulf, bishop of Rochester in the late eleventh century, for example, supervised the construction of both the Tower of London and Rochester Cathedral.[1] His contemporary, Benno II, bishop of Osnabrück, is also credited with both castle and church projects.[2] The forms and techniques of single-nave plan, thick-wall construction, intramural gallery passages, stair vises, machicolation, and crenellation, are often shared by castle and church buildings.

Nowhere can this fusion of the secular and religious realms be seen more clearly than in the twelfth-century fortified churches of Maguelone, Agde, and Saint-Pons-de-Thomières. As hybrid fortress-cathedrals and abbeys, these buildings have seldom been incorporated into the history of either ecclesiastical or military architecture. Indeed, they can scarcely be cast as

Figure 1. Map of Gallia Narbonensis.

recognizable steps along the path of church evolution as that path is usually traced, and their religious nature has generally prevented their inclusion in surveys of military design. Architectural history of the medieval period has been dominated by the study of churches. Those churches tagged as Romanesque are generally related to the outdated concept of regional schools. In this enquiry, Languedoc tends to figure as a provincial back-water. Those churches recognized as Gothic tend to be compared to devel-

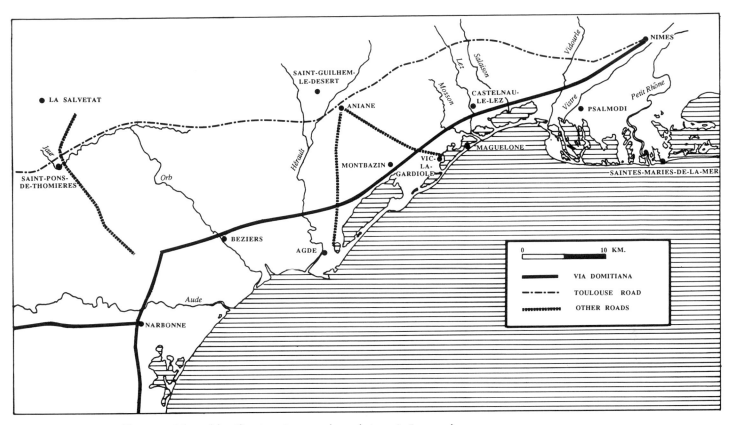

Figure 2. Map of fortification sites, roads, and rivers in Languedoc.

opments in Paris.[3] Here, Languedoc is generally held to be too remote and too tardily influenced by Parisian innovation to figure prominently. The buildings we confront in this study have thus been triply damned by their location in Languedoc, by being neither recognizably Romanesque nor Gothic, and by their military nature.

The historical circumstances in which these buildings were constructed demonstrate, however, that they participated in an intimate dialogue with important political and cultural developments. The Capetian king Louis VII, for example, began to develop contacts in the region in the mid–twelfth century. Languedoc should thus be restored to its proper status as an important political and architectural frontier (Figs. 1, 2). Our opinion of the buildings should be similarly rehabilitated. The fact that Romanesque "turns into" Gothic at a different pace and in different shapes should provide the opportunity to refine the canons of architectural history, and not simply to dismiss exceptions as aberrant. Though unusual in their specific blend of military and religious elements, the churches of Maguelone, Agde, and Saint-Pons-de-Thomières are nonetheless quite "normal" and typical of

Figure 3. Saint-Pons-de-Thomières, exterior view of the nave, south side.

many stylistic and structural aspects of twelfth-century church architecture in the south of France. These elements often differ from those found in mid-twelfth-century Paris for specific and meaningful reasons.

Churches have generally been regarded as the receivers in any exchange with military architecture. Perhaps contrary to our expectations, the fortified churches of Languedoc form an important and independent step in the evolution of fortification design, probably marking the introduction of machicolation into Western architecture, as well as the invention of an essentially new building type: the single-nave fortress-church. As we will see in greater detail in Chapter 1, churches may be fortified by the addition of a number of elements, including precinct walls, towers, or other protective devices. The fortress-church, by contrast, fuses military elements with the church so that it forms a single unit. The fortress-churches that are the object of this study are single-naved buildings wrapped with machicolated arches (Fig. 3).

Since the term "machicolation" is important and far from commonplace, we must pause briefly to define it. As Figure 4 demonstrates, machicolation is an opening that permits the passage of projectiles, stones, or other objects to be dropped on the heads of attackers. Any number of strategies can be used to create the desired slot: from timber balconies to elaborate stone-built projections resting on corbels. The technology we confront in mid-twelfth-century Languedoc is the machicolated arch (or *machicoulis sur arcs*), which is just what its name says it is: a series of arches or arcades with holes or slots at their summit. We will discuss the invention and dissemination of this form in Chapter 5.

This investigation of the machicolated fortress-churches of Languedoc has three primary aims. The first is to examine each building independently to grasp its internal evolution, to clarify the chronology of construction, and to understand the relationships between military and religious aspects in each church. When these buildings have been discussed, they have generally been considered as a unified group. Though closely related by geography and design, however, they are also distinguished by several important aspects. Maguelone and Agde were cathedrals, whereas Saint-Pons was an abbey and remained so until the fourteenth century, when it, too, became the seat of a bishopric. Both Agde and Saint-Pons were located within towns, whereas Maguelone has always stood on a remote island site. The sites of Agde and Maguelone were ports on the Mediterranean coast; Saint-Pons lay 50 kilometers inland. Although all three are single-naved, barrel-vaulted structures, their plans, elevations, and scales are radically different. Agde measures only 34 meters in length, whereas Saint-Pons originally extended more than 80 meters. Agde and Maguelone are wrapped with simple *machicoulis,* whereas Saint-Pons had an elaborate triple-tiered defensive system. These differences should encourage us to reexamine the three buildings as individual structures with independent histories.

The second aim of this study is to locate the invention of the fortress-church and to trace the early motivations for its creation and continued use. The closest parallels to the fortress-churches of Languedoc are the late-eighth-century Abbasid palace of Ukhaidir, the late-eleventh-century west façade of Lincoln cathedral, and the twelfth-century Crusader castle of Krak des Chevaliers. The chronology of contact of Languedoc with Northern Europe and the East and the directions of influence are thus important issues, requiring the researcher to take a broad, comparative view (Fig. 5).

The third objective of this study is to understand the larger (and sometimes conflicting) motivations for ecclesiastical fortification in Languedoc. It is not yet our habit to ask with any great degree of sophistication *why* a church might be fortified. Is it a defensive act in response to a threat, or a statement of control? Who poses the threat, and is that threat perceived or real? Who makes the response: the bishop or the monastic community? Whose permission do they need to fortify? Conversely, why might a fortress include a church and a monastic community? These questions – and a host of others – need to be posed. They can only be answered through a careful reexamination of the larger context of fortification, protection, and architectural creation in twelfth-century Languedoc. Only a wide-ranging contextual

Figure 4. (A) Machicolated arches; (B) Machicolation on corbels; (C) Hoarding; and (D) Portcullis.

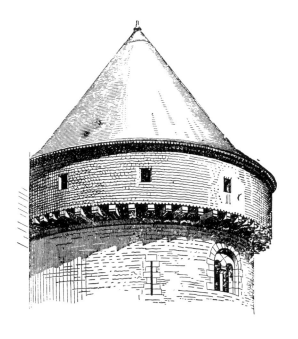

C

D

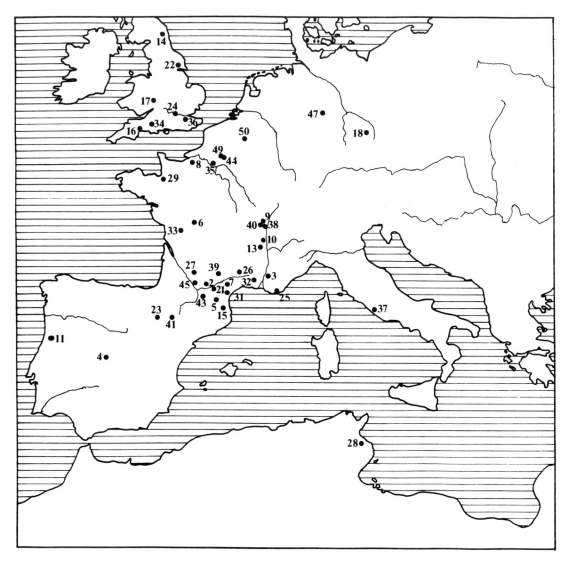

1. Abou-Gosh (Israel), Crusader church
2. Albi
3. Avignon
4. Avilà
5. Banyuls
6. Candes
7. Castelnau-Pégayrolles
8. Château-Gaillard
9. Clermont-Ferrand
10. Cluny
11. Coimbra
12. Constantinople
13. Cruas (Ardèche), fortress-church

14. Durham
15. Elne
16. Exeter
17. Goodrich
18. Gross-Comburg
19. Khirbet ed-Deir
20. Krak des Chevaliers
21. Lagrasse
22. Lincoln
23. Loarre
24. London
25. Marseille
26. Mende

Figure 5. Map of major sites mentioned in the text.

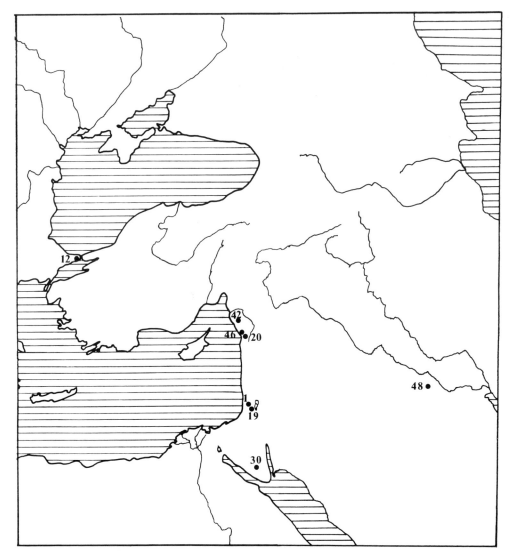

approach to these buildings permits us to read them not as eccentric architectural aberrations but as monuments expressive of their historical situations.

Religious sources of the eleventh and twelfth centuries complain of "Saracens," "pirates," and "heretics." The sources also lament the pressures exerted by secular lords of the region as well as by the mercenaries these lords first invited there, but then failed to support or control adequately. Both the organized Peace of God designating places of refuge, and the less coordinated efforts of minor religious houses to limit the powers of seigneurial competition, were motivating factors in the creation of fortifications in twelfth-century Languedoc. Bishops and abbots of the region, aided by and exploiting the expanding power of Capetian influence under Louis VII, fortified their cathedrals and monasteries and also invoked the power of relics to aid them as they became the agents of order during this period. Although defensive measures were certainly an important part of their motivation, symbolic statements of the necessity for peace and the capacity to control also formed part of their intended message. The creation of the fortress-church was thus impelled by the need to find tangible as well as political solutions to the challenges faced in Languedoc in the mid–twelfth century.

ECCLESIASTICAL FORTIFICATION IN THE MIDDLE AGES

I will say of the Lord: He is my refuge and my fortress.

(Psalm 91.1)

The link between religious refuge and fortification invoked in Psalm 91 was a potent connection during the medieval period. Many religious establishments, whether they were simple parish churches, cathedrals, monasteries, or even cemeteries, were commonly surrounded by a wall or ditch and were often provided with crenellations, iron-barred doors, fortified gates, and other elements of military defense. Under the Peace of God in the tenth and eleventh centuries (and revived in the twelfth century), churches, cemeteries, and other consecrated sites received formal rights of protection. In what was almost a physical realization of Psalm 91, a place dedicated to God acted as a fortress for those in need of refuge.

The decision to fortify a church was, however, not a matter of simple choice for the clerical patron. Permission needed to be sought and granted by the royal, local, or municipal authority. Beginning in the ninth century, permission to fortify was granted to religious patrons by the Carolingians and by their Capetian successors.[1] Italian and German monasteries were also granted the right to build and to own fortifications from the ninth century.[2] Licenses to crenellate were issued by the English chancery as early as the year 1200. Charles Coulson's study of these licenses demonstrates that monastic and episcopal patrons were every bit as eager for the privilege to fortify their buildings as were their secular counterparts.[3] Participants at church councils, however, actively debated the propriety of ecclesiastical fortification, enacting a number of statutes to prohibit the practice.[4]

MOTIVATIONS TO FORTIFY

We may wonder why a bishop might seek to fortify his cathedral, or an abbot his monastery. It is important to realize that the answers may vary with the patron, the building, its site, and its political circumstances. By way of introduction we may, however, make some general observations. The most prevalent reason for fortification was, of course, the protection it afforded against attack. On both the Mediterranean and Atlantic coasts, monasteries often erected defenses against marauding pirates, with Vikings and "Saracens" being the most frequently mentioned in medieval texts. The abbeys of Saint-Victor in Marseille, and Saint-Honorat in Lérins, for example, raised defensive towers against the eleventh-century insecurities of the Mediterranean, while the walled and elevated monastery of Mont-Saint-Michel formed a similar response at its island site off the coast of Normandy.[5]

Even monasteries with less exposed sites would be concerned about the danger of theft. As repositories of liturgical vessels, reliquaries, and other treasure, churches were especially attractive to thieves. At Lincoln cathedral, the *Liber Niger* describes two guards for the shrine of Saint Hugh, probably introduced after the theft of this important relic in 1364.[6] The sacred bones were discarded by the thieves who were apprehended after they had sold the gold and silver reliquary. Although some communities, like Lincoln, opted simply to hire "security guards," others sought more permanent architectural solutions. Precinct walls, stout doors, and treasuries placed on an upper floor of a tower all helped to thwart the recurrent problem of theft.[7]

Religious fortifications, especially those sited on military borders, might serve offensive as well as defensive functions. Fortress-churches in Aragón and Catalonia, in particular, seem to have been used to consolidate control in newly Christianized territory. As King Sancho Ramírez (1063–94) conquered strategic frontier posts in his southward expansion of the territory of Aragón, he fortified outposts such as Alquízar, Montearagón, and Loarre, providing them with churches in which he installed Augustinian canons.[8] Janice Mann has explored the ways in which the eleventh-century castle of Loarre, with its fortress-church, participated in Ramírez's frontier system.[9] The church was located directly over the only entrance to the castle and was incorporated into the most vulnerable spot in the castle precinct, visible from the Muslim frontier. Though Sancho Ramírez's castles were probably garrisoned with soldiers, the presence of a community of Augustinian canons would seem to have been an important priority in assuring the sanctity of the site and in emphasizing – especially to Muslim communities at the border – the newly Christianized nature of the territory.

In other settlements of hybrid population, churches might participate in a system of fortification designed to ensure the military supremacy of one group over another. Thus, in the early years of the Norman Conquest, castles and cathedrals were fortified to protect the new Anglo-Norman ruling class from the local Anglo-Saxons. The cathedrals of Old Sarum, Durham, Rochester, and Lincoln were all provided with defensive aspects in this period.[10] Similarly, twelfth-century Venetian colonies in the Byzantine Empire had their own churches that might be furnished with *bella propugnacula* to ensure their military effectiveness against the local population.[11]

The military aspects of Crusader churches were at least partly inspired by the desire to ensure and advertise the supremacy of the ruling Christian minority to its Muslim and eastern Christian neighbors. The cathedral of Notre Dame in Tortosa, for example, was begun in the twelfth century as a fortress-church featuring thick walls, small windows, and archer slits. The apses and two eastern bays of the existing cathedral were probably completed before Saladin took the town in 1188 and converted the cathedral to a mosque. The subsequent history of Tortosa maintained and enhanced the fortified aspect of its cathedral. In the thirteenth century, the pilgrimage to Tortosa revived, attracting donations sufficient to permit completion of the nave with the same thick walls and small windows as the twelfth-century east end. In 1265, the threat of Mamluk invasion was so great as to raise the possibility of demolishing the cathedral in order to narrow the defensive cordon for the town. Instead, the cathedral was strengthened with apsidal towers and was incorporated into the fortifications of the town.[12]

Whereas secular patrons like Sancho Ramírez or Crusader princes might found fortified churches, religious patrons might sponsor castles. As bishops became the protectors of urban justice and peace in the ninth through thirteenth centuries, they became responsible for the building of fortifications, as well as for the maintenance of armed retainers. The intensity of episcopal involvement with castle construction in eleventh-century Italy is demonstrated by an imperial diploma awarded in 1041 to the bishop of Asti which confirmed, among other properties, no less than thirty-seven fortresses.[13] In the eleventh and the early years of the twelfth centuries, bishops in France often rivaled secular castellans. The bishop of Langres, for example, amassed a veritable principality with twelve castles inside the diocese and five outside it, while the archbishop of Bourges was by far the most powerful lord of the Lower Berry, with vast ecclesiastical estates, fortifications, and an army.[14]

Permission had normally to be sought and secured for any fortification, whether secular or religious. The right of the king to license and to control the use of castles was exercised by the Carolingians and was known to the Normans, Capetians, and other rulers. In practice, the right of "rendability" had been portioned out along with other public powers, and its application varied from a formal prohibition against the castellan using the castle in a manner contrary to the king's (or lord's) interests, to full rendability, whereby the king could actually repossess the castle for a period of time.[15] The latter power was widespread in the south of France in the eleventh century, and was used by William the Conqueror in his duchy of Normandy,[16] but was not otherwise widely invoked until the later twelfth and thirteenth centuries. Under the Capetians the right of rendability was often invoked for, and linked to, the protection of churches and monasteries. In 1171, for example, King Louis VII responded to a complaint by the monastery of Cluny against the count of Mâcon by making a personal visit to subdue the offending lord. Louis' appearance in the region was very likely intended to be a conscious reminder of an earlier royal visitation. In 950, Louis IV had come to Cluny at the request of the beleaguered abbey for royal protection. Over 200 years later, Louis VII engaged in a public display of the revived rights of rendability by touring the castles of the Mâçonnais, effectively reminding their castellans of the doctrine that fortifications existed at the pleasure of the crown and in order to serve the needs of public defense.[17]

Carolingian practice, revived by the Capetians, placed the responsibility for defense on the shoulders of the nobility, who were to act on royal authorization. Among the group of aristocracy deputized for communal defense were a number of bishops and religious communities. In 1092, for example, Philip I granted to the canons of Saint-Corneille in Compiègne the royal right to oppose the building of towers or other fortifications in the town or immediate region.[18] This condition obtained outside France as well. The nuns of Shaftesbury abbey in England, for example, were obliged to support 10 knights in the mid–twelfth century.[19] During the same period, the abbey of Montecassino in northern Italy was assessed the astonishing levy of 60 knights and 200 sergeants for municipal military service.[20] As royal officials, Ottonian and Saxon counts also usurped the regalian right of granting permission to fortify. The thirteenth-century *Sachsenspiegel, Schwabenspiegel,* and the *Osterreichisches Landrecht* constantly amplified the criteria defining a castle and thus the need for a license.[21] Falling under this newly defined need for a license were any building with ditches so deep that a man could not throw earth out with a spade; wooden or stone buildings with more than three stories above ground and more than one underground; precinct walls too high for a rider to grasp the top; and any building topped by crenellations.

The licensing of fortification by royal deputies, however, created problems for many religious communities. Given the widespread danger of Viking and Islamic incursions, monasteries could not always be expected to wait for a responsible lord to solve their defensive problems for them or to grant them permission to do it for themselves. Adulterine fortifications were already a feature of the Carolingian landscape and continued to protect religious and secular communities (but to vex rulers) into the twelfth and thirteenth centuries. These unauthorized castles might be torn down, appropriated by the crown, or retrospectively sanctioned. At the monastery of Corbie, Abbot Franco undertook the building of fortifications on his own initiative in 892. In 901 he obtained from King Charles the Simple acknowledgment of his fortifications, and a guarantee of immunity for the new walls.[22] In a late-ninth-century charter of immunity for the monastery of Vézelay, the Carolingian ruler Eudes similarly gave permission for a castle the monks had already built "because of pagan persecution."[23]

Monastic communities built fortifications to protect not only their own religious establishments but also their dependent properties. The monasteries of Farfa and Sant'Ambrogio in Milan held fortified properties in the twelfth century as part of a papally sanctioned system of defense.[24] Monasteries in northern France, like the abbeys of Saint-Médard, Notre-Dame, and Saint-Jean-des-Vignes in Soissons, all possessed farms, which they fortified in the second half of the fourteenth century against the ravages of the English in the Hundred Years War.[25]

WHEN AND WHERE ARE CHURCHES FORTIFIED?

More abundant in the medieval landscape than we might initially assume, fortified churches followed certain patterns in their distribution.[26] Some regions seem to have favored ecclesiastical fortification, out of fear of attack or as a public display of political control. Others eschewed the fortification of churches, perhaps because of the security of their political situations, or out of respect for prohibitions of the practice. Periods of invasions and war had an impact on ecclesiastical as well as secular fortification. Thus, Mont-Saint-Michel, on the coast of Normandy, was initially fortified as a response to its vulnerability to Viking attack, whereas inland monasteries could be left relatively unprotected.

Though the distribution of surviving examples is far from representative, analysis of textual and pictorial sources can enhance our understanding of the medieval distribution of fortified churches. A number of churches tightly concentrated around Clermont-Ferrand provide an interesting test case for the reconstruction of a regional response to ecclesiastical fortification. Only the church of Royat survives with its early thirteenth-century machicolations and crenellations intact, but careful attention to documentary and pictorial sources demonstrates that religious fortification was a feature of this region from at least the tenth century. Surviving documents reveal that the abbeys of Saint-Austremoine in Issoire, Saint-Julien-de-Brioude, and the nearby priory of Mozat were fortified by *castrum* walls by the tenth century.[27] An engraving of Saint-Allyre in the *Monasticon Gallicanum*, made before the destruc-

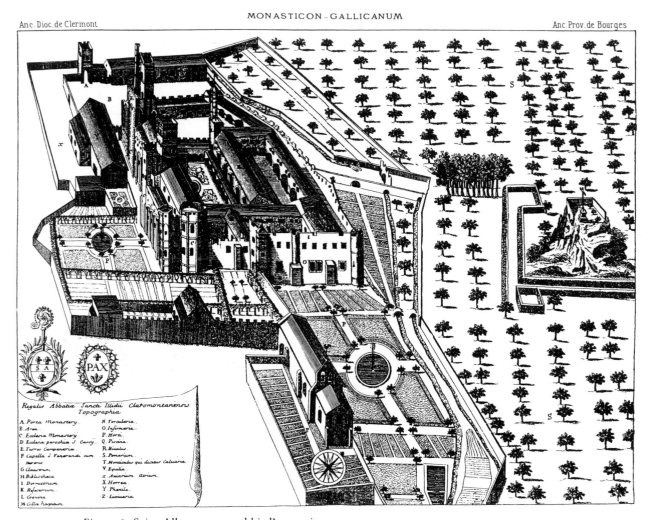

Figure 6. Saint-Allyre, engraved bird's-eye view.

tion of the complex in the Revolution, reveals that the monastery was also fortified, possibly beginning at the time of its consecration in 1106 (Fig. 6). A capital from the choir of the priory church of Saint-Nectaire (Fig. 7), which relates the story of the life of this saint, a companion of Saint Austremoine, shows the church under construction with its surrounding wall (now destroyed) and its crenellated tower (now rebuilt).[28] The documentary record for the priory of Mozat, furthermore, provides a hint of the motivations for ecclesiastical fortification in the region. As the center of a pilgrimage cult of the popular local saints Austremoine and Nectaire, abbeys profited richly from pilgrims' donations. Count Guillaume VI attacked the abbey of Mozat in 1126, provoking King Louis VI to organize an expedition in defense of the church. Some of the motivation for continued fortification of these abbeys

Figure 7. Saint-Nectaire, capital depicting the fortified priory of Saint-Nectaire.

stemmed surely from a desire to protect the pilgrimage cult sites from the rapacity of local lords.

Monastic texts provide verbal expression of the concern for protection. Amy G. Remensnyder has explored the ways in which foundation legends often reveal the defensive aims of the monastic communities who write them.[29] In several eleventh-century charters, peace is said to have been negotiated between two warring castellans by the establishment of a monastery in the territory between them. The cartulary of Conques, for example, identifies the foundation of a monastery at Clairvaux d'Aveyron as a mechanism by which peace was enforced upon the castles of Panat and Cassagnes, perched upon the two peaks which flanked the valley monastery.[30]

From the late eleventh and early twelfth centuries, church fortification began in many ways to parallel and reflect secular defense. Just as castles began to be built in stone and towns began to be surrounded with stone walls, so churches too began to be fortified in monumental form. Even here, however, the generalization must be qualified by the specific local conditions.

In Alsace and Anjou, in particular, fortified cemeteries seem to have given physical manifestation to the zone of refuge mandated by church councils to exist for thirty paces around a church.[31] As we will see, the massive stone-built fortress-churches of twelfth-century Languedoc form part of the a complex local response to threats posed by heretics, pirates, and local lords. Their thirteenth-century successors, the fortified cathedrals of Béziers, Narbonne, and Albi, continued this southern tradition of ecclesiastical fortification.

Though the fortification of churches and abbeys is not alien to the north of Europe in the early and high Middle Ages, those regions present no striking density of ecclesiastical fortification, apart from the use of precinct walls, until the fourteenth century. At that time, the areas of northern France and Flanders most threatened by seigneurial warfare and the movement of troops, witnessed not only the fortification but also the active garrisoning of churches and monasteries. Here, too, we must depend on both surviving buildings as well as textual sources to approach a more complete picture of the quality and distribution of ecclesiastical fortification. The *Annales Gandenses,* which recount the struggles between Flanders and France from 1296 to 1310, provide evidence for the fortification of churches. The *Annales* tell us that in 1304, a group of victorious Flemings returned to their own land to discover a country church "fortified and provided by the French with a garrison." Only after "fierce assault, which lasted some time," was the church eventually captured.[32] This document bears witness not only to the use of religious structures as strongholds in this fourteenth-century conflict but also to the military efficacy of the converted churches.

The Hundred Years War (1337–1453) inspired a massive campaign of ecclesiastical fortification as monasteries sought to protect themselves from the depredations of English troops on campaign and from marauding bands of mercenaries.[33] Froissart and other chroniclers make clear that churches were converted to form refuges for villagers and final retreats for defenders if the towns walls were breached.[34] The populace of Castelnaudary, for example, are said to have sought protection in the church of Saint-Michel, but the English attacked and set fire to the church.[35] When the count of Flanders captured the fortified village of Nieule, he similarly set fire to the church in which six thousand inhabitants were said to have taken refuge.[36] In several cases, however, fortified churches seem to have been more effective in their military resistance.[37] Towers and roof-platforms were specially adapted for defense during this period, and the massive stone walls and strategic placement of many churches also enhanced their military capabilities. The introduction of artillery during the Hundred Years War effectively strengthened the military suitability of such churches, whose thick walls could withstand the rebound of the cannon and whose tall towers commanded the surrounding terrain. The textual sources for the Hundred Years War reveal that churches also served as depots for stockpiling grain and other goods, which made them even more appealing as targets of enemy attack.[38] Contemporary texts also discuss the use of monasteries as fortified garrison posts.[39] The convent of La Trinité at Caen was fortified in about 1359 with walls and a ditch, and the nuns were obliged to maintain a garrison there for their own protection, and that of the region.[40] The monks of Longpont maintained a garrison of 200 soldiers and 400 cavalry under Philip, duke of Orléans for eighteen months in the late 1350s.[41] The abbeys of nearby Soissons were surrounded by walls during this period. An engraving of Saint-Jean-des-Vignes in Soissons, made in 1673, shows the complete circuit of the fortification precinct at the abbey (Fig. 8).[42] Much of this precinct wall and portions of the gatehouse at Saint-Jean-des-Vignes survive.

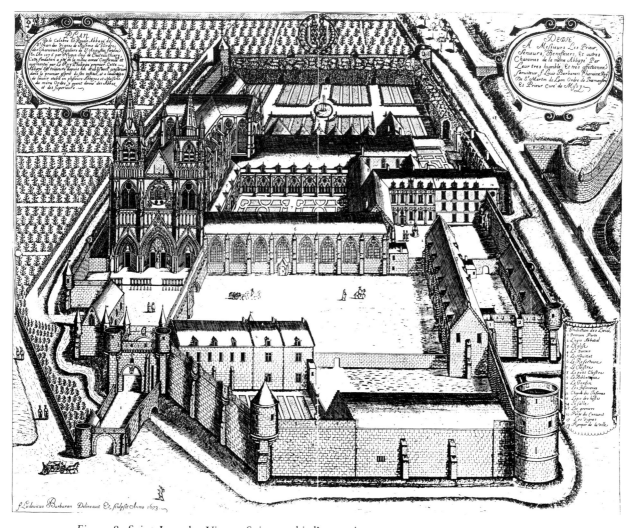

Figure 8. Saint-Jean-des-Vignes, Soissons, bird's-eye view.

Figure 9. Wimy, view of west façade.

The last phase of medieval church fortification came in the seventeenth century with the Wars of Religion.[43] The fortified churches of the Thiérache formed a direct response to this military conflict. A source from 1607 tells us that these churches were ruined

from the fault of the parishioners who used them as forts and sought refuge in them: themselves, with their families, animals, furniture, and goods, even though most of the resources of those churches had already been devoted to their fortification.[44]

With enormous towers protecting their entrances, and barnlike interiors capable of accommodating the entire village populations and their grain stores, the churches of Plomion or Wimy (Fig. 9) characterize the ecclesiastical fortifications of the Thiérache.[45] Numerous churches in the Ardennes, such as Liart, also preserve vestiges of fortification from this period. The rise in the use of artillery and a shift to more corporate military organization at the end of the Wars of Religion however, signaled a decline in the importance of ecclesiastical fortification.

MILITARY AND RELIGIOUS REALMS

The fortification of churches brings together two aspects of medieval life, the military and the religious, that we normally regard as separate. The medieval church, too, was initially adamant in its opposition to warfare and to any connection between the military and spiritual realms. If Christ came to save all peoples, a war of one group against another could only be understood as a profane campaign of aggression.

The medieval theory of "just war" developed variously and gradually.[46] The notion of a just war had classical precedents, especially in the writings of Cicero. He argued that war should be waged justly, that is, through courage and virtue rather than by treachery.[47] The early Christian Fathers grappled with the relationship of war to Christianity and found contradictory messages in the Old and New Testaments. The Old Testament would seem to champion war waged on behalf of the chosen Israelites, whereas passages in the New Testament, like the Sermon on the Mount, discouraged believers from fighting, even in self-defense. Before the conversion of Constantine, the clergy tended to condemn warfare and to proscribe participation by Christians in military endeavors. With Constantine's conversion, Christian attitudes toward warfare changed. Eusebius, bishop of Caesarea, distinguished two levels of Christian vocation: the laity, who were to preserve the peace (through warfare if necessary), and the clergy, who remained separate from such worldly preoccupations.[48] It was Ambrose, a former Roman prefect in Milan, who became the apologist for war waged in defense of Christian territory. Ambrose saw orthodoxy as synonymous with the *Pax Romana*. In his view, a clear threat was posed by pagan barbarians and heretics. Ambrose was instrumental in fostering official repression of heretics, who were identified as enemies of the state. Heretics were increasingly liable to legal restrictions and, in some cases, even to capital punishment. The Ambrosian equation of just war with the struggle of orthodoxy to suppress barbarian and heretic populations was to be of enormous importance to later medieval apologists for just war and crusade.[49]

More than any other writer, Augustine defined the notion of just war for the Middle Ages. Any attempt to summarize the attitudes expressed in the diverse writings of a mind as subtle as Augustine's is doomed to oversimplify. Moreover, Augustine explored the legitimacy of warfare through the lenses of different situations, especially as a response to contemporary Manichean thought. Yet, across his writings, Augustine found support for the legitimacy of warfare in his concept of charity. Punishment of evil-doers was permissible as long as the motivation was to prevent them from doing further evil, rather than to derive pleasure from revenge. Augustine's formulation *"iusta bella ulciscuntur iniurias,"* or "just wars avenge injuries," defined for later thinkers the limitations to be placed on just warfare.[50] The only legitimate purpose of war, according to Augustine, was to seek redress for grievances and restitution for losses. The goal was thus a return to the *status quo ante bellum* and could not include any pursuit of further rights or properties.[51]

Although the conditions of a so-called just war might legitimize military participation in the Middle Ages, any warrior who killed an opponent in battle was normally obliged to do penance for the sin of murder. Thus, the first general capitulary of Charlemagne (c. 769) stipulated:

The prince may be accompanied by one or two bishops with their chaplains. Each captain shall have with him a priest to hear the confessions of the soldiers and to impose on them penances to be performed.[52]

Medieval penitential texts demonstrate that a range of penances existed for killing in warfare, normally including fasting and prayer, lasting from forty days in the penitential of Bede,[53] to a year prescribed by Fulbert of Chartres,[54] to three years in the late-tenth-century Arundel penitential.[55] The Council of Winchester in 1076 stipulated a separate penance of one year for each victim. If a perpetrator were ignorant of the fate of a man he had wounded, he was assigned forty days' penance; if he did not know how many men he had killed, he was assessed one day of penance a week for the rest of his life. As for archers who ran the risk of not knowing the losses they had inflicted, the council required forty days' penance, repeated three times. Penance was almost invariably assigned. Despite the fact that William the Conqueror had sought and received papal approval for his invasion of England, a council of bishops assessed penitenial terms for every knight who had participated in the battle.[56]

Though penances were levied on victorious armies, important military engagements were sometimes celebrated with major religious foundations. The victories at Hastings in 1066 and Bouvines in 1214 were marked by the foundation of Battle Abbey and Notre Dame de la Victoire.[57] In both cases, the site of the victory was commemorated with a richly endowed monastery. The function of the resident monastic community included prayers to expiate the guilt soldiers incurred by killing their opponents. In these foundations, therefore, votive and penitential motives existed in fragile counterpoint with frank celebration of military success.

Although Christian apologists grappled with the legitimacy of just warfare for the laity, monks and clergy were explicitly forbidden to bear arms or to shed blood. Ambrose asserted that clerics should hold themselves far from the bearing of arms.[58] The original proscription of the Council of Chalcedon (451) remained in force and was repeated by subsequent councils and by Charlemagne's capitulary:

We absolutely prohibit clerics to bear arms and go to war, except for those who have been chosen . . . to celebrate Mass and to carry the relics of the saints.[59]

Military endeavors were repeatedly held to be antithetical to monastic life. The struggle to overcome evil was, however, often cast as a military battle, and the contemplative monk seen as a spiritual warrior. Saint Paul frequently used the metaphor of Christian life as a war with the forces of evil:

Labor as a good soldier of Christ Jesus. Let no one, soldiering for God, entangle himself in temporal affairs.[60]

The opposition between the monastic and secular "soldier" was, however, emphasized rather than blurred by the comparison. Paul applied the title of *milites Christi* primarily to Apostles and missionaries; other authors saw the martyrs as the true soldiers of Christ. Throughout the Middle Ages, however, the term was most often applied to monks.[61] Writing in the early ninth century, for example, the abbot Smaragdus pointed out the contrast between monks and soldiers:

There are warriors (milites seculi) and there are soldiers of Christ (milites Christi); but secular soldiers bear feeble and perilous arms, while those of the soldiers of Christ are most powerful and excellent. The former fight their enemies in such a way that they lead both themselves and those they kill to everlasting punishment; the latter fight evil.[62]

Smaragdus' opposition between warriors and soldiers of Christ notwithstanding, prelates who fought in military battles were not unknown. The prohibition against military involvement was difficult to apply, for example, to bishops who were also feudal lords. Merovingian bishops, like Arnould of Metz (d. 643) and Eloi of Noyon (641–60) were obliged to defend their cities. Invasions of Muslims, Vikings, Hungarians, and others put special pressures on the clergy to defend themselves and their territories. The popes especially were faced with such dilemmas. Gregory I provisioned and led his Roman troops, providing an influential precedent.[63] In 849, Pope Leo I led an army against Muslim pirates at the mouth of the Tiber.[64] In the tenth century, Pope John XII was said to have defended the city of Rome with a sword in his hand.[65] As long as these clerics merely held weapons but did not actually use them, the fine line separating a *miles christi* from his secular counterpart could be said to be preserved, but the tension was clear. The need to defend the church led increasingly to direct clerical support for, and even participation in, "just wars." Popes Leo IV and John VIII granted indulgences to any who died while defending a church.[66]

The requirement that clerical deputies maintain armies for defense of the realm led inevitably to clerical involvement in battle. Prelates are known to have aided Ottonian rulers in the tenth century, and in the Italian campaigns of the eleventh and twelfth centuries, sometimes leading armies in person and participating actively in the fighting.[67] Abbot Manso of Montecassino, who built a number of fortifications in the tenth century, is described by the abbey chronicle as habitually accompanied by a retinue of cavalry retainers. His successor, John II, personally led the attack on the town of Pignatero in 997, which had rebelled against the monastery's rule.[68] Sources tell us that in the period between 886 and 908, ten Ottonian bishops fell in battle.[69] Bishops in other regions of the medieval world also took part in battle. Odo, bishop of Bayeux (1049–97) and brother of William the Conqueror, is the most renowned example of episcopal involvement in military endeavors. Odo, however, is said to have fought with a *baculum,* a mace designed to maim but not to shed blood. He is depicted on the Bayeux Tapestry with his special mace, urging the Norman army to success.

In exceptional cases, monks might fight in defense of their church. In the early eleventh century, Bernard of Angers described a prior of Sainte-Foy at Conques who waged war against local troublemakers. Bernard clearly approved this disruption to monastic routine as a necessary and laudable expenditure of effort:

would that the lazy monk put aside his idleness and act so bravely for the monastery . . . [70]

Other writers found less to admire in clerical involvement in military endeavors. A particularly negative example was embodied by Waldric, bishop of Laon at the time of the formation of its commune in the early twelfth century. Waldric initially agreed to the formation of the commune, issuing a charter for its incorporation. He later reversed his opinion, however, and revoked his own charter. Guibert of Nogent recounts with horror the ensuing violence as the bishop and his supporters engaged in pitched battles with groups of town burghers.[71] Guibert observes of Waldric that

He showed great spirit as a fighter; but because he had wrongly and in vain taken up that other sword, he perished by the sword.[72]

Contemporaries were equally shocked by Pope Gregory VII (Archdeacon Hildebrand before his election), who engaged wholeheartedly in military campaigns during his pontificate.[73] Gregory's enthusiasm for war seems to have been almost boundless. He sanctioned and supported a number of wars of secular princes, blessing them as just and holy wars, and planned a number of campaigns in which he intended to participate personally. In 1074–5, he planned military offensives against Robert Guiscard and the Normans, against Philip I, and, as a prefiguration of the later Crusades, against the Turks. In 1080–1, he directed his energies against Ravenna, Byzantium, and Castile. He even suggested that the Truce of God be used to new and frightening purpose. Instead of laying aside arms during Lent and other holy days, he suggested that the papal armies take advantage of such periods when their enemies might be caught unaware.[74]

The Ambrosian doctrine of just war waged against pagans and heretics became newly appealing under the renewed pressure of pagan and heretic groups. In the ninth and tenth centuries, wars of this kind were accorded an exceptional status in penitential texts that excused those who battled against pagans. In similar fashion, church councils and new liturgies actively encouraged wars against pagans.[75]

The Peace of God movement began in the tenth century as an attempt to protect the unarmed, and particularly clergy and church property at all times. By the early eleventh century, the recognition that war was pervasive led to the institution of the Truce of God, an attempt to ban fighting during religious feast days.[76] The Truce first appeared at the Council of Elne (or Toulouges) in 1027 and was popularized by the synod of Arles in c. 1041. At Arles, the participating bishops prohibited Christians from engaging in combat from Thursday to Monday in recognition of Christ's Passion, on certain feast days, and in Advent and Lent.[77] In 1038, a group of peace-keepers, organized by Archbishop Aimon of Bourges, formed a militia to enforce actively the Peace.[78]

Rather than banning fighting, then, the later manifestations of the Peace of God movement tended to redirect military energies toward the main-tainence of peace and the suppression of non-Christian populations. The Crusades defined still further the medieval notion of just war, waged to defend Christian peace against pagans or heretics. In his sermon preached at Clermont in 1095, Pope Urban II summoned the knights of Europe to make an armed pilgrimage to rescue Jerusalem and the other sacred places of the Holy Land from Muslim control. To all who participated in this Crusade, he offered an indulgence, a remission of the normal penance due for sins. Though the exact terms of the crusading indulgence remain uncertain, its impact on twelfth-century theologians is clear. For many of them , the indul-gence gave papal sanction to the principle of a holy war. In such a war, killing the enemy (provided the enemy was an infidel) was not a sin requiring penance but was transformed into a positive act that could remit punishment due for other sins. Death in such a war carried the rewards of martyrdom.

This crusading indulgence represented a landmark in the medieval theory of Christian warfare. It proposed a new vocation of knighthood, which chan-neled the aggressive energies of the military aristocracy into holy war against the infidel and in so doing sanctified the military professions. As the medieval soldier evolved into a Christian knight fighting in the service of the church, descriptions of military and religious realms began to use a shared vocabu-lary. The term *miles Christi* was increasingly shifted from the monk to the knight. The military orders of the Knights Templar and the Hospitalers formed the most institutionalized expression of clerical militarism, adopting the title of *militiae Christi*. These military orders, communities of monk-knights, were a product of the crusading ethos of the late eleventh century.[79] The Knights of the Temple, or Templars as they were called, were created in the wake of the First Crusade. The inability of regular armies and the small Frankish settler population to protect pilgrims led a knight from Champagne, Hugh de Payns, to form a small standing militia for this purpose. In 1119, he and eight other companions living in Jerusalem formed themselves into a religious society for the purpose of defending pilgrims en route to the Holy Land. King Baldwin of Jerusalem sponsored the group and gave them quarters in the royal palace, which was attached to the Temple of Solomon. Hugh seems to have conceived of his group from the outset as a community of soldier-monks. They took the normal monastic vows of chastity and obedience, but they also bore arms. Battles and sieges were preceded and accompanied by prayer and fasting. The Council of Troyes in 1128 approved the group, referring them to Saint Bernard, who, in 1128, wrote their Rule. The idea of an order of fighting monks, once it had gained acceptance, gave rise to a number of other military orders, of whom the Hospitalers were the most powerful. The soldier-monks of the Templar, Hospitaler, and other military orders participated fully in the fortification and protection of Frankish Crusaders, manning sieges and battles, policing roads, and building and holding castles. Saint Bernard became an eloquent spokesman for participation in holy war, writing specifically about the Templars, but more generally about all Crusaders, that

The knight of Christ need fear no sin in killing the foe, since he is the minister of God for the punishment of the wicked. In the death of a pagan, a Christian is glorified, because Christ is glorified."[80]

Although the Templars were the earliest manifestation of the true military monastic orders, the institution had been foreshadowed by military confraternities of the eleventh and early twelfth centuries.[81] Wazo, bishop of Liège in the late eleventh century, is reported to have formed a group of warriors to defend him and his church. A similar military confraternity of nobles was founded for the protection of the monastery of La Grande-Sauve near Bordeaux in the eleventh century. Their mission included the protection of the monks, monastic property, and pilgrims visiting the house, for which they used specially consecrated swords.

Bernard of Clairvaux embodied the changing attitudes of his day regarding warfare and the participation of clerics in military conflict. Despite his enthusiastic sponsorship of the Templars, he could comment harshly on the involvement of other twelfth-century clerics in warfare:

I ask you what sort of monster is this that being a cleric wishes to be thought a soldier as well. Who would not be astonished, or rather disgusted, that one and the same person should, arrayed in armor, lead soldiers into battle and, clothed in the alb and stole, pronounce the Gospel in church.[82]

Bernard is referring specifically in this passage to one offending cleric, Stephen of Garlande, archdeacon of Paris and, from 1120 both royal seneschal and chancellor. In 1133, Stephen's vassals, possibly at his bidding, murdered two reforming ecclesiastics. Bernard was probably also making veiled reference to Suger, abbot of Saint-Denis and later to be regent of France. Suger's early career included the use of military force to recover and protect the domain of his abbey. As a result of that struggle, he held himself responsible for the deaths of many Christians.[83] Examples like these, together with the failure of the Second Crusade in 1148, dampened Bernard's initial enthusiasm for ecclesiastical involvement in military endeavors.

Despite Bernard's changing attitudes, clerics continued to be involved in military engagements of the later Middle Ages. During the Albigensian Crusade of the early thirteenth century, two northern bishops, Renaud, bishop of Chartres, and Philip, bishop of Beauvais, directed the siege of Termes, a Cathar stronghold.[84] At least eight bishops, an abbot, and an archdeacon served in the Hundred Years War.[85] Members of the clergy participated directly in the defense of fourteenth-century England, where they were required by the Crown to array separate militia led and manned by prelates.[86]

Despite proscriptions against the participation of clerics in battle, therefore, links between the religious and military realms were frequent and pervasive throughout the medieval period and accelerated during the eleventh and twelfth centuries. This link finds physical expression in the fortification of cathedrals, churches, and abbeys.

RELIGIOUS FORTIFICATION

The use of fortification in a medieval religious establishment may seem as paradoxical as a monk in battle dress. In fact, religious fortification was relatively common. Most of these fortifications no longer survive, the victims of military siege, royal demilitarization programs, Revolutionary fervor, or modern restoration. Nonetheless, as we have seen, careful examination of pictorial images, physical remains, and textual sources reveals their ubiquity. The engraved view of the monastery of Saint-Allyre near Clermont-Ferrand (see Fig. 6), for example, demonstrates that the monastery, now completely destroyed, was once furnished with machicolations on church and claustral buildings as well as with a fortified enclosure. Aerial views of the city of Canterbury reveal the ghost impressions of the fortification walls of the cathedral precinct preserved in the modern pattern of streets and houses. And, as we have seen, cartularies, records of church councils, and royal diplomas reveal the prevalence of ecclesiastical fortifications, although their physical manifestations have now been greatly changed and reduced.

The fortification of religious buildings was not the invention of the Middle Ages nor the exclusive purview of Christianity. Ancient temples were sometimes walled, the most important (at least for the Middle Ages) being the Temple of Jerusalem. The Temple Mount served repeatedly as a fortress, especially during the siege of Titus in 70 A.D.[87] Islamic *ribats* also functioned in a fashion similar to Christian fortress-monasteries.[88] Although relatively little is known of the personnel who served the *ribats*, it is believed that most were staffed by a regular military garrison aided by volunteers who combined devotional practices with combat. *Ribats* are known to have existed along Muslim borders in Spain, North Africa, and across the Middle East. Especially well-preserved examples survive at Sousse and Monastir in North Africa.[89] Early Byzantine monasteries were also commonly fortified, including the fifth- and sixth-century monasteries of Saint-Saba, Saint Catherine's of Mount Sinai, and Mount Athos.[90] High stone walls surrounded the entire monastic perimeter of all three of these sites and are especially well preserved at Mount Sinai (Fig. 10). In the early sixth century, the monasteries of the Judean desert were warned by the authorities to protect themselves against invading Muslims. This danger was invoked by Sabas, a monk and holy man, when he went to Constantinople in 531 to ask Justinian to build a fort near his monasteries.[91] A number of surviving Judean desert monasteries, like Khirbet ed-Deir, preserve walls, gatehouses, and towers that were at least partly military in form and function.[92] Later Byzantine monasteries like Saint John's on Patmos were also commonly surrounded by stone walls.

Despite the obvious advantage of stone precinct walls, many monasteries

Figure 10. Saint Catherine's, Mount Sinai, aerial view.

were protected by less permanent timber walls or earthen ditches. Where they survive, such monastic ditches have normally been identified as unfortified boundary markers. We should wonder, however, in how many cases they were originally higher and more fully defensive than we have imagined. Many monasteries reused previous secular precincts of stone or timber. The early Irish site of Nendrum was a *rath* (a secular fortified enclosure) until the early seventh century, when it was converted to a monastery. Nendrum originally maintained the form of the *rath* with its massive inner wall and two thinner outer ramparts, but the inner precinct was eventually demolished to make way for an expanded monastic layout.[93] Similar reuse is evident at the monasteries of Armagh, Kells, and Glendalough. In some cases new monastic foundations followed the *rath* plan, probably partly as the result of tradition, and partly to ensure defense.

Monastic communities in France and Germany were similarly founded within castle precincts in the tenth through thirteenth centuries. In the second quarter of the eleventh century, for example, the lord of Monton donated a plot of land within the outer court of his castle to the monks of Sauxillanges (in the Auvergne region) for the foundation of their monastery. In texts like this one, it can be difficult to distinguish a castle chapel from a monastery founded on the site of a former castle. In at least one case, however, the church of Saint-Genies de Thiers, the church predated the castle with which it later shared the precinct.[94] A number of German monasteries were also founded within castle sites given by royal, noble or even episcopal patrons. Siegburg, for example, was founded by Bishop Anno II of Cologne in 1064 in a castle in his possession. These castle-monasteries often retained the military characteristics of their sites.[95] The monastery of Gross-Comburg is the best surviving example of this phenomenon (Fig. 11).[96] Comburg

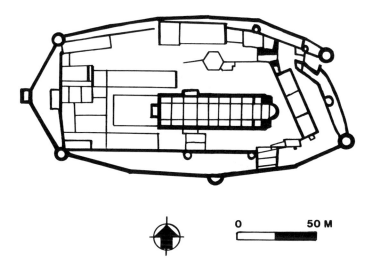

Figure 11. Gross-Comburg, plan.

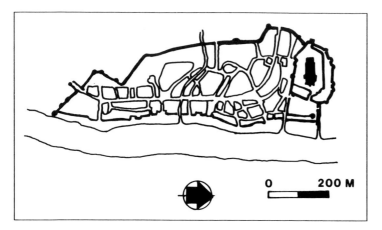

Figure 12. Tournus, town plan.

was founded in the late eleventh century as part of the monastic reform promulgated by Cluny and Hirsau. In most of these castle sites, the usual
monastic plan had to be radically adapted. Though Comburg has been
much rebuilt over its history, we can still trace much of its original layout,
constructed under Abbot Hartwig (1104–39). Some of the monastic plan
may have followed the disposition of buildings of the original castle. One
entered through the single gate, which was surmounted by a chapel dedicated to Saint Michael, the military protector. The church lay to the left,
with the conventual buildings hidden in the most defensible position behind
the church and farthest from the gate.

Burgundian monasteries were also commonly surrounded by walls in the
eleventh and twelfth centuries. At Tournus, for example, the abbey formed
a walled precinct, heavily fortified with towers that still survive in the
northern quadrant of the fortified town (Fig. 12). One documentary witness
of such fortifications in action has come down to us. An early thirteenth-
century charter for Cluny tells us that the monks threw immense stones
from the towers upon their attackers.[97]

Cathedrals were also commonly surrounded by, and even incorporated
into, fortification walls. Many cathedrals, like those at Amiens, Soissons,
Noyon, Tours, Le Mans, Rodez, or Trier, were connected (at various points
in their histories) with the Gallo-Roman walls of their towns.[98] The apse of
the cathedral of Avilà today still forms a projecting bastion of the town wall
(Fig. 13).[99] Anglo-Norman cathedrals were also fortified, normally with
precinct walls, in the period of insecurity immediately following the Norman Conquest. In 1072, Earl Waltheof constructed the castle of Durham,
"where the bishop could enclose himself with his men out of danger from
invaders."[100] The cathedral was well sited on a spur of a high hill, surrounded on all other sides by the river (Fig. 14). The new castle blocked the
only side open to the town and in so doing acted almost as a gatehouse for

Figure 13. Avila, Cathedral of San Salvador, east end.

the cathedral. These defenses were further strengthened by Bishop Ralph Flambard (1099–1128) when he built a curtain wall between the east end of the cathedral and the castle. Three years after the construction of the castle for the bishop of Durham, another bishop, Hereman of Sherborne and Ramsey, transferred his see to Old Sarum, just outside the city of Salisbury. The new cathedral, with its cloister and bishop's palace, was located within an Iron Age hillfort, reused as the Norman castle and cathedral precinct. The cathedral at Lincoln was sited in a corner of the former Roman city wall, and immediately opposite the Anglo-Norman tower. Since the castle at Lincoln was not the bishop's, the cathedral was further fortified at its west end, a feature we will discuss further below. Defensive aspects seem also to have been a priority for the new cathedral of Rochester, rebuilt by Bishop Gundulf (1077–1108). As the designer of the Tower of London, Gundulf had a certain measure of experience with fortifications.[101] At Rochester, he established the cathedral in a corner of the former Roman town wall, and close to the Anglo-Norman castle. In addition, a free-standing defensive tower formed part of the cathedral design (Fig. 15).

Towers like that at Rochester cathedral were a popular solution to the problem of defending a cathedral or church. They were widely used, especially in eleventh-century England, Catalonia, and Languedoc-Rousillon. The cathedral of Viviers was preceded by a defensive tower dating to the eleventh century.[102] Like the tower at Rochester, the west tower at Viviers was origi-

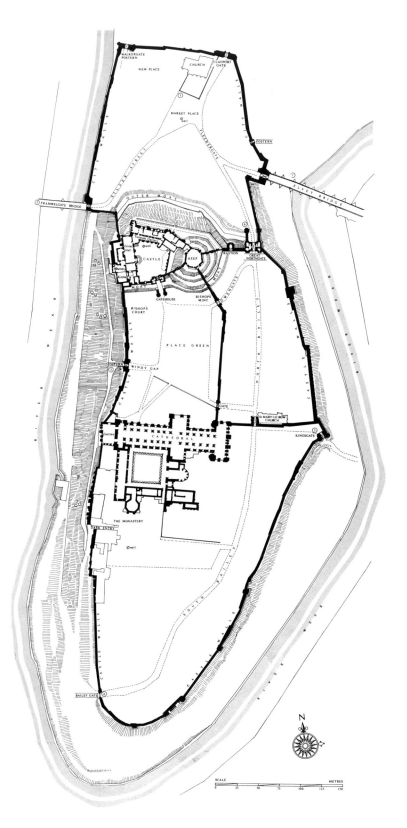

Figure 14. Durham, plan of cathedral and castle precinct.

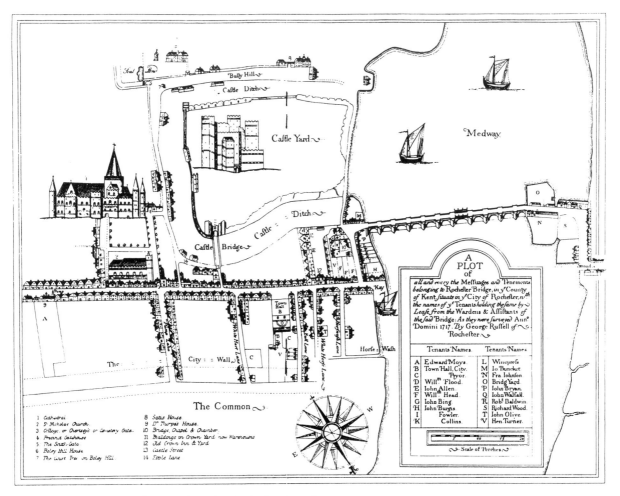

Figure 15. Rochester, plan of cathedral and castle precincts.

nally free-standing. The west front of the cathedral of Elne incorporated defensive towers, built by Bishop Udalguer in 1140.[103] One may also wonder whether the original function of the free-standing western tower at La Trinité at Vendôme or the originally independent tower now incorporated into the north tower of the cathedral of Chartres included defense.[104] Towers might also be incorporated during periods of military stress to preexisting buildings. The rather incongruous and roughly built round tower that abuts the richly decorated west façade of the church of Rampillon, for example, was probably added as a security measure during the Hundred Years War.[105]

The monastic community of Mont-Saint-Michel is one of the most renowned examples of the adaptation to a defensible island site.[106] Originally a hermitage, Mont-Saint-Michel was founded in 708 by Saint Aubert, bishop of Avranches. Saint Michael was said to have appeared to him in a dream and to have commanded him to build a sanctuary on the former

Celtic funerary mount. Saint Aubert turned to the cult site of Saint Michael in Monte Gargano and received relics from them. He instituted a pilgrim oratory on the mount, served by monks living in single cells. In the eleventh century, the Dukes of Normandy, seeking to reorganize the cult and the monastic community, founded a Benedictine house in 966. The tenth-century monks constructed a church on or near the site of Aubert's oratory, at the top of the mount. Around the church they arrayed the conventual buildings, with guest quarters underneath. The importance of the site increased with the rise of the Norman duchy and its conquest of England in 1066. Rebuilt in the late eleventh century, and again in the mid–twelfth century, the character of both the community and the site was altered by the institution of the knightly order of the Brotherhood of Saint-Michel-de-la-Mer under royal patronage in 1210. Each successive campaign, however, preserved at the top-most level all the necessary elements (church, dormitory, and an abridged cloister) that allowed the continuation of monastic life, relatively undisturbed by the military character of the site.

Friaries of the thirteenth and fourteenth centuries were also integrated with the fortifications of new towns, as we can see at Hagenau, Wiener Neustadt, San Domenico, and San Francesco in Siena, as well as in the parent house of the Franciscans in Assisi.[107] Individual churches, normally funerary in function, could also be surrounded by a wall, sometimes so close as to be practically integral with the walls of the church building. These "enclosed" churches are found primarily in the twelfth through fifteenth centuries, across Europe, from the seigneurial fortified cemetery churches of Epfig and Hunawir in Alsace, to Hordain in Flanders, to Seintein and Luz in France.[108] At Seintein, a thirteenth-century precinct wall enclosed the preexisting twelfth-century church and cemetery (Fig. 16).

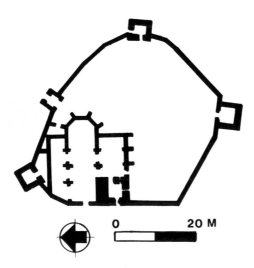

0   20 M

Figure 16. Seintein, cemetery church, plan.

ECCLESIAE INCASTELLATAE

The most common strategy for the fortification of a church seems to have been the addition of a precinct wall like that around the church and cemetery of Seintein. This solution is described in texts as early as the tenth century and persists into the late Middle Ages. By the tenth century, protected churches in France, Italy, and elsewhere are characteristically described in texts as *"castellum circumdata"* (surrounded by a castle) or as *"castra"* of the dedicatory saint. The fortification of a church thus normally entailed the creation of a fortified circuit wall, with the church contained within it. In the second half of the twelfth century, however, a new term is more commonly applied to defended churches. They are described as *"incastellatae,"* literally, "turned into a castle." Many of the churches described in this fashion seem no longer merely to have been surrounded by a wall but to have had elements of fortification incorporated into the church building itself. Aldo Settia has traced the use of this term in Italian documents and found a marked rise in its appearance in the last decades of the twelfth century.[109] In 1177, for example, the church of S. Quirico in Arrezo is described as *"invenerunt turrem ecclesie incastellatam."*[110] In 1183, an eyewitness describes the church of S. Leone di Suzzara as *"incastellatam de novo,"* and adds that *"ego vidi meis oculis betefredum super suprascriptam ecclesiam."*[111] Latin texts for the regions outside northern Italy similarly demonstrate the use of this new term, beginning in the first quarter of the twelfth century.[112] The prohibition of *ecclesias a laicis incastellari* (churches fortified illicitly by lay persons) by the Lateran Council of 1123 was undoubtedly influential in the continued usage of this term, even if the legislators hoped to limit the actual practice (Appendix 38). In 1144, for example, Henry of Huntingdon attests that Ernulf of Mandeville suffers because he has: *"ecclesiam incastellatam retinebat."*[113] Otto of Freising similarly laments, *"Ecclesiam beati Petri, omnium ecclesiarum caput, incastellare sacrilege ac profanissime non metuunt."*[114] Though some of these twelfth-century passages describing *ecclesiae incastellatae* may refer to churches fortified by the addition of a precinct wall, many now seem instead to indicate a new fusion of fortification within the church itself. Most often it was the west of the church that was furnished with towers and other protective devices. The location of the main entrance to the church at the west was probably the major factor in the fortification of that zone. The various functions of the west block as a *westwerk* or a treasury, and the location of upper chapels dedicated to the military saint, Michael, may also have provided symbolic motivations to fortify the west end.[115] One of the most impressive *westwerks* was that at La Trinité at Fécamp, built under the sponsorship of Duke Richard I (943–96).[116] Though nothing now survives,

Dudo of Saint-Quentin described it as a multistoried porch and compared it to secular fortifications.[117]

Not all western complexes with Michael chapels were, however, fortified. The west complex of Saint-Riquier, constructed by Angilbert in about 790–8, was preceded by an atrium with upper chapels dedicated to the archangels. Saint Michael's chapel lay over the principal western entrance.[118] A splendid Michael chapel was built c. 1120 in the third church of Cluny. This chapel occupied a place just above the main portal of the church and within the thickness of the western wall of Cluny III.[119] The pilgrimage churches of Vézelay and Saint-Benoît-sur-Loire both have generous upper chapels dedicated to saint Michael in their western towers. In such upper chapels, the military saint probably provided symbolic protection to an entrance that was not otherwise fortified.

A striking instance of a fortified west end occurs in the west façade of the Anglo-Norman cathedral at Lincoln. The original façade was reworked in the later Middle Ages, but much of the original eleventh-century design, with its five great arcades, still survives (Fig. 17). The north and south

Figure 17. Lincoln Cathedral, view of west façade.

Figure 18. Lincoln Cathedral, detail of west façade: machicolated arch in the southwest portal.

entrance arcades are still intact and have machicolated slots clearly visible in the soffits of their arches (Fig. 18). These machicolations were originally served by mural passages, which also communicated with the exterior by archer slits piercing the buttresses.[120] Documentary evidence supports the notion that the motivation for these elements was military. Henry of Huntingdon writes that Bishop Remigius built his church

in the upper city next to the castle . . . ; and in that strong place he built a strong church, a beautiful church in that beautiful place. . . . it was to be both fitting for the servants of God and, as the times required, impregnable to enemies.[121]

The military potential of the cathedral was realized in 1141, when King Stephen laid siege to the town. William of Malmesbury reports that during the siege of the castle, the king *"ecclesiam incastelaverat"* (made a castle of the church).[122] Though the east end does not appear to have been fortified, the cathedral was sited near the Roman town fortifications, and there is recent archaeological evidence that these walls were reinforced during the Norman period.[123]

The monastery of Saint-Pierre at Moissac is graced with a famous porch dating most probably to the middle years of the twelfth century (Fig. 19).[124] Although the richly sculpted program of the porch at Moissac is widely known, the fact that the upper story of this porch has defensive features comes as a surprise to many. The porch ensemble and its sculptures were probably originally planned for installation at the west door. It was relo-

Figure 19. Moissac, south porch.

cated, possibly because of the more protected nature of the southern entrance. The crenellations above the south porch now protect a fighting platform that communicates with the interior of the church. When the sculpture was transferred from the exposed western entrance, the arch above that door was pierced with machicolations to protect it. Scholars have often commented upon the iconographic emphasis on military triumph in the Moissac portal sculpture.[125] The fully functional crenellations reinforce the iconographic theme of military success expressed in the sculpture, while the sculpture makes articulate the defensive aspect of its setting.

The richly sculpted thirteenth-century porch at Candes is similarly surmounted with machicolations on corbels, with a *bretêche* (an individual machicolation) interrupting the gallery of sculpted saints to protect the door (Fig. 20).[126]

Perhaps the most widely recognized example of the fusion of military and religious elements is the west façade of Saint-Denis (built c. 1135–40). There, a crenellated parapet surmounts the famous triple portal and rose window (Fig. 21). These defensive elements were included, in Abbot Suger's

Figure 20. Candes, north porch.

Figure 21. Saint-Denis, west front.

words, "both for the beauty of the church, and, should circumstances require it, for practical purposes."[127]

FORTRESS-CHURCHES AND FORTIFIED ABBEYS

Most medieval churches were fortified in selected areas such as the precinct or the west entrance, but a few are especially remarkable in their fusion of protective and religious functions. Palace and castle chapels are prime examples of such a fusion. The Anglo-Norman chapels within the Tower of London (Fig. 22) and Colchester Castle were fully incorporated into the defensive system of their castle buildings. The apses of the chapels formed projecting bastions, and the galleries of the upper chapels were connected to the defensive gallery systems of the rest of each keep.[128] Similar examples of chapels fused within their castle precincts can be found in later structures, such as the twelfth- and thirteenth-century Crusader chapel at Krak des Chevaliers, Edward I's thirteenth-century Welsh castle of Beaumaris, or the original fourteenth-century castle chapel at Pierrefonds.

Gatehouses were often provided with chapels incorporated within or directly adjoining the structure. At Goodrich castle in England, the thirteenth-century chapel is located in the tower next to the gate. At Harlech castle in Wales, built by Edward I in 1283–90, the chapel has been placed directly above the fortified gate itself and, in fact, could only be used when the portcullis was in its lowered position.[129]

Like castle and gatehouse chapels, other churches fused military and reli-

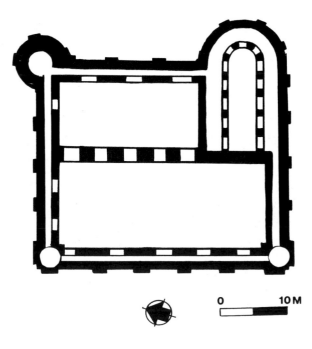

0   10 M

Figure 22. Tower of London, plan at gallery level.

gious aspects. An elegant design is used at the tiny bastide church of Rudelle (Fig. 23), built in the late twelfth and early thirteenth centuries, and converted into a fortress in the fourteenth.[130] There an unaisled nave is surmounted by an upper hall or chapel. A crenellated fighting platform protected by a series of *bretêches* crowns this exceptionally economical tower-church. The late fourteenth-century castle chapel at Vez is similar to Rudelle in plan, with its two-storied elevation. Despite extensive restoration in the nineteenth century, the original plan and elevation of the chapel can be reconstructed with the aid of physical evidence and older views.[131] Vez provides an interesting example of site planning. The chapel originally projected as an eastern arm of the residential *logis*. This eastern arm was divided into two stories: a service undercroft and an upper chapel, with a machicolated *chemin de ronde* on the roof. Perhaps as a result of adding an oriented chapel to a preexisting building, the chapel at Vez now stands immediately opposite the entrance to the castle, which is located at the eastern limit of the precinct wall (Fig. 24). As such, the chapel site necessitates that it function as a protective buffer between gate and residence.

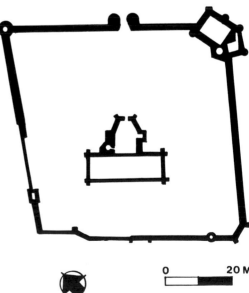

Figure 23. Rudelle, exterior view.

Figure 24. Vez, castle plan.

Twelfth-century fortress-churches fused religious and defensive elements in a manner similar to those of castle and palace chapels. The late twelfth-century church of Banyuls in the Pyrénées demonstrates one of the simplest solutions to the design of a fortress-church, with plain, thick walls and very few windows or other openings.[130] Such simplicity is a feature of many Crusader fortress-churches, such as the church of Abou-Gosh (Fig. 25). This Crusader church is a simple boxlike structure with massive walls almost 3 meters thick, probably constructed by the Hospitalers between their acquisition of the terri-

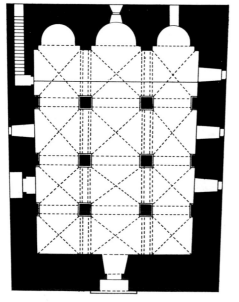

Figure 25. Abou-Gosh, exterior view, and plan.

tory in 1141 and the conquest of Saladin in 1187.[133] All of the twelfth-century cathedrals of Portugal, including those of Coimbra, Lisbon, and Evora were similarly fortified with thick walls pierced by few windows and topped by crenellations.[134]

The use of machicolations wrapped around the exterior of the church, together with a crenellated fighting platform on the roof was the solution favored in the fortress-churches of Languedoc such as Maguelone and Agde. This solution was more elaborate and permitted the defense of the entire building by a relatively small garrison.[135] Saint-Pons-de-Thomières employs an even more complex system of superimposed gallery passages provided with machicolated openings. Despite the self-sufficient nature of these buildings, they were linked to larger systems of fortification, either to urban or monastic precinct walls, and sometimes to both. This type of fortification had wide currency from the eleventh through thirteenth centuries. The small fortress-church of Cruas, for example, is completely protected by thirteenth-century machicolations that were added to the eleventh- or twelfth-century fabric, which was in turn incorporated into the town walls (Fig. 26).

Figure 26. Cruas, exterior view.

Figure 27. Narbonne, Cathedral of Saint-Just, exterior view.

The southern fortified cathedrals of Narbonne, Béziers, and Albi mark the culmination of the southern French fortress-church. The single-nave gothic cathedral of Saint-Just in Narbonne, begun in 1272, combines northern French Rayonnant style with southern Gothic forms.[136] On the exterior, this combination results in the fusion of flying buttresses springing from buttresses linked by crenellated bridges (Fig. 27). The chevet of the thirteenth-century cathedral of Saint-Nazaire in Béziers is also a single-naved structure wrapped with machicolated arches, and its west front is crowned with a crenellated *machicoulis* (Fig. 28). These thirteenth-century machicolations of the cathedral at Béziers may have been inspired by the twelfth-century machicolations of the canonial buildings of the cathedral complex, which we will discuss later.

Begun in c. 1282 by Bishop Bernard of Castanet, the single-nave cathedral of Sainte-Cécile at Albi was explicitly military in its design (Fig. 29).[137] The cathedral dominated the city. Situated on the crest of the hill, it was protected on the north by the episcopal palace and claustral buildings that extended to the river. The enormous west tower protected the adjoining flank of the cathedral, with the comital castle across from it. The town touched the cathedral only toward the east, but access could only be gained from the town through the main south door, originally defended by its own drawbridge. Since the cathedral was probably never completed, we cannot

Figure 28. Béziers, Cathedral of Saint-Nazaire, exterior view.

Figure 29. Albi, Cathedral of Sainte-Cécile, Albi, exterior view.

analyze the upper system of fortification, which may have been planned to include a crenellated roof platform. The upper elements we see today are the result of nineteenth-century elevation of the roof level which was necessitated by water damage to the vaults. Drawings made previous to those restorations demonstrate the unfinished character of the cathedral, with its timber roof resting directly on the projecting buttresses. Whatever its original upper termination, the cathedral at Albi proclaimed the military power of orthodoxy against the local threat of Albigensian heresy, wrapped with its heavy semicircular buttresses, protected at its base by a heavy talus, and entered only by a single fortified door.

SYMBOLIC ASPECTS OF PROTECTION

Protection was not only afforded in the Middle Ages by the physical application of military elements but could also accrue from the patron, the saint-protector, or from the invocation of various symbolic elements. The Pope was one of the most important medieval *defensor ecclesiae*. A number of monasteries were placed under direct papal protection in the eleventh through thirteenth centuries. As a physical expression of this protection, papal sponsors might fortify their properties. In the mid-twelfth century, for example, Pope Eugenius III (1145–53) and his successors initiated a program of fortification in the Roman countryside (the *castra specialia ecclesiae*).[138] The language of papal conveyance often emphasized the defensive aspect of papal sponsorship. When Pope Gregory VII recorded the donation of the monastery of Maskarans (near Poitiers), he reports that he has

received it into the jurisdiction and defense of the apostolic see . . . .Therefore we command that no one shall presume to trouble the aforesaid place, fortified by its apostolic sponsorship, but that it shall remain in peace and free from any disturbance under the protection of Saint Peter, to whose jurisdiction it belongs.[139]

Indeed, the language of defense became almost formulaic in eleventh- and twelfth-century monastic foundation charters, royal diplomas, and edicts of church councils, as well as the papal bulls (see, for example, Appendixes 3, 6, 24, 30, 32, and 34–41).

Specific prayers or liturgies could also afford protection, or could be used to reinforce military ideologies. As we have seen, military vocabulary was a commonly used analogy for the description of spiritual endeavors, from Saint Paul's *milites Christi* onward.[140] Barbara Rosenwein has argued that Cluniac liturgy channeled military aggression by casting the monks as spiritual soldiers in the struggle against the devil.[141] Dedication liturgies often likened the church to the militarized Heavenly Jerusalem of the Book of Revelations. Analogously, images of the Heavenly Jerusalem in twelfth-century manuscripts of Augustine's *Civitas Dei* represented the celestial city as a fortified enclosure.[142]

Saints and relics were often intimately linked with weapons and warfare. Religious phrases and saints' names were often invoked as battle cries, and religious symbols were used on military banners. *"Kyrie Eleison"* was shouted at the outset of battle in Germany from at least the ninth century. Battles fought in defense of religious property often called upon the saint to act as protector. The *Miracula sancti Benedicti* tell us that the troops defending a Benedictine priory called out to Benedict and that the saint provided protection "like a rampart."[143] The clergy also established liturgies for the blessing of weapons. Pontificals from the mid–tenth century onward contain formulae for the consecration of banners, swords, and other weapons. One such eleventh-century *oratio* exhorts:

Hearken, Oh Lord, to our prayers and bless this sword with which your servant desires to be girded in order to defend and protect churches, widows, and orphans and all the servants of God against the cruelty of pagans.[144]

As we have seen, the swords of the eleventh-century confraternity at La Grande-Sauve were specifically blessed for the protection of the monastery and its patrons.

Relics, particularly those of the patron saint of the church, were viewed as both requiring and affording protection. In a number of cases, relics were transferred to a more secure monastery to protect them, or at least that is the interpretation often given by monastic apologists for the "liberation" of the relics they describe. When the body of Mary Magdelene was translated from Provence to Vézelay in the eleventh century, for example, Count Gérard of Burgundy and Abbot Hugo of Vézelay sent a monk to fetch the relics that were said to be in danger of desecration at the hands of the "Saracens."[145]

Monastic communities not only sought "custody" of relic-saints to protect them; the monks were also eager to exploit the defensive capabilities of these saints. By praying for the nobility, monasteries made themselves worthy of secular support and protection. When that support was withdrawn, they could and did appeal to their spiritual patrons for recourse. Patrick Geary has demonstrated the ritual power of relic humiliation to coerce improved behavior from recalcitrant barons.[146] In the face of attack or dispute with a noble, relics were taken from their places on the altars and were laid prostrate on the floor, providing striking visual reminder of the "humiliation" accorded to the saint by the transgression of the baron. At the same time, the doors of the monastery were closed, its services suspended, and its bells sounded continuously. The withdrawal of honor from the monastic community, these actions proclaimed, was equivalent to the dishonoring of the patron saint. The humiliation of the relic-saint was witnessed by the local community, and the attendant actions in turn influenced public opinion on the dispute. The force of local sentiment often pressured the offending noble to reach an understanding with the monastery. Although evidently not effective in every instance, saints (through their relics) could thus provide not only protection but redress for wrongs.

Relics played a prominent role in the Peace of God. At the councils and popular assemblies of the Peace, relics were often brought to encourage and sanction the proceedings:

Crowds of common people without number . . . hurried there. In order that the devotion of these people might be increased on their journey, men of faith began to bring the bodies of saints as well. . . . This was done, moreover, so that our leaders could make a proclamation about a certain count, Landric by name, concerning the booty he had stolen from our blessed protector.[147]

According to the *Miracula sancti Benedicti,* Archbishop Aimon swore an oath on the relics of Saint Stephen and required his followers to do the same, when he formed his militia to fight against the violators of the peace.[148] When Aldebert III became bishop of Mende in c. 1151, he found his cathedral surrounded and threatened by secular fortifications. Bishop Aldebert enlisted the aid of a newly discovered relic to help subdue rival secular powers and ensure the peace.[149] The *Chronicon de gestis,* written between 1165 and 1170, tells us that the cathedral at Mende was literally surrounded by secular fortifications. Aldebert bought back lands from secular lords and fortified the town, though not, it seems, the cathedral itself. In addition to the reacquisition of alienated lands and the building of fortifications, Aldebert tried to control the abuses of seigneurial power that plagued him and the town of Mende. These included the secular control of episcopal and canonial offices at Mende, which Aldebert effectively ended, and the violence of what the *Chronicon de gestis* terms "pirates, brigands, and mercenaries." Aldebert reprimanded feudal barons who broke the Peace he sought to maintain. For example, he besieged and took the castle of Garde-Guérin, which was operating as a stronghold for brigands. The knights who inhabited the castle were obliged to come to Mende to implore pardon at the feet of the bishop. Soon after the town of Mende was fortified, it was attacked by a group identified in the *Chronicon* as "Brabançons, Basques, and Aragonais." Though Aldebert wished in many ways to reclaim for himself the independent feudal powers of the bishop-counts of Gévaudan, he also allied himself with Louis VII in 1161, receiving regalian rights in a diploma of that year.

In 1170, a definitive solution to Aldebert's problems was reached. In digging a well near the cathedral, a crypt containing a lead sarcophagus was discovered. The body found within was reportedly missing a bone: in fact, the *Chronicon* reports that it was the very bone from the body of Saint Privat that was the relic of the high altar of the cathedral, installed there in the early years of the twelfth century. The discovery was heralded as the miraculous recovery of the body of the martyr-bishop of Mende, Saint Privat. This discovery appeared to contemporaries to be witness to the divine favor in which Aldebert was held, and this more than anything seemed (at least to the author of the *Chronicon*) to subdue the brigands and to calm the revolt of the lords of Gevaudan. Aldebert almost immediately received the submission of all his enemies. Aldebert's use of relics to subdue his opponents parallels the strategies of religious fortification used by many of his contemporaries. The relics of Saint Privat, just like the walls of fortress-churches, were able to invoke not only divine protection but also secular cooperation. Both were used as potent "weapons" of the twelfth-century Peace of God.

Even in the absence of relics, certain saints were held to act as protectors. Relics of the incorporeal angel-saints were, of course, unobtainable. The sponsorship of Michael, Gabriel, Demetrios, and other military saints was, however, felt to ensure protection.[150] As we have seen, many upper chapels, like those at Vézelay or Saint-Benoît-sur-Loire, were dedicated to Michael. The elevated placement of chapels dedicated to Michael is said to commemorate his appearance on Monte Gargagno, the chief location of his cult, but in medieval France it may also be a physical reminder of the elevated cult site of Mont-Saint-Michel. Conveying a variety of meanings, the image of Saint Michael seems to have been used by some patrons to evoke his protection against physical and spiritual threats.[151] Representations of the military angel-saint seem to have been especially popular in twelfth-century Burgundy and are most often located near the entry to the church, either as reminders of a Saint Michael chapel above or as a more economical replacement for it. Examples are found, for example, on the consoles of the portal lintel at Montceau-l'Etoile and Perrecy-les-Forges, and in the tympanum of the church of Saint-Michel-d'Entraigues. The use of Saint Michael as a "protective device" is made most explicit at Saint-Vincent of Mâcon (Fig. 30), where a twelfth-century capital in the porch bears an image of the archangel brandishing his sword with the inscription:

"The demon tries to slip inside; the angel blocks his path."[152]

As we have noted, the sculpted portal program of the crenellated porch at Moissac (c. 1120) presents themes of military victory. Marcel Durliat first connected the Moissac porch (see Fig. 19) with a triumphal event. Noting the unusual presence of crenellations, he suggested that these military elements may have been intended to dramatize the recent victory of the monks

Figure 30. Mâcon, Saint-Vincent, porch capital of Saint Michael.

over their lay rulers in a struggle over rights to the tower that surmounts the porch.[153] Linda Seidel has connected the form of the porch with the Roman Arch of Titus and has suggested that the arch assumed potent meaning at Moissac as a model for the triumph of the First Crusade.[154] Many sculpted cloister programs, such as those at Moissac, include images of Old Testament and contemporary warriors. Though the interpretation of cloister programs such as these is complicated (and well beyond the scope of this study), we must note the prevalence of warrior imagery on churches that are provided with other functional and symbolic elements of fortification. A reconsideration of such images may demonstrate that the triumphal imagery of Moissac was less unusual than we have supposed. The churches of Auvergne, which were fortified with surrounding walls, are especially rich in sculpted capitals representing warriors. At Saint-Julien-de-Brioude, for example, several nave capitals depict armed warriors.[155] The military aspects of both the church and the sculptural program at Saint-Julien may commemorate the life of the martyred Saint Julien who was, before his death, a Christian soldier garrisoned at nearby Vienne.

Although fortification was most often designed as a functional and effective protection against a perceived threat, it might also express symbolically the possession of power and the capacity for control. The simple fact of fortification might be enough to discourage attack. This "deterrence factor," as modern military advisers continue to argue today, could provide sufficient motivation for a community to pay its significant cost. The symbolic values associated with crenellations has been documented. By at least the thirteenth century, and probably long before, crenellation was recognized as the architectural expression of noble rank. The English royal chancery controlled the right to crenellate, normally limiting its use to royal and aristocratic patrons. In some cases, the application of crenellations to religious establishments might advertise the aristocratic position of the higher clergy. In other cases, it might be held appropriate to the divine lordship of the church.[156]

Other fortified elements seem to have gained specific symbolic associations in the twelfth and thirteenth centuries. The machicolated arch, for example, had a marked geographic distribution in southern France. The form may thus have been recognized by contemporaries as a regionally specific expression of power. A group of churches in the Rouergue, including Notre-Dame de l'Espinasse in Millau, Saint-Pierre de Nant, and Saint-Michel in Castelnau-Pégayrolles (Fig. 31), are wrapped with heavy continuous arcades on the exterior.[157] These arcades resemble machicolated arches, but none of them seem ever to have had functional openings. If this is the

Figure 31. Castelnau-Pégayrolles, church of Saint-Michel, exterior view.

case, the arcaded churches of the Rouergue may have been intended to be "read" as symbolic protection rather than put to use in military conflict. A similar solution may have been adopted in the architecture of thirteenth-century Languedoc, where unfortified churches such as the Dominican church of the Jacobins in Toulouse or the cathedral of Perpignan are capped with machicolations, perhaps in order that they might be read as images of religious austerity and defense.

CONCLUSION

In the Middle Ages the links between the religious and military realms were frequent and pervasive. Clerics might participate in battles, but more often they fortified their churches and cathedrals. They built walls, invoked saints and relics, or applied sculptural messages to control the forces of disorder and to encourage peace. The fortification of churches and other religious establishments formed part of the changing medieval reactions to war and peace, to crusading ideology, and to a developing xenophobia directed at heretics, "Saracens," and other outsiders. We will see these themes emerge in our analysis of the larger context of fortification in Languedoc in Chapter 2, as well as in Chapter 3, in our more detailed analysis of the fortress-churches of Maguelone, Agde, and Saint-Pons-de-Thomières.

THE LARGER CONTEXT: LANGUEDOC IN THE TWELFTH CENTURY

The pressures that inspired ecclesiastical fortification in twelfth-century Languedoc were multiple and interconnected. The textual records for Maguelone, Agde, and Saint-Pons-de-Thomières describe threats from "Saracens," pirates, heretics, and foreigners, beginning in the eleventh century. The *Chronicon* for Maguelone, for example, speaks of fear of Saracen pirates at Maguelone during the late-eleventh-century episcopacy of Arnaud:

In the time of the Lord Arnaud, bishop of Maguelone, the church at Maguelone was not inhabited, out of fear of the Saracens. For there was a seaport . . . through which Saracen galleys had free access to the island, and frequently carried off from there whatever they might discover. And there were four chaplains assigned there who . . . celebrated Mass there, but lately do not dare to be at church out of fear of the pirates. (Appendix 7)

Suger of Saint-Denis expressed similar concerns after his visit to the abbey in 1118. In his *Life of Louis the Fat,* he reports that Maguelone is

a tiny island in the sea, for which there sufficed with single bishop and priests, a scanty and contemptible household, unique and isolated, . . . nonetheless very well fortified . . . with a wall because of the attacks by sea of the roving Saracens. (Appendix 5)[1]

In a royal diploma of 1173, Louis VII awarded to Bishop Guilhem of Agde

permission . . . because of fear of the Saracens, and because of the frequent incursion of evil men, for the making of towers, fortifications, walls, posterns, and the protections of gates and ditches, and whatever you shall have recognized to be helpful to (the defense of) the church and the city itself. (Appendix 24)

In 1164, the prior of Saint-Pons-de-Thomières sent an appeal to Louis VII and to Pope Alexander III for aid in the "burdens of grievances" the abbey was experiencing (Appendix 31). Two problems are identified in the letter: the absence of the abbot, Raymond of Dourgne (1151–81), and an "immoderate burden of debt." The direct participation in 1165 of Abbot Raymond in the Council of Lombers (a council called expressly to counter the Albigensian heresy) suggests that heretics may also have played a role in the abbey's troubles.[2]

THE PRESSURES

Saracens, Heretics, Brigands, and Pirates in the Textual Record

The complaints recorded in the texts for Maguelone, Agde, and Saint Pons form part of a larger body of contemporary texts that attribute disorder to the actions of Saracens, heretics, brigands, pirates, and mercenaries. Thomas Bisson has characterized the period as a "medieval crime wave."[3] Secular control of disorder seems to have been largely ineffective, and crime seems often to have been attributed to "outsiders": pirates if by sea, brigands if by land.[4] These complaints were also symptomatic of a growing xenophobic attitude that channeled military aggression into warfare against Saracens, heretics and other outsider groups.

The use of fortification at religious establishments was undoubtedly more prevalent in those areas of France which, like Languedoc, were vulnerable to invasion or attack. Texts referring to the fortification of both secular and ecclesiastical property often reveal the identity of the threatening parties. In Normandy and the north of France, it is the Vikings against which fortifications are raised. The *Annales Gandenses* speak of churches fortified against the pressures of seigneurial warfare between Flanders and France.[5] Texts written in the Midi, as we have seen, identify "Saracens" and pirates. The articulate nature of these texts, however, must be countered with a degree of skepticism. That threats are *perceived* is without question, but that they were real is not always certain. The reality behind the complaints about "Saracens" is particularly difficult to document. The Christian reconquest of Catalonia and Aragón resulted in the collapse of the Almoravid dynasty in the mid–twelfth century. Their successors, the Almohads, however, restored the vigor of Spanish Islam and remained a formidable presence in in the Mediterranean during the remainder of the twelfth century. The cathedral of Elne, for example, was fortified in 1144 as a direct result of Islamic attack ten years earlier. In that attack, hostages were taken, and ransom was demanded from a local nobility who seem to have been powerless to react.[6] Archaeological evidence, however, seems to indicate that Muslim presence in southern France was somewhat reduced during this period.[7] The *memory* of the Islamic invasions of the ninth and tenth centuries, kept alive in Carolingian chronicles, may have been in some cases stronger than their contemporary presence. Crusader ideology, furthermore, continued to fuel the notion of a Muslim threat.[8] The contemporary rhetoric of the crusading endeavor would have enhanced the resonance of older texts. Twelfth-century apologists reasoned that since the Muslims had taken lands belonging rightfully to the Church and the Holy Roman Empire, blame should fall entirely on this "most culpable nation."[9] Rhetoric like this may have helped to form negative perceptions of a cultural group never directly encountered by most inhabitants of Languedoc.

Foreign mercenary soldiers were, however, a much more familiar and problematic presence in the region. Mercenaries included men from Aragón, Brabançon, Flanders, Gascony, and elsewhere. They were hired initially to supplement or to replace feudal armies by southern counts and local lords (as well as by the king of Aragón), but they frequently continued their pillaging after local wars had ceased.[10] Few secular lords, including the count of Toulouse or the king of Aragón, seemed able to control the intermittent violence of petty princes, barons, and other quasi-autonomous powers.

Blame for mounting disorder in the area was also laid at the feet of the heretics, who were certainly a more frequent presence in the twelfth century.[11] In the first half of the century, the heretical preachings of Pierre de Bruis and Henri de Lausanne attracted the attention of the clergy outside the Midi. Later in the century, the Cathar heresy in particular gained a powerful foothold. The reasons for the popularity of the Cathars are complicated but may in part be related to the support and, in some cases, the active encouragement of the local aristocracy. The condemnation of heretics at the Council of Lombers in 1165, for example, was not supported by the nobles of the region, many of whom were present.[12] Count Raymond VI of Toulouse, in fact, is said to have kept two Cathar spiritual advisers, and several of the clergy in his territory were even reputed to be believers or sympathizers.[13] The popularity of the Cathar heresy grew until the early years of the thirteenth century, when its suppression was urged by Pope Innocent III. In 1204, papal legates Pierre de Castelnau and Arnold-Amaric began a systematic extermination of the Cathars, calling on King Philip Augustus and Count Raymond VI to participate. Both Philip and Raymond declined, with the result that Raymond was formally excommunicated by the legates. Raymond yielded, but soon after (in 1208) Pierre de Castelnau was murdered. This event precipitated the Albigensian "Crusade," as it was called by the Pope. During this bloody period, Béziers was besieged and fell in 1209, with a horrible massacre of its inhabitants. Too late, the Pope tried to divert the Crusaders to the reconquest of Spain and the Holy Land. Carcasonne, Narbonne, and other cities surrendered in fear before the savagery of the Crusaders.

Despite the accusations of violence, however, heretics seem by and large to have been a fairly peaceful group. Cathar *perfecti,* in fact, were forbidden to kill even in self-defense and, though the lower order of *credentes* might bear arms, Cathar pacifism in general denied the very notion of "just war."[14] Much of the violence encountered in the texts, in fact, seems to have been directed *against* heretics rather than fostered by them. The textual record reveals that ecclesiastical patrons were nervous about heretics and that heretics were identified as threats by orthodox communities, but even the most partisan monastic texts seldom support the notion that heretics attacked religious establishments on their own.

Heretics were, however, often protected by local nobles who were fully capable of initiating trouble all by themselves. Raymond-Roger, count of Foix, for example, was said to have sacked the cathedral of Seu d'Urgel in 1198 "with the cathar band of his uncle Arnau, viscount of Castellbó."[15] It is unclear from the text whether Raymond-Roger's band were truly cathar in religious belief, or merely labeled "infidels" because of their actions. Raymond-Roger also besieged the monastery of Pamiers (this time accompanied by his own men). He occupied the claustral buildings and cruelly mistreated the canons.[16]

Count Raymond VI of Toulouse persecuted abbeys from Moissac to Montauban, burning a church full of faithful in the diocese of Carpentras. He also pillaged several churches in the region of Orange and was responsible for the fortification of the cathedral of Rodez for his own secular purposes. Raymond was finally excommunicated by Pope Celestin III for having destroyed several churches dependent upon Saint-Gilles and for having built the nearby fortified tower of Mirapetra to control the abbey.[17] Roger II Trencavel, viscount of Béziers, was equally active, sacking the abbeys of Saint-Pons and Lagrasse, and imprisoning the bishop of Albi.[18]

The ideological conflation of these local heretics and heretic-sympathizers with "Saracen infidels" in twelfth-century texts led to a new equivalency of many Christian and non-Christian groups. The actions of some Christians, including local nobility and foreign mercenaries, rendered them equivalent to pagans. As we will see, the very term "heretic" came to have a broader meaning in the mid-twelfth-century Peace of God, encompassing other groups marginalized for religious as well as nonreligious reasons.

THE RESPONSES

Fortification and Incastellamento

One response to the varied threats faced by communities in the twelfth century was fortification of churches, villages, and even cemeteries.[19] Beginning perhaps as early as the ninth century, and certainly by the late tenth century, such sites were transferred to higher elevations and were surrounded by walls.[20] Texts begin to refer to *"castra,"* though an easy equivalency between the terms and the new physical sites is not always possible or advisable.[21] This phenomenon of increasingly defensible habitation sites is generally known as *incastellamento*.[22] As we have seen, churches actively participated in the search for effective solutions to the problems of defense.

While Maguelone, Agde, and Saint-Pons are generally discussed as fortified *churches*, it is important to note that all three formed integral parts of larger fortified complexes: at Maguelone with the abbey, and at Agde and Saint-Pons, with the town as well. Machicolation at Maguelone, for example, was employed not only around the walls of the church building itself, but also around the now-destroyed precinct walls, enclosing not only the bishop and canons, but conversi, livestock, and cemetery as well (see Fig. 33).[23] In the more heavily populated contexts of both Agde and Saint-Pons, cathedral or abbey walls were continuous with town fortifications. As fortified ecclesiastical settlements, Maguelone, Agde, and Saint-Pons participated in a larger regional and Mediterranean development. The specific forms chosen by these abbeys and cathedrals were new and different from those of their neighbors, but their existence and location can only be properly understood as part of a regional system of fortification.

A full understanding of the distribution of fortification in twelfth-century Languedoc is, of course, hindered by the partial and fragmentary survival of castles and other fortified sites, as well as their frequent destruction and subsequent rebuilding. Study of twelfth-century fortification must thus involve a number of research strategies: the detailed analysis and phasing of surviving medieval fortifications, the excavation of these fortified sites,[24] study of texts mentioning *castra*,[25] most fruitfully combined with archaeological fieldwalking and excavation to confirm the physical presence of fortifications.[26] Aerial reconnaissance has also aided not only in the identification of individual fortifications but also in the analysis of their larger relationships to one another, to boundaries, and to roads.[27] This latter study is now helped greatly by the publication of Pierre Clément's study of roads in Languedoc.[28]

The mapped results of archaeological and historical survey in the region reveal a dense distibution of fortified sites across the area (see Fig. 2). This distribution has been variously interpreted by scholars. Clusters of fortifications have been seen by A.R. Lewis and Monique Bourin as expressions of the development of quasi-feudal authority consolidating territory in the region.[29] Fredric Cheyette, however, has observed that these groupings were seldom controlled by a single castellan or family. He notes the construction of fortifications separated from larger settlements, and argues that their distribution may indicate the control of roads and other access routes.[30]

Given the fragmentary character of the evidence and the varied conclusions of the interpretative scholarship, it is premature to posit any but the most tentative hypotheses about the relationship between ecclesiastical and secular fortification. Nevertheless, we can observe that the larger pattern of religious fortifications seems to be related to that of secular castles. It is not impossible that fortified churches formed part of an integrated system of defense made up of secular castles, toll stations, fortified habitations, and other protected sites. A fuller identification and analysis of the distribution of church-fortresses in Languedoc will be found in Chapter 5.

A fortified castle or town is generally regarded to be a functional expression of power made by ruling authority to counter fear of an outside threat. Like most such generalizations, this one is only partly accurate. Fortification in Languedoc – especially of churches – was the result of various motivations: responses to perceived threats, as well as proclamations of power and control made by bishops and abbots. The locus of power in the second quarter of the twelfth century, however, was shifting. In specific terms, this meant that in towns across the south of France, responsibility for defense was in the process of being transferred from the bishop to the *consulat* (or commune). By the thirteenth and early fourteenth centuries, the *consulats* had generally assumed responsibility for municipal fortification.[31] To understand fully the phenomenon of church fortification in Languedoc, one must remain cognizant of the shifting "patrons" of military defense, and of the wider regional context for fortification throughout the twelfth century.

The Twelfth-Century Peace of God

As a corrective to the solution of military defense, the medieval church sponsored an organized pacifism. The Peace of God movement, begun in the tenth century, attempted to regulate warfare and to exclude military conflict from religious establishments, including churches, monasteries, and cemeteries.[32] The Peace, for example, generally reserved a perimeter of thirty paces around such sites, which became identified as religious refuges.[33] The Peace was revived and reorganized in the period of c. 1140–1230 as a remedy to the weakness of lay powers to deal effectively with violence, especially in the south of France. The twelfth-century incarnation of the Peace differed from its predecessor in the degree of community involvement. This new "organized peace," as Thomas Bisson has called it, was institutionalized and regularized to clarify its territorial limitations and to enforce the financial support for the maintenance of security. Early examples for this enforcement are found in the establishment of judges of the Peace in the Gevaudan, in taxation to support the Peace in Perigord, and the oaths for the Peace found throughout France.[34] Peace-keeping confraternities and militias were organized, and taxes were instituted to defray the costs of increased security measures.[35] Although religious establishments were fortified as part of the earlier Peace initiatives, it was the reorganized Peace of the twelfth century that motivated the new mid-twelfth-century fortifications at Maguelone, Agde, and Saint-Pons.

Following Carolingian precedent, the king and the princes held at least titular responsibility for the defense of their principality. As king, Louis VII was also responsible for the defense of the entire realm and was owed service by the territorial princes. Nominally, he still held control over all fortifications in the realm and had the right of rendability, which assured his authority to seize any castle or fortified site necessary during periods of military pressure.[36] In practice, however, it was the church that organized the twelfth-century counterattack in defense of peace, especially in the south of France. The lords themselves were largely powerless against their petty vassals and certainly against the bands of roving and unemployed mercenaries in the area. Two groups were particularly important in the revived and reorganized twelfth-century Peace of the south of France. The Templars were active in raising taxes to fund security measures and were also energetic in building fortified churches.[37] The bishops of the south of France were also powerful spokesmen for the revived Peace. The Capetian alliance with the bishops in this endeavor enhanced their prestige and ultimately their influence in the Midi. As we will see below, Louis participated actively in the promotion of the Peace, but it was the Church (and the bishops in particular) who took the lead.

Both papal and local councils of the eleventh and twelfth centuries legislated the Peace.[38] Councils of the mid- to late twelfth century, however, made more explicit the regulations governing the Peace, and the identification of groups seen as threatening or violating it. In 1179, for example, the Third Lateran Council, in direct response to the crises of the Midi, formulated seven statutes on the Peace (Statutes 21 through 27).[39] The first two statutes were repeated virtually verbatim from previous councils, but the subsequent five statutes were original formulations by this council to organize lay and clerical reactions to the crisis. These new statutes attempted to control the perceived violence of Saracen pirates, heretics, and mercenaries, but in so doing, they forged a new and useful equivalency among those disparate groups.[40] The language of Statute 24 reveals this new attitude:

Cruel greed has so seized the minds of some that, when they might glory in the Christian name, they supply the Saracens with arms, iron, and the timber for galleys, and become equal to them or even superior in malice. . . . (They are) subject to excommunication for their iniquity. (Appendix 39)

Statute 27 first excommunicates heretics and all who defend them and then goes on to consider mercenaries:

Concerning the Brabantians, Aragonese, Navarese, Basques, Coterelles, and Triaverdians, who practice such enormity upon Christians that they would defer neither to churches nor to monasteries, nor to widows or children . . . but in the manner of pagans would ruin and destroy everything, similarly we decree that those who would have employed them or shall have kept them throughout the regions in which they rave so madly, shall be publicly denounced . . . throughout the churches, and shall be held subject to exactly the same sentence and punishment as the aforesaid heretics. (Appendix 40)

In other words, those who broke the peace like pagans were subsumed under the title of pagans. As a corollary, heretics were also to be regarded as violators of the Peace. This language is directly related to crusading ideology, and indeed the links between the Peace and the Crusades have often been noted. The councils, in particular, made explicit this connection by calling Christians to reject infidels of every definition. In other words, the task of discrimination was simplified by the equation of Saracens, local heretics, and any violent individual.

The rules of a local "crusade" were thus invoked against heretics, pirates, mercenaries, and native brigands, as well as those who hired or supported them. This association of heretics, pirates, and brigands is found increasingly in texts of this period. Archbishop Pons of Narbonne excommunicated heretics and pirates together in 1179.[41] Louis VII condemned both heretics and unemployed mercenaries identified as "Brabançons and Coterelles" in 1162–3, and again in 1171–2.[42] The Council of Montpellier in 1195 placed them all under anathema:

All heretics, Aragons, bands called mainades, pirates, as well as those who procure arms . . . for the Saracens.[43]

The Peace of God and the Fortification of Churches

We might assume that churches would automatically be fortified against these threats to peace, and as part of the reaction to this local "crusade," but this is only partly true. The relationship of the Peace of God to the actual fortification of churches is more complicated than it might initially seem. Again, the records of local and papal councils provide useful insights to the process.

The frequent and increasing appearance of terms such as *ecclesia incastellata* or *ecclesia munitione* demonstrate that the practice of fortifying churches was known by at least the eleventh century.[44] This terminology is encountered especially often in the late eleventh and twelfth centuries, indicating that physical protection of ecclesiastical property was increasingly sought after by church officials at this time. The records of church councils reveal, however, that churches were sometimes fortified by secular powers for their own use. As we have seen, for example, Raymond VI, count of Toulouse, fortified the cathedral of Rodez for secular purposes. Similar abuses of religious refuge gave rise to legislation *against* the practice of church fortification. The Council of Elne (or Toulouges), for example, clearly distinguished between legitimate defense of churches and the misuse of ecclesiastical fortification:

This is the peace confirmed by bishops and abbots. . . . no man shall infringe upon a church, nor space, nor cemetery, nor dwellings which are or will be in the circuit of the church, up to 30 paces. We do not place those churches, however, under this protection, in which castles have been or will be made: indeed, those churches in which robbers or thieves have gathered booty or spoils, or dwell there for wrong-doing, and return from it. (Appendix 34)

This interdiction from fortification was repeated by a number of local councils and was followed by the First Lateran Council of 1123:

We . . . prohibit by Apostolic authority that churches be fortified by laypersons or converted to profane use. (Appendix 38)

The proscription against ecclesiastical fortification was repeated at both the Third Lateran Council in 1179 and the Council of Avignon in 1209 (Appendixes 39–41).

The reaction against fortified churches may be understood as part of the attempt to guard against the installation of a secular castle within an ecclesiastical precinct, in defiance of the true aims of the Peace movement. The limitation on ecclesiastical fortification may also have been influenced by the contemporary Gregorian reform in its efforts to curtail the secular possession of churches.[45] The fortification of churches as a protection against the threats of pirates, heretics, or mercenaries was not, therefore, always perceived as an automatic or even natural response. The use of religious fortification must thus be seen as a conscious choice, carrying political as well as religious implications.

Louis VII and Capetian Intervention

The intervention of the king, Louis VII (1137–80), in Languedoc in the mid–twelfth century, was influential both for the development of the Peace and for the use of ecclesiastical fortification.[46] Though Languedoc may at first seem relatively far removed from the Capetian sphere of influence in the Ile-de-France and Aquitaine, Louis VII in fact initiated the royal influence in Languedoc that would be consolidated by his successor, Philip Augustus. Louis granted privileges to bishops of Agde and Maguelone and received an appeal from the royal abbey of Saint-Pons.[47] Louis' contact with these churches reflects the more general phenomenon of his growing interest and influence in the south, and, conversely, of the desire of southern clerics to appeal to royal authority.

The second son of Louis VI, the future Louis VII, was educated at the cathedral school in Paris, probably because he was originally destined for an ecclesiastical career. The death of his brother Philip in 1131 changed that career, making him heir to the throne, to which he succeeded as a youth in 1137. William, Duke of Aquitaine had, on his deathbed, left his daughter Eleanor in Louis VI's custody; she was married to Louis VII just before his accession. Chroniclers describe Louis VII as a just and pious man, in terms similar to his more famous great grandson, Louis IX.[48] Though his contemporaries found much to praise in Louis VII, modern historians have been less enthusiastic. Louis has been criticized for allowing his wife, Eleanor of Aquitaine, and his advisers, Abbot Suger and Bernard of Clairvaux, to influence his actions. His participation in the disastrous Second Crusade, his decision to remain in the Holy Land after the crusade, his divorce from Eleanor, and the subsequent loss of Aquitaine have all contributed to the monarch's tarnished reputation. Marcel Pacaut notes rightly, however, that Louis' early consolidation of royal prestige and property paved the way for the eventual triumphs of his son Philip Augustus.[49] In Languedoc, in particular, his skillful political maneuvering permitted the consolidation of Capetian influence where there had been no effective royal presence since the Carolingian era.

Louis accomplished this, first of all, by developing and maintaining important relationships with powerful lords of the Midi, and especially with the counts of Toulouse.[50] His protection of southern churches often countered the power of these southern lords, but his presence had to be supported and tolerated by them as well. Between 1137 and 1148, Louis struggled with Count Alphonse-Jourdan of Toulouse, but from 1148, relations with the new count, Raymond V, improved. After their shared conflict with Roger Trencavel (1152–4), relations between the count and the king were excellent.[51] In 1154, Louis gave his sister Constance in marriage to Count Raymond V of Toulouse. In these years Louis aided his new brother-in-law against the intrigues of King Henry II of England and the counts of Barcelona.[52]

During this time, Louis became allied to other important families of the region: the Melgucil, the Posquières-et-d'Uzès, the Lunel, and the Anduse, among others.[53] In 1163, following the end of war with Barcelona, came new royal alliances with the house of Guilhem de Montpellier and the viscountess of Narbonne, Ermengarde, as well as numerous other nobles of the region. After 1165, however, Count Raymond V and the house of Toulouse broke with the king. War between the houses of Saint-Gilles and Narbonne broke out in 1165 as well. Most of the noble families took part, but many continued to wish for peace, and it was in this interest that many families, including the Montpellier and the Narbonne, kept up relations with Louis.[54]

One way in which Louis consolidated his contacts with southern nobility during this period was by advancing members of their families to episcopal office.[55] Nearly half the bishops of Maguelone and Agde during the late eleventh and twelfth centuries came from the local nobility (see Table 1). Louis was instrumental in the election of Jean de Montlaur to the see at Maguelone in 1159, and he actively supported both Guilhem de Minerve (1162–73) and Pierre de Montpeyroux (1173–94) to the bishopric at Agde. Louis promoted members of the nobility to other sees throughout Languedoc as well. He supported two members of the Montpeyroux, the comital family of Lodève for bishoprics: Gaucelin-Raymond to the see of Lodève (1162–91) and, as we have seen, Pierre to the bishopric of Agde (1173–91). Four bishops were drawn from the Posquières-et-Uzès family, all of them sons of Raymond-Doyen (brother-in-law of Count Alphonse-Jourdan of Toulouse) and uncles of Raymond V of Toulouse: Albert, bishop of Nîmes (1141–80), Raymond, bishop of Uzès (1154–88), Pierre, bishop of Lodève (1155–61), and Raymond, bishop of Viviers (1157–70). Louis also backed the viscounts of Narbonne by promoting Bérengar (1156–62) as archbishop of Narbonne. Bérengar succeeded an important figure from the house of Anduse, Pierre (1150–5), brother of Bernard of Anduse. Bernard was the second husband of Ermengarde, the viscountess of Narbonne, who was largely responsible for fostering the close political ties between Louis VII and the house of Narbonne.

Most of the episcopal elections in which Louis played a role took place in the decades of the 1150s and 1160s. It is principally in these two decades, and especially between 1154 and 1165 during the period of greatest ties with Count Raymond V of Toulouse, that we must see the era of Louis' greatest concern with (and ability to act in) Languedoc and the south of France. It is precisely during this period, I will argue, that the fortifications of Maguelone, Agde, and Saint Pons were under construction.

Louis seems not to have intervened in abbatial elections, aside from those houses where the abbot and bishop were identical. At Maguelone, as we have seen, Louis was instrumental in the election of Jean, a member of the important Montlaur family, who reigned as abbot-bishop from 1159 to 1190. Louis' strategy in his connections with other abbeys seems instead to have been a policy of alliance. Louis placed a number of southern abbeys under royal protection, sometimes styling himself or being adopted as, "founder." The monastery of La Bénisson-Dieu, for example, was in fact established by Saint Bernard in 1138 but was placed under royal protection in 1140–1, at which time Louis inserted himself as its founder.[56] Other southern monasteries accorded royal protection and privileges by Louis included Saint-Gilles (1163–4), Saint-Julien-de-Brioude (1138), and Ville-magne (1156).[57] In this sponsorship of southern abbeys we see a corrollary to Louis' policy of familial alliance enacted through episcopal elections. Both Maguelone and Agde profited from Louis' interest in Languedoc. It is only Saint-Pons, already a royal foundation, that seems to escape Louis' immediate interest.

Louis VII also promoted the revived Peace of God, probably as a result of contact with the southern peace movement. In Soissons in June 1155, he initi-ated a "peace for the whole realm."[58] The preceding year, Louis had traveled in Spain and cannot have been ignorant of the efforts of the cardinal-legate Jacintus to promote the Truce and Peace in Catalonia.[59] On his return trip to France, Louis visited several episcopal cities and may have witnessed a settle-ment of hostilities between the viscountess Ermengarde and the legate-arch-bishop of Narbonne (in January 1155). Louis' efforts must also be seen in the light of episcopal requests for royal protection. Between 1155 and 1174, most of the bishops and several abbots of the province of Narbonne (many of whom owed their elections to Louis) sought and obtained royal protection. Seven episcopal churches, for example, received this award: Maguelone in 1155–6, Uzès in 1156, Nîmes and Narbonne in 1157, Lodève in 1157 and 1162, Mende in 1161, and Agde in 1173–4.

Louis' motivation in these awards of protection seems to have been directed at the secular lords of the episcopal cities. At Agde, for example, Bishop Guilhem was specifically accorded privileges that would normally belong to the viscount, whose name is conspicuously absent from the diploma (Appendix 24).[60] The king was thus not appropriating rights for himself, but was alienating them *away from* the local lord to his ecclesiasti-cal ally. Louis' support for the church strengthened his royal position by weakening that of competing secular powers.[61] At the same time, however, he approved members of those families to the episcopate, thereby softening the blow and diffusing the negative effect upon local nobility. It was, in effect, a "divide and conquer" policy from which the church benefited in the short run, and the monarchy in the long run.

At Maguelone, where the bishops had been freed from secular power since the eleventh century, the intervention of the monarch took a different form. Instead of according protection away from a local lord and awarding it to the loyal bishop, Louis took Maguelone under his direct jurisdiction. This could only be accomplished where, as at Maguelone, there was no real secular power to challenge him. In episcopal sees where there was a very strong lord with whom Louis was not allied, Louis did not intervene, even when invited to do so by bishop or community. For example, in 1169,

Bishop Artaud of Elne wrote to complain that the kings of France had not concerned themselves with the protection of his cathedral church. Louis replied to thank the bishop for his letter, but seems to have done nothing further, evidently not wishing to cross the powerful count of Roussillon.[62] The selective intervention we see exercised for Elne may also have been the case at Saint-Pons-de-Thomières. We know the prior of Saint-Pons appealed to Louis for aid, but no record of a reply is preserved, and none may have been sent.

The granting of royal permission for ecclesiastical fortification, and active support of the episcopally sponsored Peace of God, helped both to undercut comital powers and to consolidate those of the king. The rhetoric of defense was consciously invoked by Louis VII in his acts issued in favor of the Languedoc churches. In his diploma for Maguelone, he proclaimed:

concerning places transferred to divine worship . . . we show ourselves well disposed toward . . . defending. (Appendix 6)

His diploma for Agde similary declares:

So that everything mentioned above be kept whole and undiminished for you . . . , we order (it) to be fortified in the strength and authority of our charter and royal seal. (Appendix 24)

The fortification of Maguelone and Agde (and, to a much lesser degree, Saint-Pons) must therefore be seen in the context of a larger royal agenda, enacted in the third quarter of the twelfth century.

THE BUILDINGS AND THE DOCUMENTS: MAGUELONE, AGDE, AND SAINT-PONS-DE-THOMIERES

The fortress-churches of Maguelone, Agde, and Saint-Pons-de-Thomières were integrally involved in the political, social, and religious developments of mid-twelfth-century Languedoc. As three of the major cathedral and abbey churches of the region, they attracted important patrons and resident clergy, hosted kings and popes as visitors, amassed great wealth and prestige, and commissioned impressive architectural complexes. Though other churches and abbeys in the region may have shared their importance and their military aspects, the survival at these three great churches of both documentary and physical evidence of their mid-twelfth-century phases permits a fuller analysis than is possible for other buildings. We will focus in this chapter on a full "reading" of the fabric of each building as well as of the relevant archival sources for each community. In this endeavor we will make frequent reference to primary material. Resumés of the building histories of Maguelone, Agde, and Saint-Pons, from their foundation to the twentieth century, precede the more detailed analysis of the twelfth-century phases of each building. In this regard, we will discuss in detail the observations recorded in the new surveyed plans, measured elevations, and analytic section drawings produced for this book. The most important texts have been assembled in the Appendixes in both the original Latin as well as in new English translations. Identification of the twelfth-century phases of Maguelone, Agde, and Saint-Pons is only possible through detailed analysis of the buildings, careful reading of the archival sources, and critical reevaluation of the secondary sources.

Previous analysis of these buildings has tended to link unquestioningly selected texts to the fabric. The survival of a chronicle for Maguelone, a royal diploma for Agde, and a charter of accord for Saint-Pons-de-Thomières have suggested dates for Maguelone in the mid- to late twelfth century, but for Agde and Saint-Pons in the 1170s. A more critical reading of these documents, together with an analysis of a fuller range of documents for all three buildings (and for Agde in particular) suggests that their construction began somewhat earlier, in the second rather than the third quarter of the twelfth century. This redating is not radical, but it has important implications for the ways in which we understand the patronage of these buildings and the motivations for their construction. As we have seen in the preceding chapter, Louis VII was influential in the region by co-opting processes that have already been initiated by important families and bishops of the region. We will see that at Maguelone and Agde, Louis granted permission retrospectively for fortifications that were already under construction.

Previous scholarship has tended to consider Maguelone, Agde, and Saint-Pons-de-Thomières as a unified group of fortified churches. It is important to recognize, as we will in this chapter, that all three form part of larger fortified precincts. Though closely related by their location and design, the three communities are to be distinguished by a number of significant differences. Maguelone adopted the Augustinian rule in its eleventh-century reform. Agde was a community of secular canons, whereas Saint-Pons observed the Benedictine Rule. Maguelone and Agde were cathedrals, whereas Saint-Pons remained until the fourteenth century an abbey in the diocese of Narbonne. Agde and Maguelone were ports on the Mediterranean coast, whereas Saint-Pons lies 50 kilometers inland. Their plans and elevations also have significant differences. Although all three are single-naved, barrel-vaulted structures, Maguelone is a triple-apsed basilica 45 meters long. Agde has a disaxial transept with no apsidal projection and measures only 34 meters in length. Saint-Pons has lost its original eastern termination (which was probably tri-apsidal) but even in its truncated form extends an impressive 67 meters from west to east, and must have stretched to over 80 meters in the twelfth century. The spans of the buildings' vaults are also different: 10 meters at Maguelone, 12.6 meters at Agde, and nearly 15 meters at Saint-Pons. Perhaps the most striking differences for our purposes lie in the defensive systems of the three buildings. Agde, and Saint-Pons are situated in towns, and their fortifications are linked to municipal defenses, whereas Maguelone is isolated on a remote island. Although Maguelone and Agde are wrapped with simple machicolated arches, Saint-Pons originally had a much more elaborate triple-tiered defensive system. All of these differences encourage us to examine these fortress-churches individually as well as conjointly.

MAGUELONE

The fortress-cathedral and abbey of Maguelone, situated on an island close to the Mediterranean coast, is one of the earliest machicolated buildings in France (Fig. 32). Machicolation was employed not only around the walls of the church building itself but also in the thirteenth-century entry towers, bishop's palace, and precinct wall. Protection was afforded not only by the physical fortifications but also by papal sponsorship, awarded in the late eleventh century. In the twelfth and thirteenth centuries, Maguelone became one of the wealthiest and most illustrious houses of Languedoc.

History of the Site

The origins and early history of Maguelone remain somewhat obscure. The island site, today silted up and nearly deserted, seems never to have been

Figure 32. Maguelone, aerial view of the church.

heavily populated, although it seems to have been a known port. The adjoining coastal zone was important for salt, fishing, and sailing.[1] From the Roman through the medieval period, Maguelone marked the intersection of two main roads: the Via Domitiana and the *ager publicus* (see Fig. 2). Only in the early eleventh century was a bridge constructed to link the island with the mainland.[2] The creation of an episcopal seat on the island, between the dioceses of Nîmes and Agde, was a relatively late installation for a southern bishopric.[3] Its creation, most likely in the late sixth century, was probably a result of an adminstrative reorganization of the province and diocese of Narbonne.[4] Like much of Septimania, Maguelone seems to have been susceptible to invasion from the sea, especially by Visigoths and Muslims. Most scholars interpret lacunae in the list of seventh- and eighth-century bishops for Maguelone as evidence of insecurity at the site. We do know that the Visigothic king Wamba besieged the port in 673 during his campaign for the reconquest of the province of Narbonne. The Chronicle of Moissac details the devastation of the region by the "Saracens" in the eighth century. In the 730's, the Chronicle says that Charles Martel took the island and destroyed it.[5] During this period of insecurity, the episcopal seat was transferred to Substantion, modern Castelnau-le-Lez. Maguelone, however, would seem to have retained some importance during the Islamic conquest of the eighth century, since chronicles refer to it as a "Saracen port."[6] By the end of the ninth century, the counts of Melgueil, residing at Maugio, had taken over the bishopric, controlling revenues and the naming of the bishop, often from their own ranks. Pierre de Melgueil, for example, served as bishop of Maguelone and Substantion from 999 to 1030 (see Table 1).[7]

The abbatial history of Maguelone begins with the eleventh-century reform, led by Bishop Arnaud (1032–60). Under his energetic direction, the canons serving the cathedral adopted the Augustinian rule, making the house an abbey as well as a cathedral.[8] Until this time, Maguelone appears to have been deserted, with the community based at Substantion and controlled by the counts of Melgueil. Pope John XIX referred to the church in 1032–3 as "reduced to nothing," perhaps an exaggeration, but certainly an indication of reduced circumstances (Appendix 1). In 1085, however, Count Pierre de Melgueil restored to the cathedral-abbey all rights and properties taken from it by his ancestors (Appendix 2). This restoration of alienated property was a common phenomenon in the reform period. As part of his (re)foundation gift, he placed himself under papal protection, awarding his county and the alienated bishopric to the apostles Peter and Paul, and to Pope Gregory VII and his successors. This donation was officially accepted in 1088 by Pope Urban II, who returned the county to Pierre, and the bishopric to the abbatial community in the person of Bishop Godfrey (1080–1104) (Appendix 3). This series of acts established Maguelone as a pontifical fief, guaranteeing free episcopal election to the canons. Maguelone thus became a community remarkably free of secular intervention, although, as we will see, both the local nobility and the royal house of the Capetians continued to exert influence throughout the twelfth century.

The Capetians, as we have seen, allied themselves to both the church and local families by according royal privileges to the community and by supporting members of noble families to the bishopric. Bishop Godfrey was energetic in participating in church councils in France and Italy, including those held in Narbonne in 1090, at Clermont in 1092, and again in 1095, when the First Crusade was announced. Godfrey maintained important links with Pope Urban II, and attended the Council of Rome in 1099. He died on crusade to the Holy Land and was buried at Tripoli.

On his way from the council at Clermont in 1096, Pope Urban II visited Maguelone, and praised it as "second only to the Roman Church" (Appendix 4).[9] Urban returned the port of Maguelone to the abbey, awarded indulgences to those buried in its cemetery, and conferred the papal arms (the keys of Saint Peter) on the chapter.[10]

These papal commentaries and awards not only provided Maguelone with Roman and papal connections, it made of the island a convenient refuge for popes fleeing the investiture controversy and the factions of Rome. The bishops of Maguelone cultivated links to the papacy. During the episcopacy of Bishop Galtier (1104–28), for example, Pope Gelasius II visited Maguelone (in 1118) and received there two powerful churchmen, Pons de Melgueil, infamous abbot of Cluny, and Suger, emissary and soon to be abbot of Saint Denis.[11] Pope Callixtus II visited in 1119, when he celebrated the same solemn feast of Saint Peter (June 29) that Urban II had initiated 23 years earlier.[12] Pope Innocent II probably also visited the island in 1130.[13] Bishop Raymond (1129–58) accompanied the pope to several councils, including those at Saint-Gilles, Clermont, and Etampes. Pope Alexander III came twice during his flight from Rome: once in 1163 when he consecrated the high altar, and again in 1165.[14] Bishop Jean de Montlaur was present at the Lateran Council of 1179, presided over by Alexander.

The new prestige of Maguelone, stemming from its papal connections, led to wealth. The territorial importance of Maguelone was based on rich fishing rights, salt collection, tolls, and donations, all of which were frequently reaffirmed in papal confirmations. The growth of the abbey and its reputation also resulted, as we shall see, in new construction in the twelfth and thirteenth centuries: a larger cathedral, a two-story cloister with claustral ranges, and a logis for the bishop and his guests.

In the thirteenth century, Maguelone remained a staunch catholic stronghold against the Albigensian heresy. Pierre de Castelnau, papal legate to Languedoc, whose death in 1208 at Saint-Gilles launched the outbreak of war in the Albigensian Crusade, was an archdeacon of Maguelone. Though royal and papal connections enhanced Maguelone's power and prestige in the twelfth and thirteenth centuries, reversals were seen in the fourteenth and fifteenth centuries. The kings of Majorca, lords of Montpellier, as well as the kings of France, increasingly limited the privileges and independence of Maguelone. Increasing financial woes and the more frequent absence of canons from the abbey for duties at the papal court in Avignon led to a decline in community life and to abuses of its practice. To counteract this in 1331, Bishop Jean de Vissec issued the reforming *Statutes* that now furnish valuable information on fourteenth-century life at the abbey (Appendix 11).[15] Though the *Statutes* may have remedied irregularities at Maguelone, they could not counteract the increasing attraction of the new town of Montpellier, with its university, markets, and financial vigor. Maguelone was garrisoned during the Hundred Years War and began to slip into oblivion (Appendix 12).

The last bishop of Maguelone, Guillaume Pellecier (1526–68), was adviser and ambassador to King François I at Rome. Having received the king at the island of Maguelone, he impressed upon him the need to transfer the see to the larger city of Montpellier. This transfer was effected in 1536, with the permission of Pope Paul III. At the time, the canons expressed their wish to have the buildings sold and destroyed to mark their definitive abandon. This was not done, and in 1562 Huguenot troops occupied the abbey until they were expelled by royal forces, who themselves left behind a garrison for several years. In 1632, Richelieu received a royal order from Louis XIII to destroy the medieval fortress, but with specific instructions to spare the church itself. He dismantled what remained of the abbey and the fortified aspects of the church, including its towers and machicolations, leaving only the core of the church itself intact.

The precinct walls were sold in 1708 by the chapter to serve in the construction of the Rhone-Sete canal. A last involuntary guest from the East was lodged at Maguelone in 1720, when Mehemet Effendi, treasurer of the Sultan and ambassador to Louis XV, was held in quarantine at Maguelone because of an outbreak of plague at Sete. During the Revolution, Maguelone was seized and sold as a "bien national." The building was classed early by Monuments Historiques, in 1840, but repairs were not forthcoming until the site passed into private hands.[16] In 1852, it was bought by Frédéric Fabrège, who excavated the island, publishing his results in a three-volume study. Fabrège also rebuilt portions of the cathedral and replanted the island with trees. These actions saved the church from ruin and the island from further loss of topsoil, but the reconstruction obscured much of the architectural evidence of the walls, while the planting of trees has undermined archaeological layers. In 1875, Fabrège and his family restored the cathedral to service. Repairs sponsored by Monuments Historiques began in the 1940s, with the first recorded repairs being the rebuilding of the *machicoulis* on the west façade. These repairs were interrupted by the threat of German occupation of the island. Maguelone was given to the diocese of Montpellier at the close of the war in 1949. Repairs from water damage, as well as reroofing of the apses and towers was accomplished in the 1950s. The 1960s saw the restoration of the nave and the recovering of the nave roof. The Compagnons Association de Travail, a charitable group, took over the site in 1969 and currently run a training farm on the island.

The Building Fabric

The abbey of Maguelone stood alone on its island site surrounded by a walled enclosure (Figs. 33, 34). The earliest surviving elements on the site seem to belong to the eleventh-century church, probably the cathedral built by Bishop Arnaud (Fig. 35). A southern tower, now known as the "tower of Saint Augustine," may originally have formed the transept of this church. Although partially ruined in its upper stories, this tower preserves a chapel on the ground story, built of small ashlar blocks and capped with a barrel vault. The chapel is joined to the twelfth-century nave by a series of heavy

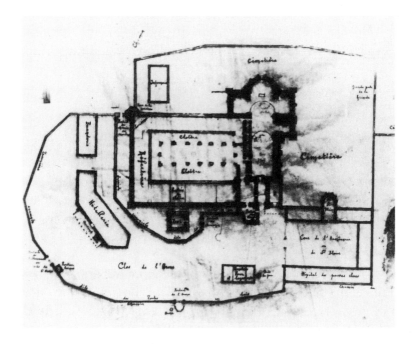

Figure 33. Maguelone, reconstruction plan of the abbey. (Fabrège plan)

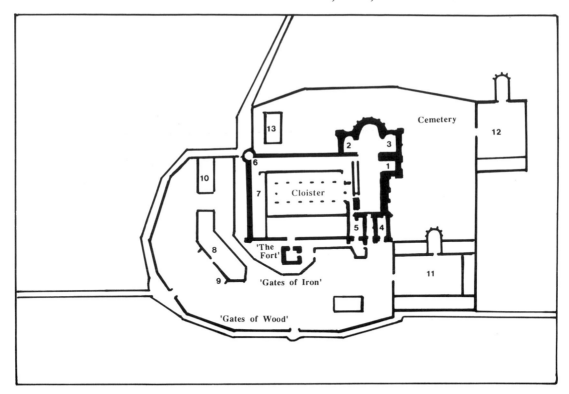

1. Tower of Saint Augustine (Chapel of Saint-Michel above)
2. Tower of Saint Sepulchre (Chapel of Saint-Pancras above)
3. Tower of Sainte-Marie
4. Tower of Saint-Jean
5. Tower of the Bishop
6. Kitchen
7. Refectory
8. Reception building
9. Lavabo
10. Wash House
11. Almonry
12. Collegiate of La Trinité
13. Infirmary

Figure 34. Keyed redrawing of the Fabrège plan.

semicircular arches. The junction between the two campaigns is evident not only in the change in ashlar size and type but also by a straight joint at the inner arch of the entry. Nineteenth-century excavations revealed an apse (now painted in red on the floor of the nave). If these measurements are correct, the earlier apse stretched across nearly the entire span of the present nave. The apse was most likely the eastern termination of Arnaud's eleventh-century cathedral.

The phases of the twelfth-century campaigns can be observed in breaks in the interior fabric. A campaign break between the choir and nave is visible in a suture line just to the west of the north stair door (Fig. 36). The change this break reveals is also observable in several differences between choir and nave construction. The choir is built of smaller stone, without the use of header-stretcher alternation that is a hallmark of the nave. The crowns of

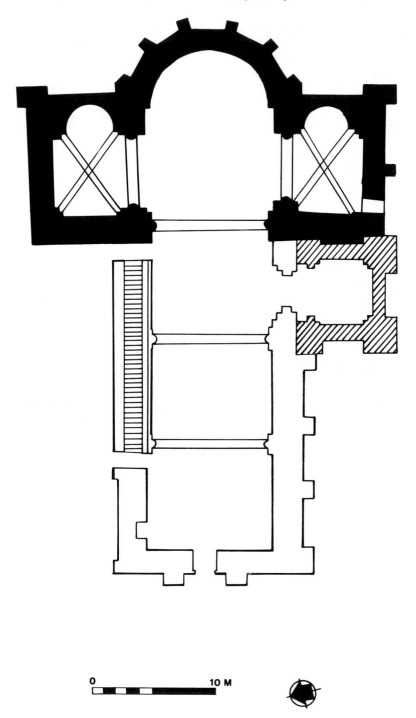

Figure 35. Maguelone, phased plan of the church. *Diagonal shading:* Eleventh-century; *Black:* Early twelfth-century; *Outline:* Mid- to late twelfth-century.

Figure 36. Maguelone, detail of north wall, showing campaign break and gallery opening in vault.

the vaults are slightly but perceptibly lower in the choir. Though all of the original capitals in the church are Corinthian, the application of decoration differs slightly in the nave, transepts, and choir. The unity of the whole building, however, is remarkable, especially in light of its apparent construction under three successive prelates over nearly fifty years.

The use of two different stone types in the fabric of Maguelone has led some specialists to conclude that the machicolations are not integral with the building and that a fourth campaign is present. However, this is demonstrably not the case. A golden, very shelly limestone is used predominantly on both the interior and exterior, whereas a denser, grey limestone known locally as "cold stone," is reserved for the southern and western machicolations (and is also found in the earlier "tower of Saint Augustine"). Because of the difference in building stone, it has been suggested that the fortifications were "wrapped" around preexisting walls.[17] Machicolations of the northern, cloister side, though less extensive, and far less well preserved, appear to have been constructed of the same golden shelly limestone as the walls. Examination of the exterior fabric around the rest of the building, moreover, makes clear that the cold-stone blocks of the southern and western machicolations are integrally coursed and bonded with the walls.[18] It is therefore clear that both stone types were used simultaneously in all three twelfth-century campaigns. It is likely that the use of a more durable stone was reserved for the outer machicolations, which were most directly exposed both to the harsh sea wind as well as to potential military attack.

The cathedral's interior is an unaisled hall of generous proportions, measuring almost 45 meters in exterior length, nearly 10 meters in width, and just under 20 meters in height (Fig. 37). The nave is divided into three bays. The two westernmost bays support a tribune, and the easternmost bay opens to the south into the tower of Saint Augustine. The apsidal projection of the choir is polygonal at the exterior. Apsidal chapels in the flanking transepts are contained within the thickness of their eastern walls. The walls throughout the building are remarkably thick (2.5 meters) and contain on the northern side a stair-passage that leads to the tribune and upper cloister

Figure 37. Maguelone, interior view, showing gallery in south wall.

Figure 38. Maguelone, interior view to the south, showing archer slits in tribune.

at the second story and then up another stair passage to the roof platform at the third story. This roof platform, which provided access to the machicolations, was probably originally crenellated.

The southern wall of the building is even more complex. There another passage with small archer slits permitted defense of the exposed flank. This passage is now blocked, but the openings remain intact (Fig. 38), and careful examination reveals the interior walls of the passage still visible within the rubble blocking. The course of this passage is now unclear, but it may well have led originally into the tower of Saint Augustine, which still preserves portions of gallery passages and a blocked stair on its upper level (Fig. 39).[19]

A number of towers crowned the church at Maguelone. In addition to the eleventh-century tower of Saint Augustine, a tower rose over each transept arm. The north transept is slightly disaligned from the rest of the east end, perhaps the result of reuse of the foundations of a predecessor tower from Arnaud's church. In the thirteenth century, towers were also added to the west front. These towers provided additional altar space in the cathedral. With a community of Augustinian canon-priests, all of whom were required to serve Mass daily, the provision of multiple chapels would

Figure 39. Maguelone, exterior view from the south, showing upper gallery.

have been a necessity.[20] The fortified aspects of these galleries and towers are explored further in Chapter 4.

Archival Sources

The sources for Maguelone are particularly rich, including the episcopal cartulary and a collection of the papal bulls relevant to the community. Two chronicles of the history of the abbey are also preserved. Through the efforts of A. Germain and J. Rouquette, many of these sources have been published. A number of inscriptions also survive or have been excavated on the site.

A chronology for eleventh- and twelfth-century construction at the site is proposed by a near-contemporary text: the *Chronicon magalonense vetus* written in the mid- to late twelfth century, after the accession of Jean de Montlaur in 1158 (Appendix 7).[21] The phases proposed in the *Chronicon,* providing early, mid- and late-twelfth-century campaigns, replacing an eleventh-century cathedral, would seem to match, in very general terms, the building campaigns identified in our discussion of the fabric. According to the colophon of the *Chronicon,* the text was composed by a canon of Maguelone, the sacristan named Bertrand. The *Chronicon* contains information about Jean's four predecessor bishops: Arnaud, Godfrey, Galtier, and Raymond, as well as about the reign of Jean himself. With its near-contemporary date, the document is of particular importance for architectural historians. Much of what Bertrand reports he either saw himself or may have heard from eyewitnesses. Bertrand also seems to have been a reliable and interested observer of the building process. Unfortunately, Bertrand reappears only once in the cartulary as a witness to a charter, limiting further precision about his life or connection with the building process.[22] It must be emphasized, as well, that recent archaeological research is providing us with a much clearer picture of the complexities of medieval monastic construction. This evidence suggests that church and claustral buildings like those at Maguelone would have been planned, partially built, and rebuilt in stages much more complicated than most medieval texts would have us believe. The assignment of discrete pieces of the church at Maguelone to successive abbots by the author of the *Chronicon* thus reflects in general ways the progress of construction but probably cannot (and was not intended to) provide an accurate picture of surviving and reused fabric in each campaign.

Two inscriptions survive, which are often cited as providing further textual precision for the dates of construction at the cathedral. However, neither can be taken to advance our understanding of architectural phases. The first inscription is found on the border surrounding the carved lintel that now decorates the west portal of the church (Appendix 9). The marble lintel has a long inscription in Latin verse, with a date of 1178, and is signed in a sort of code by "B D III VIIS," or "B. of Trèves." It has been suggested that "B" stands for Bertrand, the sacristan and author of the *Chronicon,* but this is unlikely.[23] The date of 1178 on the lintel has also been taken as marking the date of completion of the nave. With the construction dates suggested by the textual sources discussed below, completion of the nave in 1178 is entirely possible. The fact that the lintel has been incorporated with other pieces of sculptural spolia into a new, thirteenth-century ensemble, however, discourages this hypothesis. That the lintel was originally planned and executed to mark a door is likely, but its present context provides no independent evidence for the date of completion of the nave.

A second inscription is often discussed as relating to the chronology for construction for Maguelone. It is found on the funerary monument for Jean de Montlaur, who died in 1190.[24] The slab is presently reused as the tribune altar (Appendix 10). The epitaph inscription also mentions a Bertrand, though it is certainly too much to hope, as have previous commentators, that all of these Bertrands are the same person. It is, however, noteworthy that the dates of the *Chronicon* and of both inscriptions all fall within the period of 1178–90. All three seem to have been commissioned during the reign of (or at the very end of) Jean de Montlaur's episcopacy. All three texts, then, bear witness, if not to a single "author/architect" named Bertrand, at least to a community with literary pretensions.

In the fourteenth century, Arnaud of Verdale, bishop of Maguelone from

1339–52 incorporated the text of the *Chronicon* into his *Catalogus episco-porum Magalonensium* (Appendix 8). The *Catalogus* also includes copies of original charters, confirmations, poetry, and other original sources. Arnaud of Verdale had access to original sources now lost, but his fourteenth-century text is, of course, to be used only with caution to reconstruct our picture of the twelfth-century community or its buildings. Many of the dates cited by Arnaud of Verdale, for example, are incorrect (see Table 1). My analysis will depend on the *Chronicon,* with infrequent appeal to the expanded information of the *Catalogus*.

The *Chronicon* tells us that bishop Arnaud (1032–60) restored the community, which "was not inhabited, out of fear of the Saracens." This report of abandonment echoes the evidence provided by the letter of Pope John XIX, saying that the church at Maguelone had been "reduced to nothing because of sin" (Appendix 1). The *Chronicon* reports that Arnaud restored the community and instituted the Augustinian rule, despite some opposition from the community. He built a bridge, linking the island with the mainland, and began construction on the church as well as some canonial buildings. The fourteenth-century *Catalogus* adds that Arnaud began the fortifications of the abbey, but there is no contemporary witness to this assertion. Arnaud would seem to have restored not only the fabric of the abbey but also its reputation, which began to flourish from this period.

Bertrand succeeded Arnaud in 1060 and reigned until 1080, when he was deposed because of the crime of simony. For this reason, Arnaud of Verdale deems him unworthy for inclusion in his *Catalogus*. It may be that the author of the *Chronicon* felt similarly, since he is entirely absent from that text. Despite his crime, the cartulary reveals that Bertrand was responsible for the acquisition of several important properties for the community (Table 4). Bertrand was succeeded by Godfrey (1080–1104). The *Chronicon* reports that bishop Godfrey continued the work of Arnaud, but does not credit him with any significant construction of his own.

The *Chronicon* assigns the beginning of twelfth-century construction to Abbot Galtier (1104–28), its continuation to his successors, Raymond (1129–58) and Jean de Montlaur (1159–90). Galtier is said to have rebuilt "from the foundations" the "head" of the church, presumably the chevet, as well as its three "choirs" (the apses) and the north transept tower (dedicated to Saint-Sepulchre). To the north of the chevet, Galtier is also said to have begun "from the foundations" the cellar, refectory, and dormitory. The *Catalogus* adds the observation that the predecessor church "menaced ruin."

The *Chronicon* reports that Galtier's successor, Raymond, enlarged the church, raising the remainder of the north transept tower begun by Galtier and the corresponding south transept tower (dedicated to Sainte-Marie). He is credited with the construction of the main altar and the episcopal throne in the choir. The chapter room, cistern, and cloister foundations are all attributed to Raymond, as well as the *lavatorium* located within the cloister. Outside the claustral complex, Raymond is also said to have built the wall around the "court" or cloister, the walls and gates that enclosed the lay cemetery, and several subsidiary houses: the mill house and at least two reception structures.

Despite Raymond's impressive construction activities, the *Chronicon* reports that his successor, Jean de Montlaur, found the church "ruined" upon his succession in 1159. Jean is said to have "demolished" the old church and to have rebuilt "a new one . . . from the greater portion." Given the descriptions of work accomplished by his predecessors, and the phases we have observed in the fabric of the church, it is likely that Jean built much of the nave but that he left intact the eastern portions of the church, which had just been completed. Further precision may be provided by the visit of Pope Alexander III in 1163 when he is said to have consecrated the high altar that stood within the newly completed east end.[25]

Church dedications, and especially papal ones, are notoriously unreliable as a measure of the completion of building campaigns, since they coincided more often with papal availability than with the progress of architectural campaigns.[26] Nonetheless, the congruence of information in the texts suggests strongly that the east end of the cathedral of Maguelone was largely complete by c. 1163 but that more work remained to be done in the west. It may be that the eleventh-century nave built by Arnaud stood until the time of Jean de Montlaur and that it was this portion of the church that Jean found "ruined" upon his accession.

The episcopal cartulary and papal bulls also preserve evidence of the construction and dedication of the church at Maguelone, and of the special rights accorded the community by municipal, royal, and papal patrons.[27] Donations and testaments (willed gifts) given to the bishop and the community indicate an especially rich period of prosperity under bishops Raymond and Jean de Montlaur (see Table 4). Maguelone enjoyed royal and papal protection, the support of local nobility, and the leadership of capable abbot-bishops. In 1155 King Louis VII, renewing the privileges accorded by his father and his ancestors, placed the church and its goods under his protection (Appendix 6). In his diploma, he stresses the protective aspect of this agreement, saying, "Concerning places transferred to divine worship, we show ourselves well disposed toward . . . defending." In both the diploma of 1155 and the one issued the following year, Louis not only stressed his oath of protection but added the threat of interdiction to any secular power who would challenge it. Several years later, Louis backed Jean, a member of the illustrious Montlaur family, for the bishopric. Subsequent acts confirmed Louis' intention to take this cathedral abbey under direct royal jurisdiction.[28]

The award of papal protection in 1085 (Appendix 3) had elevated Maguelone to a select group of papally sponsored abbeys, best known of which was Cluny. Though many of the papal houses in France were Cluniac, a significant number were also drawn from the new orders of the eleventh- and twelfth-century reform. As we have seen above (in Chap. 2), the language of these donations often emphasized the defensive aspect of this arrangement. Thus Pope Urban stresses the "special protection of the Roman Church" awarded to Maguelone.[29]

The designers of the church and abbey at Maguelone seem to have been especially conscious of their links to Rome and the papacy and to have expressed this connection in visual as well as verbal language. Pope Urban's letter of 1096 (Appendix 4) provides the first explicit link to Rome, characterizing Maguelone as "second only to the Roman Church." As we have seen, many of Maguelone's bishops maintained contacts with the papacy, attending church councils in Rome, going on papally sponsored crusades, and receiving popes at the island of Maguelone. The church of Maguelone is replete with classicizing features. Though some of these features may be said to participate in a loosely defined local style that drew from classical sources, the connections with Rome and things Roman were quite conscious and deliberate on the part of Maguelone's bishops and chapter. Not only does the use of enormous vaulted spaces and acanthus capitals remind the viewer of Rome, the nave is built in a technique that derives ultimately from Roman practice: a header-stretcher arrangement known locally as *opus Monspelliensis*.[30] The very dedication to the church to saints Peter and Paul certainly underlines a connection with Rome. Pauline and Petrine iconography is advertised in the west portal, composed of reused relief sculpture sometime after the thirteenth century.[31] The jambs of the portal are composed of two reused bas-reliefs representing Saint Paul on the left, and on the right, Saint Peter holding his papal keys (Fig. 40). These two figures may originally have formed part of a single round-headed tympanum, altar, or ambo. The classicizing style of the figures with their crisp drapery patterns suggests that they were carved in the eleventh century. The choice of Saint Peter with his keys may have been inspired not simply by the dedication of the cathedral but also as a reminder of the new papal connections of Maguelone expressed in Pope Urban II's gift of the papal keys and in the seal of the chapter which represented a hand holding the keys of Saint Peter.

Papal sponsorship, royal connections, and revenues from local nobility, therefore, combined to allow Maguelone to become one of the most illustrious religious communities of Languedoc during the twelfth and thirteenth centuries. Its defense was accomplished not only through the addition of

Figure 40. Maguelone, detail of west portal: Saint Peter.

physical walls and machicolations but also through verbal oaths of papal and royal protection.

AGDE

Until the replacement of its original fighting platform in 1967, Agde was the best-preserved example of a southern fortified cathedral. Even now, with its stone platform replaced, it remains an eloquent reminder of episcopal power in twelfth-century Languedoc (Fig. 41). The rich survival of medieval testaments for Agde and the existence of copies of both the episcopal and chapter cartularies permit us to reconstruct the chronology of construction for the cathedral, as well as to trace the historical context for its fortification. Instead of the papal connections that were emphasized at Maguelone, the bishop of Agde seems to have appealed primarily to Carolingian precedent. The falsification of a ninth-century charter, together with the rebuilding of the cathedral, originally constructed in the ninth century, bears witness to a "Carolingian revival" in both text and stone.[32]

Figure 41. Agde, aerial view of cathedral.

History of the Site

The ancient port city of Agde was founded on the Hérault river in the sixth century by Greek settlers from Marseille, who named their town "Agathé Tyché," or "Good Fortune." The medieval city was sited on the center of the ancient town, with medieval streets following the paths of their ancient predecessors, and the foundations of ancient fortifications forming the base for the medieval precinct walls (Fig. 42).[33]

The diocese of Agde was established by the early sixth century, but it was not until the the late ninth century that the testament of Apollonius (written in 872), attests to a church with dedication to Saint Etienne in Agde and to the existence of a group of canons.[34] It seems that the first church built on the site of Saint-Etienne was constructed in the late ninth century and that it was this church that was reconstructed in the course of the twelfth century.

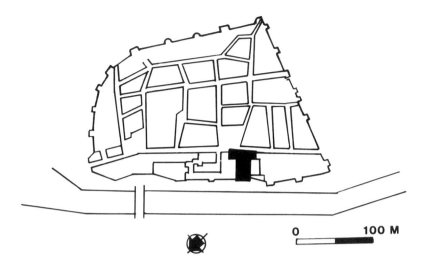

Figure 42. Agde, plan of town.

0   100 M

In 1847, in the process of repaving the choir, an apse was discovered, equal to the nave in diameter. This apse was probably the eastern termination of the Carolingian church (Fig. 43).[35]

From its inception, the cathedral chapter drew its members from the highest levels of Agathois society, receiving not only the support of the bishop but also the protection of the viscount. Bishops, too, came from the local nobility, with members of the Marseillan and Soubeiras families, the viscounts of Minerve, and the lords of Montperoux providing bishops to the city (see Table 1). Initially the viscounts of Agde supported the cathedral chapter, but stresses in that relationship appeared in the last half of the twelfth century. The viscount of Agde was, until 1151, also the viscount of Béziers. In that year, the title was divided between two brothers, Bernard Aton and Raymond Trencavel. From this period the viscounty no longer corresponded to the diocese of Agde. The viscounty fell into decline in the late twelfth century, reaching a nadir in 1187, when Bernard Aton bequeathed the viscountship and its appurtenances to bishop Pierre, with the consent of Raymond Trencavel, who held the viscounty in fief. The bishop held secular as well as religious dominance in Agde from this time until the thirteenth century, when the consulat began to gain increasing power and royal recognition.

The cathedral church was rebuilt in the twelfth century but had its final dedication only in the mid–fifteenth century, when the ceremony was performed by Bishop Etienne de Roupy on 8 July 1453. After being sacked during the Wars of Religion, it was heavily restored by Bishop Balthasar de Budos, who made a number of drastic changes to the interior of the cathedral in the 1620s. He moved the altar to the west, opened a door to the east, and installed *boiseries*. The south tower, damaged in 1581, collapsed in 1661. The cathedral of Agde was classed by Monuments Historiques in the 1840s. An attempt to acquire the cloister in order to protect it was

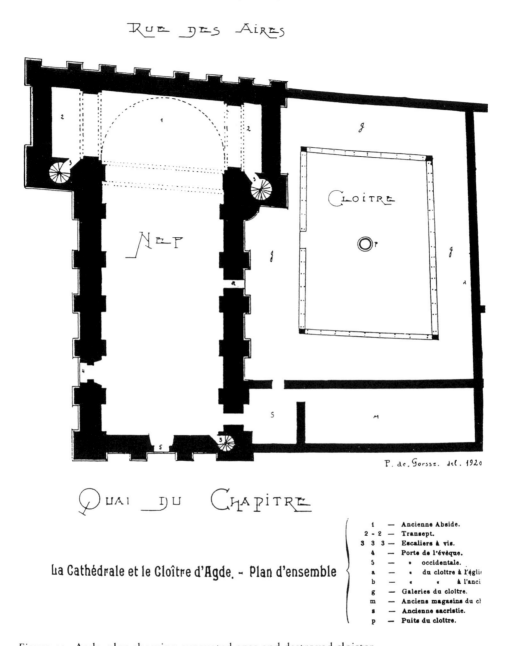

Figure 43. Agde, plan showing excavated apse and destroyed cloister.

launched in 1851 but was not successful. This cloister, virtually destroyed by vandalism in the 1860s, was subsequently demolished. Several remaining fragments were later reused in the modern terrace to the south of the church.[36] In 1896, Monuments Historiques undertook a campaign of reconstruction at Agde, involving the renewal of the west façade and the interior. Houses built on the quai against the west front were dismantled, one of the damaged machicolations was rebuilt, and the modern door now opening onto the quai was pierced. The chevet door opened by Bishop Budos was closed, and the lower portions of the interior pilasters, cut away by Budos' *boiseries,* were rebuilt. The roof, a continuing worry, was repaired, and the crenellations of the north tower were repointed. After unsuccessful attempts to repair the medieval fighting platform in 1910 and again in the 1930s, the stone roof was removed and replaced with tile in 1967.[37]

Building Fabric

The cathedral of Saint-Etienne is sober in design and appearance. It is built of a very dark and coarse volcanic stone that reinforces the severity of design and the restrained decoration of the entire building. Saint-Etienne is wrapped with *machicoulis* terminating in crenellations at the roof level (Fig. 44). Pierced only by small windows and archer slits on the upper stories, the exterior aspect is relentlessly fortresslike. This defensive aspect is understandable given the site of the cathedral, right on the inlet of Agde's port.

At Agde (as at Maguelone) some scholars have suggested that the machicolations were added to a preexisting church.[38] Analysis of the building fabric, however, makes clear that the machicolations at Agde, like those at Maguelone, bond integrally with the rest of the building. On the other hand, unlike Maguelone, there is no evidence of mural passages at Agde, where a thinner wall design made them inadvisable. Multiple stair vises seem instead to have served the necessities of circulation from ground level to the roof-platform.

On the interior, the cathedral has an unaisled nave, 34 meters long and 12.6 meters wide (Fig. 45), surmounted by a pointed barrel vault. A generous western bay (which now supports a modern organ loft) precedes the rest of the nave. The main stair vise for the building is contained in the thickness of the southwest buttress, at the southern corner of the west façade. The nave itself continues in five further bays. The nave is short (26.5 meters internally), with only a single transverse arch between the third and fourth bays. This single arch suggests that the process of construction was relatively compressed, requiring only a single centering support for vault construction. Both the reduced length of the building and its constructional aspects suggest that building was rapid, possibly under threat of attack.

Though the fabric of choir and nave bond, the choir is disaxial, probably to accommodate the preexisting street pattern (Fig. 46).[39] Several authors have argued that this disaxiality is evidence that the choir is a later addition. The presence of the predecessor apse discovered in 1847 has added fuel to this hypothesis.[40] The coursing of the fabric of both nave and choir are, however, completely integral, leaving no room for doubt about their contemporaneous construction. The excavated apse, located within the existing choir, almost certainly belonged to the Carolingian cathedral, as already

Figure 44. Agde, exterior view of the church from the southwest.

suggested. The transept arms were originally both capped with towers, although the southern one collapsed in the seventeenth century. The walls of the north transept are exceptionally thick, probably to support the tower and to protect the adjoining bishop's palace. Both eastern stair vises are contained within the thickness of the transept walls.

The windows of the nave bays were originally small and round-headed.

Figure 45. Agde, interior view of the church to the east.

Only in one northwestern bay does the original profile survive (Fig. 47). The pointed barrel vault is unelaborated, except for the single transverse arch, which is supported on decorated corbels. The crossing arch is decorated with carved capitals probably reused from the Carolingian cathedral. These capitals are carved of a white marble, unlike the greyer stone used for the twelfth-century transept capitals.[41]

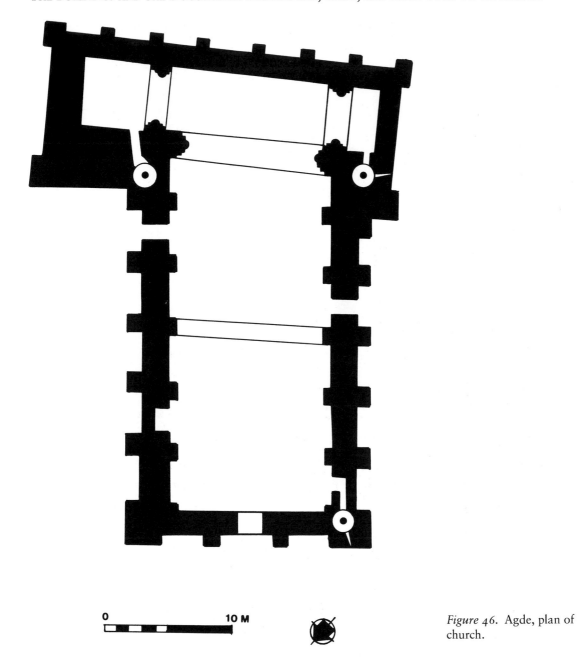

0   10 M

Figure 46. Agde, plan of church.

Archival Sources

The rich survival of medieval documentation for Agde, including copies of both the episcopal and capitular cartularies, permits us to establish a chronology of construction for the cathedral, as well as to trace the historical context for its fortification.[42] The history of the cathedral of Agde is that of a complicated and protracted struggle among bishop, viscount, and cathedral chapter.

Figure 47. Agde, interior view of the church to the west, showing northwest bay with original elevation.

Throughout the twelfth century, Agde's chapter remained remarkably independent of the bishop, allying themselves against him and with the viscount. Two interesting documents provide insight into the three-part struggle, especially as it relates to the construction and fortification of the cathedral. A false charter, allegedly issued by Charles the Bald in 848, purportedly awarded rights and properties to the bishop, at the expense of the viscount (Appendix 23).[43] As such, the forgery reflects not only an interest in Carolingian tradition but also the political aims of the bishop in the third quarter of the twelfth century. Rights virtually identical to those in the forgery were ratified by Louis VII in a diploma of 1173 (Appendix 24). This similarity has led Raymonde Foreville and André Castaldo to suggest that the charter may have been forged just before 1173, with the express purpose of influencing Louis VII.[44] In light of what Louis' diploma calls "fear of the Saracens and the frequent incursions of evil men," Louis gives bishop Guilhem the power to fortify the church and the city, including "the making of towers, fortifications, walls, posterns, and protections of gates and ditches and whatever you shall have recognized to be helpful to (the defense of) the church and city itself." Architectural historians have used this diploma to date the commencement of fortifications.[45] But the text in fact only gives *permission* for those fortifications; it does not say that they are *begun* in this year and in fact suggests the opposite. The Latin, "quae est constructa," suggests that Louis grants these rights to a church that has already been built.

In the absence of the diploma, we would search for other documentation for the construction of the buildings, which is, in fact, readily available in the form of donations and "testaments" (willed gifts) recorded in the cartularies of the bishop and chapter (Tables 2–3, and Appendixes 13–22, 25).[46] The frequency of donations to Saint-Etienne, relatively evenly spaced throughout the tenth and eleventh centuries, accelerates in the first quarter of the twelfth century. In 1122, Bishop Bernard makes a substantial donation of several churches to his chapter.[47] By the 1140s and 1150s, donations and testaments have clearly accelerated. This somewhat more generous pace of donation continues until the last quarter of the twelfth century. Fewer donations and testaments are recorded from the 1180s to the 1230s, and the gifts tend to be smaller or to involve exchange or sale rather than outright donation.[48]

Several of the donations and testaments reveal, more specifically, the destination of the donation "ad opus Sancti Stephani" (see Table 2).[49] The range of these donations is interesting, with donors drawn from many social classes, including the bishop himself, canons of the community, knights, and men and women of unspecified rank. Gifts are as generous as 1,000 solidi or as modest as 20 solidi. Donations also include precious objects of church plate and vestments, or even measures of grain. In the earliest of these testaments, Etienne of Mèze, chaplain of that town, pledges half his fortune to the works of Saint-Etienne of Agde as he departs on Crusade (Appendix 13). The testament of Ermengaud, bishop of Agde, was witnessed in 1149 (Appendix 15). Ermengaud speaks specifically about the "rebuilding of the church of Saint-Etienne" and gives a thousand melgorian solidi "for the completion of the choirs (apses)."[50] Guilhem Rainard, a canon of Saint-Etienne, awards 500 solidi and a collection of rich objects to the cathedral *opus* in 1155 (Appendix 17). Two gifts in 1160 offer measures of grain: Marie de Mermian offers one measure of corn (Appendix 20), whereas Guiraud de Touroulle pledges a measure of wheat to the cathedral works (Appendix 21).

In his testament of 1172, Bertrand, a canon of Saint-Etienne, seems especially eager to find a scheme to convert debts owed to him to cash for the cathedral *opus* (Appendix 22).[51] Bertrand's will indicates that he is owed two debts or pledges of repayment, both for 1,000 solidi. The first is owed in tithe to Bertrand by the parish of Saint-Sever and is apparently an annual payment, the proceeds of which in the future are to be divided between the ongoing project of Saint-Etienne's building fund (700 solidi) and the bishop of Agde (300 solidi). Moreover, the individuals responsible for the cathedral *opus* shall have control over the debt owed by Saint-Sever until the 700 solidi have been paid in full to the fund. The second debt seems to be a personal debt owed to Bertrand by Pons of Becciano. Here, too, Bertrand is resourceful in designing alternative schemes of repayment to benefit the *opus* of Saint-Etienne. Bertrand is willing to waive the conditions of the debt in order to raise cash quickly for the building fund. He offers Pons the opportunity to acquit himself of the debt by paying only half the pledge in a single lump sum of 500 solidi. If, however, Pons cannot raise the entire amount, Bertrand has another scheme by which he will sell the pledge, again at a loss of 50 percent, to the bishop. If the bishop can pay 500 solidi at once, he may collect the thousand solidi from Pons, making 500 solidi in the bargain. Regardless of who purchases the debt, Bertrand stipulates that the 500 solidi accruing to his estate shall be divided between the works at Saint-Etienne (300 solidi) and Raymond of Pressano (200 solidi). Finally, if neither Pons nor the bishop is willing or able to purchase the debt, then Pons shall continue to owe a thousand solidi to the estate and to repay it on schedule, with two-thirds of the proceeds to be donated to the works of Saint-Etienne.

The donations "specified" to the cathedral *opus* are found from 1147 to 1176-7, and therefore indicate a campaign of construction that began well before Louis' diploma, and that may have been nearing completion at the time of its issuance. Certainly Bertrand's repayment schemes seem to indicate a cathedral building project that is well under way in 1172. In this regard, it is important to underscore the integral nature of the construction of the church and its fortifications. The fortifications were not added, as some scholars have argued, to a predecessor building, but were constructed at the same time as the walls.

The evidence of charters and testaments suggests strongly that Louis' diploma of 1173 for Agde ratified construction that had begun at least twenty-five years earlier. Rather than seeing the diploma as marking the onset of construction, it should perhaps be taken as an indication of its near completion. This process of retrospective ratification, as we shall see, is consonant with the ways in which Louis VII asserted control in the south of France by co-opting rather than by initiating political processes. It is, in fact, typical of a Capetian method of retrospective acknowledgment of fortifications (and is in fact not uncharacteristic for the period in general). French royal licenses often gave permission for castles that already existed. In 1118, for example, Louis VI issued a license for fortifications already built on lands owned by the abbey of Saint Denis.[52] This process of retrospective licensing allowed the Capetians to revive the notion of royal initiative without challenging established procedure. At Agde, in particular, it allowed Louis to insinuate royal power at the expense of local comital control, without overtly engaging in such a struggle. Louis' diploma protected the episcopal fortifications against destruction by the viscount. By allying himself with episcopal power in Agde, Louis tacitly contributed to the demise of comital control, which, as we have seen, was already in decline. The earlier chronology of construction at Agde offered here parallels the dates of construction at Maguelone and also fits with a similar chronology of construction and fortification at Saint-Pons-de-Thomières.

SAINT-PONS-DE-THOMIERES

A royal monastery almost from the moment of its foundation in 936 (Appendix 30), the Benedictine house of Saint-Pons-de-Thomières maintained contacts with the Capetians throughout its history. Not only do the machicolated arches surrounding the church survive, but portions of the abbey and town fortifications are extant as well (Figs. 48, 49). The fortified church at Saint-Pons also preserves the most complete example of a two-tiered system of mural passages, probably originally combined with an upper crenellated platform.

History of the Site

Saint-Pons-de-Thomières is located in the Somail Mountains, about 50 kilometers north of the coast at Narbonne (see Fig. 2). The monastery and its small associated town lie at the source of the Jaur river, on the slopes of the Puech d'Artanac mountain, between Castres and Béziers. The site of the monastery itself is cut into the slope of the town's hill, with the north side of the church embedded in the hill, which has been terraced to receive the abbatial palace on the highest platform, the church on the intermediate one and the claustral complex on the lowest.

The foundation charter indicates that the monastery was founded in 936 by Pons, Count of Toulouse, and his wife Garsinde (daughter of Odo, the

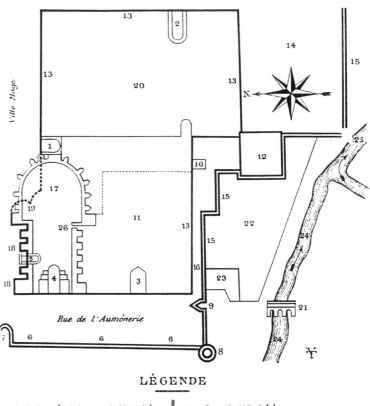

 Figure 48. Saint-Pons-de-Thomières, plan of abbey fortifications.

LÉGENDE

1 _ Porte d'entrée de la cour de l'Evêché.
2 _ Ancienne porte du Monastère.
3 _ Porte majeure du Monastère.
4 _ Grande porte de l'Eglise Cathédrale.
5 _ Porte du Nord.
6 _ Emplacement des maisons du Chapitre.
7 _ Porte du Foirul.
8 _ Tour St Benoît.
9 _ Portanelle.
10 _ Porte faisant communiquer le Monastère avec l'Evêché.
11 _ Emplacement du Monastère.
12 _ Tour du Comte Pons.
13 _ Mur du Monastère.
14 _ Cour de l'Evêché.
15 _ Mur de la Ville.
16 _ Chemin des Douze - Pans.
17 _ Emplacement du chœur de 1550, détruit en 1567.
18 _ Partie fortifiée de l'Eglise.
19 _ Emplacement de l'abside romane.
20 _ Cours, jardins et pré du Monastère.
21 _ Pont Rouge.
22 _ Jardin de l'Evêché.
23 _ Fournial du Monastère.
24 _ Ruisseau d'Aguze.
25 _ Rivière du Jaur.
26 _ Porte faisant communiquer l'Eglise avec le Cloître.

viscount of Narbonne).[53] Odo had a special devotion to Saint Pons, martyred near Nice in A.D. 257. The couple appealed to Arnould, abbot of the Benedictine monastery of Saint Gérard in Aurillac, who sent monks including Otgier, the first abbot, as well as relics of Saint Pons. Saint-Pons-de-Thomières became a royal abbey three years after its foundation when king Louis IV d'Outremer awarded it privileges and placed it under royal protection.[54] From this date, donations increased. Among the important donors were the archbishop of Narbonne and the bishop of Béziers.

The zenith of architecture and of religious life at Saint-Pons occurred dur-

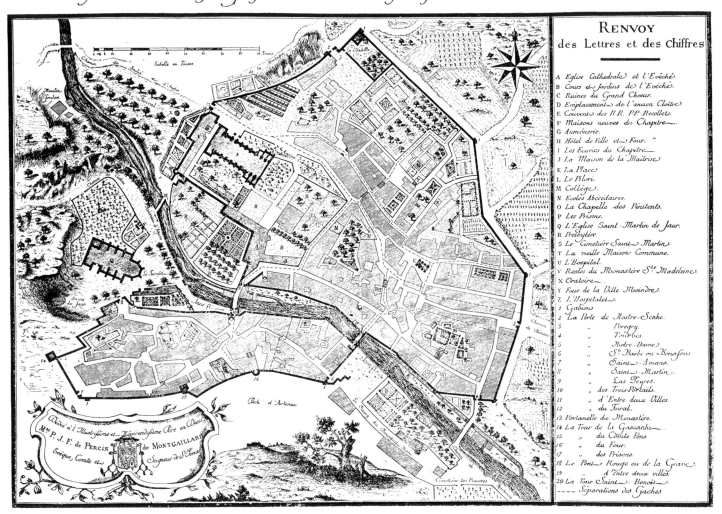

Figure 49. Saint-Pons-de-Thomières, plan of town fortifications.

ing the second half of the eleventh century. Frotard, abbot of Saint-Pons from 1060 to 1099, was an able administrator who became papal legate to Gregory VII in 1077 and who often acted as papal ambassador and mediator.[55] Under Frotard, Saint-Pons enlarged its holdings within France and also became the mother church of several Catalan monasteries, including Saint-Martin-de-Lez (given to Saint-Pons in 1070 by Bernard, count of Besalu), Sant-Benet-de-Bages (probably given at about the same time by Sanche Bérengar, brother of Raymond Bérengar who was a monk at Saint-Pons), Sant-Cugat-del-Vallès and the fortified convent of Sant-Pere-de-Roda (given fifteen years later), and finally Huesca (given in the late eleventh century).[56] The attendant rise in wealth funded a new campaign of building at Saint-Pons, which seems to have begun under Frotard sometime in the late eleventh century. We know that the church was dedicated (even if not fully complete) by Pope Urban II on 24 June 1096, after preaching the crusade at Clermont-Ferrand and Toulouse.[57]

Frotard's successors, Pierre Bérengar (1100–30), Aimeri II (1130–44), and Bérengar I (1146–51), must have overseen the completion of the church, funded by further donations, especially by the Bérengar family.[58] During the period between 936 and 1170, the monastery was under the protection of the counts of Toulouse. Donations, monks, and especially abbots were drawn from the highest levels of society, and the abbey became one of the most powerful of the region (see Table 1).[59] Raymond of Dourgne was especially active in his participation at church councils, including those held at Toulouse in 1161 and Montpellier in 1162, and the Council of Lombers in 1165, where heretics were anathematized. In the mid- to late twelfth century the abbey suffered from struggles with Roger Trencavel and other local lords, as well as from increased heretic activity in the region. Nonetheless, the community seems to have maintained control over its numerous and far-flung properties.

In 1318, Pope John XXII promoted the abbey to the rank of cathedral see. No new construction is documented for this period, and rebuilding campaigns of the fifteenth through eighteenth centuries have obscured any physical traces. At the end of the fifteenth century, Bishop Antoine Gaudet pulled down the Romanesque choir and began the rebuilding of a new and larger choir, as well as a new cloister. Construction continued under his successors, François Guillaume de Clermont-Lodève, and from 1534, Alexandre Farnèse. Surviving documents in the Archives de Saint-Pons tell us that construction was still in progress in 1551.[60] On 1 October 1567, however, Huguenot troops sacked the newly rebuilt abbey, reducing the new choir and cloister complex to ruins. Three of the towers were also dismounted at this time, and the fortification walls of the town were also partially taken down.

Many years elapsed before the church was restored. A wall was raised in 1604 to separate the nave from the ruined choir. Early in the eighteenth century, under Bishop Louis des Bertons de Crillon, the ruins of the choir were pulled down, the high altar was transferred to the west, and the last two bays of the west, including the narthex, were walled off to form a vestry. The present neoclassical facade was erected where the chancel arch had stood (Fig. 50). Between 1768 and 1771, the reoriented "choir" was lavishly decorated, enclosing the last five nave bays with a wrought-iron grille by Philippe Bongue, a Montpellier locksmith. The church lost its cathedral status in 1790. The conventual buildings to the south, newly restored in the seventeenth century, were pulled down to make way for the present main road (the Grand'rue) in the eighteenth century.[61] The celebrated historiated capitals of the cloister were dis-

Figure 50. Saint-Pons-de-Thomières, aerial view from the northeast (eighteenth-century façade is at the east on the site of the destroyed chevet).

persed at this time. The abbatial palace of the seventeenth century to the north still stands and is the present headquarters of the National Park Service of Haut-Languedoc. Restoration work was undertaken by Monuments Historiques in 1839–41, when the roof of the church nave was reconstructed. It was probably at this time that the defensive galleries of the upper level were subdivided and that the openings of the lower galleries into the church were blocked. Plaster was removed from the narthex in the 1980s, and the narthex passages were reopened, although plans to rejoin the narthex to the nave, described in the archives for 1947, were never realized.

Building Fabric

The church of Saint-Pons-de-Thomières is a vast unaisled hall, covered with a pointed barrel vault carried on transverse arches (Fig. 51). Though its dimensions vary, it now measures on average 67 by 15 meters. In the twelfth century, the church would have extended over 80 meters, making it nearly twice as long as both Maguelone and Agde (Fig. 52).[62] As we have seen, the original form of the church has been obscured by the reconstruction (and deconstruction) campaigns of subsequent centuries.

The twelfth-century core of the church consists of a generous narthex block flanked by towers at both north and south. These towers, at least in their lower courses, formed part of the predecessor church of the eleventh century. The "preordained" placement of these towers probably accounts for the disalignment of the narthex bay. The narthex is separated from the nave by a narrow transitional bay that accommodates the stair turrets added to the towers in the twelfth-century campaign. This bay is now cut through and blocked from the nave by the closure wall of the mid–eighteenth century, added when the narthex was converted into a vestry. The nave proper consists of six bays, not counting a seventh, which joins the western towers. Five of these bays are currently contained within the eighteenth-century choir enclosure. Although the windows have been widened, one bay on the northern side (Fig. 53) preserves the original interior elevation.

Figure 51. Saint-Pons-de-Thomières, interior view toward the east.

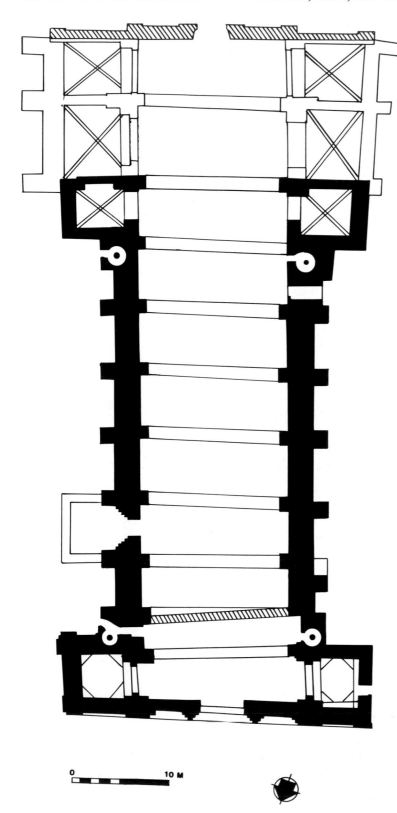

Figure 52. Saint-Pons-de-Thomières, phased plan of church. *Black:* Twelfth-century; *Outline:* Fifteenth- and sixteenth-century; *Diagonal shading:* Eighteenth-century.

0   10 M

The exterior also preserves evidence of a number of architectural phases. The present towers reuse the lower courses of towers from the predecessor building. As was common for eleventh-century churches, no access to the upper stories of these towers was provided apart from ladders. In the twelfth-century rebuilding, stair turrets were added to each tower against their western faces as part of the gallery and machicolation system (Figs. 54, 55). The apse of the eleventh-century church probably extended between the eastern towers and occupied what is now the first of two Gothic bays. These two bays, wider and longer than their Romanesque neighbors, open into cross-vaulted side chapels. They, in turn once formed part of the generous Gothic choir, but are now blocked by the mid-eighteenth-century "façade."

Evidence for the successive eastern terminations of the church is available from two excavations, but the results of these investigations have never been fully published, and must be interpreted with caution. Excavations at the time of the 1950 Congrès archéologique revealed the remains of a curving wall in the two easternmost bays (Fig. 56). The location of this wall was discussed and illustrated by Marcel Durliat in his article for the Congrès, and the wall was identified as the eastern termination of the eleventh-century church.[63] The trajectory of this wall, however, would carry it far beyond the

Figure 53. Saint-Pons-de-Thomières, interior view of northern bay, showing original elevation.

Figure 54. Saint-Pons-de-Thomières, exterior view of the nave, north side.

Figure 55. Saint-Pons-de-Thomières, exterior view of the nave, north side, detail.

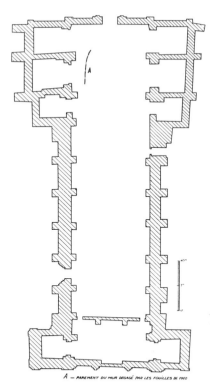

Figure 56. Saint-Pons-de-Thomières, plan of church from 1950 *Congrès archéologique,* showing excavated apse, marked *A* on the plan.

A — PAREMENT DU MUR DEGAGÉ PAR LES FOUILLES DE 1950

R. Grau del.

shallow proportions usual for eleventh-century apses. Its placement, more-over, just underneath the surviving springer of the Gothic vaults, suggests that it is instead the foundation for the sixteenth-century chevet.[64] Excava-tions on the present parvis of the church, just outside the eighteenth-century "façade," have revealed foundation walls for this chevet. These walls, unfor-tunately, were never surveyed, and only a brief but valuable sketch plan by A. Granier records their appearance.[65] This spacious eastern termination began at the outer walls of the side chapels of the Gothic choir and extended, with five radiating chapels, over 20 meters to the east (Fig. 57).

Many scholars, including J. Sahuc and A. Granier, have identified two campaigns of construction in the eleventh- and twelfth-century walls: an ear-lier unvaulted church, encased by later buttresses. The machicolations are interpreted by these scholars as part of a second phase, added partly to fortify the church and partly to support the vault.[66] Sahuc's published plans and sec-tions reveal this hypothesis, showing an earlier wall thickened at the exterior. Careful inspection of the fabric of the walls, however, reveals no such breaks. With the existence of the gallery system, moreover, the opportunity for exami-nation within the walls is ample. Stonework, mortar, and coursing are all integral through the walls of the building. The gallery and fortification system at Saint-Pons is therefore integral with the construction of the nave.

A number of doors, original and later, provide access to the church and

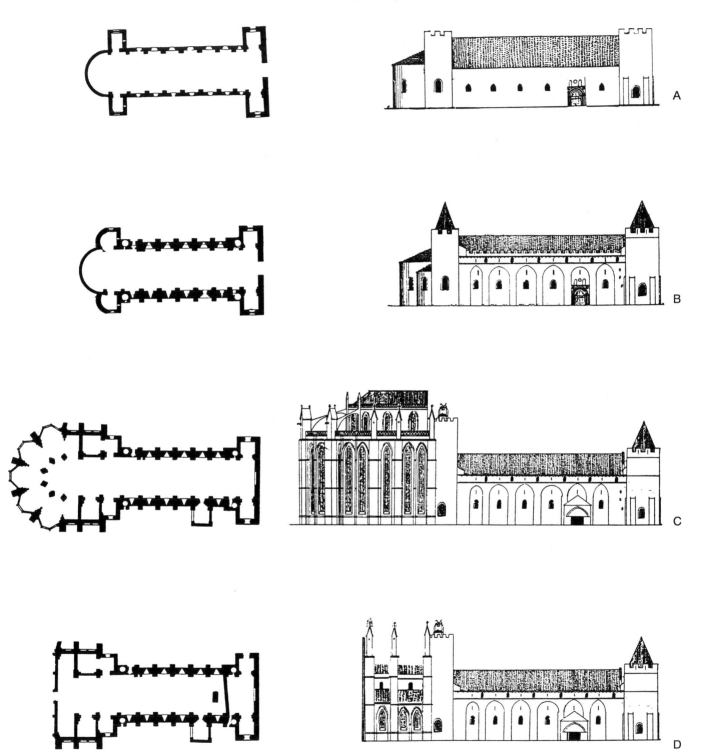

Figure 57. Saint-Pons-de-Thomières, phased sequence of plans and reconstruction views: (A) Eleventh-century; (B) Twelfth-century; (C) Fifteenth- and sixteenth-century; (D) Eighteenth-century.

permit us to trace patterns of movement. The church was originally entered through the now-blocked western narthex. The narthex has a triple portal, but the fabric of the walling of the outer arches indicates that only the central arch was originally pierced by a door. The cloister was originally reached only through the south door, which opens from the narthex. (The modern door in the south wall was cut through at a later period.) A large northern door, also decorated with eleventh-century sculpture and covered with a porch, opens toward the former episcopal palace. Two other doors, providing access to the stair turrets also open to the exterior on this side. Their construction seems original and integral with the twelfth-century turrets. It may have been that the northern side of the church acted as the construction site during the twelfth century, with these small doors acting as entrances serving the builders.

Since the fortification system at Saint-Pons is discussed in greater detail in Chapter 4, only a brief descriptive resumé is provided here. The elaborate two-tiered system of mural passages at Saint-Pons, probably originally capped by an upper crenellated platform, provided a much more complete defensive system than the machicolations at Agde and Maguelone.[67] The lower gallery (Fig. 58a) is contained within the north, south, and west walls of the church and originally opened to the exterior as well as the interior of the nave. The upper gallery passage is contained only within the south and north walls (Fig. 58b). It protects the exterior by large round-headed windows, arrow slits, and machicolated slots. The measured section drawings (Figs. 59, 60) show the relationship of the two galleries built within the walls of Saint-Pons. Saint-Pons probably always had a gabled timber roof. The flat stone fighting platforms at Agde and Maguelone would have been undesirable because of the harsher and wetter climate in the mountains. The complex gallery system at Saint-Pons would also have rendered another fighting platform extraneous.

The gallery system is best appreciated on the northern side of the nave, where it survives with machicolations and arrow slits virtually intact (see Fig. 54). The fact that eastern and western towers were already in place may have constrained the placement and design of nave buttresses on both the north and south sides, where their spans are slightly irregular. This irregularity results in an uneven cadence for the machicolated arches, which are variously round-headed or slightly pointed. Repair and rebuilding have no doubt exaggerated the original differences still further. The exterior elevation of the south wall of the nave is not as well preserved. Along with the monastic cloister that formerly adjoined it, the south elevation has seen a protracted and complex building history. Every time the claustral complex was destroyed or rebuilt (and we know that such changes occurred in the fifteenth and sixteenth centuries), the southern wall of the church was

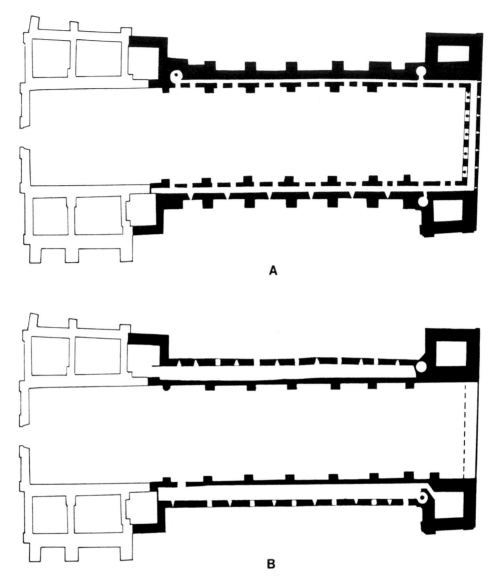

Figure 58. Saint-Pons-de-Thomières: (A) Plan of lower gallery; (B) Plan of upper gallery. *Black:* Twelfth-century; *Outline:* Later fabric.

affected. Two of the southern buttresses of bays 4 through 7 are quoined with the same white stone as the eighteenth-century east "façade." These buttresses also project in a manner similar to the eastern chapels and façade, which indicates that they were all rebuilt (or at least repaired) as part of the same eighteenth-century reconstruction campaign. The southern wall, furthermore, projects outward (southward) toward the west. This curve is most obvious in the upper levels of the building. It is clearly visible to the naked eye and is measured and recorded on the plan I have drawn for

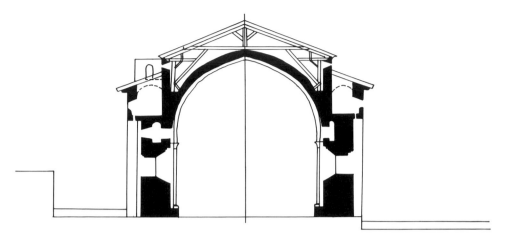

Figure 59. Saint-Pons-de-Thomières, section of church.

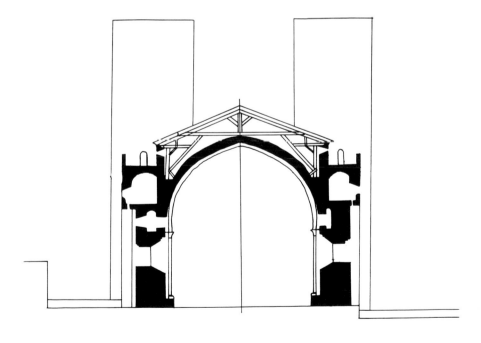

Figure 60. Saint-Pons-de-Thomières, reconstruction section.

the galleries (see Fig. 58). The outward bulge is probably the result of building and rebuilding in the cloister area.

The abbey church of Saint-Pons evolved from a relatively simple, but spacious, towered eleventh-century structure to a machicolated fortress-church in the twelfth century. In turn, it became a grandiose Gothic cathedral, which was truncated and reoriented, but still impressive in its final eighteenth-century phase (see Figs. 50 and 57).

Archival Sources

Because few early records survive, the history of Saint-Pons is much more difficult to reconstruct than that of the two comparable cathedral-fortresses of Maguelone and Agde.[68] No cartulary survives. Few archives survived the Wars of Religion, and those that did were as likely to be discarded as conserved. Of the limited remaining documents catalogued by Sahuc in his *Archives de la Ville de Saint-Pons,* many are no longer to be found in the Archives Municipales. Two texts important for the construction history of the site have, however, been preserved. The first is a short letter, apparently now preserved only in the *Recueil des Historiens des Gaules et de la France.* In it, the prior of Saint-Pons (identified only as "A") appeals to Louis VII as well as to Pope Alexander III (who was at that time in France) for help, "in the burdens of grievances" the abbey was suffering (Appendix 31).[69] A response is not preserved from Louis, and it is possible that he did not wish to interfere in this matter.[70]

The second text important to the construction history of Saint-Pons is a charter that provides information on the twelfth-century chronology of the abbey (Appendix 32). In 1171, it says, a disagreement had arisen between Raymond, abbot of Saint-Pons and Roger Trencavel, viscount of Béziers. Raymond had built an unauthorized castle at La-Salvetat-sur-Agout, bordering the lands of Roger.[71] Roger as a result "destroyed the estate of the monastery, by attack of arms and with his army," and demanded the immense sum of 30,000 melgorian solidi as ransom. Arbitration by an assembly of lords and bishops at Béziers set the terms of settlement. Raymond was encouraged to pardon Roger and his accomplices, and was to pay an annual sum. Roger, called "penitent," was required to recognize the abbot's right to the castle at La-Salvetat and was to permit the community to "improve, strengthen, and modify" the monastery and to fortify its enclosure. The agreement, however, limited the inhabitants of this strengthened monastic cloister to "abbot, monks, and brothers and serfs." The abbot was also obliged to agree not to use the castle at Salvetat to make war on Roger.

The charter has become one of the pivots of the architectural history of the building, and it must thus be discussed with some care. The document does not specifically mention damage to the church, but instead indicates that the estate of the monastery is "destroyed." The monastery receives, with this arbitration, permission to strengthen and fortify itself, though no real precision is given by the text on the location and type of fortifications. Most scholars have taken this to indicate the moment of fortification of the church and abbey, but this is not what the text says and is probably not what it means.

Both the letter of 1164 and the charter of 1171 mention local threats, and the charter refers to the existence of the fortified residence at La-Salvetat. It is likely that Raymond would have initiated the fortification of his abbey before or at the same time as his occasional residence, since both were perceived to be protective measures against regional troubles. Since Abbot Raymond clearly fortified La-Salvetat without consulting Roger Trencavel, it is difficult to imagine why he would have waited for Roger's permission to fortify his abbey and church. The charter of 1171 thus supplies another example of retrospective sanction for the existence of ecclesiastical fortification, this time a coerced permission granted by the local count rather than a voluntary one issued by the king.

CONCLUSION

Our detailed reexamination of the sources and fabric of Maguelone, Agde, and Saint-Pons reveals significant differences in their sites, as well as in the circumstances of their respective patrons, designs, and construction. Despite these differences, we see a significant similarity in the ways in which protection is organized and sanctioned. Aggressive steps are taken to fortify the church and abbey at Maguelone under Galtier, Raymond, and Jean de Montlaur in the 1120s through the 1190s. At Agde, a similar sequence of construction begins in the 1120s under Bishop Bernard and continues under Ermengaud and Guilhem into the 1170s. The sequence of construction at Saint-Pons-de-Thomières is somewhat more difficult to trace, given the paucity of surviving texts. Nonetheless, it would seem that fortification is under way by the 1160s, if not before. Religious fortification, then, is initiated by bishops and abbots in the course of the mid–twelfth century. Louis VII begins, first at Maguelone in 1155, and later at Agde in 1173, to proclaim support for these bishops by his retrospective sanction of existing campaigns of episcopal protection. Perhaps echoing this royal initiative, Roger Trencavel issues approval for similar protective measures at Saint-Pons-de-Thomières in 1171. The actual garrisoning and functioning of these fortifications is the subject to which we turn in the next chapter.

THE MANNING AND OPERATION OF FORTRESS-CHURCHES

The student of any fortified enclosure must keep two groups in careful perspective: those who are inside, and those who aspire to that coveted position. The "included" and "excluded" normally comprised competing groups of people, but valued possessions, livestock, and even supernatural protectors could form part of the medieval equation. Fortress-churches also participated in the competition between "inside" and "outside" groups. With the fortified abbeys of Maguelone, Agde, and Saint-Pons-de-Thomières, the "outsiders," identified textually, were "Saracens," pirates, brigands, and heretics.[1] The principal "insider" was the bishop or abbot. The cathedral chapters of Maguelone and Agde and the monastic community of Saint-Pons were normally "inside" with the bishop. The relationship of the chapter to the bishop could, however, become strained. The cartulary for Maguelone preserves evidence of conflicts between the bishop and chapter, especially in the second half of the twelfth century.[2] At Agde, the bishop and chapter were in direct conflict during much of the eleventh and twelfth centuries.[3]

Disputes often arose from the designation of certain groups as "insiders." In 1168, the provost of Maguelone brought a complaint to Jean de Montlaur, bishop of Maguelone. The provost alleged that the bishop's knights entered areas of the monastery that should remain closed to them and that they stole some of the abbey's table knives.[4] At Saint-Pons, the arbitrated agreement between Abbot Raymond of Saint-Pons and the viscount Roger Trencavel stipulated that, in addition to the bishop and monks, only the abbey's serfs were permitted in the cloister (Appendix 32).

"Insiders" could also be much more prosaic, as several documentary accounts relate. A fortified church, or even a church with a relatively solid

Their intentions are, in fact, quite simple. They say that they would like for us to be outside and for them to be inside.

Drawing by Sempé. Copyright © 1984, The New Yorker Magazine, Inc.

tower, could be designed or converted to serve as a storehouse for everything from church treasure to grain and even farm animals. The Anglo-Saxon Chronicle, for example, records a theft from the tower at Peterborough in 1070, indicating that valuables were kept there.[5] A complaint addressed in about 1260 by Guy de Severac to Alphonse, count of Poitiers and Toulouse, against Vivian, bishop of Rodez, reveals the myriad ways in which a church might be used as protection. Bishop Vivian, "with his troops" chased an opponent to a church, where the man sought refuge. The bishop broke down the doors of the church and excommunicated the peasants of the town who, the text reports, having no other stronghold but their church, had stored their grain within.[6]

One other "insider" group commonly protected within fortified churches was the patron saint and other spiritual affiliates, who were physically present in their relics.[7] We know that the monastery of Saint-Pons-de-Thomières possessed relics of its patron, the third-century martyr saint, Pons, as well as another martyr, Saint Aubin, and other saints.[8] In 1079, Peter, count of Melgueil, pledges a gift to the community of Maguelone "and the holy relics kept there."[9] Though the identity of these relics is not specified, the presence of multiple altars at both Maguelone and Agde would have necessitated relics for their consecration. Relics of the patron saints of Maguelone, Peter and Paul, and Stephen at Agde are likely to have been possessed. The frequent contact that the community of Maguelone enjoyed with the papacy makes their possession of relics of Peter and Paul a highly likely possibility. These relics may have taken the form of actual bones, or of "touch relics" (liturgical vestments or other objects touched to the bones of the saints conserved in Rome).

Although there survives very little information about the relics at Maguelone, Agde, or Saint-Pons-de-Thomières, the use of fortified churches like those in Languedoc as refuges for saints as embodied in their relics can be documented in several cases.[10] During the ninth-century Norman harassment of monasteries along the coast, a number of relics came to the fortified abbey of Saint-Savin-sur-Gartempe, which, because of its fortifications, was the only abbey not to have been pillaged. In 1392, under threat of the invading English, the monks of Cadouin took their prize relic of the holy shroud to Toulouse, center of the French resistance, where they installed the relics in the fortified church of the Taur. The fortification of the small church of Vénerque may perhaps be explained at least in part by its ownership of several important relics. A late residue of the original motivation to fortify may be found in eighteenth-century procession ritual for Vénerque. The ritual stipulates that when the reliquary containing the bones of Saint Phébade, bishop of Agen, was carried in procession, it should always be accompanied by armed men to protect it. Examples such as these provide rare glimpses of the motivation to protect relics. Once defended, as we have seen, the saints might in turn offer protection to their "host" monastic community.

The existence of a system of fortifications enclosing and protecting "insiders" from the perceived threats of "outsiders," poses the question of the use and surveillance of those fortifications. Who assigned and who performed sentinel duty, as well as the more permanent tasks of garrisoning in times of attack? Were monks part of the garrisoning force? How did the insiders move about the building in order to defend themselves? Who bought weapons, and who used them? Who were the insiders responsible for maintenance of the fortifications? What was the relationship of church fortifications with those of the town, especially when, as at Agde and Saint-Pons, they were continuous? Though the sources are seldom as expressive as we might like on questions such as these, careful analysis, particularly of the buildings themselves, but also of the relevant texts, can provide some answers.

MAGUELONE

Physical evidence for the movement of people and, by extension, for the defense of the buildings at Maguelone is found in the fabric of the church. The towers, stairs, and gallery passages still survive, but are now only partially complete. The machicolations that wrap around the twelfth-century church are only part of the vast fortified system that formerly enclosed the entire abbey complex. Results of excavations by Frédéric Fabrège in the late nineteenth century, and by Jean-Claude M. Richard in 1967, provide further physical information about the plan and fortification of the claustral precinct.[11] A labeled reconstruction plan drawn by Fabrège (see Fig. 33) provides valuable information on the outer fortifications, though it must be used with caution.[12]

Textual description of the fortifications and its garrisoning is found in the abbey *Statutes,* written by Abbot Jean de Vissec in 1331 as part of his reform of the abbey (Appendix 11). The *Statutes* describe the surrounding walls, punctuated by a single main door that was opened only certain hours of the day. This text is invaluable for the precision it offers about the location and often the function of certain military features. As a fourteenth-century document which aimed to reform community practices, however, it must be used with caution in any attempt to reconstruct twelfth-century garrisoning procedures.

Military elements were already a feature of the eleventh-century cathedral before the machicolated twelfth-century church was built. As we have seen, Suger, when he visited in 1118, attested that the church was already "well fortified" by that time (Appendix 5).[13] The eleventh-century tower, attributed to Arnaud, may have formed the south transept of the eleventh-century church and may have functioned as a protective element in that building. It was certainly incorporated into the defensive system of the twelfth-century cathedral. The ground story of the tower has only small window apertures; no provision was made for access from the exterior. At the upper story, the tower originally had a chapel dedicated to Saint Michael, the military saint. The dedication alone, therefore, argues for a protective function for the tower.[14] When the tower was incorporated into the corner between the south transept and the nave of the twelfth-century church, both the upper and lower chapels of the earlier tower were linked to the successor building. The lower chapel opened directly into the nave by

Figure 61. Maguelone, interior of the church, nineteenth-century view to the west, showing upper gallery with timber balustrade before reconstruction.

a generous arch, and the upper chapel opened into a small upper chapel built within the thickness of the nave wall. At present inaccessible, these small chapels were probably originally reached by timber gallery projections extending from the tribune, as was the case in the nineteenth century (Fig. 61), and as is shown on the Fabrège plan (see Fig. 33). The communicating arch between the southern nave chapel and the earlier chapel of Saint Michael (now blocked) is clearly visible from the interior and exterior, as are the stairs descending from the nave chapel into the chapel of Saint Michael. The two chapels are shown communicating in Fabrège's plan.

Gallery and stair passages form an important part of the defensive system at Maguelone. To the south, a stair built within the thickness of the wall leads upward to the tribune and upper cloister. Ascent then continues to the roof in a second stair that is also built within the thickness of the wall (Fig. 62). The roof, now simply covered, almost certainly originally had a crenellated platform like the one that still survives at Agde (see Fig. 66). These galleries and stairs, of course, not only aided in the surveillance of the church and island, they also permitted the movement of monks around the church, facilitating in particular their movement to and from the upper tribune and cloister. To the exposed, southern side, another set of gallery passages survive, although they are much less well preserved. Portions of a passage survive at the level of the springing of the vault, at the juncture between the tower of Saint Augustine and the nave. This passage now opens into the nave by one of the square-headed apertures still visible from the interior (see the top left of Fig. 37). Though ruined and blocked, it was

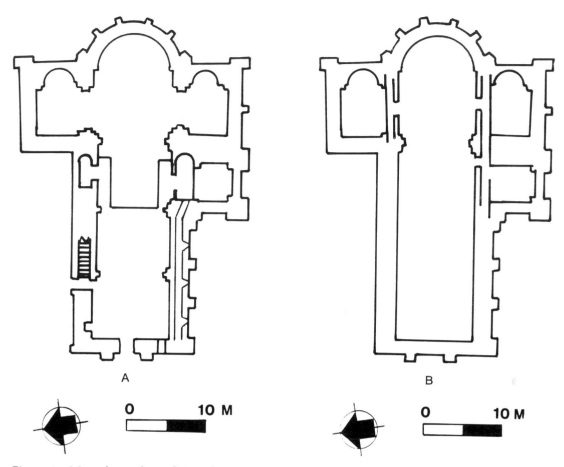

Figure 62. Maguelone, plans of (A) tribune and (B) upper levels, showing gallery system.

clearly built to link tower and nave at the highest level and to provide a system of surveillance and communication between exterior and interior. The plans of the ground and upper stories (see Fig. 62) demonstrate the system of stair and gallery passages contained within the thickness of the wall. The presence of another square-headed window on the opposite, northern side of the nave suggests that the passage originally wrapped around the entire church. This uppermost gallery system was most likely blocked during the modern reconstruction of the roof.

Beneath this passage, that is, at the second-story or tribune level, are the blocked remains of what appears to have been another gallery built within the thickness of the wall. Curious square-headed apertures now open from the tribune to the church's southern flank (see Fig. 38). Located beneath the windows, the function of these small apertures have long been a source of puzzlement. They are similar to archer slits and as such would have protected the exposed southern flank of the church. Their placement, nearly 2 meters above the floor level of the tribune, however, would have made shooting out of these slits difficult without a raised platform. Moreover, the thickness of the wall and the narrowness of the slits would have made visibility problematic. It is difficult to imagine the installation of an archer's platform in the tribune, when the obvious solution of a gallery passage was known and available. Careful inspection, in fact, reveals the presence of rubble fill, measuring 1.5 meters, on the interior of each aperture. Either the squared apertures were cut after the construction of the wall to provide extra surveillance, revealing the rubble core of the wall, or (more likely) the wall was originally built with a gallery passage, now blocked with rubble, that would have permitted defenders access around, rather than through, the tribune.[15] The interior windows would have provided air circulation and communication to the archers in the passage.

Galleries and doors permitted communication with other parts of the abbey as well. The northern nave chapel, built in the thickness of the wall (like its southern counterpart) opened originally into the upper cloister by a door that still survives. A generous door in the western wall originally opened into the southwest tower that was added in the thirteenth century and that is now known as the "tower of the bishop."

Towers formed another important element in the defense of the abbey. In addition to the tower of Saint Augustine, both transept arms were capped with towers containing upper chapels. With the expansion of the cloister in the thirteenth and fourteenth centuries, towers were also added to the west front of the cathedral (Fig. 63). According to the Fabrège plan (see Fig. 33), the northeast corner of the cloister was marked by a tower, guarding the gate, and the main entrance to the cloister was preceded by an enormous tower, built by the early fourteenth century, known as the Fort. Since only

Figure 63. Maguelone, exterior view, southwest.

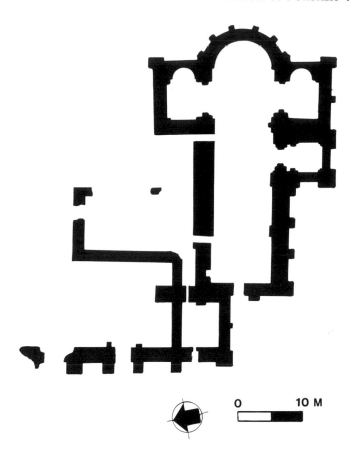

Figure 64. Maguelone, excavation plan of the site.

0   10 M

portions of the tower of Saint Augustine, the transept towers, and one of the western towers survive, and none to their original elevation, we must remain ignorant about the nature of their top stories. A crenellated fighting platform was the most likely solution, probably combined with machicolated slots. The thirteenth-century western tower, the tower of the bishop, in fact, still preserves machicolation of a profile similar to that which surrounds the twelfth-century portions of the church. The same fortification element seems thus to have been used at Maguelone from the first half of the twelfth through the fourteenth century, providing aesthetic as well as technological continuity despite extended campaigns of construction. Given this conservatism of forms at Maguelone, we may (with all due caution) assume that most of the towers at Maguelone were originally capped by machicolated and crenellated platforms.

The excavations of 1967 revealed projecting buttresses along the west face of the claustral block (Fig. 64).[16] Although their original elevation cannot be determined with certainty, the reconstruction of these buttresses as machicolated is very likely correct. If so, these machicolated buttresses would have continued the defenses of the thirteenth-century western towers.

Furthermore, the presence of a machicolated arch on the western face of the church, now blocked within the thirteenth-century tower, indicates that the entire west front of the church was machicolated in the twelfth century. It may be possible to reconstruct the original cloister plan of the twelfth-century abbey, based on the plan of its successor (see Figs. 33, 34). The curious contraction of the thirteenth-century cloister aisle within the much larger claustral block may indicate that the line of the earlier cloister was preserved, at least in plan. The thirteenth- (and fourteenth-) century campaigns of reconstruction, preserving the foundations of the predecessor cloister aisle would then have expanded toward the west so that the original outer western wall of the cloister became the inner wall of the thirteenth-century cloister aisle. The exterior wall of the twelfth-century cloister may well have continued this line of machicolations, as did its thirteenth-century successor.

The church was flanked to the east and south by the infirmary and cemetery zone. Projecting from the west of the claustral complex was the Fort, a square tower. Encircling this tower, and stretching back to the postern door at the northeast corner of the claustral complex, and westward to the west façade of the church was the canonial precinct, called the walls of iron after descriptions in the *Statutes*. An outer perimeter wall, the so-called walls of wood, enclosed the outer precinct. The church and claustral elements, then, formed the kernel of a fortified enclosure, probably wrapped with machicolations in the twelfth century and more certainly by the late thirteenth. Around this tightly fortified precinct were wrapped the "walls of iron" and the "walls of wood." This use of concentric rings of fortification is an early and effective example of a principle hailed as an innovation in secular fortifications of the following generation.

The *Statutes* provide information on the fourteenth-century garrisoning of the watch, providing for a sentinel night and day to watch the coast:

The provost ought to have in the fort a man . . . who will remain in the fort itself day and night, and with waking diligence would guard the island. . . . Also the provost ought to have a man . . . who shall trumpet the hours of the night. . . . Also the provost is held (responsible) to have and keep many other watchers, if many are necessary for watching. Also he ought to provide for a ladder for climbing up to the same tower, and a rope with a bread-basket or box or flat basket in which necessary supplies go up. . . . Also the provost ought to provide, toward the guarding of the church and island, for machinery . . . and trebuchets and stones and shields and lances, catapults, and all types of arms, and other provisions necessary . . . since he would have custody of the whole island and fort for the entire year. (Appendix 11)

Though the *Statutes* indicate that guards should be hired laymen assisted by "serfs of the priory," the use of brothers from the community as sentinels is also described. It is interesting to note the absence of any mention of galleries or stairs, with the need for ladders and lifting mechanisms clearly recorded. It is possible that the *Statutes* record only the procedures for the outer precinct wall, but it is more likely that it lists only the materials to be provided by the prevost, omitting the access systems that already existed in the defensive system of the twelfth century.

As we have seen, Maguelone was threatened during the Hundred Years War with invasion. The charters of the early fourteenth century are full of limitations imposed on the king's soldiers, and of protests from the bishop about the levying of troops from his lands.[17] King Philip commanded the refortification of the island in 1341

for the sake and defense of the kingdom. . . . You are bound to the said lord our king, to the extent that with no other delay you cause the fortification of the island of Maguelone . . . to be repaired and fortified with goods and sufficient garrisons, arms, and supplies, such that no lack could be found (Appendix 12).

In the sixteenth century, we recall, the see of Maguelone was transferred to the larger city of Montpellier. Although the canons wished to have the buildings destroyed, Huguenot troops occupied the abbey in 1562. These troops were in turn expelled by royal forces, who themselves left behind a garrison for several years. In 1632, Cardinal Richelieu carried out the royal order to destroy the medieval fortress, dismantling the abbey buildings and the towers and machicolations of the church.

AGDE

The fortified system at Saint-Etienne, Agde, was much simpler than that at either Maguelone or Saint-Pons. Simple machicolated arches rise directly to a roof platform where openings allowed projectiles to be dropped on "outsiders" (Fig. 65). A lowered passage behind crenels and merlons also protected the defenders (Fig. 66). It is curious that there is no tower directly on the water, but the two high towers over the transepts (only the north one survives) allowed ample surveillance over both the port and the town.

There is no evidence of gallery or stair passages built within the walls at Agde. The thinner walls (just under 2 meters at Agde, opposed to over 2.5 meters at Maguelone and Saint-Pons) would not have encouraged their use. Instead, the main fighting platform of the nave roof was reached by stair vises in the inside corners of the towers and nave and at the southwest corner of the nave (now blocked but visible on the roof). No windows pierce the ground level of the nave or choir, and only relatively small windows open into the episcopal and canonial precincts to the north and south, respectively. Only a single window each (see Fig. 44), placed high in the wall, illuminated the chevet, exposed to the street and, at the west end, exposed to the port.

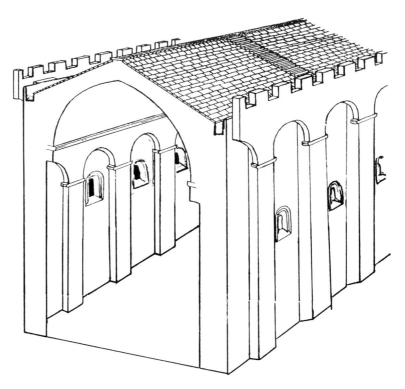

Figure 65. Agde, axonometric section.

Figure 66. Agde, roof of the church, showing machicolation slots.

The fortified west front of the cathedral formed part of the municipal fortifications along the river (see Fig. 42). The canonial cloister and episcopal palace originally participated in this defensive line. The cloister (see Fig. 43) was dismantled in the nineteenth century, and the bishop's palace, too, has been changed greatly by its conversion into a hotel and shops. We cannot be certain of the shape and military elements of the canonial or episcopal defenses, but it seems certain that they were fortified, possibly with machicolations, or perhaps with simple crenellated enclosure walls. It is likely that a wallwalk connected the fortified roof platform of the cathedral with the cordon for the town wall, although details of this system have been entirely obliterated by the blocking of the interior stairs in the west front of the cathedral and the remodeling of the palace walls. The fortified abbey of Agde was therefore primarily effective from the west front toward the river, which formed the greatest threat. Secondarily, the east end provided defense from the street, if the walls of the town were breached, or if the town revolted. Finally, the church itself could act as a donjon of last resort, protected as it was from all sides, even from the adjoining cloister and episcopal palace.

The large number of medieval documents surviving for Agde allows us to penetrate the military management of the city as well as to trace its development across the twelfth through fourteenth centuries. Several fourteenth-century texts are especially valuable for our reconstruction of twelfth-century fortifications because they provide detailed descriptions of the walls so that towers and lengths of wall may be localized. This textual information has been charted by André Castaldo.[18] The combined evidence of seventeenth-century maps and surviving lengths of town wall permit us to reconstruct the plan of medieval Agde (see Fig. 42). From this map, we can appreciate the manner in which the cathedral and its precinct formed the western extremity of the municipal fortifications.

The volatile changes in the balance of power within medieval Agde that we have traced above were reflected in shifting responsibility for the city's defenses. In the mid–twelfth century, the chapter and the viscount vied with the bishop for control of the city. Guilhem de Minerve, supported by Louis VII as an episcopal candidate in 1165, had further solidified relations with the Capetian monarch by 1173. In his diploma of that year, Louis granted the bishop permission to fortify not only the church but also the walls and gates of the city (Appendix 24).[19] By 1187, Guilhem's successor, Bishop Pierre de Montpeyroux, had consolidated his position as master of the city and viscounty. In July of that year, Raymond V, count of Toulouse, conceded the viscounty and all its attendant rights to the bishop.[20]

The diploma of 1173 awarded to Bishop Guilhem a third of the dominion over the city (conserving two-thirds for the king and omitting mention of the viscount). In his diploma, Louis VII warns that no count or viscount or their representative may usurp these episcopal rights, expressly including the towers and fortifications of the town in the enumeration of protected rights. It therefore seems that from at least 1173, the bishop of Agde was recognized as the secular and religious authority of the city and as solely responsible for the fortification of the cathedral as well as the town.

Also rising in the late years of the twelfth century, however, were the forces of the commune (or the *consulat,* as it is more commonly styled in the south.)[21] The consulat at Agde, which developed relatively late, is first encountered in the texts in about 1207. Royal influence supported the bishop in the twelfth century but then shifted increasingly throughout the thirteenth and fourteenth centuries to the consulat. For this latter period, the documents allow us to understand, in relatively precise fashion, the balance of power between the bishop and consuls, especially as it relates to the fortification of the town.[22]

By the mid–thirteenth century, despite the growing power of the *consulat,* the bishop seems to have retained his authority over the fortifications. In 1236, arbitration fixed the duties and rights of consuls and bishop, stating clearly that the bishop should continue to hold the keys to the city (Appendix 26). The record of this debate makes clear the unwillingness of the consuls to pay for the repairs to the fortifications, arguing that it had always been established practice for the bishop and chapter to pay for these necessities. The consuls argued that the "Eglise d'Agde" (now viewed corporately as the bishop and chapter) had always considered the walls of the town as their "property."[23] In 1267, this custom was again invoked. The bishop was proclaimed as holding sole responsibility for the organization of lookouts, guards, and repair. In 1286, the situation seems to be in flux, specifically over the issue of the costs of repair. Threat of war with Aragón, which brought devastation in that year, seems to have impelled fresh concern over the state of the walls and defenses. According to legend, Roger de Loria led a fleet up the Hérault river, took the town, and executed all the male inhabitants. All later accounts of this tragedy depend on a single source, written in 1321, thirty-five years after the massacre. In this document, Philip V is described as having received a report from the consuls of Agde of massive destruction from the war (Appendix 27). Houses, walls, and the town fortifications had still not been repaired, according to them, and this situation had left the town open to attack by "pirates of the Catalans, Italians, Saracens . . . and others." This situation was described as being dangerous not only for the town, but for the region and all of France generally. Since the inhabitants felt they could not pay for repairs, they petitioned the king and the inhabitants of adjoining castles and villages of the diocese of Agde to contribute. This document demonstrates that, by 1321, episcopal responsibility for the upkeep of the walls had crumbled like the very walls themselves. No longer viewed as the property of the bishop, the town fortifications are seen as the responsibility of the consuls, the king, and the diocescan region. In 1332, as part of the solution to the funding problem, an *Oeuvre Commune* was established to finance fortification repair (Appendix 28).[24]

The account of a detailed inspection of the walls in 1356, fueled by the threat of the English invasion of the Hundred Years War, provides a final glimpse of the fortified town of Agde, called in this text, the *magna fortalicia* of the region.[25] This document signals a further weakening of the bishop's control over the fortifications. The consuls, eager to win royal support for their responsibility over the walls, sought the expert counsel of two law professors from the University of Montpellier. The king decided for the consuls, awarding them possession of the keys to the gates as well as responsibility for repairs. The consuls appointed a *capitaine d'armes* to oversee the garrisoning of the walls (Appendix 29).[26]

Although the texts provide a relatively detailed glimpse of military concerns in medieval Agde, they do not tell us what we would most like to know about the garrisoning of the church as well as the town. The information they provide about the shift in responsibility from the bishop to the *consulat* may have been reflected in a reduced dependence on cathedral fortifications in communal defense of the thirteenth and fourteenth centuries. Rather than providing a single picture of the shape and organization of the military affairs in the city, the documents for Agde demonstrate the ways in which those situations were immensely fluid and responsive to change, even within the relatively short space of twenty-five years.

SAINT-PONS-DE-THOMIERES

The church of Saint-Pons had a much more complicated system of fortification in the twelfth century than did either Maguelone or Agde. The predecessor church (dating to the eleventh century, and possibly earlier) had a nave surrounded by towers that survive in their lower courses in the present church. These towers, though much rebuilt, demonstrate that the earlier church at Saint-Pons had upper chapels, like Maguelone, and perhaps also featured lookout and fighting platforms.

The eleventh-century towers were integrated into the complicated machicolation system of the twelfth-century nave. Spiral stairs were added as part of the new machicolated nave (see Fig. 55). These spiral stairs not only permitted easier access to the upper stories of the towers, they also facilitated communication with the various levels of the gallery system of the nave.

The vast unaisled nave of Saint-Pons is surrounded by an elaborate two-tiered system of mural passages, probably originally capped by an upper crenellated platform. This system provided a much more elaborate, and possibly a more fully functional, arrangement than the machicolated systems at Agde and Maguelone. The lower gallery (see Fig. 58a), built within the north and south nave walls, originally communicated with the nave by relatively generous, round-headed windows that are now blocked but that are still visible within the gallery (and, in the proper light, from the nave). This lower gallery continues around the narthex, where it receives more elaborate arched openings into the narthex (Figs. 67, 68). Archer slits open from this level to the exterior and are visible in the west façade (Fig. 69). The upper gallery passage opens outward to the south and north, with both round-headed windows and arrow slits. Beneath each arrow slit is a square machicolation that opens on the crown of each exterior arcade (Figs. 70, 71). The measured section drawing (see Fig. 59) shows the relationship of the two galleries built within the walls of Saint-Pons. A surviving door opening from the northeast tower above the upper gallery probably originally led to a third, upper level. The reconstruction section (see Fig. 60) therefore shows an upper crenellated platform capping the walls and framing the timber roof. Given the climate in the mountains of Saint-Pons, the resulting drainage problems no doubt ultimately encouraged the suppression of this upper level.

The town of Saint-Pons-de-Thomières was separated from at least the twelfth century into the *Ville Mage* and the *Ville Moindre*. Fortification of the town enclosed both these areas, and can still be traced in the town of

Figure 67. Saint-Pons-de-Thomières, interior view of narthex, showing gallery.

Figure 68. Saint-Pons-de-Thomières, western passage of lower gallery.

Figure 69. Saint-Pons-de-Thomières, detail of west façade showing archer slits which open from the lower gallery.

Figure 70. Saint-Pons-de-Thomières, machicolation, north side (exterior view of slot shown in Fig. 71).

Figure 71. Saint-Pons-de-Thomières, machicolation, north side (interior view of slot shown in Fig. 70).

Saint-Pons today (see Fig. 49). Two towers survive, although much rebuilt, and several lengths of wall survive, built into modern houses. Today, houses incorporating the town wall almost touch the west front of the fortress-church. These two systems were undoubtedly originally unified, providing further protection to the most vulnerable spot of the church, and making the arrow slits of the narthex gallery an integral part of this western defensive system. The town and abbey fortifications are specifically mentioned in the agreement of 1171, where the inhabitants of the abbey are limited to the monks, servants, and their families (Appendix 32).

By the time of the fourteenth-century *Livre des Libertés et Franchises,* the responsibility for the walls rested with the inhabitants of the town, as part of their duty to the crown (Appendix 33).[27] As at nearby Agde, the town of Saint-Pons witnessed growing secular adminstration and waning episcopal control of the town walls during this period. The Hundred Years War impelled restoration of the walls. The *Livre des Libertés* for Saint-Pons tells us that, at this time, various dependencies within the diocese held responsibility for specific lengths of the town walls. During the Wars of Religion, the gates of the town were opened to the invaders by the townspeople, who traded the sack of the abbey for the safety of the town itself.

CONCLUSION

Though the documents provide only tantalizing glimpses of the three abbey-fortresses of Maguelone, Agde, and Saint-Pons-de-Thomières in operation, we can draw some tentative conclusions. Responsibility for the fortifications of both the church and town in the twelfth century seems to have rested with the bishop or abbot, as the feudal as well as spiritual overlord of the municipality. By the end of the thirteenth century, the *consulats* of Agde and Saint-Pons had begun to usurp these military responsibilities. Maguelone is the exception in this instance. Freedom from secular intervention provided by papal protection, together with its virtually deserted island site, ensured that at Maguelone, the bishop retained control of all fortification walls. Even at Maguelone, however, pressures from the burgeoning town of Montpellier led to conflict in the fourteenth century. Monks and canons would seem to have had only a supervisory capacity in the normal garrisoning and surveillance of the precincts at Agde and Saint-Pons, although exceptions may again have been more frequent at the sparsely populated Maguelone.

Careful analysis of the surviving building fabric and the archival sources for Maguelone, Agde, and Saint-Pons-de-Thomières permit us to reconstruct some of the ways in which they functioned not only as monastic and cathedral churches but also as military fortresses.

THE ARCHITECTURAL CONTEXT: SOURCES AND PARALLELS

In contrast to the aisled plans, multistoried elevations, and ribbed vaults of early Gothic architecture in the north of France, church design in Languedoc in the second half of the twelfth century tended to favor wide and aisleless two-storied basilicas with flat expanses of uninterrupted wall.[1] The interior of Saint-Pons-de-Thomières, for example, is a large, unified volume nearly 15 meters wide (see Fig. 51). The surface of the walls encasing the interior space is interrupted only sparingly. Each bay is defined by the linear organization of vertical pilasters that carry transverse arches. Within each bay, small nave windows signal an otherwise undifferentiated second story. Round-headed windows originally opened into the nave to mark the presence of the lower gallery level, but the skeletal support of the building is otherwise unarticulated. The slightly pointed barrel vault, like the nave walls, features large flat areas of undecorated surface masonry.

Wide spans and planar surfaces seem to have been a feature of architecture in the Midi as early as the ninth century. These elements continued to dominate southern Gothic architecture of the mid-twelfth and thirteenth centuries. In this sense, the division between Romanesque and Gothic is less clearly defined in southern French architecture, or perhaps it is better to observe that the terms "Romanesque" and "Gothic" are less useful in describing the architectural history of Languedoc. Scholarship on the architecture of the region has tended to focus on the rise of Gothic style and on the contribution of the Cistercians and Mendicant orders in this development. In this chapter we will focus instead upon twelfth-century building style in the Midi without prejudice toward its architectural successors. We will also examine the varied sources and parallels for the major constituent elements of twelfth-century architectural style, looking first at the single-nave vaulted basilica and the attendant use of galleried passages and stair systems. Finally, we will examine the sources and distribution of machicolated monuments and the implications of this distribution and chronology on the connections between medieval East and West.

THE SINGLE-NAVE VAULTED BASILICA

Maguelone, Agde, and Saint-Pons are all typical in their use of a pointed barrel vault supported on simple transverse arches.[2] The immense breadth of these aisleless naves, which range from nearly 10 meters at Maguelone to 12.6 meters at Agde to just under 15 meters at Saint-Pons, can be appreciated if we compare them to contemporary northern Gothic cathedrals. The central nave vessel at Sens (c. 1145–64), which was remarkable for its size, measured 15.25 meters across, only slightly broader than Saint-Pons. Among the great Gothic cathedrals of northern France only the 16.3-meter width of the nave of Chartres (designed in c. 1194), surpassed the central span at Sens. Though modern historians tend to emphasize the Gothic conquest of height, vaulting large spans was an early and enduring preoccupation in northern Gothic design.[3] In this regard, southern builders can be seen to participate in at least one of the design motivations of northern Gothic at the same time that they rejected others.

The preference for stone vaulting over wide naves in both northern and southern buildings created special stresses on their walls. The magnitude of both the load and the thrust increases with the widening of the span.[4] This problem was created – and solved – in both fortified and unfortified churches in the region. The unfortified abbey church at Silvanès, for example, has a vaulted nave 14.17 meters in span (Fig. 72).

The military function of these buildings may have necessitated certain aspects of their designs. The provision for security might be manifested in a stone platform replacing a timber roof, which also reduced the threat of fire. Transverse arches tend to be used very sparingly, with, for example, only a single transverse arch in the nave of Agde cathedral. Such limited use of transverse arches signals not only a restrained surface aesthetic but also a relatively rapid pace of construction. If the distance between each transverse arch represents the extent of a unit of wooden centering, it also bears witness to the extent of each building campaign. This extensive (even wasteful, by normal standards) use of centering may have been mandated in some cases by the desire for rapid completion of a fortified building.

Roman and Early Medieval Sources

The use of extensive mural surfaces, the relative lack of articulation, and the taste for wide vaulted spaces in these buildings have a complicated history.

Figure 72. Silvanès, interior view.

We must look to three main sources: (1) vaulted Roman architecture; (2) Carolingian and early Romanesque architecture in the Midi and Mediterranean; and (3) secular fortification design. The relationship of twelfth-century church design to Roman design is especially problematic. No specific structural parallels for the vaulting system in these buildings, for example, can be located in Roman architectural tradition. Not a single pointed and longitudinal barrel vault constructed of ashlar survives, and it possible that one never existed. Nonetheless, the close visual similarities between the Languedoc buildings and Roman vaulted interiors in the arrangement of space, in proportion and in the handling of the wall encourage us to pursue the connection. The closest surviving parallel, both geographically as well as structurally, is the so-called "temple of Diana" at Nîmes.[5] Probably built in the late first century B.C. (but possibly as late as the second century A.D.), the "temple" most likely served as a library or reception hall within the grand fountain complex of the Roman city of Nîmes. The central vessel, 14.52 meters in length and 9.55 meters in span, is vaulted with an unusual system of cut ashlar blocks (Figs. 73, 74). Each alternating "arch" of the barrel vault projects from the recessed surface of the vault in a manner similar to transverse arches. Scholars have been divided in their opinions on the structural aspects of this vault, which has no immediate parallels, but it seems clear that the "transverse arches" (if they can be so called) did not function in the same constructional manner as later

Figure 73. Temple of Diana, Nîmes, view.

Figure 74. Temple of Diana, Nîmes, section and plan.

transverses.[6] The central nave of the structure is flanked by very narrow barrel-vaulted passages that originally contained stairs or ramps. Despite the differences in vaulting technology and profile, the general proportions and treatment of space are remarkably similar to those of the Languedoc churches.

It is useful in this context to consider the medieval "afterlife" of the "temple of Diana."[7] The fountain complex of Nîmes fell into disrepair in the late antique period. In the solitude of this newly suburban zone, the "temple" building alone seems to have survived largely intact. In 987 it was given by the aptly named Fontaine, bishop of Nîmes, to a community of Benedictine nuns for the establishment of their convent, Saint-Sauveur-de-la-Font. The nuns adapted the "temple" as their convent church without substantial modifications, except for the removal of the stairs or ramps of the side corridors. The edifice remained intact and in use as a church until the late sixteenth century. In the "temple of Diana" we thus have preserved a parallel that is remarkably close to the Languedoc churches geographically, functionally, and structurally. Its span is almost precisely equal to that of Maguelone, and the use of small gallery-like passages make their sections very similar. Despite some differences, the existence of a wide-span, vaulted Roman interior, contemporaneously in use as a monastic church, make the "temple of Diana" one plausible source for the design of medieval single-nave churches.

Barrel vaults were common in other Imperial and late Roman basilicas, reception rooms, and bath buildings, although concrete (rubble and pozzolana mortar) seems normally to have been preferred to ashlar masonry.[8] Concrete barrel vaults were employed in basilicas, receptions rooms, and baths in Imperial and late Roman architecture. The side chambers of the Basilica of Maxentius, the reception rooms of Domitian's and Flavian's palaces on the Palatine, the Portus Aemeliana, and the Markets of Ferentino, all preserve concrete barrel vaults. The closest Roman parallels for the pointed barrel vault of the Languedoc churches are preserved in domed rather than longitudinal monuments. The fourth-century "temple of Minerva Medica" in Rome is a centrally planned monument with a pointed dome spanning 24.5 meters. Another so-called temple of Diana, in Baia has a concrete vault with pointed profile. This building, part of a nymphaeum complex, has a span of almost 30 meters.

Early Christian churches, like the fourth-century basilica of Martres-Tolosane also continued the preference for wide spans (in this case 9 meters).[9] Large-span halls were also an aspect of palace architecture in early medieval tradition, though these were not certainly vaulted. The papal palace in Rome, as well as the Lateran palace, may have had vaulted halls. Carolingian palace design continued this trend with the Aula at Aachen.

These parallels illustrate that the taste for wide spans and the technology for barrel vaulting was known in the Roman and early medieval period. The proximity of buildings like the "temple of Diana" in Nîmes to the Languedoc churches demonstrates that the general design and proportions of these Roman interiors could have been influential in the creation of similar spaces in the twelfth century, even if the specific technology of vaulting was not adopted in all of its details. Early Christian churches of the region were undoubtedly important in the continued use of the wide-span nave, although Roman and Carolingian reception rooms and halls, especially those that had been converted to religious use in the Middle Ages, probably formed the most influential sources.

Architecture of the ninth to eleventh centuries functioned both as an intermediary for Roman forms as well as an independent source. Although evidence for these buildings is fragmentary and sometimes difficult to interpret, it is clear that wide single-nave interiors were found by the early eleventh century in a number of churches in the regions of Languedoc and Provence, and somewhat earlier in the adjacent territories of Catalonia and Aragón.

The closest early Romanesque sources for Maguelone, Agde, and Saint-Pons may, in fact, be themselves, that is to say, the predecessor buildings on the same three sites. All three earlier churches seem to have been wide single-nave structures. Maguelone and Agde preserve excavated evidence of apses spanning nearly the same width as the twelfth-century successor cathedrals.[10] These apses probably date to the ninth century for Agde and to the eleventh century for Maguelone. Although we cannot be certain of the plan of their naves, and thus cannot rule out aisled structures, reconstruction as single-naved churches is entirely possible. For Saint-Pons, we have more surviving fabric. Extant towers of the tenth- to eleventh-century church were reused in the twelfth-century campaign, as were, apparently, the foundation courses of the nave walls. At Saint-Pons, as well, the wide span of 14.91 meters would seem to have been predetermined by the location of towers and foundations that the twelfth-century builders wished to reuse (see Fig. 57). All three buildings, therefore, have wide naves to some degree conditioned by predecessor buildings. These earlier churches were, however, probably not vaulted until the twelfth-century campaigns.

The ambitious scale of wide spans (though without vaulting) is found in Spain by the mid–tenth century, and in Mediterranean France by the early eleventh century. The regions of Catalonia and Aragón in northern Spain were linked ecclesiastically and architecturally to southern France in the tenth and eleventh centuries. Tenth- and eleventh-century regional councils and church dedications were normally attended by bishops from France and Catalonia, normally including prelates from Maguelone, Narbonne, Agde, Vic, and Elne. This trans-Pyrenees community was reinforced by the domains of important monastic houses, like Saint-Pons or Aniane, which held significant domains in Catalonia and Aragón. Both the single-naved plan and pointed barrel vaults are known relatively early in Catalonia.[11] The single-nave church is ubiquitous in northern Spain, although examples are not always of wide span nor consistently vaulted. The single-naved plan is especially favored by Sancho Ramírez and his family. It is used at the late-eleventh-century castle church of Loarre as well as at the convent church of Santa Cruz de la Séros, which was under construction by 1095. Although aisled, several mid-eleventh-century castle churches share a similar interior aesthetic with the Languedoc churches. Santa Maria in Roses and Sant Miquel de Fluvia have a triple-apsed plan similar to that of Maguelone and have pointed barrel vaults with transverse arches in the central aisle of the nave.

Impressive examples of wide single naves (most unvaulted) are found in many of the early medieval cathedrals of the south of France. The earliest Romanesque nave at Aix-en-Provence has been identified and reconstructed as a large single vessel 30.30 meters long and 11.80 meters wide surmounted by a flat timber ceiling (Fig. 75).[12] Although nothing survives of the pre-Gothic cathedral of Saints-Just-et-Pasteur in Narbonne, it may have been a single-naved structure as wide as 20 meters. The predecessor cathedral is known through a long *procès* that describes the negotiations that took place from 1345 to 1361 between the cathedral chapter and the town *consulat* over the construction of the new fourteenth-century cathedral.[13] The document describes the location of the old cathedral to the south of the

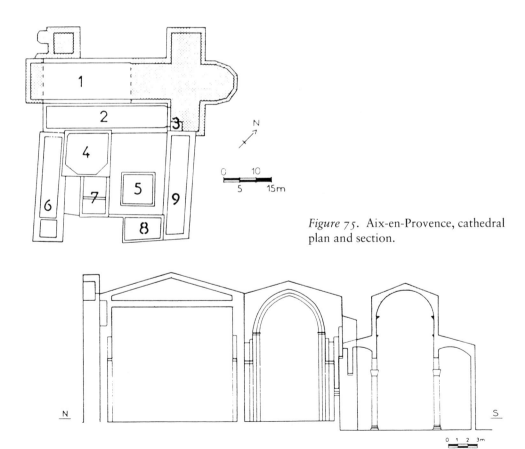

Figure 75. Aix-en-Provence, cathedral plan and section.

present church, on the site of the Gothic cloister. Given the precisions of the text and our knowledge of the site, we can reconstruct the earlier church as occupying a site roughly 33 meters long by 20 meters in width. It is not clear, however, whether the nave filled the entire available area. The *procès* also does not tell us whether the church was vaulted, but it does say that it was low and that it had a "single nave":

dicta ecclesia vetus erat valde et brevis et bassa et stricta, unicam navem habens.

We must wonder, however, about the precision of this fourteenth-century terminology, especially in light of another document of 1255 that speaks of the "destruction of six arches and piers of the church of Saint-Just." Nonetheless, the structure may have been a single vessel of between 12 to 20 meters.[14] Even more problematic than the plan and width of the early cathedral at Narbonne is the date of its *unicam navem*. Scholars have claimed it variously as fifth-, ninth-, late eleventh- or twelfth-century. Long attributed to the Carolingian archbishop Théodard, the cathedral may instead have been a late-ninth-century rebuilding of the fifth-century basilica erected by Bishop Rusticus in the mid–fifth century, as the *Vita Theodardi* would seem to suggest. The complexities of construction phases at Narbonne prevent us from identifying precisely the date and form of this important church.

Other cathedrals and abbeys seem to have used wide, single-naved plans. The eleventh-century cathedral of Lavaur may have been an aisleless basilica 14 meters in span.[15] The cathedral of Saint-Jean-le-Vieux in Perpignan was rebuilt in the early eleventh century as a *nef unique* 9.5 meters wide.[16] Several major abbey churches, including those at Caunes-Minervois, Arles, and Moissac, had single-naved plans. Though the nave of Caunes-Minervois was rebuilt in the fourteenth century, the surviving early eleventh-century apse implies a wide nave of about 11–12 meters, and the location of the surviving twelfth- to thirteenth-century porch would leave little room for aisles in the original nave. The fourteenth-century nave probably reproduces the eleventh-century original in its original dimensions and may reuse its foundations.[17] The abbeys of Saint-Trophime at Arles and Saint-Pierre in Moissac may also have had wide naves in the Carolingian period.[18]

Even "minor" parish churches might be major in span. The parish church of Saint-Etienne-de-Tersan in Azille (Aude) had an early eleventh-century single nave 12.5 meters in width.[19] The single nave of the parish church at Saint-Martin at Moissac had a span of 7.8 meters.[20]

A single-span plan was not, however, the only available alternative. It is important to remember that churches of aisled plan were also used widely in the region. The eleventh-century cathedral of Sainte-Cécile in Albi survived next to its Gothic successor until the sixteenth century. This *vieille église* was built of ashlar and was probably aisled.[21] The choice of a single nave should thus be seen as just that: a choice selected from alternatives, and not a regional imperative.

The return to vaulting wide single naves in Languedoc appears to have been a feature of the twelfth century. The cathedral of Saint-Nazaire in Béziers, with its span of 13.88 meters, was built in the second quarter of the twelfth century (Fig. 76).[22] The *Chanson de la croisade albigeoise* makes clear that this twelfth-century church was vaulted and provides the date of the vault's collapse following the siege of the town in 1209 when the church was burnt.[23] The church may have been fortified like its thirteenth-century successor, since surviving fabric of the canonial precinct (see below) was provided with machicoulis. Yves Esquieu has shown not only the presence of a *nef unique* at the old cathedral of Béziers but has also demonstrated the manner in which the single nave supplanted the basilical plan in Béziers in the course of the twelfth century.[24] The church of Saint-Jacques in Béziers was begun with aisles, but finished as a single nave of 10.86-meter span.[25] It was vaulted with pointed barrel vault and transverse arches. The nearby abbey of Saint-Papoul was similarly begun in the mid–twelfth century as an aisled basilica but converted to a *nef unique* 14 meters in span.[26]

The spacious, vaulted single naves of Maguelone, Agde, and Saint-Pons-de-Thomières therefore continue a rich regional architectural heritage that had Roman, Carolingian, and early medieval predecessors. Though neither their use of vaults nor their employment of wide naves can be identified precisely as Roman features, the spacious monumentality of these interiors res-

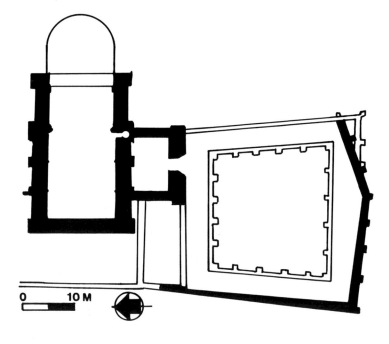

0   10 M

Figure 76. Béziers, plan of twelfth-century cathedral of Saint-Nazaire and claustral complex. *Black:* Twelfth-century fabric; *Outline:* Gothic.

onates as classicizing in effect if not also in intent. The taste for monumentality was probably formed early by ancient monuments and was reinforced during the late antique period by basilicas such as Martres-Tolosane. The taste for spaciousness, flat surfaces, and grand openings was reinvigorated during the Carolingian period with the construction of major cathedrals such as Perpignan, Aix, and possibly Narbonne, and of abbeys such as Saint-Trophime at Arles. During the eleventh century, this taste was continued in cathedral construction, reinforced by developments in Catalonia, and possibly by the adaptation to Christian use of antique monuments such as the "temple of Diana." With the reintroduction of vaulting, these spaces became once again truly monumental.

In Maguelone, Agde, and Saint-Pons, a familiarity with Roman vocabulary is clear, and is further established by the use of Corinthian capitals, double-torus bases, and other decorative elements. The Carolingian and early Romanesque past is also important for all three of the buildings. Saint-Pons was an important royal foundation of the Carolingian period, and reminders of that prestigious past are likely to have been favored. At Agde, the Carolingian past was so powerful as to have inspired a forged charter. Marble Gallo-Roman capitals were reused in the crossing at Agde and were copied in the limestone capitals of the transept arms. As we have seen, the predecessor buildings of the three fortress-churches may have been preserved in the foundation courses of twelfth-century rebuilding. The functional presence of reuse does not negate the possibility that such elements were chosen consciously or meaningfully. As argued above, the elements of wide, aisleless, and vaulted construction at Maguelone may have been meant to be consciously reminiscent of Rome, and in particular with the Rome of the reform papacy who actively supported and visited Maguelone.

Fortifications as a Source

The popularity of the single-naved plan may also be indebted to its military suitability. Since at least the tenth century (and probably earlier), secular tower fortifications consisted of square or rectangular, thick-walled structures, sometimes with wall passages for interior access. Contemporary towers such as Saint-Aulary in Languedoc may have at least partly influenced the ecclesiastical choice of a short nave, with an open and accessible plan.[27] Of course, with its original length of over 80 meters, Saint-Pons is anything but short, so this parallel is not all-encompassing. Nonetheless, it should not be surprising that fortresses might inspire designers of fortress-churches.

The hall plan adopted by these fortified churches was particularly appropriate to their military purpose, as it removed the obvious impediment of the side aisle from the trajectory of missiles dropped from the machicolated slots above

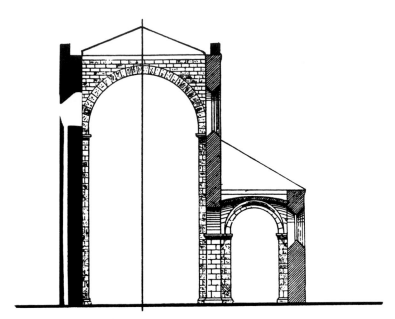

Figure 77. Comparative section of aisled and hall church.

(Fig. 77).[28] In other words, an aisleless plan permitted closer surveillance and protection of the nave walls of the church. Of course, the attachment of claustral buildings and other subsidiary structures normally left only the north nave walls exposed to outsiders. The fact that the south walls of the churches were also provided with machicolations indicates that the church was intended to function as the castle keep, or refuge of last resort, for the abbey.

The combined functions of these fortress-churches, however, enlarged the repertoire of military forms beyond pure defense. The use of the gallery, for example, may have been partly due to military needs; partly to the structural solution of vault support; partly to nonmilitary circulation of monks during services; and very possibly to a combination of all three.

Galleries and Gallery Passages

One of the characteristic features of the fortress-churches of Languedoc is the use of mural passages or stairs built within the thickness of the wall.[29] Unlike the northern examples, where the gallery was linked to a growing complexity of the elevation design, the southern use of the gallery was most often allied to the development of wide vaulted halls, largely unarticulated by colonettes or buttresses, and undivided by aisles.

Very early examples of mural passages can be found in the pre-Roman Scottish stone fortifications known as duns and brochs.[30] Their walls are generally solid and thickened at the base, while further up they divide into inner and outer walls, the space between being taken up by small rooms, stairs, and galleries. A good example of such a gallery is preserved at the broch of Dun Telve. Though examples of this tradition of stone-built, galleried fortification is not documented beyond the early second century A.D., it is not impossible that local vernacular traditions in northern Europe may have continued this form.

The use of mural passages to serve and access vaults and domes were widely known and used in Roman Imperial architecture. In these Roman examples, passages were most often used in combination with stair vises. Stairs were often concealed in the mass of the wall, or revealed in turrets. The Pantheon has a passage just above the springing of the vault, as does the basilican Baths of Diocletian. The "temple of Diana" in Nîmes had stairs or ramps housed in small barrel-vaulted corridors to either side of the vaulted nave (see Figs. 73, 74). The passages of the Porta Nigra at Trier are the closest late Roman example to the galleries under consideration here. At the Trier gate, passages with openings on two sides allow simultaneous surveillance of the interior and exterior of this fortified gatehouse (Fig. 78). It may be significant that the Trier gate, too, was converted into a church in the medieval period.

Stairs vises and gallery passages were also used in Islamic fortification. The outer walls of the Abbasid palace of Ukhaidir had mural galleries supported by rows of machicolated arches (see Figs. 81, 82). This provision for machicolated passages along the entire length of the gallery, linked by stairs, is consonant with the technique used in the Languedoc churches and in particular with the design of Saint-Pons (see below).

Passages with stair vises began to be used in northern European architecture in the mid-eleventh century in both ecclesiastical and military architecture. It is during this period that intramural stairs connected with passages begin to provide an interconnected system of communication in the upper parts of churches and castles. In the south, however, the earliest examples date somewhat later, to the end of the eleventh and the twelfth centuries.

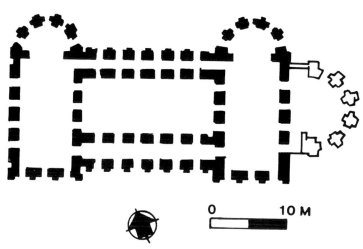

Figure 78. Porta Nigra, Trier, plan at upper story.

0   10 M

Figure 79. Distribution map of surviving machicolated monuments.

Saint-Pons-de-Thomières provides an example of this transition. The towers of the eleventh-century church of Saint-Pons originally had no stairs, with access probably provided by ladders. In the twelfth-century rebuilding, these towers were conserved, and stairs were incorporated into the projecting machicolations next to each tower (see Figs. 54, 55).

Nonfortified churches also began to share in this technology. At Saint-Jouin-de-Marnes, for example, a stair is incorporated into the angle of the nave and north transept, in a wall especially widened to receive it as at Maguelone. In the upper wall, the vise prolongs into a straight stair connected to a passage that opens into the nave above the springing of the

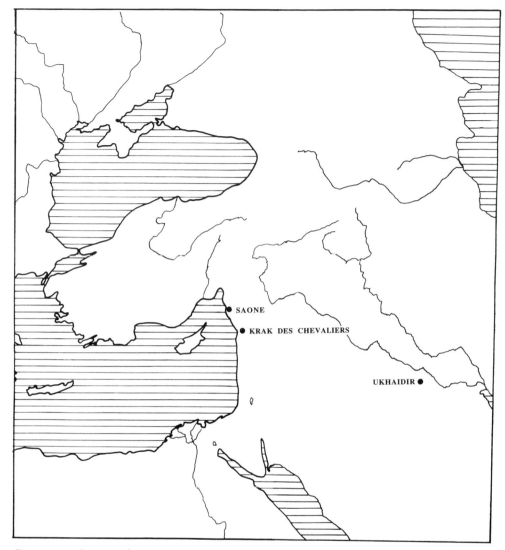

Figure 79. (Continued.)

vault.[31] The Cistercian abbey of Silvanès has a similar gallery passage at the
height of the springing of the vault (see Fig. 72).

MACHICOLATED MONUMENTS OF THE MEDIEVAL EAST AND WEST

The origin and development of the technique of machicolation has never
been fully traced.[32] The fact that machicolation, and related elements, are
used in Roman, Byzantine, Islamic, and Western medieval buildings, of both
ecclesiastical and secular natures, requires of the researcher a broad comparative approach (Fig. 79). Related to the development of machicolation

was the technology of wooden hoarding – wooden platforms built into the top of the wall – and portcullises – openings which normally allowed doors to be raised and lowered through vertical slots (see Fig. 4c). Hoarding may be thought of as machicolation written in timber, the portcullis as machicolation in the singular.

The Sources of Machicoulis sur arcs

The Romans knew and used the defensive technology of stone-built gates with portcullises. Polybius, Livy, and Vegetius all describe such slots (which they called *cataracta*).[33] *Cataracta* are described as useful not only in trapping the enemy but also in dousing fires set by attacking forces. Though the texts mention the technology, few extant examples survive. The Herculaneum gate at Pompeii (before 78 B.C.) had a portcullis, as has the late Roman gate of Qasr ash-Sham'a in Cairo.[34] The architectural elevation of most late Roman gates remains, however, virtually unknown. Surviving evidence does not suggest that the Romans expanded the use of the defensive slot beyond the gate to the exterior wall, although again we are impeded by the lack of extant examples in elevation. It is possible that some of the more closely spaced precinct tower-buttresses might have been capped by machicolations. One possible example is the late Roman burgh of Szentendre on the Danube frontier, where the projecting buttresses are only 4 meters apart, an easy span for a machicolated arch.[35]

If machicolations have been ignored in the scholarship, the history of toilets has been positively suppressed. Yet these "service slots" (known in polite scholarship as "garderobes") were ubiquitous and highly visible features of fortification design. The similarity in design between the *machicoulis* slot and garderobe openings suggests that the former is indebted to the latter. Garderobes may have inspired not only the form of delivery but also the rich array of projectiles from which defenders might chose.

The vast majority of Armenian garrison forts incorporate a "slot machicolation" (a gap between two coursed arches rather than a simple opening) in their entrances (Fig. 80). This technique is closely related to the portcullis, and is, in effect, a portcullis without the vertically sliding door. The Armenian castles are difficult to date precisely, but most were probably constructed during the eleventh through thirteenth centuries.[36] In the opinion of R. Edwards, who has studied them most closely, the slot machicolation was an Armenian invention, with the first extant example at the fortress of Van Kalesi in the seventh century.[37] If this is the case, much of what we attribute to Islamic or Crusader invention may be ultimately indebted to Armenian design.

The closest Eastern parallel to the machicolated arches used in the Languedoc churches (and especially to the galleried system at Saint-Pons) is the Abbasid fortified palace of Ukhaidir, located about 120 miles south of

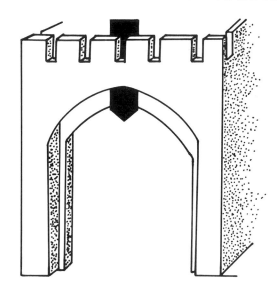

Figure 80. Armenian slot machicolation, diagram (arrow indicates passage of projectile).

Baghdad (Figs. 81, 82).[38] The palace of Ukhaidir, probably begun around 778 A.D., used a virtuouso system of machicolated galleries supported on round-headed arches, facing to the exterior and interior. The result is a series of continuous machiciolations very similar in aspect and function to the fortification system at Saint-Pons. Gateways at Ukhaidir also incorporated portcullises. The outer walls of Ukhaidir were originally about 19 meters in height and about 2.6 meters thick, with projecting buttresses supporting machicolations on both inner and outer faces. As a result, the width of the gallery is about 4.5 meters. On the exterior side of the barrel-vaulted galleries are recesses measuring 1.4 meters in width and 50 centimeters in depth. Every fifth recess opens into a small round chamber in the top of each tower; the other contained arrow-slits. In each of the four corners of the enclosures are staircases (now largely ruined) linking the galleries that run around the entire circuit of the palace. The galleries could also be reached by the double staircases that flank the gateways in the eastern, southern, and western sides. This provision for machicolated arches accessed from the interior by galleries linked by stairs, is particularly close to the design of Saint-Pons-de-Thomières.

The nearby fortification of Ashtan (c. late eighth century) had portcullis gates but no machicolated passages. Earlier machicolations can be found in Islamic architecture, as, for example, at Umayyad Qasr al Hayr East (early eighth century), but these, like the gates of Cairo, are single machicolated openings supported on corbels.[39] Later palaces following the plan and design of Ukhaidir, such as Lashkari Bazar (Afghanistan, eleventh century),[40] or the caravanserai of Ribat-i-Malik (Central Asia, c. 1068–80) also use mural passages, but not in the masterful combination with machicolation found at Ukhaidir.

Figure 81. Ukhaidir,
view of machicolations.

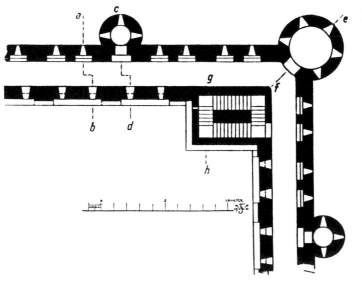

Figure 82. Ukhaidir,
plan, detail.

Links between Medieval East and West

It is all very well to suggest formal and functional parallels between Ukhaidir and Saint-Pons-de-Thomières, but a link between Baghdad and Languedoc demands substantiation. The standard link between East and West during the twelfth century, that of the Crusades, does not fully satisfy, since the palace of Ukhaidir lay far to the east of the Crusader kingdoms. Ukhaidir was, however, located along the Euphrates spice routes, which were used throughout the medieval period. Contact with the West was therefore not an impossibility. It is not improbable, moreover, that Byzantine fortifications, perhaps even in Constantinople (and almost certainly in the hinterlands), may have adopted the technique of machicolated galleries, though I am unaware of surviving examples.[41]

Westerners, including Crusaders, may have seen Eastern machicolations like those at Ukhaidir and may have been thus inspired to use the technique in their own fortifications in the East. Crusader castles such as Saone and Krak des Chevaliers all used machicolated arches, but, as we will see below, the problem of chronology is a vexed one, and the directions of influence between East and West are far from certain.

It is important to recall at this juncture that the Holy Land was far from remote to many of the prelates of Languedoc. Many bishops were present at the councils that promulgated the Crusades, and a number even went on Crusade. Three bishops from Maguelone, Arnaud, Godfrey and Galtier, went on Crusade. Whereas Godfrey and Galtier died and were buried in the Holy Land, Arnaud returned to Maguelone after his visit (although he died shortly afterward). The cartularies of both Maguelone and Agde preserve a number of testaments from members of the communities departing on Crusade (see Appendix 13), as well as donations made to the Holy Sepulchre. Prelates from across the Mediteranean also convened at church councils. In particular, the Lateran Council of 1179 brought together over 300 bishops, who together with abbots and other dignitaries brought the entire membership to nearly a thousand. Among those present were Jean de Montlaur, bishop of Maguelone, and Pope Alexander III, who had twice visited Maguelone. The East was represented by Archbishops William of Tyre, Heraclius of Caesarea; Bishop Albert of Bethlehem; Peter, the prior of the Holy Sepulchre; and others. Contact between Languedoc and the East was thus a regular feature of the life of prelates in the twelfth century.

Machicolations were used in the twelfth-century phases of construction of the fortress of Krak des Chevaliers (Fig. 83).[42] One of the rectangular towers that survives from a twelfth-century campaign has three machicolated arches at its base (Fig. 84). When this tower (the north tower, marked "A" on the plan) was incorporated into the thirteenth-century rebuilding,

Figure 83. Krak des Chevaliers, view showing surviving machicolations on twelfth-century tower.

its machicolations were blocked. Although the hilltop site of Krak des Chevaliers was probably inhabited and possibly fortified from a very early period, nothing is known of its history before the eleventh century. The castle was founded by the Emir of Homs and occupied by a Kurdish garrison from 1031. Krak was briefly occupied by Crusaders in 1099 on their way to Jerusalem. In 1109, Tancred of Antioch captured the castle, but ownership quickly passed to the Counts of Tripoli in 1112. It was briefly but unsuccessfully besieged by Alp Arslan, Sultan of Aleppo, in 1115. In 1142, Count Raymond II of Tripoli ceded the castle to the Hospitalers. The defenses were extensively rebuilt after this change in ownership, and after an earthquake in 1157. At this time, the castle was adapted for monastic use with the addition of a cloister and refectory. The castle repelled Arab attacks in 1163 and 1167, but a second earthquake in 1169 necessitated renewed

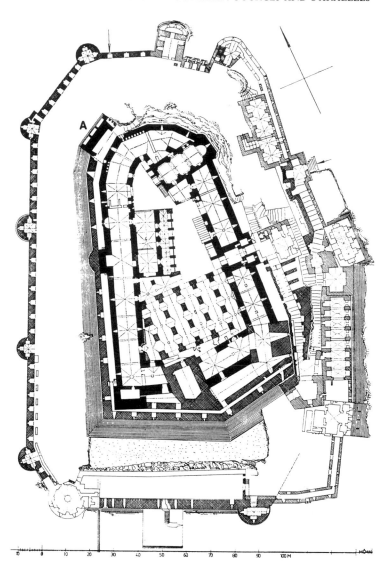

Figure 84. Krak des Chevaliers, plan.

reconstruction, which began with financial assistance from King Vladslas of Bohemia. In 1201, further earthquake damage led to the reconstruction of the outer defensive wall, the addition of the talus to the south and west, and the construction of the large storehouse in the center of the keep.

The machicolated arches of the north tower may be dated only relatively, that is, by their placement embedded in the thirteenth-century talus, and stylistically (by their square shape, no longer favored in most thirteenth-century Crusader designs). No independent documentation exists, however, to identify either the patron or the building campaign to which they belong. The phase of heavy rebuilding under the Hospitalers and after the earthquake of 1157, or that following the second earthquake of 1169–70, remains the most likely, but a construction date earlier in the twelfth century is not impossible. Obviously the date of construction bears importantly in our discussion of the sources of Western machicolation. If the machicolated tower of Krak dates to the early twelfth century, then it may have acted as an influence on the design of the Languedoc churches. If, instead, the tower belongs to a later campaign, it may be a parallel reflection of earlier machicolations. We must also consider the possibility that the design of Krak and other Crusader castles was influenced by the Languedoc churches.

It certainly seems that the initial design of the machicolated arch came ultimately from the East, from monuments like Ukhaidir and other lost early examples. Once machicolations were used in the West, however, it is possible that these Western machicolated monuments figured more prominently in the minds of castle designers. In this way, machicolations may have been exported from and "reimported" back to the East by successive waves of Crusaders and other travelers. As the staging ground for pilgrimage, trade, and crusading activity, the Mediterranean regions of Provence and Languedoc hosted a large share of the travelers headed to the East. The last glimpse many Westerners had of their homeland would have been the machicolated fortifications that protected the French coast. It may have been that memory which was recreated in the Holy Land in the design of some Crusader fortifications.

The Crusader fortification of Saone provides one piece of evidence to support the notion that the *machicoulis* was known in the Levant in the early twelfth century.[43] The castle of Saone is the best-preserved example of early Crusader design, since it was captured by Saladin in 1188 and never reverted to Crusader hands. (It also conserves significant portions of the predecessor Byzantine castle, built after the capture of the site by Emperor John Tzimices in c. 975.) In the first quarter of the twelfth century, perhaps after the capture of nearby Lattaqia in 1108, it was captured by the Franks, who concentrated on reinforcing the main northeast face. There they built the narrow entrance gate ("A" on the plan, Fig. 85), and the adjoining keep. One could reach this gate only by a bridge that spanned the deep natural fosse. The bridge was supported on a natural outcrop (or really upcrop) of rock that now stands alone like an obelisk. In addition to a bent entrance, a legacy of Byzantine design, the gate is protected by a portcullis, which is, after all, a singular machicolated arch.[44] This portcullis therefore probably dates to the first quarter of the twelfth century, almost certainly before 1180.

The fortified Templar and Hospitaler sites of Krak des Chevaliers, Saone, and other Crusader fortress-monasteries provide a close parallel to the Languedoc fortified abbeys in their combination of fortified church and abbey complex. Krak and Saone provide examples not only of the use of machicolations but of the fortification of abbey sites. It has been suggested that a parallel – and perhaps a prototype – for the fortified monastery of a

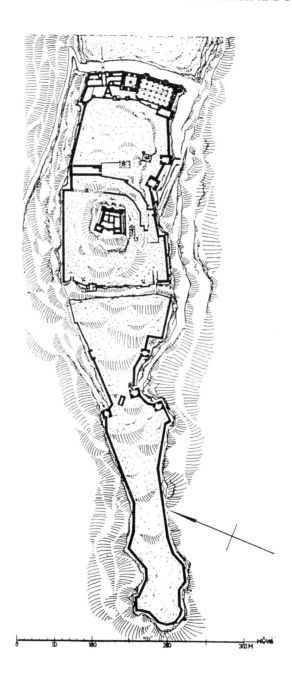

Figure 85. Saone, plan.

fighting order of monks is found in the Islamic world in the "ribats," border fortresses staffed by monks from the ninth-century Aghlabid period. A series of ribats is known in North Africa. Of those erected at Tripoli, Sfax, Monastir, Bizerte, and Sousse, the last is the best preserved.[45] At Sousse, a vaulted sanctuary is located over a machicolated entrance gate. Contact between North Africa and Languedoc has not been pursued by scholars, but connections are certainly possible.

The date of fortifications, and the direction of influence, remains an unre-solved issue in the relationship between Languedoc and the Holy Land. Byzantine and Islamic fortifications as well as Crusader monasteries played a role in the East, while both secular and religious fortresses were influential in the West. It is likely, moreover, that the relationship involved influence from Languedoc upon the East, as well as the reverse.

The Introduction of Machicoulis into Europe

By the mid–twelfth century, then, a reciprocal relationship would seem to have been established between the southern French fortress-churches of Maguelone, Agde, and Saint-Pons-de-Thomières and Crusader fortifications. The fortress-monasteries of Krak des Chevaliers and Saone preserve early examples of machicolated arches. Crusaders would seem to have been the primary carriers of Armenian, Byzantine, and Islamic invention to the West, and back again to Frankish fortifications in the Holy Land. In this connec-tion, it is interesting to recall the intimate relationship between the Templars and the organization of the Peace tax,[46] as well as the ubiquity of fortified churches and monasteries sponsored in both the East and West by the Tem-plars and Hospitalers. Though the military orders certainly are not alone in their sponsorship of the Peace of God and the fortification of churches, they are likely carriers of at least some ideas between East and West.

Earlier machicolations are known in the West, however, and other visual and functional influences on the design of the machicolated fortress-churches must also be considered. In this discussion, we must distinguish between the single machicolated portcullis or arch and the series of arches (machicolated or otherwise) that comprise an arcade. Twelfth-century builders, however, may not in all cases have made the same distinction.

Continuous Arcades: Antioch, Trier, Milan, and the Churches of the Rouer-gue. The continuous arcade of the Byzantine walls of Antioch would have been a memorable image, especially to veterans of the First Crusade. Though the summits of the arches at Antioch are not in fact machicolated, the connec-tion of continuous arcading with effective fortification is made palpable there. Other Byzantine precinct walls used continuous arcading, though more com-monly on the interior of the wall, as at Sergiopolis or Constantinople, where the arcading served as support for the wallwalk, or *chemin de ronde*.

The Lombard brick architectural tradition of Milan, northern Italy, and the Roman Rhineland also preserves a number of arcaded exterior elevations that appear very similar to machicolated arches, despite their lack of functional openings. The basilica at Trier is the best-known example (Fig. 86), but the fourth-century church of San Simpliciano in Milan (originally unaisled) is also

Figure 86. Trier, Basilica, exterior view.

persuasive as a visual parallel.[47] The audience hall at Trier was originally surrounded by porticoed courtyards, and San Simpliciano had a cloister at least by the twelfth century, making their comparison to the Languedoc abbeys even more compelling. A close functional parallel also existed in Trier, in the gallery passages of the fortified Porta Nigra (see Fig. 78).

Closer at hand were the churches of the Rouergue: Notre Dame de l'Espinasse in Millau, Saint-Michel in Castelnau-Pégayrolles, and Saint-Pierre in Nant.[48] These buildings, with their heavy arcaded buttresses supporting the pointed barrel vault of the interior (see Fig. 31), have a number of parallels with the Languedoc churches. The direction of influence between the two groups of buildings remains an open question. Although they have been assigned to the late eleventh century because of papal consecrations, it is also possible that the surviving fabric of these buildings belongs instead to the mid- or late twelfth century. The Rouergue churches may have provided a model for the arcaded exterior (though unfortified), or they may be later, "demilitarized" versions of the Languedoc buildings.

The West Façade of Lincoln Cathedral. A lone eleventh-century example of machicolated arches exists in the west façade of Lincoln Cathedral (see Figs. 17, 18).[49] This important early example must be examined with some care. As we saw in Chapter 1, the cathedral of Lincoln was described by Henry of Huntingdon as "a strong church . . . and, as the times required, impregnable to its enemies."[50] The cathedral was begun under Bishop Remigius (1067–92) at the transfer of the see from Dorchester-on-Thames. It is likely that Remigius began building soon after the transfer of the see. By 1092,

Remigius wished to have a dedication performed, perhaps because he felt his death to be imminent. Remigius, in fact, died before the ceremony could take place, and the dedication was not performed until after the appointment of his successor, Robert Bloet, in 1093. While the dedication is no guarantee of the cathedral's completion, it would seem to have been largely finished since by the time of Henry of Huntingdon, it was described as *"iam perfectam."* A fire may have damaged the new cathedral in 1123, soon after the accession of Bishop Alexander (1123–48), but the sources are contradictory on this point.[51] In 1140, Lincoln castle was taken from King Stephen by Ranulph, earl of Chester. The king marched to Lincoln where he was received by Bishop Alexander, took the castle, and also "made a castle of the church." The earl, however, escaped from the castle, brought reinforcements, and defeated the king. It was at this time that the city was sacked and the cathedral probably burned. Following the conflict, Bishop Alexander received Stephen's opponent, Mathilda. An agreement was reached that left the castle in the hands of the earl. It is likely that at this moment the earl would have wished to prevent the continued use of the cathedral as a fortress and that the bishop would have been anxious to repair his cathedral and to protect it from further damage. In 1141, therefore, there existed both a need to repair the cathedral and very possibly the desire to reduce its military appearance and capability. Henry of Huntingdon recounts in his *Historia* the manner in which Bishop Alexander

so remodeled with subtle workmanship his church, which had been damaged by burning.[52]

While the repairs to the church were probably still in progress, in 1144, King Stephen again laid siege to the castle. On this occasion, however, there is no record that the church was called into military service. The change in Bishop Alexander's loyalties, together with the as-yet-unrepaired damage to the cathedral may have rendered military use of the cathedral impossible.

Whereas the eastern portions of Remigius' cathedral have all disappeared, substantial portions of eleventh-century fabric remain in the west end, encased in Bishop's Alexander's remodeling and surmounted by the later Gothic screens and towers. The west end would seem to have formed a projecting west block or *westwerk* slightly wider than the eleventh-century nave (Fig. 87). The west block measured 34 by 19 meters externally. The façade wall is divided externally into three main bays by triple doorways set into massive arched projections nearly 4 meters deep. The central door opened into the nave bay, with the outer doors providing direct access to the aisle bays. Though this façade organization echoes Norman façades like that at Saint-Etienne at Caen, the deeply carved aspects of the façade are anomalous. Even more unusual are the slits provided in the soffits of the

Figure 87. Lincoln Cathedral, west front reconstruction.

arches over the side doors (see Fig. 18). The middle bay has now been rebuilt but no doubt originally rose higher as it now does, and was probably also originally protected by a slit machicolation. The arched bays are carried around the south side of the west block, and smaller niches are also carved into the outer buttresses, but no evidence of machicolations is visible in the remaining arches. The north wall was a flat screen wall containing chambers, and possibly garderobes, within it. The western wall and the interior faces of the portals are pierced with rectangular archer slits.

The upper stories of this *westwerk* are difficult to reconstruct, especially in light of the extensive remodeling in the twelfth century and later periods. Eleventh-century fabric is preserved in the lower courses of the spiral stair contained within the southwest corner, as well as in mural chambers of the west wall. Though the surviving mural chambers and passages are largely rebuilt in the twelfth century, it would seem that the lateral machicolations were served by individual chambers. The central door, if originally machicolated, would have been served from a higher level, most probably from a roof-platform. The connection with the nave is unknown, as is the degree of fortification applied to the eastern portions of the cathedral. Certainly, a fortified *westwerk* alone would have been impractical and must originally have been combined with a fortified precinct wall or ditch.

The location of the cathedral directly across from the castle may have necessitated its fortification. The proximity of the castle in 1141 must have suggested to Stephen that the church be converted to a temporary siege-work. Stephen used one of the towers of Hereford Cathedral in similar fashion in his siege of that city in 1140:

The citizens ran about wailing when they saw the church yard dug up to make a rampart for the fortified post. . . . They mourned also at seeing the tower, from whence they had been accustomed to hear the peaceful and harmonious sounds of the church bells, now converted into a station for engines of war.[53]

As we saw in Chapter 1, other Anglo-Norman cathedrals seem to have been furnished with military features: Durham with its defensive site and curtain wall (see Fig. 14), Old Sarum with its reused Iron Age precinct, and Rochester with its tower (see Fig. 15). Among the most plausible models for the fortified *westwerk* of Lincoln Cathedral are secular fortifications such as the Tower of London (see Fig. 22) and Colchester Castle with their gallery passages. The location of the fortifications at Lincoln may be sought not only in the obvious choice to fortify the point of entry, but also in the fortified and quasi-fortified west areas of contemporary church and secular architecture. The use of a modified westwerk has also been suggested for Winchester, and it may be that the cathedral there was similarly fortified.[54] Lincoln's western block is essentially a fortified gatetower fused with the "keep" itself. The upper stories of surviving monastic gate houses at Lorsch in Germany or Sancti Quattro Coronati in Rome all provide persuasive parallels. But the most convincing source for the Lincoln design, and for the provision of machicolated slits above the doors, is found in castle gates. Gate towers of the castles of Exeter, Bramber, and Lincoln itself all precede the entry. The gate at Exeter (Fig. 88), begun in 1068, had a deeply recessed arch protecting the entrance, with a chamber above, possibly provided with a machicolation.[55] The west gate of Lincoln Castle itself has two deep buttresses projecting in front of the entrance, but later rebuilding prevents a full reconstruction of the upper elevation. Similarities in the masonry suggest that the cathedral and castle may be nearly contemporaneous works possibly by the same masons.[56] Thus, the west front of Lincoln Cathedral may have adopted ecclesiastical and secular forms for a new purpose in the later years of the eleventh century.

Anglo-Norman England of the late eleventh and early twelfth centuries was a period of insecurity and instability, ruled by an outsider class of newly elevated Normans. We see here a similar combination of insecurity

Figure 88. Exeter castle gate, view.

and desire to advertise control as we do in a generation later in Languedoc. The existence of a similar source mandates that we address the possibilities for contact between the two. First, how similar is Lincoln to the Languedoc churches? Fortification at Lincoln seems to have been applied primarily to the west end and to the areas directly above the doors. In this sense, the *machicoulis* function as individual portcullis slits (though without a sliding closure door) more than as a unified system of machicolated galleries as at Ukhaidir or the Languedoc churches. It also seems that Lincoln may have restricted its built defensive aspects to the west end (although probably connected to a circuit wall or ditch). If this was indeed the case, Lincoln participated in a long and venerable tradition of protecting the most vulnerable western zone. Despite these dissimiliarities, however, Lincoln provided an example of a fortified cathedral par excellence: one which had proved its military suitability in the conflict of 1141. It also provided a model for the use of machicolations applied to a religious building, despite the limited and "singular" nature of those machicolations.

Nonetheless, Lincoln also provided a "negative" example of religious fortification. The presence of fortifications in the cathedral opened the church to attack and ultimately resulted in its partial destruction. We must wonder about the impact of the Lateran Council of 1123 upon Bishop Alexander's thinking. Did the prohibition of religious fortification at that council change his mind about the suitability of fortress-churches? How changed was the aspect of his remodeled cathedral at his death in 1148?

We must finally also question how much of the formerly fortified cathedral was available as a model after the reworking under Alexander. The transmission of this source is a problematic one. Contact between England and Languedoc was, however, relatively frequent. Though Bishop Alexander does not seem to have visited the south of France, we know that he visited Rome in 1144.[57] The joint participation of clerics from Lincoln (or their counterparts in England) and Languedoc at religious councils is the most likely occasion for contact to occur. We know, in fact, that many of the bishops of Maguelone participated in international councils at which English prelates were present.[58] Bishops Godfrey, Galtier, and Jean de Montlaur from Maguelone are all documented as witnesses to major church councils. Raymond of Dourgne, abbot of Saint-Pons-de-Thomières was present at international councils in 1161 and 1162. Those councils which treated the problems of ecclesiastical fortification provide the most persuasive occasions for the debate over the fortifications at Lincoln to have had an impact on the fortress-churches of Languedoc. In this instance, the Lateran councils of 1123 and 1179 are particularly important. No witness list is preserved for the Lateran Council of 1123, but we know that over 200 bishops and prelates attended. A witness list is given for the Lateran Council of 1179.[59] Jean de Montlaur, bishop of Maguelone, is attested as present at this council along with a number of English bishops.[60] It is therefore likely that both the "positive" and the "negative" aspects of Lincoln's fortification would have been known to prelates from Languedoc.

Niort and Château-Gaillard. Machicoulis sur arcs began to appear with some frequency in Western architecture in the course of the twelfth century. The earliest machicolated monuments in the West have usually been identified as the castles of Niort and Château-Gaillard. Neither Niort nor Château-Gaillard, however, have true machicolated arches, nor are they the earliest examples of this technology. The chateau of Niort (Fig. 89) was constructed by Henry II Plantagenet (1154–89).[61] (The two towers were originally independent of each other; the logis between the two was added in the fifteenth century, possibly replacing a much smaller gatehouse.) Machicolations spring from the rounded corner projections of each tower, are cut awkwardly into the fabric of the towers, and thus seem to be later additions (Fig. 90). Their design is in any case not linked to the technique of machicolated arches supported on buttresses found in southern churches and enclosures.

Figure 89. Niort, exterior view showing machicolations.

Figure 90. Niort, detail of south machicolation.

Château-Gaillard was built relatively late in the twelfth century, by Richard the Lionhearted (1189–99). There, a series of rising, trapezoidal projections are found on the donjon (Figs. 91, 92). Viollet-le-Duc reconstructed these

Figure 91. Château-Gaillard, exterior view.

Figure 92. Château-Gaillard, exterior view, detail of tower.

Figure 93. Château-Gaillard, reconstruction.

projections with machicolations, but on-site examination reveals serious flaws in his interpretation (Fig. 93).[62] Not a single springer survives to suggest machicolations or indeed any masonry superstructure. No interior stairs or galleries, moreover, afforded access to the putative *machicoulis* at Château-Gaillard. The projections are unlike any other surviving machicolated supports, and instead seem more likely to have supported timber hoarding.

The secular fortifications we have examined do not present evidence of early and consistent use of machicolations. The secular castles traditionally cited as the earliest *machicoulis,* Niort and Château-Gaillard, are neither as early (nor as machicolated) as previous scholars have supposed. It is interesting to note, by contrast, the predominance of early machicolated religious fortifications. The fortified monasteries of Krak des Chevaliers and Saone are the prime examples of machicolation in the Levant. In the West, cathedrals and abbeys such as Lincoln, Maguelone, Saint-Pons-de-Thomières and Agde stand out as the leaders in the early exploitation of machicolation. In both Europe and the Holy Land, then, religious use of machicolation appears to have been earlier than, and seems to have predominated over, secular usage of the technology. Ecclesiastical use, then, would seem to have been the vehicle for the adoption of machicolation into secular fortifications in the second half of the twelfth century.

Distribution of Machicolated Monuments in Languedoc

Maguelone, Agde, and Saint-Pons-de-Thomières now stand as exceptional religious fortifications within the larger context of secular castles and fortified habitation sites of Languedoc. Other churches and abbeys of the region, however, undoubtedly shared the same motivations and forms of defense. It is, of course, in the nature of fortification to be attacked, dismantled, and rebuilt, often with forms that are more advanced. The twelfth-century distribution of fortifications has thus been radically transformed. Nonetheless, the presence of excavated buildings with projecting buttresses like those of the three Languedoc churches, or buildings rebuilt in their upper stories but preserving lower profiles similar to those buildings, encourages the supposition that more churches were originally wrapped with machicolated arches than now survive. Many of these were likely to have been dependencies of the three Languedoc churches, and to have followed the technological and stylistic lead of the parent church. Others were likely religious establishments that found themselves in geographical and political circumstances similar to Maguelone, Agde, and Saint-Pons, and therefore turned to similar solutions. A short catalogue of such buildings follows.

Dependencies of Maguelone. The distribution of parishes and abbeys dependent upon Maguelone is recoverable through surviving cartularies and papal confirmations. While several studies have examined aspects of Maguelone's dependencies, no full study of the evidence has yet been accomplished. The diocese of Maguelone stretched along the Mediterranean from Lunel to Sete, and extended inland as far north as Ganges (see Fig. 2). Its dependencies, established through gift, acquisition, and other means, was not entirely coincident with the diocescan boundaries, but repeated it in large measure.

Vic-la-Gardiole. The small parish dependency of Sainte Léocadie in Vic-la-Gardiole is one of the few surviving examples of a small-scale machicolated church (Fig. 94).[63] Now partially obscured by telephone and power lines, and bypassed by a modern highway, the church and its attached canonial buildings crown the small rocky outcrop of its village, and would originally have dominated the nearby coast. The early history of the church at Vic-la-Gardiole is virtually unstudied, and its documentation remains largely unpublished. A church of S. Leocadis de Vico is mentioned in the cartulary of the benedictine

Figure 94. Vic-la-Gardiole, exterior view.

monastery of Aniane.[64] A church of the same dedication is given to Maguelone in a papal bull of 1095 sealing an accord between the abbot of Aniane and Godfrey, bishop of Maguelone. Permission is granted to the lords of Vic to build a castle in the region, while reestablishing Maguelone's claim to the church of Sainte-Léocadie in a charter of 1161.[65] The dedication of the church to Saint-Léocadie of Toledo is rare in Languedoc, and may reflect the Spanish connections of Aniane in the eleventh century. It may also result from the protection of relics of a community fleeing the Islamic reconquest, but the texts unfortunately remain silent on this latter point.

Built of large blocks of very shelly limestone, Vic is a modest rectangular box in plan, but an imposing fortress in elevation. Still attached to the north are the remains of rebuilt canonial residences. To the southeast a low modern sanctuary has been added, as well as a later tower to the southwest. One can nonetheless still recover the original plan of the church. My survey of the building reveals that the church measures 24.42 meters in interior length by 7.32 meters in width (Fig. 95).[66] Three nave bays are separated from the square-ended chancel by projecting pilasters. The walls are 2 meters thick (2.37 meters at the west door). The original roof probably had a near-flat fighting platform like that surviving at Agde. The disjunction at

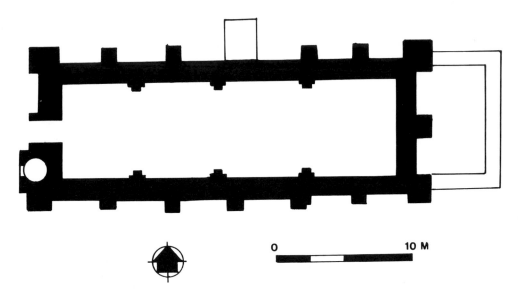

Figure 95. Vic-la-Gardiole, plan.

Vic between the six bays of the exterior machicolation and the four interior bays is similar to that found at Maguelone. This lack of correspondence of inner and outer bays was undoubtedly related to the problem of correlating usable geometries for the interior vaulting with functional spans for the machicolated arches. The solution is neither elegant nor aesthetically unified, but it is fully functional. Despite the later tower built into the front of the church on the southwest corner, one can see that the coursing of the machicolations is integral with the fabric of the church. This observation leaves no doubt that the *machicoulis* were built at the same moment as the nave walls. The form and design of the extant machicolated arches, with slightly projecting springing blocks, allies this small parish church with the larger cathedral-fortresses at Agde and Maguelone. Like them, Vic also has a partially preserved canonial precinct, presumably also originally incorporated in the fortifications.

Although the most likely building date for the existing fortress-church of Vic is the mid- to late twelfth century, it must be emphasized that documentary sources provide no independent confirmation of that date. This small fortified church probably copied directly the forms of its mother church, Maguelone, and perhaps participated with it in a system of coastal protection.

Montbazin. Also a dependency of Maguelone, the church of Montbazin probably began as a chapel to the hilltop *castrum* known from 1113.[67] The church belonged to Maguelone from 1144, when it is listed as a donation in an accord between Bishop Raymond and his chapter.[68] By the thirteenth century, it had become the seat of an important priory.[69]

The church is built integrally with the northern precinct walls of the castrum (Fig. 96). The north castrum door, with its two portcullis slits, in fact,

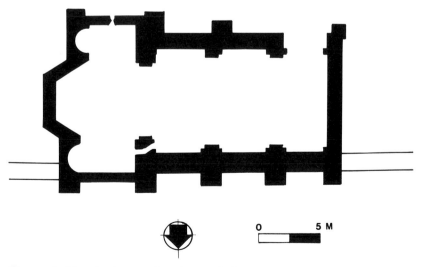

Figure 96. Montbazin, exterior view, and plan.

lies directly under the polygonal apse of the chevet. The machicolated nave (only the lower buttresses of which survive) also served as the castrum wall. Although the dates of about 1113–44 provided by the cartulary evidence may be the construction dates for both the castrum and the church, we must remain cautious, keeping in mind the frequent rebuilding of fortification walls. The church at Montbazin may provide an early experiment leading to larger solutions at Maguelone and elsewhere, or it may be a later reflection of its parent church. It provides an interesting parallel for the incorporation of the church with the municipal fortifications that we see in the larger fortress-churches of Maguelone, Agde, and Saint-Pons. Both the style and location of the machicolations at Montbazin are consonant with a date sometime in the twelfth century. If correct, Montbazin constituted another link in the chain of ecclesiastical fortifications along the coast between Maguelone and Agde.

Montaubérou, Castelnau-le-Lez, and Saint-Jean-des-Cucules. No other dependencies of Maguelone preserve extant machicolated elevations, but three churches have buttresses that indicate the possibility of having been machicolated before later rebuilding of their upper courses. Saint-Pierre de Montaubérou was confirmed as a property of Maguelone in Pope Urban III's Bull of 1095. The church has five unaisled bays, with a terminal eastern apse. Each bay is marked at the interior and exterior by projecting buttresses that could have originally been linked by machicolated arches.

Castelnau-le-Lez, a dependency of Maguelone, became the cathedral seat during the ninth and tenth centuries. After the repatriation of the bishopric back to Maguelone, the church of Notre Dame at Castelnau-le-Lez was rebuilt.[70] The projecting buttresses of the nave now support fourteenth-century machicolations, matching in their design and profile those which spring directly from corbels in the rebuilt chevet (Fig. 97). The lower courses of the exterior buttress, however, are integral with the original fabric of the nave, suggesting that the twelfth-century church may also have been machicolated.

Like Castelnau-le-Lez, the church of Saint-Jean-des-Cucules, also a dependency of Maguelone, was refortified in the fourteenth century in a style reminiscent of the twelfth century (Fig. 98).[71] These may have been a reflection of *machicoulis* at the mother house of Maguelone or a reconstruction of original twelfth-century fortifications at Saint-Jean-de-Cucules itself.

Dependencies of Agde and Saint-Pons-de-Thomières. Like Maguelone, the diocese of Agde was not always coincident with its patrimony, which can be reconstructed from surviving cartularies and papal confirmations. The diocese was a relatively small one, wedged between the dioceses of Maguelone

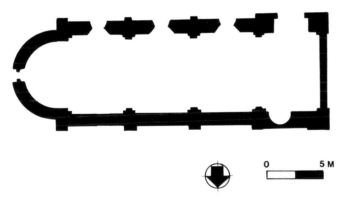

0   5 M

Figure 97. Castelnau-le-Lez, exterior view, and plan.

and Béziers (see Fig. 2). Laure Gigou, who has reconstructed the major outlines of the dependencies of Agde in the twelfth century, has found a rise in
the construction of churches by the bishop coincident with his rise in power
in the third quarter of the century.[72]

Saint-Pons was not a cathedral see until the fourteenth century, but was
from its foundation a royal abbey. Typical of important early monastic foun-

Figure 98. Saint-Jean-des-Cucules, exterior view.

dations with royal backing, its dependencies extended very widely from Languedoc to Aragón. Given the existence of a number of machicolated dependencies of Maguelone, it is remarkable that no dependencies of Agde or Saint-Pons-de-Thomières preserve twelfth-century machicolation, although some may well have been originally fortified in this manner.

Dependencies of Aniane. The abbey of Aniane was one of the earliest and most important monastic foundations in Languedoc. As such, it shared with and often rivaled the achievements of the abbeys of Maguelone, Agde, and Saint-Pons-de-Thomières. The parish church of Celleneuve was a dependency of the monastery of Aniane, and unlike Sainte-Léocadie of Vic, remained in the possession of the abbey. Celleneuve's location close to Maguelone (and today in the very outskirts of Montpellier) made it a valuable and jealously guarded property for Aniane.[73] Though the present crown of machicolations resting upon corbels clearly dates to the fourteenth century, the buttresses that support the walls belong to the twelfth-century campaign. It is possible that these originally supported machicolated arches, although the span of over 6 meters would have been rather wide for such a design.

Psalmodi and Its Dependencies. The Benedictine monastery of Psalmodi was located to the east of Maguelone, between Aigues-Mortes and Saint-Laurent d'Aigouze. In 1099, Pope Urban II freed Psalmodi from Saint-Victor in Marseilles and established its independence. Urban also confirmed the monastery's possession of sixty churches and priories. By 1212, its domain had increased to nearly 90 properties stretching from the Pyrenees to the Alps.[74]

The foundation courses of the abbey of Psalmodi demonstrate that the abbey church may have been fortified with machicolated arches. Though only the south wall of the final phase of the church at Psalmodi survives in elevation, excavations have revealed the plan of the twelfth-century church (Fig. 99).[75] The presence of projecting buttresses in this plan, together with the

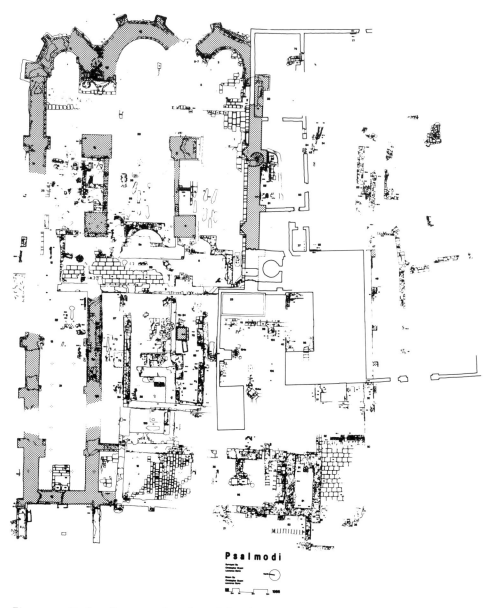

Figure 99. Psalmodi, excavation plan of church.

exposed site of this important abbey, originally very close to the sea, suggests that its buttresses may originally have been capped with machicolated arches.[76]

Dependencies of Psalmodi may have followed the lead and participated in the fortification system, of the mother house. Two churches belonging to the abbey of Psalmodi were, in fact, fortified: Saint-Pierre-de-Joncels, which preserves buttresses that were probably capped by *machicoulis,* and Saint-Bonnet-du-Gard, whose apse and transepts were fortified and crenellated in the twelfth century.

Saintes-Maries-de-la-Mer. The church of Saintes-Maries-de-la-Mer has machicolations supported by consoles on the west and east ends. The machicolations rest on the exterior buttresses of the twelfth-century church only in the nave (Figs. 100, 101).[77] Evidence of donations indicates that the church was under construction by c. 1172–5. The first documentary mention of the fortification of the church, however, is provided by an act of Raymond Berengar V, count of Provence, giving permission for the construction of fortifications in 1244. Damaged several times, the church and its fortifications were partially rebuilt in 1386, 1399, and 1410.[78] A fourteenth-century date for the present fortifications at Saintes-Maries-de-la-Mer accords well with the rebuilt examples of *machicoulis* at Saint-Jean-des-Cucules or Castelnau-le-Lez, but, like them, Saintes-Maries-de-la-Mer may also have had machicolations resting on its original exterior buttresses. Certainly, its exposed site directly on the Mediterranean suggests a continual need for fortification.

Fortified Monastic Enclosures. Churches, of course, were not the only ecclesiastical buildings to have been fortified in the twelfth century. As we have already observed, the canonial and monastic buildings of Maguelone, Agde, and Saint-Pons-de-Thomières were surrounded by walls that were, in some cases, machicolated. The canonial precinct at Vic, the abbey of Psalmodi, and that at Saintes-Maries-de-la-Mer may also have been similarly protected, although not enough survives to be certain.

Four southern examples provide physical evidence for machicolation on precinct buildings: the canonial precincts of the cathedrals of Béziers and Aix-en-Provence, the claustral complex of the abbey of Lagrasse, and (later) the papal palace at Avignon. These surviving canonial enclosures preserve evidence for a fortification practice that was undoubtedly more widespread.

The canonial precinct at Béziers was fortified by 1147, when the canons obtained the permission of the viscount to "hold a door in the wall that surrounds the houses of the community."[79] Previously, the only entrance had been controlled by the viscount and his castle. Eighteenth-century views show this door, and close to it, two Gallo-Roman towers reused in the

Figure 100. (left) Saintes-Maries-de-la-Mer, exterior view from the northeast.
Figure 101. (right) Saintes-Maries-de-la-Mer, exterior view from the west.

medieval precinct wall. Today all that survives is the wall that surrounds and supports the southern arm of the cloister (Fig. 102; also see Fig. 76). This wall, probably begun in the first half of the twelfth century, includes the four lower arches to the west, as well as the higher one, placed an an angle, to the east (Fig. 103). The final two arches have been rebuilt in restorations to the cloister above.

The cathedral of Aix-en-Provence also preserves, within the later northern tower, evidence that at least the north side of the cathedral was fortified with machicolations, a system of fortifications that was linked with other walls to protect the entire canonial zone from the rest of the town (see Fig. 75).[80] Documentary evidence indicates a date of construction for the machicolations to c. 1175–91.

The abbey of Lagrasse also has a dormitory protected on its outer face by machicolated arches. This dormitory, together with many of the claustral

Figure 102. Béziers, view of machicolated canonial precinct.

Figure 103. Béziers, detail of machicolated arches of canonial precinct.

buildings, was constructed in the late thirteenth century. The use of machicolations on its eastern exterior wall demonstrates the continuity of this technology in Languedoc.[81]

Figure 104. Avignon, papal palace, exterior view (the *Vieux Palais* of Benedict XII is to the left).

The papal palace in Avignon, constructed in the fourteenth century, had machicolated arches surrounding the exterior (Fig. 104), and even protecting interior courtyards and cloisters. While the towers are surmounted with machicolations on corbels, most of the palace is encircled by wide, flat buttresses supporting sharply pointed arches. The buttresses and arches exist as a separate plane in front of the wall proper. The *machicoulis* are served by a roof platform running around the entire palace. The dominant use of *machicoulis* on the papal palace did much to repopularize this form in the fourteenth century, particularly in the south of France and among papal dependencies. One such copy is found at the priory of Champdieu (Loire), where both the church and canonial enclosure were fortified with *machicoulis sur arcs* in the fourteenth century.

Geographic Distribution

Cathedrals (Maguelone and Agde), abbeys (Saint-Pons-de-Thomières and possibly Psalmodi), churches (Vic-la-Gardiole and Montbazin), as well as canonial precincts (Béziers and Maguelone), can be shown to have been fortified with machicolated arches in the twelfth century. Other buildings, now lost, certainly shared this technology. Increased work on the identification and phasing of fortified castles and churches will aid in our analysis of the pattern of fortification in twelfth-century Languedoc. At the present state of knowledge, we can note that Maguelone, Agde, Vic, Montbazin, Psalmodi, and Saintes-Maries-de-la-Mer all dominate ports and are all located in close proximity to the Roman road, the *Via Domitiana,* which ran parallel to the coast (see Fig. 2). The proximity of these religious buildings to sea and land routes of transportation made them vulnerable to both pirates and brigands, but also provided them with advantages in controlling the landscape. This proximity undoubtedly contributed to the choice of their site in the first place. Once chosen, however, the sites of these fortified buildings permitted them to participate in the larger process of fortification of similar nodal points in the twelfth-century landscape. The coastal sites of Agde, Vic, Maguelone, Psalmodi, and Saintes-Maries-de-la-Mer, in particular, may have belonged to a punctuated sentinel system for the immediate coastline.

Located farther inland in the Black Mountains, Saint-Pons-de-Thomières is the unusual site in this pattern. Saint-Pons does, however, reflect a similar congruence of water and land routes. The abbey is found on the road from Toulouse to Nîmes, at its juncture with the river Jaur. This crucial site on communication and trade routes may have impelled both the need and the desire to fortify the abbey and town in the mid-twelfth century. This reconstruction of the larger context of fortification in twelfth-century Languedoc (although necessarily incomplete) permits us to expand our understanding of the larger context and functions of machicolated fortress-churches.

CONCLUSION

The culture of medieval France was undoubtedly as complex and contradictory as our own. One of the primary tasks of the historian is to create a framework for keeping track of innumerable events, forms, and people and for mapping the complex interactions among these elements. This framework provides a structure by which we organize and – we hope – make sense of a past that can be similar to our own experience but that can also be quite alien. The frame, however, can also become a limit to vision. For example, the failure of past historians of Western medieval Europe to consider aspects of the medieval East, the place of women, or the evidence of material culture have produced views of the Middle Ages we now see as flawed. Similarly, the conventional frame of architectural history has marginalized buildings in Languedoc that are unusual according to standards more appropriate to the north than to the south of France.

A close reading of the uses and meanings of the fortified church in Languedoc has forced us to reevaluate some of the canons of architectural history. The fortress-church has demanded that we integrate the study of military and ecclesiastical architecture, reconsider the motivations for a host of architectural forms, rescue Languedoc from its position as a provincial backwater, reexamine the links between medieval East and West and between the North and South, and reevaluate the stylistic concepts of Romanesque and Gothic.

Though they have languished outside the preserve of mainstream architectural history, the fortified churches of Agde, Maguelone, and Saint-Pons-de-Thomières played central roles in the ecclesiastical, political, and architectural history of Languedoc. As hybrid fortress-cathedrals and abbeys, they participated in the regional development of a system of fortified protection and added a new structural solution to the arsenal of twelfth-century defensive strategies. The "invention" of the fortress-church in twelfth-century Languedoc, and its use of the machicolated arch, introduced an economical and effective system of fortification to Western Europe. With its ultimate source in Eastern prototypes, this technology developed rapidly in the climate of military and architectural exchange during the Crusades that united the various cultures of the eastern and western Mediterranean even as they were locked in combat.

Independent analysis of Maguelone, Agde, and Saint-Pons has allowed us to grasp their significant differences and to reconstruct the twelfth-century phases of construction at each of these fortress-churches. We have identified slightly earlier dates of construction than have previously been proposed, with Maguelone under construction from c. 1120 to c. 1190, Agde from c. 1120 to the 1170s, and Saint-Pons-de-Thomières from at least the 1160s. We have not only clarified the chronologies of construction but have explored the relationships between the military and religious aspects in each building, identifying the ways in which they functioned as fortresses and as churches.

Our analysis of political and religious structures in twelfth-century Languedoc has revealed the larger context of religious fortification. Secular and religious fortifications participated in a larger regional system of *incastellamento*. The fortification of Maguelone, Agde, and Saint-Pons, at a moment when the very existence of fortified churches was under scrutiny in papal and local councils, signaled a deliberate decision on the part of their patrons. This choice was linked to the new, reorganized peace initiatives of the second half of the twelfth century, sanctioned (albeit retrospectively) by Capetian royalty. Our examination of the dynamics of power and control in mid-twelfth-century Languedoc has highlighted the central position of the bishops in the acquisition of power and the creation of regional control. Though the bishops of Agde and Maguelone and the abbot of Saint-Pons all appealed to Louis VII for aid in maintaining the peace, they also exploited a variety of military and ideological strategies to contain the perceived threats of "Saracen" pirates, heretics, local lords, and their unemployed henchmen. The abbots of Saint-Pons used arbitration, participation in councils, and the pain of excommunication to exert control over heretics and uncooperative local nobility. The bishops of Agde appealed primarily to Carolingian precedent against the incursions of both viscount and disruptive chapter. Although the bishop-abbots of Maguelone also sought and received royal diplomas and participated in Councils, they seem primarily to have exploited the prestige and power of their papal connections.

The forms used by the fortified churches of Languedoc, especially the machicolated arch and unaisled plan, were at once functional and expressive. These forms were repeated in the region because they were effective, both militarily and symbolically. The machicolated arch advertised the possession of power and was possibly recognized as a specifically southern architectural expression. Its use at the major cathedral sites of Maguelone and Agde, as well as at Aix-en Provence and Béziers, ensured recognition for the form in the twelfth century. Machicolations continued to predominate in the thirteenth- and fourteenth-century southern cathedrals such as Albi (see Fig. 29). Although many thirteenth- and fourteenth-century buildings bear the exterior vocabulary of fortification (machicolation, heavy buttresses, and a dearth of windows), these elements were not always functional. As they now exist, for example, the *machicoulis* on the west front of the cathedral of Béziers have neither a fighting platform for access nor slots for "delivery" of projectiles, rendering them completely unusable for military purposes (see Fig. 28). It is possible that the nonfunctional nature of these military elements was a deliberate strategy developed in an era when church councils regularly proscribed the fortification of churches.

It is interesting to note that the distribution of *machicoulis sur arcs* in the twelfth through fourteenth centuries lies predominantly in the south of France (see Fig. 79).[1] The Capetians seem to have eschewed the machicolated arch.[2] They seldom used machicolation, as far as we can tell, even in royal fortifications in Languedoc, where wooden hoarding and crenellated parapets were preferred. The Capetians, and other northern military patrons, may have recognized in the *machicoulis* a specifically southern expression of power.

The adoption of machicolations on the papal palace in Avignon in the fourteenth century (see Fig. 104) ensured both the popularity of *machicoulis* and its connection with the south of France. The resurgence of the machicolated exterior in the fourteenth century may be largely attributed to the Avignon popes, many of whom were themselves from southern France. Benedict XII, the patron of the *Vieux Palais* in Avignon was especially influential in this connection. The former Jacques Fournier was born near Toulouse, and served as abbot of Fontfroide and as bishop of Pamiers and of Mirepoix, before his election to pope in 1334. After rejecting plans to restore the papacy to Rome, Benedict fixed the curia even more firmly in Avignon, appointing five French cardinals and arranging for the transfer of the entire papal archives from Assisi to Avignon. He began the construction of a permanent palace at Avignon, designed to be both administrative center and stronghold of the papacy. With its massive towers and blank exterior walls wrapped with *machicoulis*, Benedict's palace invoked the vocabulary of ecclesiastical fortification initiated at Maguelone, Agde, and Saint-Pons-de-Thomières and converted it to new papal expression.[3]

The single-nave plan also had a long popularity in southern France, used widely (though not exclusively) in southern French cathedrals and abbeys. The single-nave design may have been adopted for its defensive suitability, permitting the unimpeded function of the new machicolated system. The use of a wide and aisleless interior plan may also have advertised an allegiance to classical and Carolingian vocabulary. As we have seen, the tradition of the single-naved building was rich in the Roman, Carolingian, and early medieval architectural heritage of the Midi. To the viewer in twelfth-century Languedoc, this classicism may have resonated most powerfully as the Rome of papal reform and orthodoxy, in which these churches were deeply invested. A revival of Carolingian architecture makes sense at precisely the moment when Louis VII began to reassert Carolingian forms of royal authority in the south of France. The connection of the aisleless plan with the symbolic vocabulary of fortification may have been a more important stimulus for its continued popularity. Whatever its ultimate sources and meanings (which were undoubtedly multiple and complex), the adoption of the single-nave plan in important buildings of the mid-twelfth century ensured the survival and popularity of that plan in southern Gothic buildings of the next generation.

Through fortress-churches, therefore, bishops and abbots of the region sought to exert control in the face of threats from "outsiders" identified as "Saracens," pirates, heretics, and brigands. These insecurities formed part of a larger development of communal identity, of which the Peace of God movement, the Crusader indulgence, and the fortress-church were all manifestations. The fortification of Maguelone, Agde, and Saint-Pons would thus seem to have been principally intended to discourage violence rather than to participate in it. Defensive measures were undoubtedly an important part of the motivation to fortify, but positive statements of ecclesiastical power and regional peace also seem to have been part of the intended message. A fortified church made a striking visual statement by the bishop or abbot in his capacity as the local advocate of peace. The functional, military capabilities of such a building made it an effective deterrent for the use of military force. In other words, the more functional a fortress-church was, the less likely that it would ever have to be employed in military conflict. Ironically, the trappings of war rendered Maguelone, Agde, and Saint-Pons-de-Thomières all the more eloquent as instruments of peace.

APPENDIXES

Sheila Bonde and
Michael Gleason

MAGUELONE

APPENDIX 1

Letter of Pope John XIX (excerpt), 1032–3

Johannes episcopus, servus servorum Dei, omnibus bonum facientibus in ecclesia Magalonensi, ad honorem apostolorum principis Petri et doctoris gentium Pauli dedicata et dedicanda . . . Supraedictam Magalonensem ecclesiam, peccatis exigentibus, ad nihilum redactam audivimus; unde, valde dolemus, quia ecclesiarum desolatio, Christianorum detrimentum esse dignoscitur; ob hoc quidem, tam ecclesie supraedicte, quam et omnibus circumcirca degentibus. suggere volumus Christianis, ut in restauratione hujus ecclesie laborent. Peccatorum namque suorum veniam et indulgentiam promereri et justo Judice apostolica auctoritate spondemus cuicumque de propria hereditate, vel de propriis bonis offerendo, aut de beneficiis ipsius reddendo, ecclesiam supradictam relevare nisus fuerit. Nam unam et similem mercedem accipiet, qui propria offeret, et quia beneficia ecclesie reddet in commune; et benedictione pariter et absolutione apostolica fruetur.

Quod si aliquis episcopus, vel cujuscumque dignitatis homo, quod ibidem oblatum fuerit, pravo ingenio alienare, usurpare, vel vendere voluerit, maledictione anathematum percellatur, habeaturque extraneus a Christianorum consortio et regno Dei.

PRINTED SOURCES

A.C. Germain, *Arnaud de Verdale, Catalogus episcoporum magalonensium* (1881), 62–4.

John, bishop, servant of the servants of God, to all who do good within the church of Maguelone, already dedicated, and about to be [re]dedicated to the honor of Saint Peter, prince of Apostles, and to Saint Paul, doctor of nations . . . We have heard that the aforesaid church of Maguelone is reduced to nothing because of sin, at which news we are deeply saddened since the ruin of churches is recognized to be the detriment of Christians. For this reason moreover we wish to suggest to the Christians of this aforesaid church as much as to all those dwelling roundabout that they work toward the resoration of this church. For we guarantee with apostolic authority that pardon and indulgence of his sins be promised by the just Judge to whoever shall have tried to relieve the aforesaid church by donating from his own property or from his own goods or by returning [anything] from his benefices. For one and the same reward shall he receive who would have offered his own things and because he shall return the benefices to the church for general usage, and to one and all, we offer apostolic benediction and absolution.

But if any bishop, or man of whatever rank with wicked intent shall have wished to alienate, usurp or sell that which shall have been offered in this same manner, may he be stricken with a curse [as] anathema and may he be held excluded from the company of Christians and from the kingdom of God.

F. Fabrège, *Histoire de Maguelone*, 1 (1894), 106–7.

C. DeVic and J.J. Vaissete, *Histoire générale de Langue-doc* 4 (1874), 161.

J. Rouquette and A. Villemagne, ed., *Bullaire de Maguelone*, 1 (1911), 1–2.

APPENDIX 2

Donation by Count Pierre de Melgueil, 1085

In nomine sanctae et individuae Trinitatis, Patris, et Filii, et Spiritus sancti. Ego Petrus comes Melgoriensis pro redemptione animae meae, necnon et parentum meorum, uxoris quoque et filii dono Domino Deo, et beatis apostolis ejus Petro et Paulo me ipsum et omnem honorem meum, tam comitatum Sustantionem, quam episcopatum Magalonensem, omnemque honorem eidem episcopatui appendentem, sicut ego, et antecessores mei comites hactenus, habuimus et tenuimus in alodium; ita utrumque, quantum juris mei est, dono et trado ego per alodium sanctae ecclesiae Romanae, et sanctis apostolis Petro et Paulo, necnon et Papae Gregorio VII et omnibus successoribus ejus, qui in sede apostolica per meliorem partem cardinalium, et reliqui cleri, et populi fuerint canonice et catholice electi et consecrati; ut praedictus comitatus Sustantionis et episcopatus Magalonensis jure proprio sit beatorum apostolorum Petri et Pauli; ego autem praedictum comitatum habeam per manum Romani Pontificis sub illius fidelitate, et singulis annis, pro censu persolvam unciam auri optimi.

Similiter quoque et filius meus, vel quilibet alius omnis, qui ex hereditario jure mihi successerit, praedictum comitatum per manum Romani pontificis ad fidelitatem illius teneat, et praedictum censum, id est unciam auri optimi singulis annis persolvat.

Sit vero in potestate Romani pontificis, in episcopatu Magalonensi, quem placuerit episcopum juste et canonice ordinare, et per eam auctoritatem ejus liceat Magalonensi ecclesiae, juxta constitutiones, et decreta sanctorum patrum, personam probabilem et idoneam ad regendum populum, et res ecclesiasticas, liceat, inquam, et ex hoc, et deinceps qualem dixerimus, probabilem et idoneam personam in episcop[at]um eligere absque mei, vel alicujus heredum aut successorum meorum contradictione.

Si quis autem heredum, aut successorum meorum contra hanc donationis, et confirmationis nostrae authoritatem, et privilegium insurgere prae-

In the name of the holy and indivisible Trinity, Father Son, and Holy Spirit. I, Pierre count of Melgueil, for the redemption of my soul and also of my parents and my wife and sons, give to my Lord God, and to the holy apostles Peter and Paul, myself and all my honor as count of Substantion and that of the bishop of Maguelone and all the honor that pertains to the bishopric of Maguelone, just as I and my ancestral counts, until now have had and have held in allod; thus both, as much as is of my rule, I give and hand over through allod to the Holy Roman Church and the holy apostles Peter and Paul and also to Pope Gregory VII and to all his successors who have been elected and consecrated in canonical and catholic fashion in the Apostolic seat through the majority of cardinals and the rest of the clerics and the people; so that the aforesaid county of Substantion and the bishopric of Maguleone may be under the personal control of the blessed apostles Peter and Paul. I however may hold the aforesaid county through the hand of the Roman pontiff under his trust and as tribute in successive years I will pay a measure of the best gold.

Similarly also my son or whoever else who from hereditary right shall have succeeded me, shall hold the aforesaid county through the hand of the Roman pontiff at his loyalty, and the aforesaid rent, which is, he shall pay a measure of the best gold for individual single years.

Thus truly may it be in the power of the Roman pontiff in the bishopric of Maguelone to ordain [as] bishop justly and canonically whom[ever] it shall have pleased, and may it be permitted through its authority of this church of Maguelone according to the rules and decrees of the Holy Fathers [to elect] a likely and suitable person for ruling the people and church matters, may it be permitted, I say, from now and in succession to elect such a person we shall have declared [to be] likely and suitable into the bishopric without contradiction from me or from any of my heirs or successors.

sumptuosq(ue) et obviare, quod absit, attentaverit, et de praedicto comitatu dominum suum Romanum pontificem esse debere recognoscere noluerit, et praenominatum censum de comitatu eidem unciam auri, singulis annis persolvere recusaverit, aut in libertate ecclesiastica de substituendo canonice episcopo in episcopatu Magalonensi ei contradictor extiterit, non valeat vindicare quod injuste repetit, et persolvat mulctam, quam sancta lex Romana per Theodosium, Arcadium, et Honorium promulgatam decrevit, et insuper ecclesiasticae subjaceat disciplinae, quam velut sacrilegus, et sanctae ecclesiae destructor incurrit.

Fecit autem praedictam donationem de comitatu et episcopatu ego Petrus comes vice beati Petri, et Romani pontificis in manu Petri Albanensis episcopi Romani legati, et Gotafredi Magalonensis episcopi per investituram annuli mei, et Frotardi abbatis Tomeriarum anno Incarnationis MLXXXV. indictione VII. V calend. mensis Maii. Actum per manum Stephani + Signum Dalmatii. + Signum Raimundi. Signum Pontii de Monlaur. Petrus signavit. Adalmodis comitissa confirmavit. Signum archdiaconi. Raymundus comes filius ejus firmavit. Isti omnes ex praecepto comitis firmaverunt ante altare S. Petri. Testes Orgerius archidiaconus et Deodatus canonicus, testis Gothofredus episcopus, in cujus manu factum est.

MANUSCRIPT SOURCE

Archives départementales de l'Hérault, Cartulaire de Maguelone, Reg. C, fol. 70 r.

PRINTED SOURCES

Gallia Christiana VI (1739), Instrumentum no. 11, 349–50.
J. Rouquette and A. Villemagne, eds., *Cartulaire de Maguelone*, Vol. 1 (1912), no. 14, 18–20.

APPENDIX 3

Urban II's acceptance of Pierre de Melgueil's donation (excerpt), 1088

Urbanus episcopus servus servorum Dei, Gotofredo Magalonensi episcopo, ejusque successoribus in perpetuum. . . . Tibi itaque, frater Gotofrede Magalonensis episcope, Magalonensem ecclesiam, tuisque successoribus canonicis sub Romana libertate specialiter permansuram jure perpetuo confirmamus. . . .

However, if any of my heirs or successors shall have attempted to rise up presumptuously against this authority and privilege of donation and of our confirmation and to obstruct it, may that be absent, and concerning the aforesaid county, shall not have wished to acknowledge that his lord ought to be the Roman pontiff, and shall have refused to pay the named rate for the county [an ounce of gold for individual years], or in the ecclesiastical freedom of canonically substituting the bishop in the bishopric of Maguelone, he shall have stood [as a] contradictor to it, may he not be able to defend what he unjustly has reclaimed, and may he pay the fine that the Holy Roman Law promulgated through Theodosius, Arcadius, and Honorius has decreed, and in addition may he be subject to church discipline like that which an idolatrous destroyer of the Holy Church incurs.

However, I, Pierre, viscount of the blessed Peter and of the Roman pontiff, made the donation of the county and the bishopric in[to] the hand of Peter Alban, legate of the Roman bishop, and [the hand of] Godfrey bishop of Maguelone through investiture of my ring, and [to the hand of] Frotard, abbot of Thomières in the year of the Incarnation 1085 in the seventh indiction before the month of May [April 27]. Done by the hand of Stephen. + The sign of Dalmatus. + The sign of Raymond. + The sign of Pons of Montlaur. Pierre signed. Adalmodis the countess confirmed. The sign of the archdeacon. Count Raymond his son confirmed. All by order of the count confirmed before the altar of Saint Peter. Witnesses [were] Orgerius the archdeacon and Canon Deodatus, witness [was] Bishop Godfrey, in whose hand this has been made.

Bishop Urban, servant of the servants of God, to Godfrey, bishop of Maguelone, and to his successors in perpetuity. . . . Thus for you, brother Godfrey, bishop of Maguelone, and for your canonical successors under Roman privilege specifically, we confirm in eternal law, the church of Maguelone to remain to you. . . .

At bonae memoriae comes Petrus Dei timore compunctus, B. Petro, ejusque vicariis ex toto episcopatum reddidit, et scripti actione refutavit, comitatum quoque, qui sui juris erat, sub jure B. Petri eiusque vicariorum per testamenti paginam dereliquit, . . . ut haeredes sui Romani pontificis milites fieret, et ex ejus manu comitatum obtinerent; quod si haeredum successio destitisset sub Romani pontificis ordinatione, et Magalonensis cura episcopi haberetur. . . . Magalonensis igitur episcopatus, et Sustantionensis comitatus investituram ex manu fraternitatis tuae vice praedicti comitis per annulum recipientes, et ejusdem comitatus donationis constituta religiosa firmantes, praedictam ecclesiam, atque comitatum sub B. Petri, et Romanae ecclesiae protectione specialiter confovendum suscipimus. . . .

Ad ostensionem autem specialis hujus acceptae a Romana ecclesia libertatis, ex episcopatu unam auri unciam quotannis Lateranensi palatio tu, tuique successores persolvetis. Datum Romae XIX. (XIV?) cal. Januarii per manum Johannis diaconis sanctae Romanae eccles. . . . anno Domini M. LXXXVIII. pontific. ejusdem Urbani primo.

MANUSCRIPT SOURCE

Archives départementales de l'Hérault, Cartulaire de Maguelone, Reg. E, fol. 149.

PRINTED SOURCES

Gallia Christiana, VI (1739), Instrumentum no. 12, 350–1.
J. Rouquette and A. Villemagne, ed., *Bullaire de Maguelone*, 1 (1911), 6–11.

But Count Pierre, of good memory, compelled by the fear of God, returned his entire episcopate to Saint Peter and to his vicars, and renounced by charter his countship also, which was under his jurisdiction, and bequeathed by means of a charter of testament under oath of Saint Peter and his vicars, . . . that [his] heirs would become soldiers of the Roman pontiff, and would hold the countship from his hand; but if the succession of heirs should cease under command of the Roman pontiff, it should be held in the care of the bishop of Maguelone. . . . Therefore, the bishopric of Maguelone and the countship of Substantion, invested by the hand of your fraternity, the aforesaid viscount, by means of the ring, and confirming the religious decrees of the donation of the same count, we take up [as things] to be cherished the aforesaid church and the countship specifically under the protection of Saint Peter and of the Roman Church. . . .

As evidence, moreover, of this special privilege received from this Roman church, from the episcopate one ounce of gold yearly to the Lateran palace you and your successors shall pay. Dated at Rome on the nineteenth (fourteenth?) day before the calends of January (December 14 or 18), by the hand of John, deacon of the Holy Roman Church . . . in the year of Our Lord 1088, in the first (year) of the pontificate of that same Urban.

APPENDIX 4

Letter of Pope Urban II (excerpt), 1096

Anno MCXVI, in vigilia apostolorum Petri et Pauli, Urbanus papa II, qui ad visitandas et confirmandas Galliae ecclesias Alpes transiverat, ad preces dicti Gothofredi episcopi intravit Magalonam, ibique stetit per quinque dies; et tunc secunda die adventus sui, scilicet dominica, congregato totius pene Magalonensis episcopatus clero, et populo sermone facto, assistentibus archiepiscopis Pisano et Tarraconensi, ac episcopis Albanensi, Signensi, Nemausensi et Magalonensi, praesentibus comite Sustanionensi, Guillelmo Montispessulani domino, et aliis terrae nobilibus, totam insulam Magalonensem solemniter consecravit, et omnibus

In the year 1096, on the vigil of saints Peter and Paul, Pope Urban II, who, for the [purpose of] visiting and confirming the churches of Gaul, had crossed the Alps, came to Maguelone at the request of the said Bishop Godfrey, and there he stayed five days; and on the second day of his visit, namely, Sunday, with almost the entire clergy of the episcopate of Maguelone having been gathered, and with a sermon having been made to the people, with the assisting archbishops of Pisa and Tarragon, and also with the bishops of Alba, Sigena, Nîmes, and Maguelone, with the count of Substantion, Guilhem lord of Mont-

in ea sepultis et sepeliendis absolutionem omnium delictorum concessit, et multa alia privilegia eidem ecclesiae donavit; et secundo loco post Romanam ecclesiam honorificandam decrevit, et ut se fideles de quibuscumque locis ibidem sepeliri facerent, diligenter monuit; et tunc constitutum est ab ipso Gothofredo episcopo, ut in commemoratione ac veneratione processionis hujusmodi singulis annis a clero et populo hac die in circuitu dictae insulae processio solemnis fiat, et duodecim pauperes reficiantur.

pellier and other nobles of the region being present, he solemnly consecrated the whole island of Maguelone, and he granted absolution of all sins to all who had been buried in it or would be, and he gave many other privileges to the same church; and he decreed [it to be] second only to the Roman church for honoring, and he diligently urged that the faithful from anywhere else should cause themselves to be buried in that same place; and then it was ordered by Bishop Godfrey himself in commemoration and veneration of this procession in successive years that there be a solemn procession on this day by the clergy and the people in a circuit of the said island, and that twelve paupers be fed.

PRINTED SOURCES

A. Germain, *Maguelone sous ses évêques et ses chanoines* (1869), 16, fn. 1.

J. Rouquette and A. Villemagne, ed., *Bullaire de Maguelone*, 1 (1911), 24–5.

APPENDIX 5

Letter of Abbot Suger (excerpt), 1118

Qui cum navali subsidio – pauperie quippe multa angebatur – applicuisset Magalonam, artam in pelago insulam, cui superest solo episcopo, clericis et rara familia contempta, singularis et privata, muro tamen propter mare commeantium Sarracenorum impetus munitissima civitas, a domino rege, quia jam adventum ejus audierat, destinati mandata deposuimus, diem certam locumque Viziliaci mutui colloquii, cum ejus benedictione, quia regni primatis obtuleramus, gratanter reportavimus.

When he with naval support – he was of course much troubled by poverty – had steered toward Maguelone, a tiny island in the sea, for which there sufficed with a single bishop and priests a scanty contemptible household, unique and isolated, an episcopal see nonetheless very well fortified by the lord king with a wall because of the attacks by sea of the roving Saracens, because he had already heard of his arrival we – having been designated – laid down his commands, and we happily reported a certain day and place of Vézelay of mutual assembly with his blessing, because we had met the prominent men of the kingdom.

MANUSCRIPT SOURCE

MS. A: Bibliothèque Mazarin 2013; MS. B: Paris BN lat. 17546.

PRINTED SOURCE

Suger, *Vie de Louis VI le Gros*, ed. and trans. by Henri Waquet (1929), 200–3.

APPENDIX 6

Diploma of Louis VII addressed to Raymond, bishop of Maguelone (excerpt), 1155

In nomine Sanctae et individue Trinitatis, Ludovicus Dei ordinante providentia, Francorum imperator Augustus, Raimundo, Magalonensi episcopo eiusque successoribus canonice substituendis, et

In the name of the Holy and undivided Trinity, Louis, august emperor of the Franks by the ordaining providence of God, to Raymond, bishop of Maguelone, and his successors elected canonically,

eiusdem ecclesiae sancto conventui in perpetuum. Si erga loca divinis cultibus mancipata ad largiendum et defensum benignos nos exhibemus, praemium nobis aeternae remunerationis ab auctore omnium Deo rependi non diffidimus. . . . totam insulam in qua ipsa ecclesia sita est, cum suis pertinentiis et quidquid in mari vel in stagnis eadem ecclesia juste possidere videtur. . . . Adicimus etiam huic nostro rescripto, ut nulles comes, nullus princeps, nulla alia laica potestas, in clericis totius Magalonensis episcopatus, aut in aliis eiusdem ecclesiae hominibus, sive in locis ad eandem ecclesiam pertinentibus justicias. albergas, toltas, sive aliquas alias injustas exactiones post huiusmodi nostri decreti rescriptum temerario ausu accipere praesumat. . . . . Haec autem omnia donavit atque concessit Ludovicus rex Francie Raimundo Magalonensi episcopo, Magalone, in capitulo . . . apud Arzacium, . . . , V idus februarii, . . . die mercurii, anno Dominicae Incarnationis MCLV.

and the holy community of his church in perpetuity. If, concerning places transferred to divine worship, we show ourselves well disposed toward distributing and defending, we do not despair of the recompense to us of an eternal reward to be repaid by God the author of all things . . . The whole island on which the church is situated and whatever in the sea or in the marshes this same church is rightly seen to possess. . . . And we add also to this our statement that no count, no prince, no other lay power may presume with bold daring to accept among the clergy of the whole bishopric of Maguelone or among any other men of this church or in places belonging to this church, the rights, lodgings, tolls, or other unjust payments after the statement of this our decree. . . . Louis, king of France, gives and concedes all these to Raymond, bishop of Maguelone in the chapter of Maguelone, at Arxacium, in the fifth day before the ides of February (February 9), on the day of Wednesday, in the year of the Lordly Incarnation, 1155.

MANUSCRIPT SOURCES

Paris, Archives Nationales, J 339, and Montpellier, Archives départementales de l'Hérault, Cartulaire de Maguelone, Reg. D, fol. 296 r., and Reg. E, fol. 97 v.

PRINTED SOURCES

Gallia Christiana, VI (1739), Instrumentum 21, cols. 357–8.
A. Teulet, ed., *Layettes du Trésor des Chartes* I (1863), no. 141.
C. DeVic and J.J. Vaissette, eds., *Histoire de Languedoc*, V (1875), no. 610, col. 1193.
A. Luchaire, *Etudes sur les actes de Louis VII* (1885), no. 340.
J. Rouquette and A. Villemagne, eds., *Cartulaire de Maguelone*, 1 (1912), no. 44, pp. 185–7.

APPENDIX 7

Chronicon Magalonense vetus (excerpt), written by Canon Bertrand, sacristan at Maguelone, during the abbacy of Jean de Montlaur (1158–90)

[Tempo]ribus domini Arnaldi, Magalonensis episcopi, Magalonensis ecclesia non habitabatur, timore Sarra[ce]norum. Erat enim ibi portus maris, qui dicitur gradus, per quem galee Sarracenorum liberum habebant accessum ad insulam, et frequenter inde asportabant quaecumque inve-

In the time of the Lord Arnaud, bishop of Maguelone, the church at Maguelone was not inhabited, out of fear of the Saracens. For there was there a sea port, which is called a harbor through which Saracen galleys had free access to the island, and frequently carried off from there

niebant. Et erant ibi constitui quattuor cappellani, qui singulis ebdomadibus, circa terciam, celebrant ibi missam, non ausi celerius ecclesiae [adesse], ob timorem piratarum. Quod videns, dominus Arnaldus bone memorie, secum recogitans, mentem compunctus, maximum adgressus est opus. Predictum enim gradum lapidibus obstrusit. Deinde pontem construxit, per quem advenientes liberum haberent adhitum. Post, parrochianos suos convocavit, et eos ut elemosinis suis Magalonensem edificarent ecclesiam admonuit: quod et factum est. Multi enim, ejus admonitione, mansos suos, appennarias suas, terras et vineas suas, pro redemptione peccatorum, dicte ecclesiae contulerunt.

Consequenter construxit ecclesiam. Hic turres jecit, hic muros undique fecit; omnes offi[ci]nas, quotquot erant ibi necessarie, ibi edificare fecit. Tunc operam dedit ut canonicos regulares ibidem constitueret. Cui canonici seculares respondebant quod pusillum patrimonium esset, [et] non sufficeret regularibus canonicis. Eo enim tempore erant ibi duodecim canonici et XII prebende, et non amplius. Quibus episcopus dixit: "Deus et ego tantum dabimus eis, quod sufficiet." Et emit stagnum a quadam Melgoriensi comitissa, de suo proprio, et dedit canonicis pulmentum, retentis sibi decimis et dominio. . . . Et dum ita ad canonicos regulares in instituendo communiam constitueret, viam universe carnis ingressus est.

Deinde dominus Gotafridus, bone memorie episcopus, in episcopatum ei successit, et quod dominus Arnaldus bone memorie in instituendo ordines regularium canonicorum, et in contribuendo eisdem de beneficiis suis minus perfecerat, ipse supplevit. Ipse enim instituit de novo ibi canonicos regulares. . . .

[Gotafrido] in episcopatum successit dominus [Galterius bone] memorie. . . . Hic videns ma[teria]m veterem ecclesie Magalonensis, caput ecclesie, tres choros et turrim Sancti Sepulcri a fun[damen]tis edificarent. Cellarium, reffectorium, dormitorium a fundamentis perfecit; ultra se[ptem] milia solidos ibidem de suo proprio expendit. Et omnes fere capas sericas, planetas [ser]icas, dalmaticas sericas, optima pallia, peroptima capeta, libros Evangeliorum deauratos, crucem auream et argenteam, que in festivitatibus ponitur super altare, et calicem aureum continens quatuor marchas auri et amplius, et vestimenta pontificalia peroptima eidem ecclesie contulit. . . .

Cui vita functo in episcopatu dominus Raimundus bone memorie successit; qui quod

whatever they might discover. And there were four chaplains assigned there who in successive weeks around [the hour of] Terce celebrated Mass there, but lately do not dare to be at church out of fear of the pirates. Seeing this, Lord Arnaud of good memory, reflecting with himself, devoted [in] mind, undertook the greatest work. For he obstructed the aforesaid inlet with stones. Then he built a bridge by which visitors might have free approach. Afterward, he called together his parishioners, and exhorted them so that with their alms they would [re]build the church of Maguelone, and this was done. For many, at his instigation, pledged to the aforesaid church their houses, their appurtenances, their lands and vines, for the redemption of sin.

Consequently, he built the church. Here he raised the towers, and here he made walls on all sides; there he caused to be built all monastic buildings, however many were necessary. Then he paid attention so that he would establish the regular canons in that [same] place. The secular canons responded to him that their estate was poor and not sufficient for regular canons. At this time there were 12 canons and 12 prebends and not more. To them the Bishop Arnaud said, "God and I, we will give them as much as will suffice." And he bought the marsh from a certain countess of Melgueil and gave the proceeds from it to the canons, having kept for himself the tithe and dominion. . . . And when thus he had arranged for the regular canons in instituting communal possession, he went the way of flesh generally.

Then Lord Godfrey, a bishop of good memory, succeeded him in the episcopate, and what the Lord Arnaud of good memory had not at all finished in instituting the orders of regular canons and in contributing to them from his own benefices, he completed. For he himself there instituted again the regular canons and gave them [many properties]. . . . (There follows a list of possessions.)

Lord Galtier of good memory succeeded Godfrey in the episcopate. He, seeing the ancient material of the church of Maguelone, [they] built from the foundations the head (chevet) of the church, three choirs (the apses) and the tower of Saint Sepulchre. He finished from the foundations the cellarium, refectory and dormitory. He spent over seven thousand solidi of his own, and gave it to the church. He also gave to the church, for example, all of his silk caps, plain silks, dalmatian silks, his best pallium, his very best cape, gilt

vixit, religioni et ordini operam dedit, et ecclesiam multis modis ampliavit. Capitulum Magalonense de novo fecit. Cisternam, que ibi est, peroptimam fecit. Turrim Sancti Sepulcri a muris superioris [consumavit, et turrim Sancte Marie similiter a muris superexaltavit, et] turrim Coquine a fundamentis fecit. Altare Beati Petri, et cathedram episcopalem, que retro altare est, et lavatorium, quod est in claustro, fecit. Murum, qui est novus, in cortina fecit. Muros et portalia, que claudunt cimiterium laycorum, fecit. Domum molendini, et domum in qua recondientur lecti lignei, et domum in qua recipiuntur equi adventientium, juxta pontem fecit.

Ecclesiam Sancti Desideri communie dedit. Ecclesiam de Molinis communie dedit. Honorem Guillelmi Ebrardi de Coconeto ad opus communie emit. Optimis libris, optimis capis sericis, optimis planetis, optimis dalmaticis, optimis palliis, optimis capetis, optimis vestimentis et ornamentis ecclesiam ditavit et ampliavit. In fine vite sue, octuaginta marchas argenti ecclesie Magalonens dedit.

Mortuo domino Raimundo, Magalonesi episcopo, Johannes in capitulo Magalonensi [electus fuit in episcopum. . . .] Adhec, cum dominus Johannes factus esset episcopus, videns ecclesia, ruina minari, cum parrochianis suis super ejus reedificatione locutus est, et operi ecclesie triginta milia solidorum sua diligenti provisione et cura offerri ad haec usque tempora fecit, et de suo proprio XXVIII modios grani et vini dedit; et ex his ecclesia vetus demolita est, et nova ex majori parte constructa.

Qui istas et alias melioriationes episcopi Magalonensi ecclesie contulerunt. . . .

MANUSCRIPT SOURCE

Survives in a single manuscript copy inserted into Vol. 2, Archives départementales de l'Hérault, Cartulaire de Maguelone; Reg. B; fols. 257 v–259 v.

PRINTED SOURCES

A. Germain, "Chronique inédite de Maguelone," *Mémoires de la Société archéologique de Montpellier,* 3 (1853), 357–70.

A. Germain, *Maguelone sous ses évêques et ses chanoines* (*Mémoires de la Société archéologique de Montpellier,* 5) (1869), 659–62.

C. DeVic and J.J. Vaissete, *Histoire générale de Languedoc,* 5 (1875), cols. 55–60.

J. Berthelé, *La Vieille Chronique de Maguelone* (1908).

Evangelary books, a gold and silver cross which is placed on the altar at festivals, and a golden chalice containing four marks of gold and more, and the very best pontifical vestments.

[Galtier's] life completed, the Lord Raymond of good memory succeeded to the episcopate; he lived thus, devoting [himself] to religion and the order, and [he] enlarged the church in many ways. He built anew the chapter room of Maguelone. He made a very fine cistern [which is there]. He finished from its upper walls the tower of Saint Sepulchre [and likewise he raised up the tower of Saint Mary from its walls, and] he built from the foundations the tower of the kitchen. He built the altar of Saint Peter, and the episcopal seat that is behind the altar, and the lavatorium that is in the cloister. He made the wall around the court which is new. He built the walls and gates that enclose the lay cemetery. He built the mill house, and the house in which are stored the wooden beds, and, next to the bridge, the house in which the horses of visitors are received.

He gave the church of Saint Desiderius for the community. He gave the church of Moline into common possession. He bought the fief of Guilhem Ebrard of Coconet. He endowed and increased the church with the best books, silk *capetis,* plate, dalmatian vestments, palls, capes, vestments, and ornaments. At the end of his life, he gave 80 silver marks to the church of Maguelone.

Lord Raymond having died, bishop of Maguelone, Jean from the chapter at Maguelone was elected bishop. . . . Then, when the Lord Jean had been made bishop, seeing the church ruined, he spoke with his parishioners about rebuilding it, and he made to the works of the church 30,000 solidi from his diligent provision and care which he caused to be offered to the cure for this at this time. And from his own property he gave 28 measures of grain and wine; and the old church was demolished, and a new one was from the greater portion [re]constructed.

The bishops of Maguelone have brought these and other improvements to the church. . . .

APPENDIX 8

Catalogus episcoporum Magalonensium (excerpt), Arnaud of Verdale, bishop of Maguelone (1339–52)

Incipit Catalogus episcoporum Magalonensium, per reverendum in Christo patrem Arnaldum de Verdala, Dei providentia Magalonensem episcopum, editus et etiam publicatus. . . .

ARNALDUS

Arnaldus, hujus nominis primus, fuit electus anno Domini MXLVIII. Vixit in episcopatu annis XXX. Obiit anno Domini MLXXVIII . . .

Preterea, de ejus vita, in archivo tales versus sunt reperti:

Hic locus insignis fuit urbs, habitata malignis
   Gentibus unde ruit, quod scelerata fuit.
Carolus hanc fregit, postquam sibi marte subegit,
   Ob Sarracenos, quod tueretur eos. . . .
Inde manens annis urbs hec deserta trecentis,
   Tandem pontificem repperit artificem.
Presulis Arnaldi sit semper subdita laudi,
   Cujus nacta vicem, crevit in hunc apicem.
Hic muros jecit, turres hic undique fecit,
   Clerum divinis contulit officiis.
Ipse gradum clausit, quo predo piraticus hausit,
   Sepe latronciniis littora nostra suis. . . .

Sacerdos enim iste fuit dominus Arnaldus, bone memorie, primus hujus nominis, de quo nunc agitur, Magalonensis episcopus, qui miserabilem statum et ruinas hujusmodi, quasi in desertum positas, respiciens, et se ad sublevandas necessitates ipsas impotentem attendens, cum sibi opes ad sumptus tanti operis non adessent, presertim quod possessiones et jura episcopalia erant per nobiles et alios occupata, ad reparationem hujusmodi manus suas subito apponere non est ausus, sed suum cogitatum jactans in Domino, non absque anxietate et paupertate nimia ad sanctissimum dominum Johannem papam XX (XIX) direxit ocius, pro concilio et auxilio, gressus suos, et ei statum miserabilem sue Ecclecie explicavit. Dictus vero summus pontifex, necessitatem ipsam sedula mente considerans, consilium quod potuit negotio huic exhibuit, et omnibus populis Magalonensis diocesis, ac aliis audituris et intelligentibus, tam propinquis, quam longe positis, misit epistolam, quam per omnes episcopos confirmari et subscribi voluit, in hunc modum:

Here begins the Catalogue of the bishops of Maguelone, edited and published also by the reverend father in Christ, Arnaud of Verdale, by the providence of God, bishop of Maguelone. . . .

ARNAUD

Arnaud, first of that name, was elected in the year of the Lord 1048. He lived in the episcopate 30 years. He died in the year of the Lord 1078. . . .

Moreover, concerning his life, such verses have been found in the archive:

This place was a famous city, inhabited by evil peoples; whence it fell to ruin since it had been desecrated.
Charles crushed it, after he had subdued for himself in war, on account of the Saracens, because it used to shelter them . . .
The city, thus ruined, stayed deserted for three hundred years, until a bishop undertook its reconstruction.
May the priest Arnaud ever be given praise, having chanced upon it, it grew into this crown.
Here he threw up walls, there he made towers on all sides, He brought the clergy to their divine offices.
He himself enclosed the harbor, where the piratical marauder often drained our shores with his outrages. . . .

For that priest was Lord Arnaud, of good memory, first bishop of Maguelone of that name, from whom it now decends, who, seeing the miserable condition and the ruins of that [place], just as if it were situated in the desert, and considering himself powerless to raise the necessities, since the resources were lacking for the undertaking of such a work, especially because the episcopal possessions and rights had been seized by the nobles and others, he did not dare to set his hands at once to the repair of it, but throwing his intention upon the Lord, not without anxiety and extreme poverty toward the most holy lord Pope John XX (actually John XIX), he swiftly directed his steps and explained to him the sorry state of his church. Indeed the aforesaid sovereign pontiff, considering the extreme need with close attention, showed in this affair the foresight which he was able [to show], and to all the people of the

Johannes episcopus, servus servorum Dei, omnibus bonum facientibus in Ecclesia Magalonensi, ad honorem apostolorum principis Petri et doctoris gentium Pauli dedicata et dedicanda, salutem carissimam, cum benedictione apostolica et absolutione. Supradictam Magalonensem Eclesiam, peccatis exigentibus, ad nihilum redactam audivimus; unde valde dolemus, quia Ecclesiarum desolatio Christianorum detrimentum esse dignoscitur. . . .

Quibus peractis, idem beate memorie Arnaldus episcopus, ponens manus ad fortia, gradum prefatum lapidibus et lignis, ante omnia, claudere et obstruere festinavit. Deinde, anxietate nimia pressus, ut tam ingredientibus quam egredientibus ad dictam insulam, ad quam nullum, nisi navale, iter esse poterat, liber pateret accessus, juxta verbum propheticum, suum jactans in Domino cogitatum, tam prece, quam pretio rates conduxit, et artifices collocavit, ac per stagni latitudinem pontis stravit longitudinem, ad utilitatem hominum perpetuo permansuram, et sui nominis memoriam pereniter duraturam.

Subsequenter parochianos suos convocavit, eosdem ad eleemosynas largiendas pro reedificatione dicte ecclesie facienda piis monitis inducere non obmisit; adeo quod multi, ejus admonitione, mansos, terras, prata, vineas, census, alodia, pecunias, et alia bona sua, pro redemptione suorum peccaminum, eidem Ecclesie contulerunt; ex quibus eleemosynis et aliis bonis suis ecclesiam Magalonensem, turres, muros et omnes officinas necessarias, et fortalitia alia, que patent cuilibet intuenti, edificari solemnite fecit.

Demum, attendens quod XII canonici seculares, cum XII prebendulis, tunc in dicta ecclesia existentes, in dicta insula residere nolebant, se relegatos quodam modo reputantes, cogitavit quod regulares canonici, utpote magis vite solitarie et contemplationi dediti, ibidem melius deservirent. Induxit salutaribus monitis canonicos ipsos seculares, ut religionis beati Augustini habitum vellent assumere. Qui sibi respondebant, quod pusillum eorum patrimonium minime sufficeret ad omnes expensas regularium canonicorum hujusmodi supportandas; quibus vir Dei respondit, "Deus et ego tantum communie vestre de proprio largiemur, quod vobis et successoribus vestris sufficiet abundantur." Et tunc idem pontifex emit stagnum Magalonense a quadam comitissa Melgorii; et ipsius pulmentum, retentis sibi decimis et dominio. . . . et dum communiam ipsam con-

diocese of Maguelone, and others who would hear and understand [as much as those far off], he sent a letter, which he wished to be confirmed and undersigned by all bishops, in this fashion:

John, bishop, servant of the servants of God, to all who do good in the church of Maguelone, already dedicated and about to be [re]dedicated to the honor of the prince of the apostles, Peter, and the doctor of the nations, Paul, the most dear salutation, with benediction and apostolic absolution. We have heard that that the aforesaid church of Maguelone is reduced to nothing because of sin, at which news we are deeply saddened since the ruin of churches is recognized to be the detriment of Christians. . . .

These things accomplished, the same Bishop Arnaud of blessed memory, turning his hand to the fortifications, above all hurried to enclose and obstruct the aforesaid harbor with stones and timber. Then, oppressed by great fear as much for those entering as for those leaving the aforesaid island, there could be no travel except by sea, he opened free access, according to the prophetic word, thrusting his intention upon the Lord, as much with prayer as with money, he collected boats and gathered resources and stretched the length of a bridge along the width of the marsh perpetually for the permanent use of men and the perennially enduring memory of his name.

Afterward he called together his parishioners, nor did he omit to induce them with pious exhortation toward bestowing alms for making the repair of the aforesaid church; and to this end many offered to the same church at his admonition for the foregiveness of their sins, houses, lands, fields, vineyards, gifts, allods, moneys, and their other goods; from which alms he solemnly began to build the church of Maguelone, towers, walls, and other necessary structures and other fortifications that are apparent to anyone who looks.

Only then, remarking that 12 secular canons with 12 prebends, which then existed in the said church, did not wish to reside in the said island, considering themselves especially isolated, he concluded that regular canons, more devoted to a solitary life of contemplation, would better serve there. With helpful encouragement, he induced the secular canons so that they themselves wished to take up the habit of the order of Saint Augustine. They responded to him that their meager holdings scarecely sufficed to support all the expenses of

stitueret, ad ipsos regulares canonicos sustentandos, ivit ultra mare ad sepulchrum Domini; et inde rediens, apud Villanovam viam fuit universe carnis ingressus, et inde portatus Magalonam.

BERTRANDUS

Bertrandus fuit electus episcopus, anno Domini MLXXVIII, post obitum dicti Arnaldi; sed, propter crimen simonie, fuit ab episcopatu amotus. Quare non meretur inter alios episcopos nominari . . .

GOTHOFREDUS

Gothofredus successit in episcopatu Arnaldo primo, circa annum Domini MLXXX. . . . Vixit in episcopatu annis XXVIII. Obiit anno MCVIII. Et est sciendum, quod, anno Domini circa MLXXX, idem bone memorie Gothofredus episcpus, quod ejus predecessor Arnaldus de canonicis regularibus instituendis in Magalonensi ecclesia, morte preventus, efficere non potuit, ipse Gothofredus, Deo annuente, complevit; et ibidem canonicos regulares de novo instituit . . .

Anno MLXXXV, [quinto] cal. maii, Petrus, comes Melgorii, domino Gregorio pape et Romane Ecclesie donavit, in personis Petri, Albanensis episcopi apostolice sedis legati, et dicti Gothofredi, Magalonensis episcopi, comitatum Substantionem, et jus quod habebat in episcpatu Magalonensi, et pro dicto comitatu promisit Ecclesie Romane, pro censu annua, dare unam unciam auri.

Anno MLXXXVIII, Urbanus papa confirmavit dicto episcopo Gothofredo donationem de episcopatu et successione dicti comitatus Substantionensis, sibi factam. . . .

Anno MXCV, Urbanus papa secundus confirmavit dictis canoncis Magalonensibus multas ecclesias, sibi . . . , per episcopum Gothofredum donatas.

Anno MXCVI, in vigilia apostolorum Petri et Pauli, Urbanus papa secundus, cum, ad visitandas et confirmandas Gallie Ecclesias, Alpes transiisset, ad preces dicti Gothofredi episcopi intravit Magalonam, ibique stetit per quinque dies; et tunc, secunda die adventus sui, scilicet dominica, congregatio totius pene Magalonensis episcopatus clero, et populo sermone facto, assistentibus archiepiscopis Pisano et Tarrasconensi, ac episcopis Albanensi, Signensi, Nemausensi et Magalonensi, presentibus comite Substantionensi, Guillermo Montispessulani domino, ac aliis terre nobilibus, totam insulam Magalone solemniter consecravit, et omnibus in ea sepultis et sepeliendis absolutionem omnium delictorum concessit, et multa alia privilegia eidem Ecclesie donavit, et

regular canons; to them the man of God replied: "God and I will give from our own to your community so much that it will abundantly suffice for you and your successors." And then that same pontiff bought the marsh of Maguelone from a certain countess of Melgueil, and he gave them the proceeds, having kept for himself the tithe and the domain. . . . and when he arranged the community itself for maintaining the regular canons, he went beyond the sea to the Sepulchre of the Lord, and having returned, he followed the way of all flesh generally at Villeneuve, and [his body] was transported to Maguelone.

BERTRAND

Bertrand was elected bishop in the year of the Lord 1078, after the death of the said Arnaud; but because of the crime of simony he was deprived of his bishopric. For which reason, he does not merit to be named among the other bishops. . . .

GODFREY

Godfrey succeeded Arnaud I as bishop of Maguelone around the year of Our Lord 1080. . . . He lived as bishop 28 years. He died in the year 1108. And it should be known that, around the year of Our Lord 1080, the same Bishop Godfrey, of good memory, because his predecessor Bishop Arnaud, prevented by death, was unable to effect the instituting of regular canons in the church of Maguelone, Godfrey himself, with God approving, completed it; and he instituted regular canons there anew. . . .

In the year 1085, [five] days before the calends of May (April 27), the count Pierre of Melgueil made a donation to the lord Pope Gregory and to the Roman church, in the persons of Bishop Peter Alban, legate to the apostolic seat, and this same Godfrey, bishop of Maguelone, the countship of Substantion and the power he held in the episcopate of Maguelone, and for the aforesaid countship, he promised to pay, as annual tribute, an ounce of gold.

In the year 1088, Pope Urban confirmed the donation to the said Bishop Godfrey which the said count of Substantion had made to the bishop and his successors. . . .

In the year 1095, Pope Urban II confirmed to the canons of Maguelone the donation Godfrey had made to them of many churches. . . .

In the year 1096, on the vigil of the apostles Peter and Paul, Pope Urban II, when he crossed the Alps to visit and confirm the churches of Gaul, came to Maguelone at the entreaty of the said

secundo loco post Romanam Ecclesiam honorificandam decrevit, et ut se fideles de quibuscumque
locis ibidem sepeliri facerent diligenter monuit. Et
tunc constitutum est ab ipso Gothofredo episcopo,
ut, in commemorationem et venerationem processionis hujusmodi, singulis annis, a clero et populo,
hac die, in circuitu dicte insule processio solemnis
fiat, et duodecim pauperes reficiantur. . . . .

GALTERIUS

Galterius successit Gothofredo, anno MCX. . . .
Vixit in episcopatu annis XXIII, mensibus VIII,
diebus XXII. Obiit anno MCXXXIII, VIII idus
decembris.

   Hic religioni et ordini magnam operam dedit.
Caput ecclesie Magalonensis ruinosum fulcivit.
Turrim Sancti Sepulchri, cellarium, refectorium et
dormitorium a fundamentis fecit. Calicem
aureum, ponderis IIIIor marcharum, crucem
auream et argenteam, cappas, planetas, tunicas,
dalmaticas, pallia serica et aurea, libros et alia
ornamenta pretiosa eidem ecclesie contulit. . . .

RAYMUNDUS

Raymundus primus successit Galterio, anno
MCXXXIII. Vixit in episcopatu annis XXXIII,
mensibus III, deibus X. Obiit anno MCLXVI, II
cal. januarii.

   Hic, dum vixit, religioni et ordini navavit magnam operam, et ecclesiam Magalonensem multis
modis ampliavit. Capitulum Magalonense a fundamentis construxit; cisternam etiam fecit, et turrim Sancti Sepulchri a muris superius consum-
mavit, et turrim Sancte Marie similiter a muris
superius exaltavit, et turrim Coquine a fundamentis edificavit. Altare Sancti Petri, et cathedram episcopalem retro ipsum, ac lavatorium
claustri superioris, similiter fecit, et cortinale ac
portalia, et murum quo clauditur cimeterium laï-
corum, domum molendini, et in qua reconduntur
lecti lignei, domum conversorum, domum in qua
recipiuntur equi, juxta pontem. . . .

   Anno MCLV . . . Adrianus papa IIIIus, confirmavit eidem episcopo nominatim omnes possessiones, castra, loca et jura, tunc eidem Ecclesie et
episcopatui acquisita.

   Anno MCLVI, Ludovicus rex Francie et
imperator, confirmavit eidem nominatim castra,
loca et jura, qui tenebat.

JOHANNES DE MONTELAURO

Johannes de Montelauro, canonicus Magalonensis, castri de Montelauro, Magalonensis diocesis,
primus hujus nominis, successit Raymundo primo,

Bishop Godfrey, and stayed there for five days;
and then, the second day of his visit, being a Sunday, when nearly the entire clergy of the bishopric
of Maguelone had been brought together, and a
sermon having been made to the people, with the
archbishops of Pisa and Tarragon, and the bishops of Albano, Segni, Nîmes and Maguelone
assisting, and the count of Substantion, the lord of
Montpellier, and other nobles of the land present,
he solemnly consecrated the whole island of
Maguelone, and he granted to all who were
buried there or who will be, absolution for all
their faults, and he gave many other privileges to
that same church, and he described [it as being] in
second place after the Roman Church for honoring, and he urged all the faithful of the place to
make their burial there. And then it was established by that Bishop Godfrey that, in commemoration and veneration of this procession, every
year, on that day, a solemn procession be made
around the said island by the clergy and the people, and twelve poor be fed.

GALTIER

Galtier succeeded Godfrey in the year 1110. He
lived in the episcopate for 23 years, 8 months,
and 22 days. He died in the year 1133, the eighth
day before the ides of December (December 8).

   Galtier greatly paid attention to the priesthood
and the order. He consolidated the chevet of the
church of Maguelone which was menacing ruin. He
built from the foundations the tower of Saint Sepulchre, the cellar, refectory, and dormitory. He gave
to this same church a golden chalice of the weight
of four marks, a cross of gold and silver, chapes,
chasubles, tunics, dalmatics, silk and gold vestments, books, and other precious ornaments. . . .

RAYMOND

Raymond I succeeded Galtier in the year 1133.
He lived in the episcopacy 33 years, 3 months,
and 10 days. He died in the year 1166, the second
day before the calends of January (December 31).

   Here, while he lived, he performed great
works for the priesthood and the order, and he
enlarged the church of Maguelone in many ways.
He built the chapter room of Maguelone from the
foundations; he made a cistern, and he completed
the upper walls of the tower of Saint Sepulchre,
and similarly raised the tower of Saint Marie
from its walls upwards, and he built the tower of
the kitchen from its foundations. He also made
the altar of Saint Peter, and the episcopal throne
behind it, and the lavatorium of the upper clois-

circa annum MCLVIII; et tempore electionis sue, prout reperimus in quadam Chronica antiqua, que est in archivo episcopali, fuit magna dissensio in Capitulo, super nova creatione prepositi. . . .

Item . . . Alexander papa declaravit questionem subortam inter dictos episcopum et prepositum, super custodia munitionis Magalonensis, quam etiam Honorius papa IIIus postea confirmavit.

Item etiam Alexander papa declaravit potestatem et jurisdictionem civilem, regularem et criminalem, quam habet episcopus super dictos canonicos. . . .

Anno MCLXVIII, idem fecit compositionem cum domino Agantici, super clave et custodia cloquerii ecclesie dicti loci, et quibusdam aliis, de quibus prior dicti loci habet publicum instrumentum. . . .

Anno MCLXIII, III idus aprilus, que fuit IIIIa feria post Pascha, Alexander papa IIIus, pontificatus sui anno quarto, cum cetis cardinalibus et prelatis appulit Magalonam, et stetit ibi tribus dies, et sexta feria dedicavit majus altare in ecclesia Magalone, in honorem apostolorum Petri et Pauli. . . .

Hic vixit in episcopatu annis XXVIII, mensibus VIII, diebus XII.

MANUSCRIPT SOURCES

Seventeenth-century copies in Paris, Bibliothèque Nationale ms. lat. 11849 (Florilegium Sacrum); Paris, Coll. Peiresc, reg. XLIV; Carpentras, Bibliothèque Municipale; Nîmes, Bibliothèque Municipale; and Aix, Bibliothèque Municipale, ms. 677.

PRINTED SOURCE

A. Germain, ed., *Arnaud de Verdale, Catalogus episcoporum Magalonensium* (1881).

ter, as well as the corridor and gates and the wall by which is enclosed the lay cemetery, the house of milling, in which are stored the wooden beds, the house of the conversi, and the house next to the bridge in which horses are received. . . .

In the year 1155, Pope Adrian IV confirmed in the name of the same bishop all the possessions, castles, places, and rights then acquired by the same church and bishop.

In the year 1156, Louis, king of France and emperor, also confirmed for the same [bishop] by name the castles, places, and rights that he held.

JEAN DE MONTLAUR

Jean de Montlaur, canon of Maguelone, of the castle of Montlaur in the diocese of Maguelone, the first of that name, succeeded Raymond I around the year 1158; and at the moment of his election, just as we have found in a certain ancient chronicle that is in the episcopal archive, there was great dissension about the new creation [of the office] of provost. . . .

Moreover . . . Pope Alexander clarified the question raised between the said bishop and the provost about the custody of the fortifications of Maguelone, which was later confirmed by Pope Honorius III.

Moreover, Pope Alexander clarified power and civil jurisdiction, regular and criminal, which the bishop held concerning the said canons. . . .

In the year 1168, the same [bishop] formed an agreement with the lord of Ganges, about the key and the custody of the bell tower of the church of that said place, and certain other matters, on which the prior of that said place has an official document.

In the year 1163, on the third day before the ides of April (April 11), which is the fourth feast after Easter, Pope Alexander III, in the fourth year of his papacy, arrived at Maguelone with several cardinals and prelates, and stayed there three days, and on the sixth day, he dedicated the great altar in the church of Maguelone, in honor of the apostles Peter and Paul. . . .

Here he lived in the bishopric 28 years, 8 months, and 12 days.

APPENDIX 9

Lintel of west façade, 1178

+ AD PORTV VITE: SITIENTES QVIQ VEN-
ITE
HAS INTRANDO FORES: VESTROS
COPONITE MORES

To the port of life, come, you who are thirsting
By entering these doors, mend your ways

HINC INTRANS ORA: TVA SEP CRIMINA
   PLORA
QVICQD PECCATVR: LACRIMA2 FONTE
   LAVATVR +

B D III VIIS FECIT HOC +
ANO INC D M C LXX VIII +

Pray as you enter here, ever weep for your
   crimes
Whatever has been sinned, let it melt in the
   fountain of your tears.

B. of Trèves (III = tres viis) made this
In the year of the incarnation of Our Lord
   1178.

SOURCE

Transcription of inscription around the borders of the
   linted still *in situ* in the west façade of the cathedral of Maguelone.

APPENDIX 10

Jean de Montlaur (d. c. 1190), epitaph

+ IN HOC VASE IOANNIS (Alpha Omega)
LVX SEMPER CLARESCAT PERENNIS
QVI SPIRITVS SANCTI DONIS
PAVPERES INTRODVXIT IN SCOLIS
ET CVJVS NOBIS EFVSVS EST SANGVIS
ILLIVS PVRGET CRIMINA CARNIS
BERTRANDVS VOCATVR ILLE
QVI SIBI ELEGIT DE MILLE
HIC EU DEPOSVIT
SICVTI AD PSES POTVIT
IN PRIMA EBDA RAGSIME
ANNO INCARNACIOIS DNICE
SICVTI SCPT/ E INSILICE
QVI POSIT/S E INCAPITE
IN DIE PENULTIMO POSTREMO IN MER-
   CURIO
AB HOC MIGRAVIT SECVLO FINITO
NONDVM FEBRVARIO

In this tomb [rests the body of] Jean. (Alpha
   and Omega)
May an eternal light always shine for him
Who introduced the poor in the schools
To the gifts of the Holy Spirit,
May he whose blood has been spilled for us
Purge the sins of that flesh.
Bertrand is called
who is chosen among thousands.
He buried him here,
As he was able,
In the first week of Lent
Of the incarnation of Our Lord.
Thus as it is written on the stone
Which has been placed at his head,
He departed this age on a Wednesday,
Before the last day of February.

SOURCE

Transcription of inscription around the four sides of the
   tomb slab of Jean de Montlaur, currently
   installed as an altar in the tribune of the cathedral of Maguelone.

APPENDIX 11

Statutes of the Chapter (excerpt), Bishop
Jean de Vissec, 1331

De Preposito
De fortalicio
71. Item debet prepositus tenere in fortalicio
   unum hominem, qui dicitur *bada*, bonum et

On the Provost
On the fortifications
71. Also the provost ought to have in the fort a
   man, good and sufficient, who is called the

sufficientem, qui moretur in ipso fortalicio die et nocte, et insulam cum diligentia custodiat vigilando.

Et debet ille *bada* vocare familiam, quando est necessaria canonicis, et illis qui tenent claves, ad preceptum canonicorum.

72. Item tenetur prepositus habere et tenere unum hominem, qui dicitur *gacha,* bonum et sufficientem, qui debet tubicinare horas noctis; et ille homo debet habere namphile ad tubicunandum dictas horas.

Et dictus *gacha* tenetur facere salsas.

73. Item tenetur prepositus habere et tenere plures alios vigiles, si plures sint necessarii pro vigilando.

74. Item tenetur prepositus hedificare et rehedificare illam domum, in qua cubant dicti *gacha* et *bada;* que domus est supra turrim.

Debet etiam providere de pannis in quibus jaceant.

75. Item debet providere de scala ad ascendum supram dictam turrim, et corda cum uno panerio, vel cofino seu cabasso, cum quibus ascendunt victualia necessaria eisdem *bade* et *gache.*

Debet etiam eisdem hominibus providere de aliis *esplets* sibi necessariis.

76. Item tenetur prepositus providere, ad custodiendum ecclesiam et insulam, de machinis, seu *giens* et *trabuquetz,* et lapidibus, et scutis, et lanceis, balistis, et omnibus armorum generibus, et aliis munimentis necessariis temporibus opportunis, cum habeat custodiam totius insule et fortalicii per totum annum.

Et in octavis festi apostolorum Petri et Pauli debet habere et tenere in insula familiam prepositure cum armis, ad faciendum excubias per totam dictam insulam, et die et nocte.

De navibus et portis

77. Item tenetur prepositus tenere et habere navetas . . . ad deferendum omnia qui sunt necessaria in tota insula.

78. Item debet habere et tenere dictas navetas pro canonicis et aliis bonis hominibus, quando volunt exire insulam vel redire ad eam, propter pontis evitandum periculum. . . .

81. Item tenetur prepositus ibidem facere et reficere portas ferreas omnes, et claves, et cathenas, et vectes, excepta porta ferrea ecclesie, et exceptis aliis portis ecclesie, et infirmarie, helemosinarie et vestiarie.

bada who will remain in the fort itself day and night, and with waking diligence would guard the island.

And that *bada* ought to call the serfs, when it is necessary for the canons who hold the keys, according to canonial rule.

72. Also the provost ought to have and keep a man, who is called *gacha* [watchman], good and sufficient, who shall trumpet the hours of the night, and this man ought to have have a horn for sounding the said hours.

And the said *gacha* is held [responsible] to make [watch] upon the salt marshes.

73. Also the provost is held [responsible] to have and keep many other watchers, if many are necessary for watching.

74. Also the provost is held [responsible] to build and rebuild that house in which the said *gacha* and *bada* stay; that house is atop the tower.

He ought also to provide the bedding in which they lie.

75. Also he ought to provide for a ladder for climbing up to the said tower, and [for] a rope with a bread-basket or box or flat basket in which the necessary supplies go up to these same *bada* and *gacha.*

He ought also to provide these men with other revenues necessary for them.

76. Also the provost ought to provide, toward the guarding of the church and island, for machinery, or *giens,* and trebuchets and stones and shields and lances, catapults, and all types of arms, and other provisions necessary at suitable times, since he would have custody of the whole island and fort for the entire year.

And in the eighth day of the feast of the apostles Peter and Paul he ought to have and keep on the island serfs of the priory with weapons for keeping vigils throughout the whole said island, both day and night.

On Ships and Ports

77. Also the provost is held [responsible] to have and keep ships . . . for defending everything that is necessary on the island.

78. Also he ought to have and keep the said ships for the canons and other good men when they wish to leave the island or return to it, because of the danger, to be avoided, of the bridge.

81. Also the provost himself is held [responsible] there to make and repair all the iron gates and keys and chains and bolts, except the iron door of the church, and excepting the other doors of the church, and of the infirmary, the almonry, and vestiary.

De porterio et pontanerio

105. Item debet prepositus habere et tenere unum bonum hominem et fidelem prop porterio seu janitore, ad custodiendum portas ligneas primas, ad recipiendum raubam hospitum advenientium, et specialiter armaturas. . . .

106. Item porterius laycus tenetur notificare canonico porterio, quando aliquis ex canonicos petitur per aliquem. . . .

De helemosinario

22. Item tenetur helemosinarius cameram, que vocatur Quatuor Lectorum, tenere munitam de quatuor lectis fusteis, mundis et bonis pannis munitis . . . pro canonicis et aliis, nostram societam habentibus, recipiendis.

23. Item, quando canonici veniunt hora tarde de extra insulam, post ascencionem arcubii sive gache, debent jacere in domo helemosine, in dicta camera Quatuor Lectorum. . . .

De operario

1. Primo tenetur operarius ecclesiam Beati Petri constuere et ressarcire, et omnia alia hedificia infra portas ferreas antiquas constructa, . . . [et] omnia alia hedificia, extra portas ferreas constructa, ad communiam pertinentia.

7. Item tenetur operarius reparare et ressarcire tectum ecclesie Sancti Petri, et Sancti Augustini, et Sancti Pancracii, et turrim Beate Marie, et turrim Sancti Jacobi, . . . et quod omnes operas lapidum Capituli, dormitorii, et claustrum, et muros fortalicii, et omnia alia hedificia lapidum, que erunt ressarcienda infra veteres portas ferreas.

MANUSCRIPT SOURCE

Archives départementales de l'Hérault, Cartulaire de Maguelone, Reg. B., fol. 272 ff.

PRINTED SOURCES

A. Germain, *Maguelone sous ses évêques* (1869), 219ff. (excerpts).

J. Rouquette and A. Villemagne, eds., *Cartulaire de Maguelone,* 5 (1923), no. 1641, pp. 205–352.

On the Porter and the Keeper of the Bridge

105. Also the provost ought to have and keep a good and faithful man as porter or door-keeper for guarding the first wooden gates, for receiving the valuables of arriving guests, and particularly their weapons. . . .

106. Also the lay porter is held [responsible] to notify the canon porter when[ever] anyone of the canons is sought by anyone.

On the Almoner

22. Also the almoner is held [responsible] to hold a room, which is called the Four Beds, furnished with four wooden beds, supplied with clean and good bedclothes . . . for receiving canons and others enjoying our company.

23. Also, when canons arrive at a late hour from outside the island, after the fortress-keeper or *gacha* [watchman] has ascended, they should sleep in the almoner's house, in the aforesaid room of the Four Beds. . . .

On the Master of the Works

1. First the Master of the Works is held [responsible] to build and restore both every other building constructed within the ancient iron gates, . . . and every other building outside and all other buildings constructed within the ancient iron gates, pertaining to the community.

7. Also the Master of the Works is held [responsible] to repair and restore the roof of the church of Saint Peter, and of Saint Augustine, and of Saint Pancras, and the tower of the blessed Mary, and the tower of Saint James, . . . and all the works in stone of the chapter room, dormitory, cloister and the walls of the fort, and all other buildings of stone which will have to be restored within the ancient iron gates.

APPENDIX 12

Record of the fortification of Maguelone in the Hundred Years War (excerpt), 1341

Anno Domini millesimo trecentesimo quadragesimo primo, et die quarta mensis januarii,

In the year of Our Lord 1341, and the fourth day of the month of January, the Lord Philip, by

domino Philippo Dei gratia rege Francorum regnante.

Noverint universi, quod existentes apud Nemausum coram nobili et potenti viro domino Guillelmo de Esperiaco, milite domini nostri Francorum regis, senescallo Belicadri et Nemausi, dominus Matheus Blegeri, licentiatus in legibus, et magister Leonardus Nicholai, procuratores et nomine procuratorio, ut dixerunt, reverendi in Christo patris domini Arnaldi, Dei gratia Magalonensis epsicopi, presentaverunt quasdam patentes litteras ipsius domini episcopi . . .

. . . Habemus et habere consueverunt pacifice et quiete hactenus, et a tanto tempore citra, de cuius contrario hominum memoria non existit, in civitate, fortalitio et tota insula Magalone soli et in solidum, perturbare et salvagardiam nostram regiam, in qua nos cum dicta civitate et aliis castris, locis, fortalitiis, rebus, personis familiaribus existimus, temere offendere, ponentes, preter et contra nostram voluntatem, in dicta insula et fortalitio homines armatos, nobis ignotos, per quos domino nostro regi, regno et nobis, qui sumus sui fideles, posset periculum imminere. . . .

Ex causa defensionis regni et recognicolarum, et ut obvietur malitiis inimicorum eiusdem, prehabita deliberatione cum nostro consilio, vobis mandamus districte, sub juramento et fidelitate quibus estis astrictus dicto domino nostro regi, quatinus, absque mora aliqua, fortalitia insule Magalone et castri Melgorii, et aliorum locorum vobis subjectorum, prope fronterias, prout ad vos pertinuerit, refici et muniri bonis et sufficientibus custodibus, armis et victualibus faciatis, taliter quod in vobis nullus reperiatur defectus.

MANUSCRIPT SOURCE

Archives départementales de l'Hérault, *Cartulaire de Maguelone*, Reg. F; fol. 152.

PRINTED SOURCE

A. Germain, ed., *Arnaud de Verdale, Catalogus episcoporum Magalonensium* (1881), 379–83.

the grace of God the reigning King of the Franks.

All shall have known that, appearing at Nîmes before the noble and powerful man, Lord Guilhem of Esperiaco, knight of Our Lord the king of the Franks, the seneschal of Bellicadri and of Nîmes, Lord Matthew Bligeus, licensed in laws, and Master Leonard Nicholai, procurators, and in the procuratorial name, as they have said, of the reverend father in Christ, Lord Arnaud, by the grace of God bishop of Maguelone, have presented certain letters patent (unsealed letters) of the same lord bishop . . .

We own and they have grown accustomed to own peacefully and quietly so far and from such a time before, concerning which, the memory of men exists not to the contrary, in the city, the fortress, and on the whole island of Maguelone of soil and in solid, and to perturb the safeguard and to boldly offend our palace, in which, with the aforesaid city, and other castles, places, forts, things, persons, and servant personnel, placing, beyond and contrary to our will, on the aforesaid island and fort, armed men unknown to us through whom it is possible to threaten danger to our king, to our kingdom, and to us, who are its faithful . . .

For the sake of the defense of the kingdom, and of its known citizens, and that it be protected from the attacks of its enemies, by fore-ordained agreement with our advice, we strictly command you, under the oath and loyalty by which you are bound to the said lord our king, to the extent that with no other delay you cause the fortification of the island of Maguelone and of the castle of Melgueil, and of other places subject to you, near the frontiers, as it shall have pertained to you, to be repaired and fortified with goods and sufficient garrisons, arms, and supplies, such that no lack could be found among you.

AGDE

APPENDIX 13

Testament of Etienne, chaplain of Mèze
(excerpt), 1147

In nomine Domini nostri Jesu Christi. Anno ab Incarnatione Domini MCXLVII. Ego Stephanus capellanus de Mezoa iturus ad Sanctum Sepulchrum ita facio meum testamentum. Si in hoc itinere Sancti Sepulchri de me mesfalliebat, dimitto universum meum honorem Pontio meo nepoti. . . . Et post mortem mei nepotis, dimitto omnem meum alodem quem habeo in terminio de Mezoa, Sancto Stephano de Agathe et canonicis euisdem. . . . Et dimitto episcopo agathensi L solidos et medietatem totius mei averi dimitto ad opus Sancti Stephani de Agathe, et aliam medietatem ad opus Sancti Petri de Mezoa, ut fiat inde ecclesia et renovetur.

In the name of our Lord Jesus Christ. In the year of the incarnation of the Lord 1147. I, Etienne, chaplain of Mèze, about to go to the Holy Sepulchre, make my testament. If on the trip to the Holy Sepulchre misfortune befalls me, I grant my entire holdings to my nephew Pons. . . . And after the death of my nephew, I grant my entire allod, which I hold in the district of Mèze, to Saint-Etienne of Agde and its canons. . . . And I grant to the bishop of Agde 50 solidi, and I grant half of all my fortune to the works of Saint-Etienne of Agde, and the other half to Saint-Pierre of Mèze, so that this church may be built and renewed.

MANUSCRIPT SOURCES

Cartulaire du Chapitre d'Agde (17th-c. copies):
MS. "B," Bibliothèque municipale de Montpellier, ms. 33, 182; and MS. "C," Archives départementales de l'Hérault, Reg. G. 20, 182–83.

PRINTED SOURCE

O. Terrin, *Cartulaire du Chapitre d'Agde* (1969), no. 258.

APPENDIX 14

Testament of Bernard of Roujan (excerpt), 1147

In nomine Domini. Ego Bernardus de Rojano divido me ipsum domino Deo et beato Martino, si mortuus fuero in hac terra. . . . Divido domino Deo et ecclesiae Sancti Stephani XXX solidos ad opus, ad episcopum X solidos et cantet missam, ad hospitalem XX solidos, ad militiam X solidos.

In the name of the Lord. I, Bernard of Roujan, devote myself to hand over to the Lord God and Saint Martin, if I shall have died in that land. . . . I give to the Lord God and to the church of Saint-Etienne: 30 solidi to the works, 10 solidi to the bishop so that he may sing mass, 20 solidi to the hospital, and 10 solidi to the soldiers.

MANUSCRIPT SOURCES

Cartulaire du Chapitre d'Agde (17th-c. copies):
MS. "B," Bibliothèque municipale de Montpellier, ms. 33, 228–9; and MS. "C," Archives départementales de l'Hérault, Reg. G. 20, 232–4.

PRINTED SOURCE

O. Terrin, *Cartulaire du Chapitre d'Agde* (1969), no. 340.

APPENDIX 15

Testament of Ermengaud, bishop of Agde (excerpt), 1149.

In nomine domini, Anno Incarnationis ejus MCXLIX, regnante Ludovicus rege Francorum, ego Ermengaudus agathensis ecclesiae episcopus licet indignus sic factio testamentum . . .

Pro remedio animae meae relinquo elemosynae de communia S. Stephani campum qui fuit Raimundi Bec cum ipso prato, quae duo emi ante episcopatum, ad reparationem altaris S. Stephani et ad chorum perficiendum mille solidorum melgoriensium quos relinquo in potestate Pontii archidiaconi et Bertrandi sacristae, ut inde fideles sint adminstratores secundum meam voluntatem. Et duos cislatores et unum pallium relinquo in potestatem Bertrandi sacristae ad hoc proprie, ut de duobus cislatonibus vestes fiant ad missarum solemnia celebranda, et pallium unum quod superponatur altari S. Stephani in solemnitatibus. . . . .

Corpus meum et animam meam domino Deo et gloriosae virgini Mariae et S. Stephano dono atque relinquo, et reaedificationem ecclesiae S. Stephani relinquo duas partes aliorum omnium bonorum mobilium acque se moventium, substractis inde omnibus debitis, tertiam vero pauperibus erogandam. Hujus testamenti sunt testes rogati Pontius archidiaconis, Bertrandus sacrista, Petrus de Beciano, Johannes camerarius, Willelmus de Fabricolis, Bertrandus de Agathe, Willelmus Rainardi, Willelmus Sigarii et Deodatus de Torolla, atque Berangarius de Gigano, Johannes de Beciano hoc testamentum transtulit ex primitivo, mense septembri feria VI.

PRINTED SOURCES

Gallia Christiana, VI (1739), Instrumentum no. 13, cols. 323–4.

O. Terrin, *Cartulaire du Chapitre d'Agde* (1969), pp. LXXXIII-LXXXIV.

In the name of the Lord, in the year of His Incarnation 1149, with King Louis reigning as king, I, Ermengaud, bishop of the church of Agde, clearly unworthy, thus make [my] will . . .

For the cure of my soul I leave to the endowment of the community of Saint-Etienne a field that was of Raymond Bec the meadow itself, which two I bought before the bishopric; for the repair of the altar of Saint-Etienne and for the completion of the choirs (apses) a thousand melgorian solidi, which I leave in the power of Pons the archdeacon and of Bertrand the sacristan so that they may be faithful administrators according to my wish. And I leave two *cislatores* and one pall in the power of Bertrand the sacristan for this especially that from the two *cislatores* there be vestments for the solemn celebration of the Mass, and a pall that is placed on the altar of Saint-Etienne at feast days . . .

My body and my soul, I give and leave to the Lord God and glorious Virgin Mary and Saint Stephen, and for the rebuilding of the church of Saint-Etienne I leave two parts of all my other goods, furniture, and moveables, after all debts have been subtracted, a third truly to be left to the poor.

[As] witnesses of this will have been invited Pons the archdeacon, Bertrand the sacristan, Peter de Beciano, John the treasurer, Guilhem of Fabricolis, Bertrand of Agde, Guilhem Rainard, Guilhem Sigarus and Deodatus of Torolla, and Berengar of Gigano; John of Beciano transcribed this will from the original, in the month of September, on the sixth day of the week (Friday).

APPENDIX 16

Testament of Pierre Rainard (excerpt), 1153.

In nomine Domini. Anno Incarnationis ejus MCLIII, regnante Ludovico rege Francorum. Ego Petrus Rainardus facio testamentum meum sic. In primis dono corpus meum domino Deo et sancto Andreae, et insuper divido eidem ecclesiae Sancti Andreae pro remedio animae meae et parentum meorum C solidos melgorienses, ut ematur

In the name of the Lord. In the year of His Incarnation 1153, in the reign of Louis, king of the Franks. I, Pierre Rainard, make my testament thus. First I give my body to the Lord God and to Saint Andrew, and in addition I give a share of 100 melgorian solidi for the cure of my soul and [those of] my parents to that same church of

casula. Divido ad opus Sancti Stephani XX solidos biterrenses. . . .

Saint Andrew so that that little house might be
obtained. I give a share of 20 biterrois solidi for
the works of Saint-Etienne. . . .

MANUSCRIPT SOURCES

Cartulaire du Chapitre d'Agde (17th-c. copies):
MS. "B," Bibliothèque municipale de Montpellier, ms.
  33, 288–9; and MS. "C," Archives départementales de l'Hérault, Reg. G. 20, 291–2.

PRINTED SOURCE

O. Terrin, *Cartulaire du Chapitre d'Agde* (1969), no. 386.

APPENDIX 17

Testament of Guilhem Rainard, canon of
Agde (excerpt), April 1155.

Haec est carta sive testamentum quod Willelmus,
timens scilicet mortis periculum, fecit et scribere
jussit in hunc modum de omnibus rebus suis
mobilibus et immobilibus. Divido corpus meum
et animam meam domino Deo et beatae Mariae
et sancto Stephano, ad sepeliendum eum quingentos solidos melgoriensis monetae ad aedificia
ipsius ecclesiae, et dono capam meam de cisla-
tione ecclesiae Sancti Stephani, et scyphum meum
argenteum, et duos annulos, alterum aureum et
alterum argenteum ut inde fiat thuribulum ad
quodidianos usus. . . . .Similiter de rebus meis
sumantur quingenti praedicti solidi ad opus ecclesiae Sancti Stephani; pro sepultura et omnibus
aliis quae erunt mihi necessaria usque ad septe-
narium, divido C solidos. . . .

This is the charter or will that Guilhem, naturally
fearing the peril of death, made and ordered written in this manner concerning all of his possessions, moveable and permanent. I bequeath my
body and my soul to the Lord God and to blessed
Mary and to Saint-Etienne for burying it, 500
solidi of melgorian money [for] the buildings of
the same church, and I give my cape of *cislation*
to the church of Saint-Etienne, and my silver gob-
let, and two rings, one gold and the other silver,
so that there may be a thurible for daily use. . . .
Similarly, from my possessions may be taken the
aforesaid 500 solidi toward the work of the
church of Saint-Etienne; for burial and for all
other things that will be necessary for me up to
the *septinarium* (obituary mass for the seventh
day after death), I allot 100 solidi. . . .

MANUSCRIPT SOURCES

Cartulaire du Chapitre d'Agde (17th-c. copies):
MS. "B," Bibliothèque municipale de Montpellier, ms.
  33, 20–2; and MS. "C,"Archives départementales de l'Hérault, Reg. G. 20, 19–21.

PRINTED SOURCE

O. Terrin, *Cartulaire du Chapitre d'Agde* (1969), no. 17.

APPENDIX 18

Testament of Raymond of Foreville
(excerpt), 1157

In Dei nomine. Anno ab Incarnatione euis
MCLVII. Ego Raymundus de Forisvilla, jacens in

In the name of the Lord. In the year from His
Incarnation 1157. I, Raymond de Foreville, lying

aegritudine, cum mea bona voluntate et recta memoria, facio testamentum meum sic. In primis dimitto corpus meum et animam meam domino Deo et beatae Mariae et Beato Stephano de Agathe ut ibi sepeliatur. Divido communiae Sancti Stephani de Agathe quingentos solidos melgoriensis. . . . Divido domino meo episcopo agathensi, unum modium frumenti, operi Sancti Stephani unum modium ordei. . . .

in illness, of sound mind and right memory, make my testament thus. First I commit my body and soul to the Lord God and the blessed Mary and Saint-Etienne of Agde so that I may be buried there. I give a share of 500 melgorian solidi to the community of Saint-Etienne of Agde. . . . I give one measure of wheat to the bishop of Agde, and to the works of Saint-Etienne, one measure of barley. . . .

MANUSCRIPT SOURCES

Cartulaire du Chapitre d'Agde (17th-c. copies): MS. "B," Bibliothèque municipale de Montpellier, ms. 33, 136–7; and MS. "C," Archives départementales de l'Hérault, Reg. G 20, 135–7.

PRINTED SOURCE

O. Terrin, *Cartulaire du Chapitre d'Agde* (1969), no. 171.

APPENDIX 19

Testament of Bernard of Tongue (excerpt), April 1159.

In nomine Domini. Ego Bernardus de Tongua, viam universae carnis ingrediens, bono sensu et recta memoria, facio testamentum meum sic. In primis, dono corpus meum et animum meam domino Deo et beatae Mariae et ecclesiae Sancti Stephani de Agathe, per conversum. Divido et dono operi ejusdem ecclesiae Sancti Stephani de Agathe quingentos solidos melgoriensis monetae pro anima mea. Divido unicuique sacerdotum, sciliciet illis qui ecclesia Sancti Stephani servieunt II solidos biterrenses, unicuique diaconorum XII denarios, et unicuique puerorum III denarios. . . . Et si aliquid de meis rebus remaneat quod non sit nominatum, totum divido et dono operi praedictae ecclesiae Sancti Stephani de Agathe. Hoc testamentum fecit Bernardus de Tongua in praesentia Petri Raimundi sacristae, et Guillelmi Rainardi, et Guillelmi praecentoris, et Petri de Pomairiolis, et Guillelmi Guiraldi et Berengarii Bernardi, et Guiraldi de Andusia. Acta sunt haec anno ab Incarnatione Domini MCLVIIII, mense aprilis. Adam scripsit.

In the name of the Lord. I, Bernard of Tongue, going the way of all flesh, of sound mind and right memory, make my will thus. First, I give my body and my soul to the Lord God and blessed Mary and the church of Saint-Etienne of Agde as a convert. I share and give to the works of the same church of Saint-Etienne of Agde 500 solidi of melgorian money for my soul. I also allot to each of the priests, namely, those who serve the church of Saint-Etienne, 2 biterrois solidi, to each of the deacons, 12 denarii, and to each of the boys, 3 denarii. . . . And if something of my possessions remains that has not been named, I pledge and give all to the works of the aforementioned church of Saint-Etienne of Agde. This will is made by Bernard of Tongue in the presence of Peter Raymond the sacristan, and Guilhem Rainard , and Guilhem the precentor, and Peter of Pomairols, and Guilhem Guiraldus and Berengar Bernard, and Gerald of Anduse. These things have been done in the year 1159 from the Incarnation of the Lord, in the month of April. Adam wrote this.

MANUSCRIPT SOURCES

Cartulaire du Chapitre d'Agde (17th-c. copies): MS. "B," Bibliothèque municipale de Montpellier, ms.

33, 38; and MS. "C," Archives départementales de l'Hérault, Reg. G. 20, 36–7.

PRINTED SOURCE

O. Terrin, *Cartulaire du Chapitre d'Agde* (1969), no. 36.

APPENDIX 20

Testament of Marie de Mermian (excerpt), 1160

In nomine Domini. Anno Incarnationis euis MCLX, Lodoico regnante. . . . Ego, Maria de Mermiano, timens subitaneam mortem, bono sensu et recta memoria, facio divisionem de omnibus rebus meis mobilius et immobilius, in hunc modum. In primis dimitto et dono corpus meum et animam meam domino Deo et Sancto Silvestro de Mirmiano. Operi eiusdem ecclesiae dimitto unum sestarium de blado; capellano eiusdem ecclesiae dimitto II solidos, clericis qui me sepelient dimitto XII denarios; operi ecclesiae Sancti Stephani dimitto unam eminam de blado. . . .

In the name of the Lord. In the year of His Incarnation 1160, in the reign of Louis. . . . I, Marie de Mermian, fearing sudden death, in sound mind and right memory, make a division of all my things, moveable and immoveable, in this fashion. First, I devote my body and soul to the Lord God and to Saint Silvester of Mermian. I grant to that church one sestarium (two-and-a-half shares) of corn; to the chaplain of that church I grant 2 solidi, to the clerics who bury me I grant 12 denarii; to the works of the church of Saint-Etienne I grant one measure of corn. . . .

MANUSCRIPT SOURCES

Cartulaire du Chapitre d'Agde (17th-c. copies):
MS. "B," Bibliothèque municipale de Montpellier, ms. 33, 38–9; and MS. "C," Archives départementales de l'Hérault, Reg. G. 20, 37.

PRINTED SOURCE

O. Terrin, *Cartulaire du Chapitre d'Agde* (1969), no. 37.

APPENDIX 21

Testament of Guiraud de Touroulle (excerpt), 1160

In nomine Domini. Ego Guiraldus de Torolla, in infirmitate positus, bona voluntate et sana memoria, sic divido res meas, et testamentum meum facio. In primis dimitto corpus meum et animam meam domino Deo et beatae Mariae et sancto Stephano de Agathe ad sepeliendum et duos modios frumenti, unum episcopo et alium operi Sancti Stephani. . . .

In the name of the Lord. I, Guiraud de Touroulle, placed in illness, of sound mind and sane memory, divide my things thus, and make my testament. First, I grant my body and my soul to the Lord God and the blessed Mary and Saint-Etienne of Agde toward [my] burial, and two measures of wheat: one for the bishop and the other for the works of Saint-Etienne. . . .

MANUSCRIPT SOURCES

Cartulaire du Chapitre d'Agde (17th-c. copies):
MS. "B," Bibliothèque municipale de Montpellier, ms.

33, 115–16; and MS. "C," Archives départementales de l'Hérault, Reg. G. 20, 115–16.

PRINTED SOURCE

O. Terrin, *Cartulaire du Chapitre d'Agde* (1969), no. 142.

APPENDIX 22

Testament of Bertrand of Agde, canon of Saint-Etienne (excerpt), 1172

In nomine Domini. Ego Bertrandus de Agde constitutus in infirmitate mei corporis, bona memoria et integra mente hoc modo dispono testamentum meum. In primis relinquo corpus meum domino Deo et ecclesiae Sancti Stephani ad sepeliendum. . . . Dimitto operi Sancti Stephani septingentos solido melgorienses de mille solidis, quos habeo in decimis Sancti Severi, et volo ut opera tamdiu habeat gaudimentum pignoris totius, donec isti septingenti solidi persolvantur. Domino meo episcopo relinquo CCC solidos de praedictos pignore. De pignore M solidorum quod habeo a Pontio de Beciano ita dispono; ut si Pontius voluerit dare quingentos solidos, recuperet pignus praedictam, et alios quingentos solidos ei dimitto. Si vero Pontius de Beciano redimere noluerit, dimitto domino meo episcopo ut redimat jamdictam pignus pro quingentis solidis et habeat totum integre donec nominata pecunia ei solvatur. Isti vero quingenti solidi a quocumque praedictorum soluti fuerint, ita dividantur: CCC solidi sint operi Sancti Stephani et CC sint Raimundi de Pressano. Quod si necque Pontius, necque dictus episcopus redimere voluerit, opera ecclesiae Sancti Stephani habeat duas partes redditum et Raimundus de Preixano tertiam. . . .

In the name of the Lord. I, Bertrand of Agde, set amidst the infirmity of my body, [but] with right memory and intact mind, dispose of my testament thus. First, I leave my body to the Lord God and to the church of Saint-Etienne for burial. . . . I grant to the works of Saint-Etienne seven hundred melgorian solidi of the one thousand solidi I hold in tithe from Saint-Sever, and I wish that the works hold possession of the entire debt for the time until those 700 solidi shall be paid. To my lord bishop I bequeath 300 solidi of the aforesaid debt. Of the debt of 1,000 solidi I hold from Pons de Becciano, I thus dispose: that if Pons shall have agreed to pay five hundred solidi, he shall redeem his said debt, and the other five hundred solidi I forgive him. If in fact Pons de Becciano shall not have wished to redeem [it], I grant to my lord bishop that he may purchase the aforesaid debt for five hundred solidi and he may possess the entire thing whole until the named money be paid to him. Indeed, let those five hundred solidi be paid by whomever of the aforesaid persons, they shall be allotted thus: 300 solidi shall be for the works of Saint-Etienne and 200 shall be for Raymond de Pressano. But if neither Pons nor the said bishop shall have wished to repurchase the debt, the works of the church of Saint-Etienne shall hold two parts, and Raymond of Pressano the third. . . .

MANUSCRIPT SOURCES

Cartulaire du Chapitre d'Agde (17th-c. copies): MS. "B," Bibliothèque municipale de Montpellier, ms. 33, 31–3; and MS. "C," Archives départementales de l'Hérault, Reg. G. 20, 29–31.

PRINTED SOURCE

O. Terrin, *Cartulaire du Chapitre d'Agde* (1969), no. 27.

APPENDIX 23

Forged diploma of Charles the Bald, dated
11 August 848; forged c. 1173

In nomine sancte et individue Trinitatis. Karolus
divina ordinante providentia rex. Dignum est ut
regalis majestas suorum procerum petitionibus pio
provideat amminiculo, quatenus eos nobilitando et
provido moderamine consulendo erga sua reddat
promptiores obsequia et fideliores per omnia.
Quanto itaque est utilius et animarum necessitati
salubrius ecclesiarum honestati subvenire easque
congruis honoribus exaltari, qui quam feliciores
esse credimus sanctorum patrociniis et oratione.
Proinde noverit omnium fidelium nostrorum tam
presentium quam futurorum universitas quod adi-
ens ante presentiam serenitatis nostre Apollonius,
comes noster communis fidelis enixus postulavit
quatenus concederemus ad votum Dacberti rev-
erendissimi episcopi Agathensis ecclesie, ad sub-
jectionem videlicet sancti Stephani, tertiam partem
rerum quecumque ab ea ecclesia quondam mag-
nifici antecessores nostri abstulerant ad com-
munem suorum nostrorumque fidelium utilitatem.
Cui petitioni aurem libenter prebentes, clementiae
concedimus eidem episcopo et successoribus suis
tertiam partem in ipsis rebus, et, si ibi ecclesia constructa fuerit, prenominato protomartyri Stephano
pro nobis et pro progenie nostra ad orandum con-
donamus cum tertia scilicet parte ipsius terrae,
sane reliquam nostris usibus reservamus.

Donamus etiam prenominato pontifici et successoribus eius in ipso commitatu pulveraticum,
pascuarium, piscaticum, tam maris quam aquae
currentis volatiliaticum, salinaticum, telonei mar-
catum, tertiam partem in omnibus habendam tam
quesitum quam diligenter inquirendum. Omnia et
in omnibus de nostra potestate in Beati Stephani
rebus placabili voto transfundimus. Jubemus
etiam et regia auctoritate decernimus aut nullis
judiciarie potestatis aut cuiuscumque personae
vir, a clericis aut a laicis supra terras predicti loci
commanentibus audeat exigere mansionaticum,
pontiaticum, salinaticum, hospitalicum, nec
alicuis redibitionis curam infligere, nec inquitare
nec distringere, sed quecumque agenda sunt in
[potestate] eiusdem loci episcopum omni tempore
maneant. Ut autem hec nostrae voluntatis auc-
toritas certior habeatur, hoc serenitatis nostrae
preceptum, per quod iam dictus episcopus et successores eius ea omnia supradicta absque ulla
inquietudine aut deminoratione sempiternis temporibus possidere valeant.

In the name of the holy and undivided Trinity.
Charles, king by order of divine providence. It is
proper that the royal majesty provide for the
requests of his nobles with conscientious assistance to the extent that, by making them famous
and by advising upon their allegiances with prudent constraint he renders them more obedient
and more faithful in all matters. By so much,
therefore, is it more useful and more healthy for
the need of souls to reinforce the integrity of the
churches, and that they be exalted with appropriate honors, those whom we believe to be so much
happier by the protection of saints and by prayer.
Consequently, the entirety of all our faithful, as
much of present ones as of future, shall have
learned how, coming before the presence of Our
Serenity, Apollonius, our zealous count of the
faithful community has petitioned insofar as we
would grant at the behest of Dagobert, most reverend bishop of the church of Agde, in the jurisdiction of course of Saint-Etienne, a third part of
those things from that church our magnificent
ancestors once alienated for the common use of
themselves and our faithful. Gladly lending an ear
to his petition, we grant to this same bishop and
his successors a third part in these very things,
and, if a church shall have been erected there for
the aforesaid protomartyr Stephen (Etienne), we
devote it to praying for us and for our posterity
along with a third, naturally, of that very land; the
remainder we certainly reserve for our own use.

We also give to the aforenamed bishop and his
successors in the same county the toll, pasturage,
fishing rights, as much in the sea as in flowing
waters, bird hunting, salt making, stamping of
tolls: a third part to be had in all things to the
same extent obtained as must be carefully
requested. With an agreeable prayer we shift
everything and in all matters concerning our
power in Saint-Etienne. We also command, and
by royal authority we resolve, that no man of
judicial power or of whatever rank shall dare to
demand from the clergy or from the laity residing
in the said place (the rights of) lodging, bridge
toll, saltworks, or hospitality, nor to inflict a
charge of any payment, nor to claim as bonds-
man, nor to distrain, but those things that must
be done may remain in the power of the bishop
of that place for all time. So that this, moreover,

Et ut verius credatur et diligentius ab omnibus observetur, manu propria super firmavimus et annuli nostri impressione assignari iussimus. Signum Karoli (Monogramma) gloriosissimi regis. Teudo cancellarius ad vicem Ludovici arch-cancellarii recognavit (signum recognitionis). Datum III idus augusti, indictione V anno VIII regnante Karolo gloriosissimo rege. Actum apud Carisiacum palatium. In domino feliciter.

MANUSCRIPT SOURCES

Cartulaire du Chapitre d'Agde (17th-c. copies):
MS. "B," Bibliothèque municipale de Montpellier, ms. 33, no.3; and MS. "C," Archives départementales de l'Hérault, Reg. G. 20, no. 3.
Cartulaire de l'Evêché d'Agde: Paris, Bibliothèque Nationale, ms. 9999, no. 3.

PRINTED SOURCES

Gallia Christiana, VI (1739), Instrumentum no. 1, cols. 311–13.
C. DeVic and J.J. Vaissete, *Histoire de Languedoc*, II (1876), no. 133, col. 277–9.
Recueil des Historiens des Gaules et de la France, VIII (1869–80), no. 77, 496.
O. Terrin, *Cartulaire du Chapitre d'Agde* (1969), no. 3.
A. Castaldo, *L'Eglise d'Agde* (1970), no. 1.

APPENDIX 24

Diploma of Louis VII (excerpt), 1173

In nomine Sanctae et Individuae Trinitatis, amen. Ego, Ludovicus, Dei gratia Francorum rex, dilecto nostro Willelmo reverendo episcopo Agathensi, ejusque successoribus canonice substituende in perpetuum. Plurimum gaudemus et exultamus in Domino semper quod provida moderatoris omnium disposito usibus regni Francorum actenus bene prospexit, cum eos suae potestatis vicarios esse constituit per quod jus suum integre servetur ecclesiis, et exuberans improbitas suo tempore servetur in malis. Talibus quippe regnum Franciae rectoribus indigebat, quorum studio et sollicitudine et tirannorum retunderetur impietas, et ecclesiarum dignitas servaretur illaesa. In ipsorum namque regnorum et principum redundat opprobrium si ecclesiae Dei, quod absit, se statu quo paterentur lapsum, quae ab eis deberent jugiter suscipere incrementum. Et quia virtus petrum filios non degeneres provocat ad virtutam, gloriosissimorum regum Francorum

may be held a more definite mandate of our desire, this is Our Serenity's edict through which now the aforesaid bishop and his successors may be entitled to possess for all time everything mentioned above without disruption or diminution.

And so that it may more truly be believed and more diligently observed by all, we have moreover confirmed [it] with our own hand and we have ordered [it] to be signed with the impress of our ring. Sign of Charles (monogram) the most glorious king. Teudo, vice-chancellor to Louis the archchancellor has acknowledged. (Sign of confirmation). Dated the third day before the ides of August (August 13), in the fifth indiction, in the eighth year of the reigning most glorious King Charles. Enacted at the palace of Cariscum. Happily in the Lord.

In the name of the holy and undivided Trinity, amen. I, Louis, king of the Franks by the grace of God, to our beloved Guilhem, reverend bishop of Agde, and his successors canonically elected in perpetuity. We rejoice greatly and we exult in the Lord always because with prudent purpose of the ruler of all things He has until now well looked to the advantages of the kingdom of the Franks, since He has appointed them to be ministers of his power through which His law may be kept whole in the churches and extravagant sinfulness in His time may be checked among the wicked. The kingdom of France, indeed, was in need of such leaders, by whose zeal and concern both the impiety of tyrants might be blunted and the honor of churches might be preserved unharmed. For shame abounds among kingdoms and princes themselves, if the churches of God, may it be far off, reveal a decline from their condition, which [churches] should continually receive increase

praedecessorum nostrum vestigiis inherentes, et si impares meritis, pro nostris tamen viribus ecclesiarum commodis inhiantes, notum esse volumus tam praesentibus quam futuris quod ecclesiae Beati promartyris Stephani, et tibi Willelmo episcopo in praesentialiter et tuis successoribus, in perpetuum hac nostri privilegii auctoritate communimus, in civitate seu villa Agathensi ecclesiam, quae est constructa in honorem Beati promartyris Stephani, cum tertia parte totius dominii villae; damus licentuam in ipsa ecclesia et civitate, ob timorem Saracenorum, et propter frequentem incursum iniquorum hominum faciendi turres, munitiones, muros, posterlas et portarum tuitiones, et valles et quaecumque ecclesiae et ipsi civitati novertis expedire.

Concedimus etiam tibi et tuis burgum civitatis ipsius, sicut melius et plenius visus es habere et possidere, et licentuam claudendi muris et vallis atque portalibus. Donamus etiam tibi et tuis successoribus in ipso comitatu pulveraticum, pascurarium, piscaticum tam maris quam stagni et aquae currentis, volatiliaticum, in salinis, theloneis, mercatis, usaticis tam terrae quam aquae lesdis terris cultis et incultis, patuis, viis, stantis aquis aquarumque decursibus, silvis, pratis, et in ipso portu et ripis seu littoribus, in omnibus tertiam partem habendam tam in quaesitis quamque diligenter inquirendis, sicut melius et plenius habes, vel habere debes, ex conantione gloriosissimi Karoli antecessoris nostri, ad petitionem Apollonii comitis olim Dagberto reverrendissimo episcopo Agathensi et successoribus ejus, ex regali munificentia collata.

Jubemus etiam, et regia auctoritate decernimus, ut nullus comes, aut vicecomes, vel nuntius ejus, a clericis vel a laicis vestris in alodio praefatae ecclesiae Sancti Stephani in toto episcopatu Agathensi commorantibus, audeat exigere, albergare, vel petitionem domorum, neque bovariam vel asinariam, neque in pontibus navalibus, seu aliis, usaticum vel censum vel in salinis, neque alicujus tote vel questae, seu aliquam redhibitionis curam infligere, neque inquietare vel distringere neque firmantiam pro aliqua cause, civili vel criminali, ullo modo exigere. Sed tibi, tuisque successoribus pleno jure concedimus potestatem judicariam omnium causarum tam civilium quam etiam criminalium, seu capitalium, earumdem per ministros executionem in omnibus hominibus tuis, et canonicis ejusdem ecclesiae in suis, sine contradictione curiae saecuraris.

Concedimusque tibi, et successoribus tuis, in

from them [royalty]. And since the virtue of the fathers provokes sons not unworthy toward virtue, adhering to the footsteps of our most glorious predecessors, kings of the Franks, and though unequal [to them] in merit, nonetheless standing amazed before our advantageous resources of churches, we wish it known as much now as in the future that to the church of the blessed protomartyr Stephen (Etienne), and to you Guilhem, bishop, for the present, and to your successors, by this authority of our privilege we grant in perpetuity in the city or town of Agde, a church that has been constructed in honor of the blessed protomartyr Stephen, along with a third part of the whole dominion of the town; we give permission within the same church and city, because of fear of the Saracens and because of the frequent incursion of evil men, for the making of towers, fortifications, walls, posterns, and protections of gates, and ditches and whatever you shall have recognized to be helpful to [the defense of] the church and the city itself.

We also concede to you and to yours, the fortress of the city itself so that better and more fully you may have been seen to have and to possess permission for enclosing walls and ditches and also gates. We grant also to you and to your successors in the same county, toll, pasturage, fishing rights, as much of the ocean as in still and running water, bird hunting, salt making, taxes, market rights, easements as much of land as of water, taxes on lands cultivated and uncultivated, pastures, roads, standing waters and coursing water, forests, meadows, and in the port itself, and on banks and shores, in everything a third part to be had as much among acquisitions as things to be carefully requested; so that better and more fully you have and you should have from the undertaking of our most glosious ancestor Charles, at the request of Count Apollonius, on behalf of Dagbert most reverend bishop of Agde, and his successors, of the combined royal estate.

We command also and by royal authority we decree, that from the clergy or from your laypersons dwelling in allod of the said church of Saint-Etienne in the whole bishopric of Agde, no count or viscount or his proxy shall dare to exact [payment], to demand lodging, or tollage of farm buildings, neither for cows nor donkeys, nor usage nor tax on naval bridges or others, or on saltworks, nor of anything of the total aquisition to inflict any change of payment, nor to disturb nor distrain, nor to exact a surety in any cause,

regalibus nostris, stratas, caminos, novas fortias, praecipas illas quae fuerint in ecclesiis vel cimitariis, earumquae domibus et pertinentiis ecclesiarum, et jus prohibendi facere novas fortias in toto episcopatu Agathensi. Donamus insuper et laudamus tibi et tuis successoribus murum, posterlas et turres de Agathe cum fevalibus, et quascumque possessiones, quaecumque bona habes in civitate Agathensi et in territorio ejus et burgo, ex donatione regum, vel principum, et oblatione fidelium, seu aliis justis modis, vel praestante Domine, in futurum poteris adipisci. . . . Praeterea donamus tibi et tuis, ut te vel aliquo successorum tuorum obeunte, nulli comiti vel vicecomiti seu eorum vicariis et nuntiis, bona episcopalia, vel clericorum ecclesiae usurpare liceat, vel ecclesiam tuam, aut domos ecclesias, seu episcopales, turres seu munitiones aliquas aliqua praesumptione invadere, sed liceat canonicis ejusdem loci liberam semper electionem facere sine ulla representatione vel contradictione alicujus saecularis potestatis, sicut plenari tibi et tuis concessa sunt in privilegio Adriani papae.

Praeterea statuimus, et quicumque usque ad hoc tempus loca vel jura monasterii occupaverint, si nulla temporum curricula possit munire, per hanc nostram sanctionem possessionis interuptione facta. Ut autem omnia supradicta, vobis praedictis episcopo, et canonicis et ecclesiae vestrae, firma et semper illibata serventur scripturae nostrae et sigilli regii auctoritate et robore praecipimus communire, super inscripto nominis nostri caractere. Actum publice Parisius, anno Incarnati Verbi MCLXXIII, astantibus in palatio nostro quorum supposita nomine et signa. Signum comitis Theobaldi dapiferi nostri. Signum Mathei camerarii. Signum Guidonis buticularii. Signum Radulfi constabularii, vacante can (*monogramme*) cellaria.

MANUSCRIPT SOURCES

Cartulaire du Chapitre d'Agde (17th-c. copies):
MS. "B," Bibliothèque municipale de Montpellier, ms. 33, no. 3; and MS. "C," Archives départementales de l'Hérault, Reg. G. 20, no. 3.
Cartulaire de l'Evêché d'Agde: Paris, Bibliothèque Nationale, ms. 9999, no. 3.

PRINTED SOURCES

Gallia Christiana, VI (1739), Instrumentum no. 18, col. 328–9.

civil or criminal, by any means. But to you and your successors with full rights we concede judicial power of all cases, as much of civil as also of criminal or capital, and the prosecution of them [the cases] through ministers among all your men and among the canons of that church without contradiction by secular court.

And we grant to you and to your successors, in our royal [authority] the streets, roads, new fortifications, those which shall have been in the churches or cemeteries and in the related buildings of those churches, and the right of prohibiting the making of new fortifications in the whole episcopate of Agde. We give in addition and we approve for you and your successors the wall, posterns, and towers in Agde with its properties and whatever possessions and whatever goods you have in the city of Agde and in its territory and fortification from the granting of kings or of princes, and by offering of the faithful, or by other lawful means, and with the Lord helping you, you will be able to obtain [more] in the future. . . .

Moreover, we grant you and yours, when you or any of your successors die, that it is permitted to no count or viscount or to the proxies and legates of them to usurp episcopal goods or [those] of the clergy of the church, and to invade your church or church buildings or bishop's palace, towers, and any fortifications by any presumption, but it is permitted to the canons of that place always to hold free election without any representation or contradiction of any secular power, just as in full these things have been granted to you by a privilege of Pope Adrian.

Moreover we establish [this], as well as whoever shall have occupied the lands and rights of the monastery up to this moment, if no passage of time may be able to fortify [it], through this our blessing, an interruption in ownership having occurred. So that everything mentioned above be kept whole and undiminished for you the said bishop and canons and your church, we order [it] to be fortified in the strength and authority of our charter and royal seal in addition to the written letters of our name. Enacted officially at Paris, in the year of the Word Incarnate 1173, for those atttending in our palace signs [have been] set in place of the name. Sign of count Theobald our steward. Sign of Matthew the chamberlain. Sign of Guido the butler. Sign of Ralph the constable, while the chancellery (monogram) is unoccupied.

A. Luchaire, *Etude sur les actes de Louis VII* (1885), no. 650 (partial text).

O. Terrin, *Cartulaire du Chapitre d'Agde* (1969), no. 352.

A. Castaldo, *L'Eglise d'Agde* (1970), no. 10.

APPENDIX 25

Second Testament of Guilhem Rainard, canon of Agde (excerpt), 1176–7

In nomine Domini. Anno Incarnationis ejus MCLXXVI. Ego Guillelmus Rainardi viam ingrediens universae carnis, sana memoria et bona voluntate dispono meum testamentum. In primis dono corpus meum et animam meam domino Deo, et beatae Mariae et sancto Stephano ad sepeliendum; et divido operi Sancti Stephani M solidos melgorienses. . . .

In the name of the Lord. In the year of His Incarnation 1176. I, Guilhem Rainard, going the way of all flesh, in healthy memory and good will, arrange my testament. First, I give my body and my soul to the Lord God, and blessed Mary and Saint-Etienne for burial, and I give the share of 1,000 melgorian solidi for the works of Saint-Etienne. . . .

MANUSCRIPT SOURCES

Cartulaire du Chapitre d'Agde (17th-c. copies): MS. "B," Bibliothèque municipale de Montpellier, ms. 33, 23–6; and MS. "C," Archives départementales de l'Hérault, Reg. G. 20, 22–5.

PRINTED SOURCE

O. Terrin, *Cartulaire du Chapitre d'Agde* (1969), no. 19.

APPENDIX 26

Sentence of Bernard, bishop of Béziers and Peter, archdeacon of Narbonne, fixing the jurisdiction of the bishop and chapter of Agde in civil and criminal matters (excerpt), 1236

. . . Creatio autem tabellionum, et praeconisationes, sive erides, recognitio et coertio mansurarum et ponderum, custodis clavium civitatis et burgorum portalium ad episcopum pertinebunt. . . .

. . . The election of notaries, however, and announcements or inheritors, the investigation and enforcement of measures and weights, the guardianship of the keys of the city and of the gates of the fort will obtain to the bishop. . . .

MANUSCRIPT SOURCES

Cartulaire du Chapitre d'Agde (17th-c. copies): MS. "B," Archives départementales de l'Hérault, Reg. G. 20; and MS. "C," Bibliothèque municipale de Montpellier, ms. 23.

PRINTED SOURCES

O. Terrin, *Cartulaire du Chapitre d'Agde* (1969), no. 350.
A. Castaldo, *L'Eglise d'Agde* (1970), no. 25.

APPENDIX 27

Command of King Philip V to inspect the defenses of the city of Agde (excerpt), 1321

Consules et Universitas Civitas agathensis nobis humiliter supplicaverunt ut cum olim tempore guerre Arragonensis civitas ipsa pro magna parte destructa multorum strages habitancium in ea murique ac fortalicia ipsius diruti fuerint per Catalanos habensque non reparatis, eadem civitas cum suis habitatoribus piratarum Catalanorum, Ytalicorum, Sarracenorum, Guibelinorum aliorumque predonum pateat incursibus violenciis invasionibus et rapinis, ne dum in ipsorum scilicet nostrum et locorum vicinorum dicte civitatis ac regni totius grande periculum et terrorem, cum civitas ipsa sit in regni confinibus et maris littore situata, et ad predictorum reparationem civium et habantium dicte civitatis non suppetant facultatem eis ipsam claudendi civitatem ac muros et fortalicia reparandi, concedere licenciam et ad contribuendi in expensis ad hoc necessariis habitatores castrorum et villarum diocese Agathensis et aliorum locorum circumvicinorum. . . . Datum Parisius die XXII octobri anno Domini M CCC vicesimo primo.

The consuls and the united city of Agde have humbly entreated us, since once in the time of the war with Aragón the city itself, in large part destroyed, many residences thrown down, and the walls of the fortifications of it shattered by the Catalans, and not having [resources] for repairs, this same city with its inhabitants lies open to the violent incursions, invasions, and rapine of the pirates of the Catalans, Italians, Saracens, and Ghibellines, and of other looters, lest now into the great danger and terror of ourselves and of places near to the said city and the whole kingdom, since the city itself has been situated at the borders of the kingdom and on the shore of the sea, and toward the reparation of the said citizens and of the inhabitants of that said city, the resources are not available to them for enclosing the same city and for repairing the walls and fortifications, to grant license of incorporating in the expenses necessary to this, to the inhabitants of the castles and villages of the diocese of Agde and of places nearby. . . . Enacted at Paris, on the 12th day of October, in the year of Our Lord 1321.

MANUSCRIPT SOURCE

Agde, Archives municipales, DD: I , 145.

PRINTED SOURCE

A. Castaldo, *Le consulat médiéval d'Agde* (1974), 337–8.

APPENDIX 28

Record of establishment of the Oeuvre Commune (excerpt), 1332

. . . diversis tractatibus . . . et attenta in hac parte evidenti utilitate communi: cum diversa et plura prata . . . situata in territorio dicte ville sint in presenti sterilia seu modicum fertilia; que, si ad culturam . . . redigantur . . . utilitatibus inde provenientibus necessitati dictarum refectionem

[Among] diverse tracts [of land] . . . having been tried in this respect for the evident use of the community: since various and many meadows situated in the territory of the aforesaid town may be barren or scarcely fertile; which, if they were returned to cultivation, could suitably provide for

seu reparationem dictorum murorum et malorum passuum potent comode provideri.

the uses, then for the proceedings necessary for the aforesaid restoration and repair of the aforesaid walls and bad passages.

MANUSCRIPT SOURCE

Agde, Archives Municipales, DD: I, 469.

PRINTED SOURCE

A. Castaldo, *Le consulat médiéval d'Agde* (1974), 344–51.

APPENDIX 29

Letter from King John (Jean le Bon) granting permission for the consuls to elect a "captain" to oversee municipal defense (excerpt), 1362

Johannes, Dei gratia Francorum rex senescallo Carcassonensi vel eius locumtenenti, salutem. Ad supplicationem consulum ville agathensis dicentium quod ipsi formidant ne ad resistentiam plurimorum depredatorum seu inimicorum nostrorum, qui de die in diem per regnum nostrum et specialiter per patriam huiusmodi discurrunt, pro ipsius ville agathensis et omnium in ea habitantium bonorumque suorum tutione et custodia capitaneum constituere, prout alio tempore guerrarum nostrarum factum extitit, oporteat. . . . Datum Nemausi, die XXVIII decembris, anno Domini M CCC sexagesimo secundo.

John, king of the Franks by the grace of God, greetings to the seneschal of Carcassone or his representative. At the request of the consuls of the town of Agde declaring that they are certainly fearful toward the resistance of many looters or of our enemies, who daily overrun our kingdom, and especially the homeland of this sort, for the sake of the defense and guardianship of the same town of Agde and of all the inhabitants and their goods in it, just as it has been done in other time of our wars, may it be fitting to establish a captain. . . . Dated at Nîmes, on the twenty-eighth day of December, in the year of Our Lord 1362.

MANUSCRIPT SOURCE

Agde, Archives Municipales, BB: 17, 169.

PRINTED SOURCE

A. Castaldo, *Le consulat médiéval d'Agde* (1974), 365–6.

SAINT-PONS-DE-THOMIERES

APPENDIX 30

Foundation charter (excerpt), 936

Rege regum Domino, etc. Igitur in Dei nomine ego Pontius gratia Dei comes Tolosanus, primarchio et dux Aquitanorum, et uxor mea Garsindis, propter remedium et salutem animarum nostrarum, ut pium judicem divinum sentiamus placatum in angustiis nostris, cum venerit judicare vivos et mortuos, et pro genitore nostro Raimundo, et genitrice mea, et pro consanguineis nostris et fidelibus nostris omnibus, seu pro salute vivorum et requie omnium defunctorum fidelium damus, et concedimus omnipotenti Deo, et S. genitrici ejus Mariae, et beato Petro apostolorum principi, et S. Paulo doctori egregio, necnon et glorioso martyri Pontio, Thomeriensi monasterio, et domino abbati Otgario, et monachis ejusdem monasterii tam praesentibus quam futuris, videlicet totum allodium et totum potestativum de villa nostra dominicata quae dicitur *Thomieres*, cum ipsa ecclesia quae est fundata in honore S. Martini, cui vocabulum est *de Jauro*, et rebus omnibus pertinentibus . . .

De repetitione vero, quod fiero minime credimus, si nos immutata voluntate nostra, aut ullus de heredibus nostris, aut ulla emissa persona, quae contra hanc nostram donationem ullam calumniam generare conata fuerit, iram Dei incurrat et contra se testem et judicem habeat et sanctos ejus exactores omnes et rei defensores, et sua repetitio nullum effectum obtineat, sed haec praesens donatio firma et inconvulsa permaneat omni tempore cum stipulatione subnixa. Facta donatio ista in mense Nov. anno DCCC-CXXXVI, Dominicae Incarnationis, primo anno Ludovico rege sedem ejus regni gubernante. Signum Pontii marchionis qui hanc donationem fieri aut affirmare rogavit. Sign. Garsindis uxoris ejus consentientis. S. Ragauberti. S. Vidimi. S. Altoni. S. Malfredi. S. Raimundi.. S. de Agberto. S. Aimeriti. S. Odonis. S. Atrio. S. et Guillelmus qui hanc chartam scripsit rogatus.

PUBLISHED SOURCE

Gallia Christiana, 6, 77–8.

In the reign of the Lord of Kings, etc. Thus in the name of God, I Pons, count of Toulouse, by the grace of God, great lord and leader of Aquitaine, and my wife Garsinde, for the salvation and health of our souls, so that we, in our distress, may be able to consider the pious divine judge [to be] pleased when he shall come to judge the living and the dead, and for our father Raymond and my mother, and for our relatives and all our faithful, whether we give [this] for the salvation of the living or the burial of all the faithful dead, and we concede to the Almighty God, and Holy Mary his mother, and Saint Peter, chief of the Apostles, and Saint Paul, outstanding doctor, and also to the glorious martyr Pons, to the monastery of Thomières, and the Lord Abbot Otger, and the monks of that monastery as much [to those] present as future, clearly all allods and our entire dominion of our lordly town called Thomières, with that church which has been founded in honor of Saint Martin, to which name is "of the Jaur [river]" and all the things pertaining to it: (here follows a list of properties given to the monastery) . . .

Out of sincere urging, if we ourselves with our unchanging wish (which we believe will not happen), or any of our successors, or any other person sent [by them], will have attempted to generate any calumny against our gift, may it incur the wrath of God, and may he have against himself as witness and judge all the holy judges and defenders of property, and may his prayer receive no effect, but may this present gift be maintained for all time with this stipulation effected. This gift was made in the month of November in the year 936, of the Incarnation of the Lord, in the first year with king Louis governing the seat of his kingdom. Sign of Pons, marquis, who requests that this donation be made [and] affirmed it. Sign of Garsinde his wife, consenting [to it]. Sign of Ragaubert. Sign of Vidimus. Sign of Altonus. Sign of Malfredus. Sign of Raymund. Sign of Agbert. Sign of Aimeric. Sign of Odo. Sign of Atrius. And the sign of Guilhem who, having been asked, wrote this charter.

APPENDIX 31

Letter from "A," prior of Saint-Pons-de-Thomières, to Louis VII (excerpt), c. 1164.

Domino suo Ludovico, Dei gratia pi[usi]ssimo Francorum Regi, A. Tom[eriensis] ecclesiae prior, et universus simul conventus, quicquid in hoc saeculo felicius, et in futuro gloriosius. Diu est quod ecclesia nostra capite languido gravaminum patitur incommoda; et nisi regia manus subveniat, ultra non adjiciet ut resurgat. Duobus praecipue malis affligitur, immoderato scilicet debitorum gravamine, et pastoris desolatione. Nam, nobis inconsultis discedens, quid acturus sit ignoramus. Rogamus igitur regiam majestatem vestram, qui post Deum nullum alium praeter vos speramus solatium, ut ad dominum Papam pro nobis clametis, et legatis nostris prout necesse fuerit subveniatis, ecclesiaeque vestrae penitus destructae consilii et auxilii manum celerius porrigatis.

PRINTED SOURCE

Recueil des Historiens des Gaules et de la France, 16 (1814), no. 349, 114.

To his Lord Louis, by the grace of God most pious king of the Franks. "A," prior of the church of Thomières, having collected and also assembled whatever [may be] happier in this life and more glorious in the next. Long is it that our church with weary head suffers the burdens of grievances; and unless the royal hand assists [it], it will not increase farther so that it may rise again. By two evils in particular is it afflicted: namely, by an immoderate burden of debts and by the absence of our shepherd. For, departing from us who are unadvised, what he is about to do we do not know. Therefore, we beg your royal majesty, we who hope for no other help besides you after God, that you might appeal to the Lord Pope on our behalf, and that you might ask our ambassadors just as it will have been necessary and you might more swiftly stretch forth the hand of help and advice to our deeply wounded church.

APPENDIX 32

Charter of arbitrated peace between Roger Trencavel and Raymond, abbot of Saint-Pons, 1171.

In nomine domini Jesu anno ab ejus Incarnatione MCLXXI. Notum fit omnibus, ad quorum auditum ista devenerint, quod dominus Raimundus abbas sancti Pontii, et Rogerius illustris vicecomes Bitterensis convenerunt apud Bitterim, et compromiserunt quod de querimoniis, quas adversum se proponebant, sine contradictione facerent, quod dominus Pontius Narbonensis archiepiscopus, et Bernardus Biterrensis, et Wilhermus Albiensis episcopus dictarent, cum Petro Carcassensi, et Petro Narbonensi archidiaconis, et Ifarno Jordane, Petro de Laurano, Petro Raimundi de Altopullo, Wilhermo de sancto Felice vicario Carcassense, Pontio de Beciano vicario Biterrensi, Pontio de villari vicario Reddense, Bernardo de Cencennone, et Ugo de Romegons.

Conquerebatur enim praelibatus abbas de Rogerio vicecomite, quia multa mala intulerat monasterio S. Pontii, villam ipsius monasterii occasione armorum destruendo, et ipsum monasterium ad redemptionem triginta millium solido-

In the name of the Lord Jesus in the 1171 year from His Incarnation. Be it known to all to whose hearing these things shall have reached: that the Lord Raymond, abbot of Saint Pons, and Roger, famed viscount of Béziers have met at Béziers and compromised regarding the complaints they brought against each other, without objection they shall perform what Lord Pons, archbishop of Narbonne, and Bernard of Béziers and Guilhem bishop of Albi shall dictate, along with Peter of Carcassonne and Peter, archdeacon of Narbonne; and Ifarno Jordan; Peter of Laurano; Peter Raimund of Altopullo; Guilhem of Saint Felice, vicar of Carcasonne; Pons of Beciano, vicar of Béziers; Pons of Villari, vicar of Reddense; Berbard of Cencennone; and Ugo of Romegons.

For the aforesaid abbot complained about Viscount Roger because he had brought many evils upon the monastery of Saint Pons, by destroying the estate of the same monastery, by attack of arms and with his army, by compelling the

rum cum exercitu suo cogendo. Rogerius autem praelibatus vicecomes adversus abbatem questionem proponebat de quadam forcia, munitione, sive castro, quod dicitur Salvetat, quam juxta terram suam contra voluntatem patris sui fecerat, et adhuc faciebat: post multas autem allegationes ex utraque parte dictas, praefati auditores inter jam dictum abbatem, et praememoratum Rogerium pacis compositionem fieri condixerunt.

Ego igitur Raimundus praememorati monasterii abbas ex admonitione, et instinctu supraedictorum assessorum, per me et omnes successores meos, assensu et convenientia totius capituli S. Pontii, absolvo te dominium Rogerium vicecomitem Biterrensem, et omnes coadjutores tuos de omnibus malefactis, quas mihi in redemptione monasterii, et hominum ejusdem monasterii depraeditiones violenter fecisti, et promitto tibi saepe dicto Rogerio, sicut nobili viro et monasterio S. Pontii, et mihi per sacramentum adstricto, quod ab hac hora inantea te diligam, custodiam, et in bonis actibus tuis confervem fideliter.

Et ego similiter saepe dictus Rogerius poenitens, quod tanta mala praefato monasterio intulerim, per fidem et sine enganno absolvo et sustineo, promitto tibi Raimundo abbati S. Pontii, et successoribus tuis in perpetuum, et ut sine querela et contradictione mea meorumque successorum habeas deinceps et possideas in pace castrum, seu munitionem, quam Salvetat vocant, et pro voluntate tua tu et successores tui aedifices ibi et construas.

Et ego jam dictus abbas concedo tibi Rogerio, et tuis in perpetuum, et dono, et laudo ad feudum cum ceteris feudis, quae a monasterio S. Pontii habes et possides, albergum scilicet quinquaginta equitantibus, vel 50. solidorum Melgorensium, quod ego magis voluero singulis annis, et si tu vel nuntius tuus semel in anno praefatum censum accipere neglexeritis, ad alium annum census ille nullo modo debeat transferri. Hoc autem concedo tibi in loco, et pro loco illo, quem Salvetat vocant, ut castrum cum habitatoribus suis manuteneas et defendas, et ab hominibus tuis nullo modo verbari permittas; et si de castris, vel de terra tua aliquod malum, vel guerra saepe dicto castro advenerit, liceat hominibus de castro, et modo et successoribus meis pro viribus resisterer, et de malefactis pro posse vindicare; et si homines tuos proprios ibi habitare contigerit, servient pro voluntate tua, vel infra triginta dies a potestate mea eos penitus absolvam, et ego inde saepe dictus abbas accipio te Rogerium in Dei fide, et mea, et volo et jubeo, quod sacrista et cel-

monastery to a ransom of 30,000 solidi. Roger, however, the aforesaid viscount, brought suit against the abbot concerning a certain fort, garrison, or castle, which is called Salvetat, which he had built along his property against the wish of his father, and was building until now: but after many allegations reiterated by either party, the aforesaid delegates have arranged that a reconciliation of peace occur between the aforenamed abbot and aforesaid Roger.

Therefore I, Raymond, abbot of the aforesaid monastery, at the reproach and prompting of the said assessors, by myself and all my successors, with the assent and agreement of the whole chapter of Saint Pons, absolve you, Lord Roger, viscount of Béziers, and all your accomplices in evil deeds, which plunderings you have committed violently against me in the ransoming of the monastery and of the men of the monastery, and I promise to you the oft-said Roger, as to a noble man, and with the monastery of Saint-Pons having been bound by me upon the sacrament, that from this hour forward, I shall cherish, I shall protect, and toward your worthy undertaking I shall be steadfastly enthusiastic.

And I similarly, the often-named Roger, penitent that I have brought such troubles upon the monastery, upon oath and without fraud discharge and uphold and promise to you Raymond, abbot of Saint Pons, and all of your successors, in perpetuity, that without my or my successors challenge or objection, you may henceforth possess in peace the castle or fortress called Salvetat, and that you and your successors may build and fortify there at your will.

And now I the already mentioned abbot concede to you, Roger, and to yours in perpetuity, and I grant and I approve for a fief along with other fiefs you hold and possess from the monastery of Saint-Pons, namely, lodging for 50 cavalry or 50 melgorian solidi, which I shall have maintained even more in successive years, and even if you or your proxy in any year shall have neglected to collect the said rent, that rent should in no way be transferred to another year. This moreover I concede to you in this place, and for that place they call Salvetat, that the castle with its inhabitants you may take in hand and defend, and allow to be harrassed in no way by your men; and if from the castles or from your land any trouble or fighting to the oft-named castle shall have come, it may be permitted to the men of the castle both now and to my successors to

larius S. Pontii jurent super sancta quattuor evangelia, quod de praedicto castro de la Salvetat non faciam tibi guerram, nec aliquis mea arte, vel meo consilio, et si aliquod malefactum tibi vel tuis propriis hominibus praefato jam dicto castro, nisi pro sua defensione, factum fuerit, infra quadraginta dies sine diminutione, et sine poena emendetur; adhuc et ego Raimundus saepe et dictus abbas volens haec omnia, quae in hoc instrumento continentur, firma et rata omni tempore permanere, dono tibi Rogerio duo milia solidorum Melgorum;

et ego Rogerius volo, absolvo, promitto per me et per omnes successores meos, et cum hac charta in perpetuum laudo, ut monasterium S. Pontii cum omnibus officinis suis aedificitur, firmetur, construatur, et ad majorem munitionem, sicut melius poterit, claudatur, ita ut infra claustrum monasterii nulli alii homines praeter abbatem, monachos, fratres, cum familia sua habitionem habeant: et ego Rogerius vicecomes Biterrensis haec omnia superius me observaturum promitto, et sicut in hujus instrumenti serie continentur, per haec sancta quatuor evangelia observabo, et volo et jubeo, et obligo heredes meos ad hoc idem sacramentum abbati S. Pontii in perpetuum, nullo propter hoc munere, vel pecunia exigenda;

et ego Raimundus abbas praedictus volo et statuo per me, et per omnes successores meos, et super mandamento, abbatis jurent sacrista et cellarius S. Pontii, et faciant sacramentum simile superiori tibi Rogerio vicecomiti praedicto, et successoribus tuis. Factum fuit hoc totum secundo nonas Januarii feria secunda regnante Ludovico rege in Francia, et domino Alexandro Romae praesidente, in praesentia supradictorum.

PRINTED SOURCE

Gallia Christiana, VI (1739), Instrumentum no. 11, cols. 84–5.

resist in force, and to protect [it] from the transgressions with troops; and if it should happen that your men live there, they shall serve at your will and within 30 days I shall release them completely from my command, and next I, the oft-named abbot welcome you, Roger, on the honor of God and mine and I intend and command that the sacristan and cellarer of Saint-Pons swear upon the four Holy Gospels that concerning the aforesaid castle of la Salvetat I shall not make war on you, nor shall any other by my means or my advice, and if any crime upon you or your own men by the already named and noted castle, unless for the sake of its defense, shall have been committed, within 40 days without loss and without fine let it be corrected; in addition, I, the aforenamed Raymond, intending that all these things which are contained in this instrument remain confirmed and approved for all time, give to you, Roger, 2,000 melgorian solidi;

And I, Roger, intend, discharge, and swear by myself and all my successors, and with this charter in perpetuity I approve, that the monastery of Saint Pons with all its claustral buildings be improved, strengthened, modified, and, for its greater fortification so that it will be better able, enclosed so that within the cloister of the monastery no other men except the abbot, monks, and brothers and serfs shall have their residence; and I, Roger, viscount of Béziers, promise that I shall observe all the above and just as they are contained in the order of this instrument, by these four Holy Gospels I will abide and I intend and I command and I obligate my heirs on this same oath for the abbey of Saint Pons with no tribute to be paid after this or money to be paid;

And I, Raymond, the aforesaid abbot, maintain and determine by myself and by all my successors and by the above notification that the sacristan and cellarer of the abbot of Saint-Pons shall swear and make an oath similar to the one above for you, Roger, the said viscount, and your successors.

This has all been done on the second [day before] the nones of January (January 6), on the second day of the week (Monday), with King Louis reigning in France, and Lord Alexander presiding at Rome, in the presence of all those listed above.

APPENDIX 33

Livre des Libertés et Franchises (excerpt),
14th century

... coma las murailhas de Sanct Pons et los portalz et cavas aguessan mestier de reparatio ... de par lo Rey ... a commandar al sendix et habitans de la viala de Sanct Pons sus pena de corps ... a far los d mandamens. ...

When the ramparts of Saint-Pons and its gates and cellars begin to need repair ... by command of the King, the syndics and inhabitants of the town of Saint-Pons are held under mortal threat ... to effect said repairs. ...

PRINTED SOURCES

G. Gros, ed., *Lo libre de las libertats et franquesas de la villa et civitat de Sanct Pons* (1881).
J. Sahuc *Saint-Pons: ses vieux édifices; ses anciennes institutions* (1895), 10.

CHURCH COUNCILS

APPENDIX 34

Council of Toulouges/Elne (excerpt), 1041

Haec est pax confirmata ab episcopis, et abbatibus, et comitibus, nec non vicecomitibus, et caeteris magnantibus Deum timentibus, in episcopatu illo, videlicet ut ab ista die et deinceps nullus homo ecclesiam non infringat, necque spatium, necque coemeterium, nec mansiones quae in circuitu ecclesiae sunt aut erunt, usque ad XXX ecclesiasticos passus.

Ecclesias autem illas in hac defensione non ponimus, in quibus castella facta sunt aut erunt: eas vero ecclesias in quibus raptores vel fures praedam vel furta congregaverunt, vel malefaciendo inde exierunt, aut illuc redierunt, tamen salvas esse jubemus, donec querimonia malefacti ad episcopum illius aut ad sedem et conventum canonicorum ejusdem sedis prius perveniat. ...

Item placuit ut clericos qui arma non portaverit, aut monachos, seu sanctimoniales ullus homo invaserit necque injuriam faciat eis, vel aliqua malefacta.

This is the peace confirmed by the bishops and abbots and counts, indeed also viscounts and others greatly fearing God in that bishopric, namely, that from this day and henceforth, no man shall infringe upon a church, nor space, nor cemetery, nor dwellings which are or will be in the circuit of the church, up to 30 ecclesiastical paces.

We do not place those churches, however, under this protection, in which castles have been or will be made: indeed, those churches in which robbers or thieves have gathered booty or spoils, or dwell there for wrongdoing, and return from it; we nevertheless order to be unharmed, until complaint of crime should reach the bishop of it or the see and convent of canons of its seat.

Also it has pleased [us] that clerics who shall not have carried arms, nor monks, even if any man invades, nor should [they] do injury to them, or any crime.

PRINTED SOURCES

P. de Marca, *Marca Hispanica sive limes hispanicus* (1688), col. 1138ff.
Recueil des Historiens de la France, 11, n.ed. (1876), 510.
C. DeVic and J.J. Vaissette, *Histoire de Languedoc*, 5 (1875), no. 186, cols. 442–5.
V. Mortet, *Recueil des textes relatifs à l'histoire de l'architecture*, I (1911), 113–14 (excerpt).

APPENDIX 35

Council of Saint-Gilles (excerpt), 1042–3

Ecclesias autem quae intra castellum aut civitatem fundatae fuerint, aut in villis, aut in agris, illae videlicet in quibus aedificium ad debellandum non habetur, vel cum quibus seditio non exercetur, nec malefactorum excursus ad reparanda damna civilia vel communia fieri comprobatur, hanc pari consensu volunt et definiunt habere potestatem, ut nemo infra terminum XXX dextrorum circa ecclesias positum quicquam rapere praesumat, nec ulli personae nocenti aut innocenti malum ingerat, nisi cum ipso termino malefactor damnum intulerit.

It is approved to those churches, however, which have been founded within the castle or in the city, either in towns or in fields, those, namely, in which no edifice for making war may be had, and with whom no treachery is exercised, nor existings of criminals for renewing civil or communal crimes, this power they wish and define to have, that no one may presume to have power, so that no one placed anywhere within the limit placed around the churches of 30 right-foot [paces], nor upon any harmful or harmless person may bring harm, unless, with the boundary itself the criminal bring harm.

PRINTED SOURCES

Recueil des Historiens de la France, 11 (1876), 513.
V. Mortet, *Recueil des textes relatifs à l'histoire de l'architecture*, I (1911), 116–17 (excerpt).

APPENDIX 36

Council of Narbonne (excerpt), 1054

Anno Dominicae incarnationis MLIV. Iterum mandamus atque confirmavus ipsam treugam Dei, quae a nobis dudum constituta fuerat, et nunc a pravis hominibus disrupta esse videtur. . . .

Pacem autem a nobis sive a principibus olim constitutam, mandamus, sive firmavus ut ab hodierna die et deinceps ecclesiam nullus hominum infringat; neque mansiones quae in circuitu ecclesiarum sunt et erunt; neque aliquid ex omnibus quae infra XXX passus sunt ecclesiae et erunt, violenter auserre audeat, aut praesumeri nisi episcopus, aut cui ipsi jusseret, propter suum censum, aut propter hominem excommunicatum: excepta munitione, quae infra praedictos passus XXX ecclesiae sita fuerit ad concitandum bella et conteniones.

In the year of the incarnation of Our Lord 1054. Again we enjoin and confirm this truce of God, which had long been established by us and now is seen to be disrupted by evil men. . . .

The peace once constituted, however, by us and by princes, we enjoin or confirm, that from this day and henceforth no [one of] men may infringe upon the church; nor the dwellings that are or will be in the circuit of the churches, nor anything from all things which are or will be within 30 paces of the church, may he dare to appropriate or to occupy, unless a bishop had ordered him, because of revenue or because of [being] an excommunicated man; the garrison excepted, which will have been situated within the said 30 paces for conducting battles and dispute.

PRINTED SOURCE

J.D. Mansi, *Sacrorum conciliorum collectio,* 19 (1774), cols. 827–32.

APPENDIX 37

Council of Toulouges/Elne (excerpt), 1065

Haec est treuga et pax confirmata ab archiepiscopo Narbonensi. . . . ullus homo ecclesiam non

This is the truce and peace confirmed by the archibishop of Narbonne. . . . Any man may not

infringat, necque cimeteria, vel sacraria, XXX passuum ecclesiasticorum in circuitu uniuscuiusque ecclesiae, nisi episcopus propter hominem excommunicatum, aut propter suum censum. Si vero aliquis homo aliter infringit ecclesiam, vel spatium XXX passuum ipsius ecclesiae in praedicto episcopatu Helensi: quidquid ei commiserit emendet ut justum fuerit ipsi homini cui injuriam fecerit, et ecclesiae, in quae fecerit satisfaciat legaliter: et insuper compositionem sacrilegit Helensi componat episcopo.

Ecclesias vero illas ubi castra fuerint constructa, sive ubi fures vel rapaces congregaverunt furta vel praedam vel malefacta, tamdiu posuerunt eas jam dicti episcopi in defensione praescriptae pacis. . . .

infringe upon a church, nor cemeteries, nor shrine [within] 30 ecclesiastical paces in a circle of every church, unless a bishop because of an excommunicated man, or because of his own tribute. If indeed any man otherwise infringes upon a church or a space of 30 paces of the same church the said bishopric of Helensus: whatever he shall have committed in it, may he make amends so that it will have been fair to the man to whom he made injury, and to the church in which he committed [it] may he make satisfaction legally: and in addition he shall pay the fine of sacrilege to Bishop Helensus.

Those churches truly in which castles have been built, or where thieves or robbers gather to hide, or pillage or for evildoing, so long as they are there, the aforesaid bishops hold them to be in defiance of the prescribed peace. . . .

PRINTED SOURCES

J.D. Mansi, *Sacrorum conciliorum collectio*, 19 (1774), cols. 1041–4.

V. Mortet, *Recueil des textes relatifs à l'histoire de l'architecture*, I (1911), 115–16 (excerpt).

APPENDIX 38

First Lateran Council (excerpt), 1123

Statute XIV: Sanctorum patrum canonibus consona sentientes, oblationes de sacramentissimo et reverendissimo altari beati Petri et Salvatoris et Sanctae Mariae Rotundae, ac de aliis omnium ecclesiarum alteribus sive crucibus a laicis auferri penitus interdicimus, et sub anathematis districtione prohibemus. Ecclesias a laicis incastellari aut in servitutem redigi auctoritate apostolica prohibemus.

Following the canons of the Holy Fathers, we absolutely forbid that offerings from the most holy and reverend altar of the blessed Peter and of the Savior and of Saint Mary Rotunda and from other altars or crosses of all churches be removed by laypersons and we prohibit this under penalty of anathema. We also prohibit by Apostolic authority that churches be fortified by laypersons or converted to profane use [impressed into service to a lord].

PRINTED SOURCES

J.D. Mansi, *Sacrorum conciliorum collectio*, 21 (1776), col. 285.

V. Mortet, *Recueil des textes relatifs à l'histoire de l'architecture*, I (1911), 364.

C.H. Hefele and H. Leclerq, *Histoire des conciles* (1913), Vol. 5, 631–8

H.J. Schroeder, *Disciplinary Decrees of the General Councils* (1937), 188/543.

APPENDIX 39

Third Lateran Council, 1179

Statute 24: Ita quorumdam animos occupavit saeva cupiditas, ut cum glorientur nomine chris-

Cruel greed has so seized the minds of some that, when they might glory in the Christian name,

tiano, Saracenis arma, ferrum et lignamina galearum deferant, et pares eis, aut etiam superiores in malitia fiant, dum ad impugnandos christianos, arma eis et necessaria subministrant. Sunt etiam qui pro sua cupiditate in galeis et piraticis Saracenorum navibus regimen et curam gubernationis exercent. Tales igitur a communione ecclesiae praecisos, et excommunicationi pro sua iniquitate subjectos, et rerum suarum per saecula principes catholicos et consules civitatum, privatione mulctari, et capientium servos, si capti fuerint, fore censemus. Praecipimus etiam, ut per ecclesias maritimarum urbium crebra et solemnis excommunicatio preferatur in eos. Excommunicationis quoque poena subdantur, qui Romanos aut alios christianos pro negotione vel aliis causis honestis navigio vectos aut capere aut rebus suis spoliare praesumunt. Illi etiam qui christianos naufragia patentes, quibus secundum regulam fidei auxilio esse tenentur, damnanda, cupiditate rebus sui spoliare, praesumunt, nisi ablata reddiderint, excommunicationi se noverint subjacere.

they supply the Saracens with arms, iron, and the timber for galleys, and become equal to them or even superior in malice, since they furnish them with arms and other supplies for attacking Christians. There are even those who for their greed undertake piloting and the work of navigation in the galleys and piratical ships of the Saracens. We decree, therefore, that such persons are cut off from the communion of the church and subject to excommunication for their iniquity, [and are] to be punished forever with removal of their possessions by the catholic princes and magistrates of the cities and, if captured, be the slaves of their captors. We instruct also that frequent and solemn excommunication be preferred against them throughout all the churches of the maritime cities. They also are to be punished by excommunication who dare to capture or rob of their possessions Roman or other Christians carried on vessels on matters of business or other honest purposes. And those also who, by damnable greed, rob shipwrecked Christians instead of rendering aid as the rule of faith requires, shall be themselves subject to excommunication if they do not restore the things taken.

PRINTED SOURCES

J.D. Mansi, *Sacrorum conciliorum collectio*, 22 (1778), cols. 230–2.

H.J. Schroeder, *Disciplinary Decrees of the General Councils* (1937), 234–5; 558–9.

APPENDIX 40

Third Lateran Council (excerpt), 1179

Statute 27: Sicut ait beatus Leo, licet ecclesiastica disciplina sacerdotali contenta judicio cruentas non efficiat ultiones catholicorum tamen principum constitutionibus adjuvatur, ut saepe quaerant homines salutare remedium, dum corporale super se metuunt evenire supplicium. Ea propter, quia in Gasconia, Albegesio, et partibus Tolosanis, et aliis locis, ita haereticorum, qous alii Catharos, alii Patrinos, alii Publicanos, alii aliis nominibus vocant, invaluit damnata perversitas, ut jam non in occulto, sicut aliqui, sensum simplices attrahant et infirmos; eos et defensores eorum, et receptores anathemati decernimus subjacere; et sub anathemate prohibemus, ne quis eos in dominibus vel in terra sua tenere, vel fovere vel negotiationem cum eis exercere praesumat. Si autem in hoc peccato decesserint, non sub nostrorum privilegiorum cuilibet indultorum obtentu, nec sub aliacumque occasione, aut obla-

Just as the blessed Leo said, although ecclesiastical discipline content with religious judgment does not inflict bloody vengeances, it is, however, aided by the ordinances of catholic princes, for men often seek a wholesome cure for their souls as long as they fear that some severe corporal punishment may befall them. On account of these things, since in Gascony, in the area of Albi, in the territory of Toulouse, and in other places, the damned perversity of the heretics, whom some call Cathars, others Patarenes, others again Publicans, and others by other names, has grown so strong that no longer in secret as some [do], they attract the simple and the weak; that they, their defenders and supporters are subject to anathema we resolve, and we forbid under anathema anyone to presume to keep them in his residence, or on his land, or to aid or transact business with them. However, if they would have died in this sin, not

tio fiat pro eis, aut inter christianos recipiant sepulturam.

De Brabancionibus, et Aragonensibus, Navariis, Bascolis, Coterellis, et Triaverdinis, qui tantam in christianos immanitatem exercent, ut nec ecclesiis nec Monasteriis deferant, non viduis et pupillis, non senibus et pueris, nec cuilibet parcant aetati aut sexui, sed more paganorum, omnia perdant et vastent; similiter constituimus, ut qui eos conduxerint, vel tenuerint, vel foverint, per regiones, in quibus taliter debacchantur, in dominicis et aliis solemnibus diebus per ecclesias publice denuncientur, et eadem omnino sententia et poena cum praedictis haereticis habeantur adstricti, nec ad communionem recipiantur ecclesiae, nisi societate illa pestifera et haeresi abjuratis.

Relaxatos autem se noverint a debito fidelitatis et hominii, ac totius obsequii, donec in tanta iniquitate permanserint, quicumque illis aliquo peccato tenetur annexi. Ipsis autem, cunctisque fidelibus in remissionem peccatorum injungimus, ut tantis cladibus se viriliter opponant, et contra eos armis populum christianum tueantur. Confiscenturque eorum bona, et liberum sit principibus, hujusmodi homines subjicere servituti. Qui autem in vera poenitentia ibi decesserint, et peccatorum indulgentiam, et fructum mercedis aeternae se non dubitent percepturos. Nos etiam de misericordia Dei, et beatorum apostolorum Petri et Pauli auctoritate confisi, fidelibus christianis, qui contra eos arma susceperint, et ad episcoporum, seu aliorum praelatorum consilium ad eos decertando expugnandos, biennium de poenitentia injuncta relaxamus; aut si longiorem ibi moram habuerint, episcoporum discretioni, quibus hujus rei causa fuerit injuncta, committimus, ut ad eorum arbitrium, secundum modum laboris major eis indulgentia tribuator. Illos autem, qui admonitioni episcoporum in hujuscemodi parte parere contempserunt, a perceptione corporis et sanguinis Domini jubemus fieri alienos. Interim vero eos, qui ardore fidei ad eos expugnandum, laborem justum assumpserint, sicut eos, qui sepulchrum dominicum visitant, sub ecclesiae defensione recipimus et ab universis inquietationibus, tam in rebus, quam in personis, statuimus manere securos. Si vero quispiam vestrum praesumpserit eos molestare, per episcopum loci excommunicationis sententia feriatur; et tamdiu sententia servetur ab omnibus, donec et ablata reddantur, et de illatis damnis congrue iterum satisfaciat. Episcopi vero, sive presbyteri, qui talibus fortiter non restiterint, officii sui privatione mul-

under any protection of the pardoners of our [area of] privileges, nor under any other circumstance, shall either an offering be made for them or shall they receive burial among Christians.

Concerning the Brabantians, Aragonese, Navarese, Basques, Coterelles, and Triaverdans, who practice such enormity upon Christians that they would defer neither to churches nor to monasteries, nor to widows or children, nor to old men or boys, nor would they spare any age or sex, but in the manner of pagans would ruin and destroy everything, similarly we decree that those who would have employed them or shall have kept them throughout the regions in which they rave so madly, shall be publicly denounced on Sundays and on other days throughout the churches and shall be held subject to exactly the same sentence and punishment as the aforesaid heretics; nor shall they be received in the communion of the church unless that pestiferous society and its heresy have been abjured.

However, they shall consider themselves released from the obligations of fealty and homage, and of their whole allegiance also, so long as they [the heretics] shall persist in their iniquity, whoever is bound to them by any fault. Upon these, however, and upon all the faithful in remission of sins we enjoin that they might courageously oppose themselves to such scourges, and that they might protect the Christian people. Let their possessions be confiscated and let it be free to princes to subject men of this kind to vassalage. Those, however, who shall have died in true repentence there, let them not doubt that they will receive the remission of their sins and the fruit of eternal reward. We also, trusting in the mercy of God and in the authority of the blessed apostles Peter and Paul, for the faithful Christians who take up arms against them and, at the advice of the bishops or other prelates, by struggling to fight them, we relax the injunctions of penance for a period of two years; or if they are engaged there for a longer period, we commit the injunctions to the discretion of the bishops, to whom the care of this matter has been committed, that at their decision according to the character of the effort a greater indulgence may be granted. Those, however, who have scorned to comply with the admonition of the bishops in this matter, we order to become strangers to the reception of the body and blood of the Lord. Meanwhile, indeed, those who in the ardor of faith for battling them would have taken up a just

centur, donec misericordiam apostolicae sedis obtineant.

PRINTED SOURCES

J.D. Mansi, *Sacrorum conciliorum collectio*, 22 (1778), cols. 230-2.

H.J. Schroeder, *Disciplinary Decrees of the General Councils* (1937), 234-5; 558-9.

cause, like those who visit a royal tomb, we receive under protection of the church, and we order that they remain secure from all disturbances as much in their possessions as in their persons. If, indeed, anyone of you would have presumed to molest them, may he be stricken with excommunication by the bishop of the area and let the sentence be observed by all until the things taken be returned, and suitable satisfaction made for the injurious thefts. Indeed, bishops or priests who would not bravely have stood firm in such matters shall be deprived of their office until they have obtained mercy from the Apostolic See.

APPENDIX 41

Council of Avignon (excerpt), 1209

In nomine Domini, anno Incarnationis eiusdem millesimo ducentesimo nono, pontificatus domini Innocenti papae III, anno XII octavo id. septembris. Haec quae sequuntur, statuta fuerunt apud Avenionem in concilio generali sub Hugone Regiensi episcopo . . .

Caput IX: Propter abominationes quas vidimus et intelligimus ab illis, qui ecclesias incastellanda, domus Domini convertunt in speluncam latronam, aliquid severius constituimus contra hujusmodi praesumptores: sub anathematis poena districtissime inhibentes, ne quis ulterius, nisi forte ad repellendam instantiam paganorum, aliquam ecclesiam incastellare praesumat et attentet; immo incastellatas videlicet totam incastellaturam, et quidquid infra cimiterium aedificatum est, ad arbitrium dioecesanorum episcoporum quam celerius poterunt ad diruendum jubemus, praeter illam vel illas quas ad tuitionem parochianorum episcopis visum fuerit reservari; quae perpetuo possideantur ab eis, vel aliis personis ecclesiasticis teneantur. Si forte aliquis temerarius et violentus detentor, ecclesiam incastellatam ad mandatum sui episcopi noluit diruere, vel ei noluerit tradere possidendam: nominatim excommunicationis vinculo percellatur, et interdicti sententia supponatur tota terra ipsius.

In the name of the Lord, in the year of His Incarnation 1209 of the pontificate of Pope Innocent III, in the twelfth year, on the eighth hour of the ides of September (at eight o'clock on September 13). These things which follow have been established at Avignon in the general council [held] under Bishop Hugh Regiensus.

Statute 9: On account of the abominations which we see and understand by those who, in fortifying churches, turn the house of the Lord into a den of thieves, we declare something severe against expropriators of this sort: forbidding most strictly under pain of anathema, lest anyone further, unless by chance for repelling an attack of pagans, may presume or attempt to fortify any church; on the contrary, those fortified, namely, the entire fortification, and whatever has been built within a cemetery, at the judgment of the diocescan bishops, we appoint for immediate dismantlement, except that or those which may have been seen by bishops to be reserved for the defense of parishes, which may be possessed in perpetuity by them, or which may be held by other ecclesiastical persons. If perhaps a daring or violent person has refused to demolish the fortified church at the order of his bishop, or has refused to surrender possession [of it], let him be stricken with the chain of excommunication, and may his entire land be placed under sentence of interdiction.

PRINTED SOURCES

J.D. Mansi, *Sacrorum conciliorum collectio*, 22 (1778), cols. 783-98.

V. Mortet and P. Deschamps, *Recueil des textes relatifs à l'histoire de l'architecture*, II (1929), 210-11 (excerpt).

TABLES

TABLE 1: Regnal Dates for the Abbot-Bishops of Maguelone and Agde, and the Abbots of Saint-Pons-de-Thomières.

(The following regnal dates have been reconstructed from cartulary evidence, where available. In many cases, the exact dates are not possible to confirm.)

Abbot-Bishops of Maguelone

NAME OF BISHOP	CORRECTED DATES	DATES GIVEN (IN CATALOGUS)	FAMILY
Pierre de Melgeuil	999–1030	———	counts of Melgeuil
Arnaud	1032–60	1048–78	
Bertrand	1060–80	1078–80	
Godfrey	1080–1104	1080–1108	
Galtier	1104–28	1110–33	
Raymond	1129–58	1133–66	
Jean II de Montlaur	1159–90	(1158)–86	lords of Montlaur
Guilhem Raymond	1190–95		Guilhem, lords of Montpellier?
Guilhem de Fleix	1195–1202		

Abbot-Bishops of Agde

NAME OF BISHOP	DATES	FAMILY
Bérengar I	1068–93	
Bernard Deodat	1099–1122	lords of Pouzzoles
Aldebert	1122–30	
Raymond de Montredon	1130–43	
Ermengaud de Marseillan	1144–9	Marseillan family
Berengar II	1149–52	Soubeiras family
Pons de Montmirat	1152–3	
Adhémar	1153–62	
Guilhem de Minerve	1162–73	viscounts of Minerve
Pierre de Montpeyroux	1173–94	lords of Montpeyroux
Raymond Guilhem de Montpellier	1194–1213	Guilhem, lords of Montpellier
Pierre de Pulvérel	1215	
Tédise	1215–32	

Abbots of Saint-Pons-de-Thomières

NAME OF ABBOT	DATES	FAMILY
Frotard	1060–99	
Pierre I Bérengar	1100–30	Bérengar family
Aimeri II	1130–44	
Pierre II	1145–6	
Béranger I	1146–51	Bérengar family
Raymond of Dourgne	1151–81	
Ermengaud	1181–1205	

TABLE 2: "Specified Donations" to the Building Fabric of Saint-Etienne, Agde, in Testaments of the Cartularies of the Chapter and Bishop (See Appendixes 13–17 and 19).

DONOR	OCCUPATION	DATE	AMOUNT
Etienne	chaplain of Mèze (departing on Crusade)	1147	50 solidi
Bernard de Roujan		1147	30 solidi
Ermengaude	bishop of Saint-Etienne	1149	a field and meadow for the restoration of the altar; 1,000 solidi for the completion of the "choirs"; and precious objects
Pierre Rainard		1153	20 solidi
Guilhem Rainard	canon of Saint-Etienne	1155	500 solidi and precious objects
Raymond de Foreville		1157	one measure of wheat
Bernard of Tongue	knight	1159	500 solidi
Guiraud de Touroulle		1160	one measure of wheat
Marie de Mermian		1160	one measure of corn
Bertrand d'Agde	canon of Saint-Etienne	1172	1,000 solidi
Guilhem Rainard (second testament)		1176–7	1,000 solidi and precious objects

TABLE 3: The Pattern of Donations to Saint-Etienne, Agde.

Donations made in testaments

1068–98	Agilbert
1130	Guilhem Rainard
1147	Etienne, chaplain of Mèze
1147	Bernard de Roujan
1147	Guiraud de Mèze
1149	Ermengaud, bishop of Saint-Etienne
1149	Pons Guarin
1153	Pierre Rainard
1155	Guilhem Rainard
1157	Raymond de Foreville
1159	Bernard de Tongue
1160	Guirard de Touroulle
1160	Marie de Mermian
1172	Bertrand
1174	Adhémar
1176	Guilhem Rainard (second testament)
1203	Bérangar Bernard
1212	Raymond de Bessan

Donations, Sales, Exchanges, and Other Acquisitions to Saint-Etienne, Agde, Recorded in Both Cartularies, Arranged by Episcopal Reign

847–1031	11
1031–88	0
Bérengar I (1068–93)	3
Bernard (1099–22)	24
Aldebert (1122–30)	4
Raymond (1130–43)	13
Ermengaud (1144–9)	21
Bérengar II (1149–52)	4
Pons (1152–3)	4
Adhémar (1153–62)	20
Guilhem (1162–73)	13
Pierre (1173–94)	23
Raymond (1194–1213)	29
1213–39	20
after 1239	0

TABLE 4: Donations to Saint-Pierre, Maguelone, Recorded
in the Cartulary and Arranged by Episcopal Reign.

899	1
Pierre de Melgueil (999–1030)	0
Arnaud (1032–60)	1
Bertrand (1060–80)	2
Godfrey (1080–1104)	5
Galtier (1104–28)	5
Raymond (1129–58)	13
Jean II de Montlaur (1159–90)	27
Guilhem Raymond (1190–5)	2
Guilhem de Fleix (1195–1202)	2

ABBREVIATIONS

AB	*Art Bulletin*
BM	*Bulletin monumental*
Biget et al., 1986	J-L. Biget, H. Pradelier and M. Pradelier-Schlumberger, "L'Art Cistercien dans le Midi Toulousain," *Cahiers de Fanjeaux,* 21 (1986), 312–70.
Bisson, 1977	T.N. Bisson, "The Organized Peace in Southern France and Catalonia (c. 1140–1233)," *American Historical Review,* 1977, 290–311.
CA	*Congrès archéologique de France.*
Cartulaire de Maguelone	J. Rouquette and A. Villemagne, eds., *Cartulaire de Maguelone,* 7 vols., 1912–25.
Castaldo, 1970	A. Castaldo, *L'église d'Agde, Xe–XIIIe siècle,* Travaux et Recherches, série "Sciences Historiques," no. 20, Paris, 1970.
DeVic and Vaissete	Dom C. DeVic and Dom J.J. Vaissete, *Histoire Générale du Languedoc . . .,* new ed., 16 vols., Toulouse, 1872–1904.
Durliat, 1972	M. Durliat, "Problèmes posés par l'histoire de l'architecture religieuse en Catalogne du XIe siècle," *Cahiers de Saint Michel de Cuxa,* 3 (1972).
Durliat, 1973–4	M. Durliat, "L'architecture gothique méridionale au XIIIe siècle," *Bulletin de l'école antiquaire de Nîmes* (1973–4), 63–132.
Erdmann, 1977	C. Erdmann, *The Origin of the Idea of Crusade,* trans. M.W. Baldwin and W. Goffart, Princeton, 1977, from the original, *Die Entstehung des Kreuzzugsgedankens,* Stuttgart, 1935.
Fabrège	F. Fabrège, *Histoire de Maguelone,* 3 vols., Paris and Montpellier, 1894–1902.
Gallia Christiana	*Gallia Christiana in Provincias Ecclesiasticas Distributa; In quae Series et Historia Archiepiscoporum et Abbatum Regionum Omnium quas Vetus Gallia,* Tomus Sextus: Provincia Narbonensi, Paris, 1739. [facsimile ed., Vol. 6: Paris, 1899]
Germain, 1869	A. Germain, *Maguelone sous ses évêques et ses chanoines. Etude historique et archéologique,* Montpellier, 1860.

Hefele and Leclerq, 1913	C.H. Hefele and H. Leclerq, *Histoire des conciles d'après les documents originaux*, Paris, 1913.
Languedoc roman	*Languedoc roman (Zodiaque, la nuit des temps, XLIII)*, eds. J. Lugand, J. Nougaret, and R. Saint-Jean, 2nd ed., n.p., 1985.
MGH	*Monumenta Germaniae Historica.*
Mansi	J.D. Mansi, *Sacrorum conciliorum nova et amplissima collectio . . .*, 31 vols., Florence and Venice, 1759–98.
Mortet and Deschamps, 1911	V. Mortet, *Recueil des textes relatifs à l'histoire de l'architecture et à la condition des architectes en France au moyen âge*, 2 vols., Paris, 1911 (Vol. 2 with P. Deschamps).
PL	J.-P. Migne, ed., *Patrologiae cursus completus . . . Latinae*, 221 vols., Paris, 1844–64.
Pacaut, 1957	M. Pacaut, *Louis VII et les élections épiscopales dans le royaume de France*, Paris, 1957.
Pacaut, 1964	M. Pacaut, *Louis VII et son royaume*, Paris, 1964.
Paul, 1974	V. Paul, "Le problème de la nef unique," in *La naissance et l'essor du gothique méridional qu XIIIe siècle (Cahiers de Fanjeaux 9)*, Toulouse: Privat, 21–53.
Paul, 1988	V. Paul, "The Beginnings of Gothic Architecture in Languedoc," *Art Bulletin*, 70 (1988), 104–22.
RHF	*Recueil des Historiens des Gaules et de la France.*
Rey, 1925	R. Rey, *Les Vieilles Eglises Fortifiées du Midi de la France*, Paris, 1925.
Reyerson and Powe, 1984	K. Reyerson and F. Powe, eds., *The Medieval Castle*, Medieval Studies at Minnesota, I, Dubuque, 1984. [Reissued Minneapolis, 1991]
Sahuc	J. Sahuc, *Saint-Pons-de-Thomières: Ses Vieux Edifices, Ses Anciennes Institutions*, Montpellier, n.d. (1895). [Marseille: Lafitte Reprints, 1979]
Schroeder, 1937	H.J. Schroeder, *Disciplinary Decrees of the General Councils*, London, 1937.
Terrin, 1969	O. Terrin, *Cartulaire du Chapitre d'Agde*, Publication de la Société d'Histoire du Droit et des Institutions des anciens pays de droit écrit, no. 1, Nîmes, 1969.
Vicaire, 1969	M.-H. Vicaire, "'L'affaire de paix et de foi' du Midi de la France," in *Paix de Dieu et guerre sainte en Languedoc au XIIIe siècle* (Cahier de Fanjeaux 4), Toulouse, 1969, 102–27.
Viollet-le-Duc, *Dictionnaire*	E. Viollet-le-Duc, *Dictionnaire Raisonné de l'Architecture Française du XIe au XVIe siècle*, 10 vols., Paris: Librairies-Imprimeries Réunies, 1854–68.

NOTES

INTRODUCTION

1. On Gundulf, see W. Saint John Hope, "Gundulf's Tower at Rochester, and the First Norman Cathedral There," *Archaeologica Cantaniana,* 23–4 (1898–9); F.H. Fairweather, "Gundulf's Cathedral," *Archaeological Journal,* 86 (1929), 187–212; H.M. Colvin, ed., *The History of the King's Works,* 3 vols., London, 1963, I, 28–32; and S. Bonde, "Castle and Church Buildings at the Time of the Norman Conquest," in Reyerson and Powe, 1984; 79–96.
2. Ilse Hindenburg, *Benno II, Bischof von Osnabrück, al Architekt,* Strasbourg, 1921, though not all scholars agree with Hindenburg's interpretation of Benno's architectural involvement.
3. See Paul, 1988, for one of the earliest exceptions to this scholarly neglect.

CHAPTER 1

1. C. Coulson, "Fortresses and Social Responsibility in Late Carolingian France," *Zeitschrift für Archäologie des Mittelalters,* 4 (1976), 29–36; also his unpublished dissertation: *Seignorial Fortresses in France in Relation to Public Policy c. 864–c. 1483,* University of London, 1972.
2. On the Italian licenses, see R. Poupardin, *Etude sur les Institutions politiques et administratives des Principautés Lombardes de l'Italie méridionale (IXe–Xe siècles),* Paris, 1907.
3. C. Coulson, "Hierarchism in Conventual Crenellation: An Essay in the Sociology and Metaphysics of Medieval Fortification," *Medieval Archaeology,* 26 (1982), 69–100; 58 out of 460 licenses to crenellate, issued by the chancery between 1200 and 1536, were approved for ecclesiastical precincts.
4. See the fuller discussion of church councils in Chapter 2, and the statutes in Appendixes 34–41.
5. On Saint-Victor, Marseille, see F. Benoit, *L'abbaye de Saint-Victor et l'église de la Major à Marseille,* Paris, 2nd ed., 1966; P.-A. Fevrier, *Le développement urbain en Provence de l'époque romaine à la fin du XIVe siècle,* Paris, 1964; E. Duprat, "Essai sur les fortifications de Marseille dans le Haut moyen âge," *Mémoires de l'Institut Historique de Provence,* IV, 1927, 22; and G. Démians d'Archimbaud, "Les fouilles de Saint-Victor de Marseille," *Académie des Inscriptions et Belles-Lettres, Comptes rendus,* 1971, 87–117, and 1974, 314–46. On Lérins, see H. Maris, *L'abbaye de Lérins,* Paris, 1909; L. Cristiani, *Lérins et ses fondateurs,* Paris, 1946; and J.-J. Antier, *Lérins: L'Ile sainte de la Côte d'Azur,* Paris, 1973. On Mont-Saint-Michel, see principally, E. Corroyer, *Description de l'abbaye du Mont-Saint-Michel,* Paris, 1877; F. Enaud, *Le Mont-Saint-Michel,* Paris, 1966; Y.-M. Froidevaux, *Le Mont-Saint-Michel,* Paris, 1965; and J. Laporte et al., eds., *Millénaire monastique au Mont-Saint-Michel,* 3 vols. (of a projected 6-vol. study), Paris, 1967.
6. On the theft and subsequent security measures at Lincoln, see Charles Oman, "Secu-

rity in English Churches A.D. 1000–1548," *Archaeological Journal*, 136 (1979), 90–8; and K. Edwards, *The English Secular Cathedrals in the Middle Ages*, Manchester, 1949, 230. The royal charter on this incident is reproduced in T. Rymer, *Foedera, Conventiones, Litterae, et cujuscunque generis Acta Publica inter Reges Angliae*, 3 vols., London, 1704–35 (rpt. 1830), Vol. 3, pp. 2, 720. Guards were also employed at Ely Cathedral. Bishop Walpole's statutes of 1300 stipulate the necessity of two watchmen there. See the *Ely Chapter Ordinances*, in the *Camden Miscellany*, 17 (1940), 15.

7. On security in Anglo-Saxon towers, see H.M. Taylor, *Anglo-Saxon Architecture*, Cambridge, 1973, Vol. 3, 869ff. See also Walter Johnson, "The Secular Uses of the Church Fabric," Chap. 3 in his *Byways in British Archaeology*, Cambridge, 1912. (I am indebted to John Kudlick for this last reference.) On elevated treasuries, see the recent study by C. Kosch, "Zum spätromischen schatzkammer (dem zog Kapitelsaal) von St. Pantaleon," *Colonica Romanica*, 6 (1991), 34–63.

8. On the fortress-churches of Sancho Ramírez, see W.M. Whitehill, *Spanish Romanesque Architecture of the Eleventh Century*, 2nd ed., Oxford, 1968, 243–52; J. Salarrullana y de Dios and E. Ibarra y Rodríguez, *Documentos correspondientes al reinado de Sancio Ramírez (1063–94)*, 2 vols., Zaragossa, 1907–13; V. Lampérez y Romea, *Historia de la Arquitectura Cristiana Espanola en la Edad Media*, 3 vols., 2nd ed., Madrid, 1930, i, 443–4; and A. Kingsley Porter, "Iguácel and More Romanesque Art of Aragón," *Burlington Magazine*, 52 (1928), 111–27. The preference for placing Augustinian canons in castle chapels was marked in France and England as well. One reason for the popularity of Augustinians was undoubtedly the fact that canons were also ordained priests, and were thus able to serve Mass. On Augustinian castle chapels in northern France, see S. Bonde and C. Maines, *Protecting God from the English: The Fortification of French Monasteries in the Hundred Years War*, forthcoming. On the links between castles and monastic foundations in England, and the special preference for Augustinians, see M.W. Thompson,

The Rise of the Castle, Cambridge, 1991, 136–42.

9. On Loarre, see R. del Arco, "El castillo real de Loarre," *Linajes de Aragón*, 6 (1915) 81–90; and J. Mann, "San Pedro at the Castle of Loarre," Columbia Ph.D. dissertation, 1991.

10. For a further discussion of the fortifications of Anglo-Norman cathedrals, and of Lincoln in particular, see Chapter 5.

11. S. Borsari, *Venezia e Bisanzio nel XII secolo. I rapporti economici* (Deputazione di storia patria per le Venezie, Miscellania di studi e memorie, XXVI), Venice, 1988, 57. I am indebted to J. Schulz for directing my attention to this source.

12. T.R.S. Boase, "Ecclesiastical Art in the Crusader States in Palestine and Syria," in K.M. Setton, *A History of the Crusades*, Vol. 4, Masison, 1977, 108–10; M. Pillet, "Notre-Dame de Tortosa," *Syria*, 10 (1929), 40–51; C. Enlart, *Monuments des Croisés*, II, 395–426; and P. Deschamps, *Terre Sainte Romane*, n.p. (Zodiaque), 1964, 231–6.

13. On Asti, see R. Bordone, "L'aristocrazia militare del territorio di Asti: i signori di Gorzano," *Bolletino storico-bibliografico subalpino*, 69, 1971, 357–447. On the same phenomenon in Verona, see A. Castagnetti, *"Ut nullus incipiat hedificare forticiam." Comune veronese e signorie rurali nell'età di Federico I*, Verona, 1984.

14. On Langres, see J. Richard, *Les Ducs de Bourgogne et la formation du duché du XIe au XIVe siècles*, Paris, 1954, esp. 52; on Bourges, see G. Devailly, *Le Berry du Xe siècle au milieu du XIIIe. Etude politique, religieuse, sociale et économique*, Paris, 1973. On Archbishop Aimon de Bourbon of Bourges and his famous "peace army" of 1038, see *Les Miracles de Saint Benoît*, ed. E. de Certain, Paris, 1858, 192–8.

15. On rendability, see C. Coulson, "Rendability and castellation in medieval France," *Château Gaillard*, 6 (1972/73) 59–67; and E.M. Hallam, *Capetian France 987–1328*, New York, 1980, 98–9.

16. See the Customs of the Duchy of Normandy, cited in D. Renn, *Norman Castles in Britain*, 2nd ed., New York 1973, 14.

17. On Louis' visit to the Maçonnais, see G. Duby, *La Société aux XIe et XIIe siècles dans la région Maçonnaise*, 2nd ed., Paris, 1971,

412–15; and Jean Dunbabin, *France in the Making, 843–1180*, Oxford, 1985, 264–5. Similar reminders of the royal right to rendability occurred elsewhere. For example, both Louis VII in 1164 and Philip Augustus in 1196 intervened in favor of the monastery of Mozat, near Clermont-Ferrand, as had their predecessor Louis VI in 1126.

18. M. Prou, *Recueil des actes de Philippe I, roi de France* (Paris, 1908), 315–17.

19. On Shaftesbury, see A. Williams, "The Knights of Shaftesbury Abbey," in *Anglo-Norman Studies: Proceedings of the Battle Conference, 1985*, 214–32.

20. See E.M. Jamison, ed., *Catalogus Baronum*, Fonti per la storia d'Italia, 101, Rome, 1972, art. 823, discussed in G.A. Loud, "Military Obligation in Norman Italy," W.J. Sheils, ed., *The Church and War*, Studies in Church History, 20, Oxford, 1983, 39.

21. On the German licenses to fortify, see H.M. Maurer, "Bauformen der hochmittelalterlichen Adelsburg in Südwestdeutschland; Untersuchungen zur Entwicklung des Burgenbaus," *Zeitschrift für die Geschichte des Oberrheins*, 115 (1967), 61ff.; *Burgen im deutschen Sprachraum; ihre rechtsund verfassungsgeschichtliche Bedeutung*, 2 vols., 1976; H. Hinz, *Motte und Donjon: zur Frühgeschichte der Mittelalterlichen Adelsburg*, 1981.

22. On the Carolingian fortifications at Corbie, see M. Rouche, "The Vikings versus the Towns of Northern Gaul. Challenge and Response," in C. Redman, ed., *Medieval Archaeology*, Papers of the Seventeenth Annual Conference of the Center for Medieval and Early Renaissance Studies, Binghamton, 1989, 48; and A. d'Haenens, "Corbie face aux Vikings," in *Corbie, abbaye royale*, Lille, 1963, 187–90.

23. R. Bautier, ed., *Actes d'Etudes*, Paris, 1967, 41–5. See also Jean Dunbabin, *France in the Making, 843–1180*, Oxford, 1985, Chap. 3, 40–1.

24. On the fortifications of Sant'Ambrogio, see G. Rosetti, *Società e istitutioni nel contado lombardo durante il medioevo: Cologno Monzese*, I, Milan, 1968. On Farfa, see P. Toubert, *Les structures du Latium médiéval: Le Latium méridional et la Sabine du IXe à la fin du XIIe siècle*, 2 vols., Rome,

1973, 1074–81; I. Schuster, *L'imperiale abbazia di Farfa*, Rome, 1921, 288; and C. B. McClendon, *The Imperial Abbey of Farfa*, New Haven, 1987, 14.

25. On the fortified farms of the Soissonais, see M.-J. Salmon, *L'architecture des fermes du Soissonais: son évolution du XIIIe au XIXe siècle. Etude architecturale rurale*. Mollets-Sazeray, CNRS, n.d.; and B. Ancien, "La grande campagne de reconstruction rurale monastique en soissonais au XIVe siècle," *Mémoires de la Fédération des Sociétés d'Histoire et d'Archéologie de l'Aisne*, 17 (1971), 83–96.

26. I have concentrated in my study on the patterns of ecclesiastical fortification in Languedoc. (See Chap. 5.) I suggest here only the rough outlines of the shape of ecclesiastical fortification across the rest of Europe and the East. Much more work remains to be done on the rich archival, physical, and archaeological evidence available for this topic.

27. On the fortifications of abbeys in Auvergne, see G. Fournier, *Le peuplement rural en Basse-Auvergne durant le Haut-Moyen Age*, Paris, n.d. (1964?), esp. 145–54 (on Issoire); 160–9 (on Brioude). On the architecture, see principally, B. Crapelet, *Auvergne Romane*, 4th ed., Zodiaque, 1972.

28. On the capitals of Saint-Nectaire, see B. Crapelet, *Auvergne Romane*, 4th ed., Zodiaque, 1972, 108–9; and E. Mâle, *Religious Art in France*, Princeton, 1978, 212.

29. A. G. Remensnyder, *Remembrance of Kings Past: Monastic Foundation Legends in Medieval France*, Ithaca, Cornell University Press, forthcoming. I am indebted to Prof. Remensnyder for sharing her conclusions with me in advance of publication.

30. *Cartulaire de l'abbaye de Conques*, no. 15, p. 19. The *Cartulario de San Juan de la Pena*, ed. A. Ubieto Arteta, Textos Medievales, 6, Valencia, 1962, no. 9, pp. 37–9, describes the ninth-century foundation of San Martin de Cerceto in similar terms. These two cases will be discussed in further detail in A.G. Remensnyder, *Remembrance of Kings Past*. On the phenomenon of peace negotiated by monastic communities, see G. Koziol, "Monks, Feuds, and the Making of Peace in Eleventh-Century Flanders," in T. Head and R. Landes, eds., *The Peace of God: Social Violence*

and Religious Response in France Around the Year 1000, Ithaca, 1992, pp. 239–58.

31. On fortified cemetery churches, see the discussion later in this chapter.

32. "Nulloque comparente qui eis resisteret, infra limites terre sue reversi, ecclesiam quamdam fortem et contra eos incastratam, provisam de viris armatis et cibariis a Francis, que stabat in villa quadam campestri, que Basseida vocatur, obtinuerunt." *Annales Gandenses,* ed., H. Johnstone, London, 1951, 55.

33. On ecclesiastical fortification during the Hundred Years War, see especially P. Denifle, *La désolation des églises, monastères, hôpitaux en France, pendant la Guerre de Cent ans,* 3 vols., Paris, 1891–9; Rey, 1925, 37–47; and S. Bonde and C. Maines, *Protecting God from the English: The Fortification of French Monasteries during the Hundred Years War,* forthcoming.

34. Froissart, *Chroniques,* ed. J.A.C. Buchon, Paris, 1837; *Livre des faits du bon messire Jean le Maingre, dit Bouciquaut,* ed. J.A.C. Buchon, Paris, 1835; and *Chronique de Jean le Bel,* ed. J. Viard and E. Déprez, Paris, 1904. All are discussed in Rey, 1925, 39–44. On churches serving as a refuge for municipal populations, see, for example, Froissart, *Chronicles,* II, 58; II, 95

35. Rey, 1925, 47.

36. Froissart, *Chronicles,* II, Chap. 95; Rey, 1925, 43.

37. The church of Notre Dame in Bayonne, for example, is said to have thwarted English attack. Boucicaut, 1835; and Rey, 1925, 44.

38. "Lors furent attrapés ces paysans sur le plat pays, qui avaient fortifié églises et moustiers, et là dedans retrait leurs biens, meubles, vins, blés, avoines, chairs et autres choses, et les voulaient et cuidaient tenir et garder. Mais il leur en advint tout du contraire, car ces chevaliers et escuyers et captaines de routes y envoyèrent leurs gens qui tout prenaient." Froissart, *Chronicles,* III, 35.

39. This practice also occurred for parish churches. For example, Philippe de Mézières wrote about strengthening the church and garrisoning the tower of Saint-Pierre de Camelin while he occupied the castle at Blérancourt: "incepi fortificare et de gente mea ipsam munire." This passage is discussed by O. Caudron, "Un épisode de la Guerre de Cent Ans," *Mémoires de la Fédération des Sociétés d'histoire et d'archéologie de l'Aisne,* 29 (1984), 69–73.

40. Froissart, *Chronicles,* I, 2; II, 8.

41. A. Muldrac, *Compendiosium abbatiae Longipontis Suessionensis chronicon,* Paris, 1652, cited in L'abbé Poquet, *Monographie de l'abbaye de Longpont,* Paris, 1869, 31–3; and C. Bruzelius, "Cistercian High Gothic: The Abbey Church of Longpont and the Architecture of the Cistercians in the Early Thirteenth Century," *Analecta Cisterciana,* 35 (1979), 30–1, and fn. 123–4.

42. On the fortifications of Saint-Jean-des-Vignes, Soissons, see S. Bonde and C. Maines, *Protecting God from the English,* forthcoming. Our work on this topic was first presented by C. Maines in a paper entitled, "Protecting God from the English," in the ICMA-sponsored session on "The Representations and Concepts of War and Peace," at Kalamazoo in 1992. The surviving fortification system at Saint-Jean-des-Vignes is the object of ongoing archaeological excavation and research by our excavation team.

43. Rey, 1925, 47.

44. "Par la faute des paroissiens qui s'en servis comme de forts et s'y sont servis comme réfugiés, eux, leurs familles, bestiaux, meubles et moiens, même la plupart aiantz vendu le patrimoine desdites églises tant pour faire fortifier icelles." Archives départementales de l'Aisne, cited in J.P. Meuret, *Les églises fortifiées de la Thiérache,* Vervins, 1977, 5.

45. J. Meuret, *Les églises fortifiées de la Thiérache,* Paris, 1985; and "Note sur l'église fortifiée de Plomion," *Mémoires de la Fédération des Sociétés d'Histoire et d'Archéologie de l'Aisne,* 24 (1979), 158–83.

46. On the medieval concepts of war, see Erdmann, 1977; F.H. Russell, *The Just War in the Middle Ages,* Cambridge, 1947; and S. Windass, *Christianity versus Violence: A Social and Historical Study of War and Christianity,* London, 1964. In the discussion that follows I am dependent upon Erdmann, 1977, Chaps. 1 and 3; and J. Russell, *Just War,* 1947, Chap 1.

47. Cicero, *de Officiis,* III, 22, 86–7.

48. On Eusebius' attitudes toward war, see R.H. Bainton, *Christian Attitudes toward War and Peace,* Nashville, 1960, 84.

49. "Fortitudo, quae in bello tuetur a barbaris

patriam, vel domi defendit infirmos, vel a latronibus socios, plena sit iustitiae." Ambrose, *de Officiis Ministrorum,* i, 27, 129; P.L. 16, 66.

50. Augustine, *Quaestiones in Heptateuchum,* VI, 10; C.S.E.L., 28, 428.

51. For Augustine's complicated attitudes toward war and violence, see principally, R.A. Markus, "Saint Augustine's views on the 'Just War,'" in W.J. Sheils, ed., *The Church and War,* Studies in Church History, 20, Oxford, 1983, 1–13; R. Hartigan, "Saint Augustine on War and Killing: The Problem of the Innocent," *Journal of the History of Ideas,* 27 (1966), 196ff.; and H. Deane, *The Political and Social Ideas of Augustine,* New York, 1963, Chap. 5. Within Augustine's writings, see especially *Epist.* 139, 6; C.S.E.L. 57, 135: "Pacem habere debet voluntas, bellum necessitas." See also the *de Civitate Dei,* esp. XVII, 13; XIX, 12; and *Contra Faustum,* Book 22.

52. C. Vogel, *Le pécheur et la pénitence au Moyen Age,* Paris, 1969, 192–3.

53. Ibid., 77.

54. "De peccatis capitalibus: Si quis hominiem occiderit . . . in bello, uno anno paeniteat." PL, CXLI, 339; discussed and cited in A. Vacant, E. Mangenot and A. Amann, eds., *Dictionnaire de théologie catholique,* Paris, 1941, xiv, col. 1980.

55. "Qui in invasione patriae repugnando hostem occiderit tribus annis paeniteat." Cited in *Dictionnaire de théologie catholique,* xiv, 1979.

56. H.E.J. Cowdrey, "Bishop Ermenfrid of Sion and the Penitential Ordinance following the Battle of Hastings," *Journal of Ecclesiastical History,* 20, 1969, 225–42.

57. On these foundations, see principally, E.M. Hallam, "Monasteries as War Memorials," in W.J. Sheils, ed., *The Church and War,* Studies in Church History, 20, Oxford, 1983, 47–57.

58. Ambrose, *Epist,* 20; PL 16, 1050.

59. This statute was first formulated at the Council of Austrasia (742) and was reaffirmed by Charlemagne in his first general Capitulary of c. 769. The text (translated into French) is reproduced in C. Vogel, *Le pécheur et la pénitence,* 1969, 192–3.

60. Tim. 2: 3–4: "Labora sicut bonus miles Christi Jesu. Nemo militans Deo implicat se negotiis saecularibus."

61. Erdmann, 1977, 13.

62. "Sunt enim saeculi, sunt et milites Christi; sed milites infirma et lubrica arma; milites autem Christi fortissima sumunt atque praeclara. Pugnant illi contra hostes, ut se et interfectos aeternam perdacant ad poenam; pugnant isti contra vitia." "Commentaria in regulam sancti Benedicti," *PL,* ser. lat., Vol. 102, col. 696.

63. Gregory I, *Registrum,* II, 7, 32–4; MGH, Ep., 1.106 and 128ff. Discussed in Erdmann, 1977, 25.

64. L. Duchesne, ed., *Liber pontificalis,* II, 118.

65. P. Contamine, *War in the Middle Ages,* trans. M. Jones, Oxford, 1985, 270; and Erdmann, 1977, 15.

66. Leo IV, Epist., 28; MGH Epist. 5.601; and John VIII, Epist. 150, MGH 7.126. There is some scholarly discussion on the actual nature of these early pronouncements. E. Delaruelle, "Essai sur la formation de l'idée de croisade," *Bulletin de littérature ecclésiastique,* 42 (1941), 24–45; 86–103; 45 (1944), 13–46, 73–90; 54 (1953) 226–39; 55 (1954), 50–63, considers John VIII as a key figure in the development of the Crusading indulgence. J. Brundage, *Medieval Canon Law and the Crusader,* Madison, 1969, 22–3, argues that Leo and John offer "general absolution" instead of a true indulgence.

67. See J. Beeler, *Warfare in Feudal Europe (730–1200),* Ithaca, 1971, 219–21; and B. McNab, "Obligations of the Church in English Society: Military Arays of the Clergy, 1369–1418," in *Order and Innovation in the Middle Ages: Essays in Honor of Joseph R. Strayer,* ed. W.C. Jordan, B. McNab, and T. Ruiz, Princeton, 1976, 293.

68. *Chronica Monasterii Casinensis,* ed. H. Hoffman, MGH, SS, 34 (1980), II; 194–5, 196, 204, 240, discussed in G.A. Loud, "Military Obligation in Norman Italy," in W.J. Sheils, ed., *The Church and War,* Studies in Church History, 20, Oxford, 1983, 33.

69. P. Contamine, *War in the Middle Ages,* trans. M. Jones, Oxford, 1985, 269–70.

70. "Et utinam monachus desidiosus, deposita ignavia, ad utilitatem sui monasterii sic fortiter ageret." *Liber miraculorum sancte Fidis,* I, 26, ed. A. Bouillet, Paris, 1897, 68.

71. Guibert of Nogent, *De vita sua,* Book 3, Chaps. 7–8 (*Self and Society in Medieval*

France: The Memoirs of Guibert of Nogent, trans. C.C. Swinton Bland, ed. and corrected by J. Benton, New York, 1970, 172–5); and E. M. Hallam, *Capetian France 987–1328*, New York, 1980, 141.

72. Guibert of Nogent, *De vita sua*, Book 3, Chap. 8 (Benton, *Self and Society*, 175).

73. On the military campaigns of Gregory VII, see Erdmann, 1977, Chap. 5; and E. Delaruelle, "Essai sur la formation de l'idée de croisade," *Bulletin de littérature ecclésiastique*, 42 (1941), 24–45; 86–103; 45 (1944), 13–46, 73–90.

74. E. Caspari, ed., *Das Register Gregors VII, Monumenta Germaniae Historica, Epistolae selectae* 2, Berlin, 1920–3, IX, 4, p. 578. See also, Erdmann, 1977, 175.

75. Erdmann, 1977, 95–7.

76. On the Peace and Truce of God, see the Bibliography, Section VII.

77. Mansi, 19, 483–4.

78. For a discussion of the militia in Bourges, see T. Head, "The Judgement of God: Andrew of Fleury's Account of the Peace League of Bourges," in T. Head and R. Landes, eds., *The Peace of God: Social Violence and Religious Response in France around the Year 1000*, Ithaca, 1992, Chap. 9, 219–38.

79. On the military orders, see J. LeClercq, "Un document sur les débuts des Templiers," *Revue d'histoire ecclésiastique*, 52, 1957, 81–90; J. Riley-Smith, *The Knights of Saint John in Jerusalem and Cyprus*, London, 1967; C. Lawrence, *Medieval Monasticism*, London, 1984, Chap. 10; and A. Forey, *The Military Orders from the Twelfth to the Early Fifteenth Centuries*, Toronto, 1992.

80. "At vero Christi milites securi praeliatur praelia Domini sui, necquaquam metuentes aut de hostium caede peccatum. . . . Dei enim minister est ad vindictam malefactorum. . . . In morte pagani Christianus gloriatur, quia Christus glorificatur." Bernard of Clairvaux, *Liber ad milites Templi de laude novae militiae*, in *S. Bernardi Operi: Tractatus et Opuscula*, ed. J. LeClercq and H.M. Rochais, Rome, 1963, III, 217.

81. On the formation of the military orders and their precursors, see A. Forey, *The Military Orders*, 1992, Chap. 1.

82. PL, Vol. 182, cols. 197B-198A; and B.S. James, *The Letters of Saint Bernard of Clairvaux*, London, 1953, 116–17. This passage is discussed by C. Maines, "Good Works, Social Ties and the Hope for Salvation: Abbot Suger and Saint Denis," in P. Gerson, ed., *Abbot Suger and Saint Denis*, New York, 1986, 80.

83. On Suger's involvement in military affairs, and his subsequent penance for these deeds, see C. Maines, "Good Works," 77–94. L. Grant has also presented an interpretation of Suger's military preoccupations as these are recorded in his Life of Louis VI in an unpublished paper, "The Churchman Militant: Abbot Suger at War," presented at Kalamazoo in 1992. It is hoped that Dr. Grant will publish her study, which demonstrates Suger to have been an active castle builder.

84. See Petrus Sarnensis, *Histoire Albigeoise*, trans. P. Guébin and H. Maisoneuve, in the series *L'église et l'état*, Vol. 10, Paris, 1951, 70–80. I am indebted to C. Maines for this reference.

85. P. Contamine, *Guerre, état et société à la fin du moyen-âge: études sur les armées des rois de France*, Paris and the Hague, 1972, 171–2. See also B. McNab, "Obligations of the Church" in *Order and Innovation*, ed. W.C. Jordan, B. McNab, and T. Ruiz, 1976, 293–314, esp. 294.

86. Ibid.

87. On the Temple fortifications, see Y. Yadin, *Excavations in Jerusalem*; and P. Barbier, *La France Féodale*, Saint-Brieuc, 1968, II, 391.

88. On the *ribat*, and particularly on the similarities and differences with the military orders and their foundations, see A. Forey, "The Emergence of the Military Order in the Twelfth Century," *Journal of Ecclesiastical History*, 36 (1985); and E. Lourie, "The Confraternity of Belchite, the Ribat, and the Temple," *Viator*, 13 (1982).

89. A. Lézine, *Le Ribat de Sousse, suivi de notes sur le Ribat de Monastir*, Tunis, 1946, esp. 1–26.

90. M. Vogüe, *Syrie Centrale, Architecture civile et religieuse du 1er au 7ème siècle*, 4 vols., Paris, 1865–97; H.C. Butler, *Early Churches in Syria*, Princeton, 1929; and G. Forsyth, *Saint Catherine's Mount Sinai*, Princeton, 1979; and Y. Herschfeld, *The Judean Desert Monasteries of the Byzantine Period*, New Haven, 1992.

91. See the "Vita Sancti Johanni Hesychastae"

and the "Vita sancti Sabae," in E. Schwartz, ed., *Kyrillos von Skythopolis*, Leipzig, 1939, 13, 211. 15–22; 72, 175. 16–19. Both are discussed in Y. Hirschfeld, *Judean Desert Monasteries*, 1992, 277, fn. 30.

92. Y. Hirschfeld, *Judean Desert Monasteries*, 1992, Chap. 6.

93. F. Henry, *Irish Art in the Early Christian Period (to A.D. 800)*, Ithaca, 1965, pp. 76–84; and C. L. Neuman de Vegvar, *The Northumbrian Renaissance: A Study in the Transmission of Style*, London and Toronto, 1987, 61–2.

94. See G. Fournier, *Le peuplement rural en Basse-Auvergne durant le haut moyen âge*, Paris, n.d. (1964?), 390–2.

95. For a survey of castle-monasteries, see W. Braunfels, *Monasteries of Western Europe*, London, 1972, Chap. 8.

96. On Gross-Comburg, see E. Gradmann, *Die Kunst und Altertumsdenkmale im Königreich Württemberg*, Inventar, 1907; A. Mettler, "Die ursprüngliche Bauanlage des Klosters Komburg," *Württembergische Vierteljahrshefte für Landesgeschichte*, n.s., 20, 1911; and O. Linck, *Vom mittelalterlichen Mönchtum und seinem Bauten in Württemberg*, Stuttgart, 1953.

97. "Et a turribus monasterii lapides immensos in eum projicientes." In *Recueil des chartes de l'abbaye de Cluny*, ed. A. Bernard and A. Bruel, Paris, 1903, Vol. 6, 8.

98. On Gallo-Roman precinct walls, see A. Blanchet, *Les enceintes romaines de la Gaule*, Paris, 1907. On the incorporation of cathedrals into these walls, see A. Erlande-Brandenburg, *La Cathédrale*, Paris, 1989, Chap. 1. On Amiens, see J.-L. Massy and D. Bayard, *Amiens*, Paris, 1985. On Soissons, see G. Brunel and D. Defente, *Histoire de Soissons et des villages du Soissonais des Gallo-Romains à l'an mil*, Soissons, 1987, 5–8. On Rodez, see L. Bousquez, "Rodez," *CA*, 1937, 360–86. On Trier, see T.K. Kemp, "Grundrissentwicklung und Baugeschichte des Trierer Domes," *Das Münster*, XXI, 1968, 1.

99. On Avilá see M. Durliat, *L'architecture espagnole*, Toulouse, 1966.

100. Symeon of Durham, *Historia Regum*, ed. T. Arnold (Rolls Series, 75, 1885), 199–200; discussed briefly in R. Gem, "Lincoln Minster: Ecclesia Pulchra, Ecclesia Fortis," in *Medieval Art and Architecture at Lincoln Cathedral*, The British Archaeological Association conference transactions for 1982, Vol. 8, Leeds, 1986, 25.

101. On Gundulf, see Chap. 1, fn. 1.

102. Y. Esquieu, "Système défensif de quartiers canoniaux dans quelques cités épiscopales du Midi," *Actes du 105e Congrès National des Sociétés Savantes: Archéologie* (1980) pp. 331–45; and his unpublished doctoral dissertation, "Quartiers Canoniaux des Cathédrales dans la France Méridionale," Université de Toulouse, 1986.

103. Rey, 1925, 70.

104. On Vendôme, see G. Plat, *L'église de La Trinité de Vendôme*, Paris, 1934. That the north tower of the west façade of Chartres was originally independent of the church behind has long been recognized. Around the turn of the twentieth century, the relative sequence of the façade's construction was the subject of considerable debate. See E. Lefevre-Pontalis, "Les façades successives de la cathédrale de Chartres au XIe et XIIe siècles," *Congrès archéologique*, 1900; A. Mayeux, "Réponse à M. Lefevre-Pontalis sur son article," *Mémoires de la Société archéologique d'Eure-et-Loir*, 13 (1901–4); and E. Lefevre-Pontalis, "Nouvelles études sur les façades et les clochers de la cathédrale de Chartres: réponse à M. Mayeux," *Mémoires de la Société archéologique d'Eure-et Loir*, 13 (1901–4).

105. P. Barbier, *La France Féodale*, Saint-Brieuc, 1968, I, 163–4.

106. On Mont-Saint-Michel, see fn. 5 in this chapter.

107. On the friaries, see W. Braunfels, *Monasteries of Western Europe*, Princeton, 1980, 136–7; and G. Richa, *Notizie istorische delle chiese fiorentine divisi nei suoi quartieri*, Florence, 1754-62.

108. On the fortification of cemeteries, see especially, E. Zadora-Rio, "The Role of Cemeteries in the Formation of Medieval Settlement in Western France," in C. Redman, ed., *Medieval Archaeology*, Binghamton, 1989, 171–86; and M. Fixot and E. Zadora-Rio, eds., *L'Eglise, Le Terroir* (Monographie du CRA, no. 1), Paris, 1989. On Epfig and Hunawir, see B. Metz, "Schloss und Kirchhof: les cimetières fortifiés seigneuriaux," in *L'Eglise, Le Terroir*, 34–43. On

Hordain, See P. Demolon, "Hordain," in *L'Eglise, Le Terroir,* 59–62; On Seintein and Luz, see Rey, 1925, 147–50.

109. See principally, A. Settia, "'Ecclesiam incastellare': chiese e castelli in diocesi di Padova," *Fonti e ricerche di storia ecclesiastica padovana,* 12 (1981), 47–75; and his "Eglises et fortifications dans l'Italie du Nord," *L'église et le château. Xe-XVIIIe siècles,* Bordeaux, 1988, 81–94. These have now been reprinted, along with several other studies in A. Settia, *Chiese, Strade e Fortezze nell'Italia Medievale,* Rome, 1991. While I applaud Settia's detailed analysis of the Italian sources, I find his interpretation of the term *ecclesia incastellare* too strict. Settia argues that the term signals a new and restricted sense of fortification that begins in the latter part of the twelfth century. Earlier cases appear, particularly in the Lateran council of 1123, and the term is undoubtedly used more loosely to describe any church fortified in any manner.

110. U. Pasqui, *Documenti per la storia della città de Arezzo,* I, Florence, 1899, no. 389, p. 556; discussed in A. Settia, "'Ecclesiam incastellare,'" 48.

111. G. Tiraboschi, Memorie storiche modensi, III, Modena, 1794, no. 521, 87; discussed in A. Settia, "'Ecclesiam incastellare,'" 47.

112. No study comparable to Settia's for the non-Italian material has been undertaken. In the interim, Du Cange's *Glossarium,* and J.F. Niermeyer, *Mediae Latinitis Lexicon Minus,* Leiden, 1976, can be consulted for their entries on *Incastellare.* Mortet and Deschamps, 1911, is also of great utility.

113. Henry of Huntingdon, *Historia Anglorum,* viii, 22; ed. T. Arnold (Rolls Series, 74, 1879), 277–8.

114. Otto of Freising, *Chronicon,* vi, 31, ed. Hofmeister, 360.

115. Within the large body of scholarship on *westwerks,* see principally, H. Reinhardt and E. Fels, "Etude sur les églises-porches carolingiennes et leur survivance dans l'art roman," BM, 92 (1933), 331–65, and 96 (1937), 425–69; D. Grossman, "Zum Stand det Westwerkforschung," *Wallraf-Richards Jahrbuch,* 19 (1957), 253–65; and F. Möbius, *Westwerkstudien,* Jena, 1968. On the cult of Saint Michael, and upper chapels dedicated to that military saint, see principally, M. Crosnier,

"Culte aérien de Saint Michel," BM, 28 (1862), 693–700; and J. Vallery-Radot, "Note sur les chapelles hautes dediées à Saint Michel," BM, 88 (1929), 453–478.

116. On the Carolingian *westwerk* at La Trinité at Fécamp, see J. Vallery-Radot, *L'église de la Trinité de Fécamp,* Paris, 1928, 9–13.

117. "Mirabiliter miri scematis formae construxit (Ricardus) in honore Sanctae Trinitatis delubrem, turribus hinc inde et altrinsecus praebalteatum, dupliciterque arcuatum mirabiliter et de concatenatis artificiose lateribus coopterum." Dudo of Saint Quentin, *De moribus et actis primorum Normanniae ducum,* ed. J. Lair (Caen, 1865), 291. This passage is discussed by E. Carlson, "Religious Architecture in Normandy, 911–1000," *Gesta,* 5 (1966), 29, and in an unpublished paper by D. Stanley, "The Westwork of Notre Dame de Jumièges," 15.

118. H. Reinhardt and E. Fels, "Etude sur les églises-porches carolingiennes et leur survivance dans l'art roman," BM, 92 (1933), 343, where they cite Hariulf, Book 2, 8.

119. On the Saint Michael chapel at Cluny see J. Vallery-Radot, "Note sur les chapelles hautes dédiées à Saint Michel," BM, 88 (1929), 453–78.

120. On the west façade of Lincoln, see principally F. Saxl, "Lincoln Cathedral: The Eleventh-Century Design for the West Front," *Archaeological Journal,* 103 (1946), 105–17; J. Bilson, "The Plan of the First Cathedral Church of Lincoln," *Archaeologia,* 62 (1911), 543–64; R. Gem, "The Origins of the Early Romanesque Architecture of England," unpublished Cambridge University dissertation, 1974, 696–9; and R. Gem, "Lincoln Minster: Ecclesia Pulchra, Ecclesia Fortis," in *Medieval Art and Architecture at Lincoln Cathedral,* The British Archaeological Association conference transactions for 1982, Vol. 8, Leeds, 1986, 9–28; P. Kidson, unpublished lecture, 14 Dec. 1972, and private communication, 18 Nov. 1978; P. MacAleer, "The Eleventh-Century Facade of Lincoln Cathedral: Saxl's Theory of Byzantine Influence Reconsidered," *Architecture* (1984), 1–19; S. Bonde, "Saxo-Norman Overlap Architecture: Castle and Church Building in Mid-Eleventh-Century England," unpublished Ph.D. dissertation, Harvard University, 1982, 178–9; S. Bonde, "Castle and Church Buildings at the

Time of the Norman Conquest," in Reyerson and Powe, 1984, 79–96; and P. Miles, "Lincoln Cathedral," *Current Archaeology,* 129 (1992), 396–7.

121. "Juxta castellum turribus fortissimus eminens in loco forti fortem, pulchro pulchrem quae et grata esset Deo servientibus, et, ut pro tempore oportebat invincibilis hostibus." Henry of Huntingdon, *Historia Anglorum,* vi, 41, ed. T. Arnold (Rolls Series, 74, London, 1879), 212.

122. "Ecclesiam beate Dei genetrici de Lindocolino incastelaverat." William of Malmesbury, *Historia Novella,* ed. K.R. Potter (London, 1955), 47–8.

123. P. Miles, "Lincoln Cathedral," *Current Archaeology,* 129 (1992), 396–7.

124. See Rey, 1925, 76–9; Viollet-le-Duc, Vol. 1, 262, and Vol. 7, 290–3; A. Anglès, *L'abbaye de Moissac;* and M. Durliat, "Les crénelages du clocher-porche de Moissac et leur restauration par Viollet-le-Duc," *Annales du Midi,* 78 (1966), 433–47.

125. Marcel Durliat, "Les crénelages du clocher-porche de Moissac et leur restauration par Viollet-le-Duc," *Annales de Midi,* 78 (1966), 433–7; Linda Seidel, "Images of the Crusades in Western Art: Models as Metaphors," in *The Meeting of Two Worlds: Cultural Exchange between East and West during the Period of the Crusades,* ed. V. Goss and C. Bornstein, Kalamazoo, 1986, 377–91; Stephen Nichols, *Romanesque Signs: Early Medieval Narrative and Iconography,* New Haven, 1983, Chap. 5; and Peter K. Klein, "Programmes' eschatologiques, fonction et réception historiques des portails du XIIe Siècle: Moissac-Beaulieu-Saint Denis," *Cahiers de civilisation médiévale,* 33 (1990), 317–49, esp. 329–30.

126. See W. Götz, *Zentralbau und Zentralbautendenz,* Berlin, 1968, 319–21.

127. "Turrim etiam et superiora frontis propugnacula, tam ad ecclesiae decorem quam et utilitatem, si opportunitas exigeret, variari condiximus.," translated in E. Panofsky, ed., *Abbot Suger: On the Abbey Church of St.-Denis and Its Art Treasures,* 46–7. On the fortified aspects of the façade of Saint-Denis, see S.M. Crosby, *L'Abbaye royale de Saint-Denis,* Paris, 1953, 35; S.M. Crosby, *The Royal Abbey of Saint-Denis from its beginnings to the death of Suger, 475–1151,* ed. and completed by P. Blum, New Haven,

1987; 163, 282; von Simson, *Gothic Cathedral,* 108–10; and S. Gardner, "The Influence of Castle Building on Ecclesiastical Architecture in the Paris Region, 1130–1150," in Reyerson and Powe, 1984, 97–123.

128. S. Bonde, "Castle and Church Buildings at the Time of the Norman Conquest" in Reyerson and Powe, 1984, 79–96.

129. On the castle chapels at Goodrich and Harlech, see M.W. Thompson, *The Rise of the Castle,* Cambridge, 1991, 133. See also A.J. Taylor, *Harlech Castle,* Gwynedd, London, 1977.

130. The meurtrières on the uppermost level were added in the fourteenth century, and reworked in the nineteenth. On Rudelle, see the brief article by M. Durliat, "L'église fortifiée de Rudelle," *Bulletin de la société des études littéraires, scientifiques et historiques du Lot,* 90, 1969, 49–50.

131. B. Ancien, "Le château de Vez pendant la guerre de Cent Ans," *Mémoires de la Fédération des Sociétés d'histoire et d'archéologie de l'Aisne,* 27 (1982) 115ff.; J. Mesqui, *Ile de France Gothique. 2: Les demeures seigneuriales,* Paris, 1988, 316–26.

132. On Banyuls, see Rey, 1925, 81–3.

133. On Abou-Gosh, see C. Enlart, *Monuments des Croisés,* I, 204; T.R.S. Boase, "Ecclesiastical Art in the Crusader States in Palestine and Syria," in K.M. Setton, *A History of the Crusades,* Vol. 4, Masison, 1977, 112–13; and P. Deschamps, *Terre Sainte Romane,* n.p. (Zodiaque), 1964, 223–6. Scholars are, however, still divided on whether the church at Abou-Gosh incorporates the remains of a predecessor Roman structure.

134. On the fortified Portugal cathedrals, see A. de Lacerda, *Historia de arte romanica em Portugal,* I, Oporto, 1942, 186–204.

135. For a fuller discussion of the manning of these church-fortresses, see Chap. 4.

136. On Narbonne, see R. Rey, "La cathédrale de Narbonne," CA, 1954, 446–75. For a more detailed study of the cathedral, we await the forthcoming study by V. Paul.

137. On Albi, see principally, J.-L. Biget, "La cathédrale Sainte-Cécile d'Albi: L'architecture," CA, 143 (Albigeois), 1985, 20–62.

138. See principally, P. Toubert, *Les structures du Latium médiéval: Le Latium méridional et la Sabine du IXe à la fin du XIIe siècle,* 2 vols., Rome, 1973, II, 1068–81. See also I. Schus-

ter, *L'imperiale abbazia di Farfa*, Rome, 1921, 288; and C.B. McClendon, *The Imperial Abbey of Farfa*, New Haven, 1987, 14.

139. " Notum sit vobis nos ecclesiam sancti Petri sitam in villa que dicitur Maskarans sub ius et defensionem apostolice sedis ab ipsius fundatoribus sponte traditam suscepisse. . . . Quapropter apostolica auctoritate precipimus, ut nemo prefatum locum apostolica tuitione munitum deinceps infestare presumat, sed sub defensione beati Petri, cuius iuris est, quietus et securus ab omni perturbatione permaneat." In E. Caspari, ed., *Das Register Gregors VII, Monumenta Germaniae Historica, Epistolae selectae 2*, Berlin, 1920–3, IX. 7, 584. See also Y. M.-J. Congar, *L'ecclésiologie du haut moyen-âge*, Paris, 1968, 203–4; and I.S. Robinson, *The Papacy 1073–1198: Continuity and Innovation*, Cambridge, 1990, esp. 209.

140. Paul, Letters to the Ephesians, 6:11–12. See also J. Flori, "Chevalerie et liturgie. Remise des armes et vocabularie "chevaleresque" dans les sources liturgiques du IXe au XIVe siècle," *Le Moyen Age*, 84, 1978, 147–78.

141. Barbara Rosenwein, "Feudal War and Monastic Peace: Cluniac Liturgy as Ritual Aggression," *Viator*, 2 (1971), 129–57. See also, Michael McCormick, "The Liturgy of War in the Early Middle Ages: Crisis, Litanies and the Carolingian Monarchy," *Viator*, 15 (1984), 1–23, and his *Eternal Victory*, Cambridge, 1986.

142. On the militarized representations of the City of God, see C.M. Kauffman, *Romanesque Manuscripts, 1066–1190, A survey of Manuscripts Illuminated in the British Isles*, III, ed. J. Alexander, London, 1975; 62–3, pl. 50. On representations of the City of God generally, see A. de Laborde, *Les manuscrits à peintures de la Cité de Dieu de saint Augustin*, Paris, 1909.

143. 5.15, 212–13. This passage is discussed by T. Head, "The Peace League of Bourges," in T. Head and R. Landes, eds., *The Peace of God: Social Violence and Religious Response around the Year 1000*, Ithaca, 1992, 229–30; in D.W. Rollason, "The Miracles of St. Benedict: A Window on Early Medieval France," *Studies in Medieval History Presented to R.H.C. Davis*, ed. H. Mayr-Harting and R.I. Moore, London, 1985, 86; and in Erdmann, 1977, 91–3.

144. "Exaudi, domine, quesumus, preces nostras, et hunc ensem, quo hic famulus tuus N. se circumcingi desiderat, maiestatis tuae dextera benedicere dignare, quatinus defensio atque protectio possit esse ecclesiarum, viduarum, orphanorum omniumque deo servientium contra sevitiam paganorum aliisque sibi insidiantibus sit pavor, terro et formido." Cited in A. Franz, *Die kirchlichen Benediktionem im Mittelalter*, Fribourg-en-Brisgau, 1909, II, 293.

145. *Acta Sanctorum Bollandistarum*, 3rd ed., 62 vols, Brussels and Paris, 1863–1925, Vol. 5, 208. Discussed in P. Geary, *Furta Sacra*, Princeton, 1978, 138. Geary notes that the frequent use of threat by pagans as a narrative motif in the translation accounts lays this motivation open to suspicion.

146. P. Geary, *Furta Sacra*, 1978, and his "Humiliation of Saints," in S. Wilson, ed., *Saints and Their Cults*, Cambridge, 1983, 123–40, reprinted and translated from *Annales* 34, 1979, 27–42. See also L. Little, "Formules monastiques de malédiction aux IXe et Xe siècles," *Revue Mabillon*, 58, 1975, 377–99. Icons were also used in the defense of Byzantine cities. The defeat of the Persians in 544 was attributed to the intervention of a magical image of Christ. Another icon of Christ was carried around the walls of Constantinople by the Patriarch during the Avar siege in 626. When the city was again besieged by the Arabs, an icon of the Virgin was similarly displayed. In addition to tactical strategies, Byzantine military manuals also enumerated the defensive powers of holy icons and relics. See S. Runciman, *Byzantine Style and Civilization*, London, 1975, 78–81; J. Pelikan, *Imago Dei: the Byzantine Apologia for Icons*, Princeton, 1990, 28; and C. Oman, *The Art of War in the Middle Ages*, Ithaca, 1953. In at least one known case, a Western manuscript seems to have held a similar function. The Irish Cathach of Saint Columba takes its name from the practice since the term *cathach* means "battler." See F. Henry, *Irish Art in the Early Christian Period (to A.D. 800)*, Ithaca, 1965, 58–9; and C.L. Neuman de Vegvar, *The Northumbrian Renaissance: A Study in the Transmission of Style*, London and Toronto, 1987, 61.

147. On the council of Héry, see De diversibus casibus coenobii Dervensis et miracula s.

Bercharii, in L. d'Archéry and J. Mabillon, eds., *Acta sanctorum ordinis sancti Benedicti*, 9 vols., Paris, 1668–1701, c. 27, discussed in T. Head and R. Landes, eds., *The Peace of God: Social Violence and Religious Response around the Year 1000*, Ithaca, 1992, 4–6.

148. *Les miracles de saint Benoît écrit par Adrevald, Aimon, André, Raoul Tortaire et Hugues de Sainte Marie, moines de Fleury*, ed. E. de Certain, Paris, 1858, 5.2, 193–4.

149. On Aldebert and the fortifications at Mende, see M. Barbot, "Mende au XIIe siècle," *Revue de Gévaudan*, 1960; C. Brunel, *Les plus anciennes chartes en Langue provençale*, Geneva, 1973; C. Brunel, *Les miracles de Saint-Privat suivis des opuscules d'Aldebert III, évêque de Mende*, Paris, 1912; G. Plique, "Etude sur le chapitre cathédrale de Mende, de 1123 à 1516," *Bulletin de la Société des Lettres, Sciences et Arts de la Lozère*, 1931; C. Porée, "Les évêques-comtes de Gévaudan, étude sur le pouvoir temporel des évêques de Mende aux XIIe et XIIIe siècles," *Société des Lettres, Sciences et Arts de la Lozère: Archives gévaudanaises*, 4, 1919.

150. On the cult of Saint Michael and upper chapels dedicated to him, see fn. 115 in this chapter.

151. J. Vallery-Radot, "Note sur les chapelles hautes dediées à Saint Michel," BM, 88 (1929), 453–78.

152. "Demonius cognatur intrare, vetatur; angelus obstat ei preditus de<nse>." Cited in J. Virey, *L'architecture romane dans l'ancien diocèse de Mâcon*, 231; and J. Vallery-Radot, "Note sur les chapelles hautes dediées à Saint Michel," BM, 88 (1929), 477–8.

153. Marcel Durliat, "Les crénelages du clocher-porche de Moissac et leur restauration par Viollet-le-Duc," *Annales de Midi*, 78 (1966), 433–7.

154. Linda Seidel, "Images of the Crusades in Western Art: Models as Metaphors," in *The Meeting of Two Worlds: Cultural Exchange between East and West during the Period of the Crusades*, ed. V. Goss and C. Bornstein, Kalamazoo, 1986, 377–91.

155. On the sculpture of Saint-Julien-de-Brioude, see B. Craplet, *Auvergne Romane*, 4th ed., Zodiaque, 1972, 227–80; and Z. Swiechoski, *La sculpture romane auvergnate*, Clermont, 1972.

156. C. Coulson, "Hierarchism in Conventual Crenellation: An Essay in the Sociology and Metaphysics of Medieval Fortification," *Medieval Archaeology*, 26 (1982), 72.

157. On the arcaded churches of Millau, Nant, and Castelnau-Pégayrolles, see J.-C. Fau, *Rouergue Roman*, Zodiaque, 3rd ed., 1990.

CHAPTER 2

1. The passage is cited in Suger, *Vie de Louis le Gros*, trans. Henri Waquet, Paris, 1929, 200–3, though I have given a new translation in Appendix 5. Clearly, Maguelone was fortified by the early twelfth century, when Suger was writing. This reference may refer to the machicolated walls of the chevet which were under construction at this time, or it may simply describe the precinct walls of the abbey.

2. On the Council of Lombers and the spread of heresy in the south of France, see DeVic and Vaissete, VI, 1879, 1–5; C. Langlois, *Histoire des croisades contre les albigeois*, 1887, I, 32; and Y. Dossat, "Le clergé méridional à la veille de la Croisade Albigeoise," *Revue historique et littéraire du Languedoc*, I, 1944, 263–78, reprinted in Y. Dossat, *Eglise et hérésie en France au XIIIe siècle*, London, 1982.

3. Bisson, 1977, and personal communication.

4. The study of piracy in the Mediterranean has focused primarily on the ancient and the sixteenth-century manifestations of this recurrent problem. Few sources treat medieval piracy, although both L. Durand, *Pirates et barbaresques en Méditerranée*, Avignon, 1975, and R. Coulet du Gard, *La course et la piraterie en Méditerranée*, Paris, n.d. (c. 1980) each devote several pages to a brief survey. The work of L. Balleto has illuminated the phenomenon of piracy in southern Italy in the thirteenth century. See esp. *Mercanti, pirati e corsari nei mari della Corsica (sec. XII)*, Genova, 1978. F. Cheyette, "The Sovereign and the Pirates, 1332," *Speculum*, 45 (1970), 40–68, treats fourteenth-century piracy.

5. *Annales Gandenses*, ed. H. Johnstone, London, 1951, esp. 55, 91. See Chap. 1, this volume, for a fuller discussion of fortified churches in the *Annales Gandenses*.

6. Devic and Vaissete, IV, 227; and V, 554;

cited in P. Ponsich, "Les églises fortifiées du Roussillon," *Les Cahiers de Saint-Michel de Cuxa*, 17 (1986), 9–29, esp. 15–16. See also Villaneuva, *Viage literario*, 6, 340–1; and Bisson, 1977, 301.

7. On the presense of Islam in Languedoc, see esp., *Islam et chrétiens du Midi (XIIe – XIVe siècle)*, (Cahiers de Fanjeaux, 18), Toulouse, 1983. The hypothesis of reduced Islamic presence on the Mediterranean coast of France can only be supported by negative evidence. Researchers have noted, for example, reductions in the amount of eleventh- and twelfth-century Islamic ceramic in fieldwalk surveys, or the lack of destruction layers in habitation sites of this period. Clearly, much more work needs to be done on this subject before we can assess accurately the nature of the Islamic threat posed in late twelfth-century southern France. For a resumé of recent archaeological and documentary research on the Islamic presence in Catalonia and southern France, see J. Salrach, "L'enchâtellement de la frontière," in X. Barral i Altet, ed., *Le paysage monumental de la France autour de l'an mil*, Paris, 1987, 743–55; and J.M. Font Ruis, "Les modes de détention de châteaux dans la 'Vieux Catalone' et ses marches extérieures du début du IXe au début du XIe," in *Les structures sociales de l'Aquitaine, du Languedoc et de l'Espagne au premier âge féodal*, Paris, 1969, 63–78.

8. See Chap. 1, this volume, and H.E.J. Cowdrey, "Cluny and the First Crusade," *Revue Bénédictine*, 83, 1973, 285–311; H.E.J. Cowdrey, Pope Urban II's Preaching of the First Crusade," *History*, 55, 1970, 177–88; and B.Z. Kedar, *Crusade and Mission: European Approaches toward the Muslims*, Princeton, 1984.

9. "Summa culpabilis." See N. Daniel, *Islam and the West*, Edinborough, 1960, 112.

10. On mercenaries, see H. Géraud, "Les routiers au douzième siècle," *Bibliothèque de l'Ecole de Chartes*, III, Paris, 1841–2, 125–47; and Bisson, 1977, passim.

11. On heretics in twelfth-century France, see esp., W.L. Wakefield, *Heresy and Inquisition in Southern France, 1100–1250*, London, 1974; E. Peters, *Heresy and Authority in the Middle Ages*, London, 1980; M. Erbstösser, *Heretics in the Middle Ages*, trans. J. Fraser, Leipzig, 1984; and R.I. Moore, *The Formation of a Persecuting Society: Power and Deviance in Western Europe, 950–1250*, Oxford, 1987. For further sources, see the Bibliography, Section V.

12. R.I. Moore, *The Origins of European Dissent* (1977), 200–3; 232–7; and W.L. Wakefield, *Heresy, Crusade and Inquisition in Southern France, 1100–1250* (1974), 65–6.

13. C. Langlois, *Histoire des Croisades Albigeoises*, 1887, II, 219. Even allowing for the bias of critical northern clerics, there does seem to have been a remarkable sympathy toward the Cathars in many areas of Languedoc.

14. On Cathars and war, see P. Biller, "Medieval Waldensian abhorrence of killing pre-c. 1400," in W.J. Sheils, ed., *The Church and War*, Studies in Church History, 20 (1983) 129–46.

15. P. Ponsich, "Les églises fortifiées du Roussillon," *Les Cahiers de Saint-Michel de Cuxa*, 17 (1986), 9–29, esp. 18. See also P. de Marca, *Marca Hispanica*, cols. 518–19.

16. Pierre des Vaux de Cernay, *Hystoria*, I, 199–207, cited in Y. Dossat, "Le clergé méridional à la veille de la Croisade Albigeoise," *Revue historique et littéraire du Languedoc*, I, Albi, 1944, 276.

17. J. Guiraud, *Histoire de l'Inquisition au Moyen Age*, I, Paris, 1935, 307–9; and Y. Dossat, "Le clergé méridional à la veille de la Croisade Albigeoise," *Revue historique et littéraire du Languedoc*, I, Albi, 1944, 263–78, esp. 276; republished in *Eglise et hérésie en France au XIIIe siècle*, Variorum Reprints, 1982.

18. See Chap. 3, this volume, for a fuller discussion of Roger Trencavel and his actions at Saint-Pons. The text of his dispute with the abbey is found in Appendix 32. See also Y. Dossat, "Le clergé méridional à la veille de la Croisade Albigeoise," *Revue historique et littéraire du Languedoc*, I, Albi, 1944, 276.

19. On the fortification of cemeteries, see especially, E. Zadora-Rio, "The Role of Cemeteries in the Formation of Medieval Settlement in Western France," in C. Redman, ed., *Medieval Archaeology*, Binghamton, 1989, 171–86; and M. Fixot and E. Zadora-Rio, eds., *L'Eglise, Le Terroir* (Monographie du CRA, no. 1), Paris, 1989.

20. For an important resumé of textual and archaeological background of the phenome-

non of *incastellamento* in Languedoc, M. Bourin, "Le paysage bâti dans les campagnes bas-languedociennes: le temps de nos incertitudes," in X. Barral i Altet, ed., *Le paysage monumental de la France autour de l'an mil*, Paris, 1987, 409–14.

21. For a discussion of the relationship between documentary and archaeological evidence for early fortifications in Provence, see M. Fixot, "L'image du bâti," in X. Barral i Altet, ed., *Le paysage monumental de la France autour de l'an mil*, Paris, 1987, 671–80, esp. 677–9.

22. Within the large bibliography on *incastellamento*, see principally, P. Toubert, *Les structures du Latium médiéval: Le Latium méridional et la Sabine du IXe à la fin du XIIe siècle*, 2 vols., Rome, 1973, II, Chap. 4; A.A. Settia, *Castelli e villaggi nell'Italia padana*, Naples, 1984; A.A. Settia, "Incastellamento e decastellamento nell'italia padan, X e XI secolo," *Bolletino storico-bibliografico subalpino*, 1976, 5–26; and B. Cursente, "'Castra' et castelnaux dans le Midi de la France (XIe–XVe siècles)," in *Châteaux et peuplement en Europe occidentale du Xe au XIIIe siècle. Premières journées internationales d'histoire*, 1979, *Flaran*, I (Auch, 1980).

23. See Chap. 4.

24. The work of the Laboratoire d'Archéologie of the C.N.R.S. at the Université de Provence, esp. that of G. Demians d'Archimbaud, M. Fixot, and J.-P. Pelletier, has been pioneering in this area. Their publications are numerous. For a recent survey with bibliography, see M. Fixot, "L'image du bâti," in X. Barral i Altet, ed., *Le paysage monumental de la France autour de l'an mil*, Paris, 1987, 671–80

25. M. Bourin-Derruau, *Villages médiévaux en Bas-Languedoc*, Paris, 1987; and the recent work of A. Durand, summarized in *L'Eglise, Le Terroir*, ed. M. Fixot and E. Zadora-Rio, Paris, 1989.

26. The ongoing work of A. Parodi and C. Raynaud on the identification and phasing of late antique and early medieval sites for Languedoc, based on field-survey and textual analysis is also summarized in *L'Eglise, Le Terroir*, ed. M. Fixot and E. Zadora-Rio, Paris, 1989.

27. F. Cheyette, "The castles of the Trencavels, a preliminary aerial survey," in *Order and Innovation in the Middle Ages, essays in honor of Joseph R. Strayer*, ed. W.C. Jordan, B. McNab, and T.F. Ruiz, Princeton, 1976, 255–72; "The origins of European villages and the first European expansion," *Journal of Economic History*, 37, no. 1, 1977, 182–206; and F. Cheyette and C. Amado, "Organisation d'un terroir et d'un habitat concentré: un exemple languedocien," *Habitats fortifiés et organisation de l'espace en Méditerranée médiévale*, Lyon, 1982 (Lyon, 1983), 35–44.

28. Pierre Clément, *Les Chemins à travers les âges en Cévennes et Bas Languedoc*, Montpellier, 1989.

29. A.R. Lewis, "The Development of Town Government and Seigneurial Adminstration in Twelfth-Century Montpellier," *Speculum*, 22 (1947), 51–68 and 562–77. and M. Bourin-Derruau, *Villages médiévaux*, 1987.

30. F. Cheyette, "The castles of the Trencavels," 255–72; and "The origins of European villages and the first European expansion," *Journal of Economic History*, XXXVII, no. 1, 1977, 182–206.

31. See Chap. 4.

32. Within the extensive bibliography on the Truce and Peace of God, see in particular, E. Magnou-Nortier, *La société laïque et l'église dans la province ecclésiastique de Narbonne*, Toulouse, 1974, esp. Chap. 3; Bisson, 1977; Erdmann, 1977; A. Graboïs, "De la trêve de Dieu à la paix du roi: étude sur les transformations du mouvement de la paix au XIIe siècle," *Mélanges offerts à René Crozet*, ed. P. Gallais et Y-F. Riou, 2 vols., Poitiers, 1966, I, 585–96; and *Paix de Dieu et guerre sainte en Languedoc au XIIIe siècle (Cahiers de Fanjeaux 4)*, Toulouse, 1969. For further sources, see the Bibliography, Section VII.

33. See, for example, the Council of Saint-Gilles (1042–3): "Hanc pari consensu volunt et definiunt habere potestatem, ut nemo infra terminum XXX dextrorum circa ecclesias positum quicquam rapere praesumat." (Appendix 35), published in RHF, XI, 513; and Mortet and Deschamps, I, 116–17. On the reservation of zones of refuge, see E. Zadora-Rio, "La topographie de lieux d'asile dans les campagnes médiévales," in M. Fixot and E. Zadora-Rio, eds., *L'Eglise, Le Terroir*, Monographie du CRA, no. 1, Paris, 1989, 11–16. D. DuCange, *Glossar-*

ium Mediae et Infimae Latinitatis (entry on "*dextri*"), provides numerous examples, primarily from councils of the eleventh and twelfth centuries, of the usage of "XXX dextri" as a measure of "thirty paces" surrounding a church, and enjoying the right of asylum.

34. Bisson, 1977, 294–6; fns. 19–21.
35. On the twelfth-century revival of the peace, see principally, Bisson, 1977, as well as G. Molinié, *L'organisation judiciaire, militaire et financière des associations de la paix. Etude sur la Paix et la Trêve de Dieu dans le Midi et le Centre de la France*, Toulouse, 1912, esp. 32–40; and *Paix de Dieu et guerre sainte en Languedoc au XIIIe siècle* (*Cahiers de Fanjeaux* 4), Toulouse, 1969.
36. C. L.H. Coulson, "Rendability and Castellation in Medieval France" *Château Gaillard*, 6 (1973), 59–67.
37. Bisson, 1977.
38. For the councils, see the Bibliography, Section VIII.
39. On the Third Lateran Council, see especially, *Le troisième concile de Latran (1179): Sa place dans l'histoire*, communications présentées à la table ronde du C.N.R.S., 1980, ed. Jean Longère, Paris, 1982.
40. For this observation, and the examples which follow, I depend on Vicaire, 1969, esp. 106–9. See also E. Delaruelle, "Paix de Dieu et croisade dans la chrétienté," in the same volume, *Paix de Dieu et guerre sainte en Languedoc au XIIIe siècle* (*Cahiers de Fanjeaux* 4), Toulouse, 1969, 51–71.
41. H. Géraud, "Les routiers au douzième siècle," *Bibliothèque de l'Ecole de Chartes*, III, Paris, 1841–2, 137; and Vicaire, 1969, 107.
42. On Louis VII's actions against heresy, see the RHF, XVI, 697–8; and Pacaut, 1957, 78.
43. On the Council of Montpellier, see Mansi, XXII, 667–72; and Vicaire, 1969, 107–8.
44. D. DuCange, *Glossarium Mediae et Infimae Latinitatis* V (entry on "*incastellare*"), provides examples of fortified churches. See also discussion in Chapter 1 of this volume.
45. See Pierre Ponsich, "Les églises fortifiées du Roussillon," *Les Cahiers de Saint-Michel de Cuxa*, 17 (1986), esp. 14–19.
46. Within the large bibliography on Louis VII, see esp., A. Luchaire, *Etudes sur les actes de Louis VII*, Paris, 1885; Pacaut, 1957; and

Pacaut, 1964. See also the Bibliography, Section IX.
47. Louis confirmed royal protection for Maguelone in 1155, Bishop Guillaume of Agde sought and received royal permission to fortify Agde in 1173–4, and the prior of Saint-Pons appealed to the king in c. 1164, though it is not recorded whether Louis responded. See Appendixes 6, 24, and 31. See also Pacaut, 1957, esp. 72–77 and 129–30.
48. Cf., for example, Odo of Deuil, RHF xii, 123.
49. Pacaut, 1964, esp. 222–3.
50. I present only a brief summary of Louis' southern contacts here. For further discussion, see Pacaut, 1957 and 1964.
51. On Louis' relations with Raymond V of Toulouse, see Pacaut, 1957, 129–30; and Pacaut, 1964, 184–7.
52. Pacaut, 1957, 73–4.
53. On Louis' relations with powerful families of Languedoc, see Pacaut, 1957, 129–33.
54. Pacaut, 1957, 129–30.
55. In the early part of his reign, before c. 1152, Louis engaged in rather grandiose schemes of political intervention and control. Often criticized is his backing of the unsuccessful candidate Cadurc for the archbishopric of Bourges. Despite this unhappy example of royal interference, the remainder of Louis' episcopal appointments were handled with much greater finesse and success.
56. Pacaut, 1964, 106–7; and A. Luchaire, *Etudes sur les actes de Louis VII*, 1885, no. 65.
57. Pacaut, 1964, 106–7. For Villemagne, see A. Luchaire, *Etudes sur les actes de Louis VII*, 1885, no. 379. For Saint-Julien-de-Brioude, see Luchaire, *Etudes*, no. 220.
58. See Bisson, 1977, esp. 295–6; RHF 14, pp. 378–88; A. Graboïs, "De la trêve de Dieu à la paix du roi: étude sur les transformations du mouvement de la paix au XIIe siècle," *Mélanges offerts à René Crozet*, ed. P. Gallais et Y-F. Riou, 2 vols., Poitiers, 1966, I, 585–96, esp. 588.
59. Bisson, 1977, 295; fn. 24.
60. See Chap. 3, this volume, for a fuller discussion of the act. It is published in *Gallia Christiana*, VI, Instrumentum XVIII, cols. 328–29; A. Luchaire, *Etude des Actes de Louis VII*, 1885, no. 650 (partial text); Terrin, 1969, no. 352; and Castaldo, 1970,

pièce justificative, no. 10. The diploma is discussed in Castaldo, 1970, 68–74.

61. See Pacaut, 1957, esp. 72–7 and 129–30.

62. Pacaut, 1957, 77; *Gallia Christiana,* VI, 1049; and A. Luchaire, *Etude sur les Actes de Louis VII,* 1885, no. 598.

CHAPTER 3

1. Sources in the Archives départementales de l'Herault, Montpellier; ser. G, from the sixth to the sixteenth centuries, witness the presence of disputes over just these issues.

2. Vestiges of this bridge were still visible in 1900.

3. Fabrège's excavations revealed numerous Roman and Gallo-Roman sculpted fragments and ceramic, which led him to propose the existence of a lost Roman city at Maguelone. Excavation in 1967 by J.-C. M. Richard, however, demonstrated some Gallo-Roman presence but no city, and no habitation outside the circle of the abbey precinct. On the archaeology of Maguelone, see Fabrège; and, more recently, J.-C.M. Richard, "Maguelone, petit île, grand passé," *Archéologia,* 23 (1968), 50–5. A fuller article by M. Richard on the excavations at Maguelone is forthcoming. In the interim, an unpublished dossier at the Direction des Antiquités, Montpellier, can be consulted by appointment. I am grateful to M. Richard for sharing with me the results of his excavations in advance of publication.

4. Boetius, the first known prelate, sent a deacon to represent Maguelone at the third Council of Toledo, and went himself to the Council of Narbonne in 590. See L. Duchesne, *Fastes épiscopaux,* t. I, 307.

5. MGH, Scriptores, ed. G. Pertz, I, 292–300, esp. 292.

6. In late nineteenth- and early twentieth-century excavations of the site, Fabrège identified fragments of Islamic pottery, which may provide physical evidence for the "Saracen raiders" of early medieval texts. The excavations by J.-C.M. Richard, however, revealed no Islamic material nor any evidence of the kind of massive burning or destruction that would have accompanied a sack of the abbey in the early medieval period.

7. On the early bishops of Maguelone, see esp., L. de la Roque, *Les évêques de Maguelone et de Montpellier,* Montpellier, 1893, 1–19.

8. "Urbanus episcopus servus servorum Dei, dialectis in Christo filiis Ocgerio aridiacono, Raimundo sacerdoti, et Deodato subdiacono, ceterisque in Magalonensi ecclesia cononicam vitam professis . . . ," Bull of Urban II, 14 March 1095, published in *Gallia Christiana,* VI, Instrumentum 352–4. The bull is also discussed in Germain, 1869, 12–15; and Fabrège, I, 116–17.

9. See also L. Paulot, *Un pape français: Urbain II,* Paris, 1903, 400–1. Monastic communities owned by the papacy were listed in the *Liber Censuum,* the description of papal properties compiled by Censius in 1192. See P. Fabre and L. Duchesne, eds., *Le Liber censuum de l'église romaine,* 3 vols., Paris, 1889–1952, esp. I, 243–7; V. Pfaff, "Sankt Peters Abteien im 12 Jahrhundert," *Zeitschrift der Savigny-Stiftung für Rechtsgeschichte* 57, 1971, 150–95; and I.S. Robinson, *The Papacy 1073–1198: Continuity and Innovation,* Cambridge, 1990, 221–30.

10. The episcopal arms changed with each bishop, whereas the chapter arms remained the same. On the arms of Maguelone, see Fabrège, I, 181–91.

11. Suger's account of the island is contained in his *Vie de Louis VI le Gros,* ed. Henri Waquet, Paris, 1929. See Appendix 5. On Pons de Melgueil, see A. Bredero, *Cluny et Cîteaux au douzième siècle: L'Histoire d'une controverse monastique,* Amsterdam and Maarssen, 1985.

12. While at Maguelone, from the 20 to 30 June, Callixtus signed three acts in favor of Saint-Gilles and sent a letter to the canons of Besançon. See DeVic and Vaissete, II, 383, 635; Germain, 1869, 17; and Fabrège, 218–19.

13. Pope Innocent came to the region following a prolonged stay in Pisa and Genoa, possibly stopping at Maguelone before moving on, by 11 September, to Saint-Gilles. See DeVic and Vaissete, II, 405; and Fabrège, 237.

14. "Anno MCLXIII III idus aprilis, que fuit II feria post Pascha, Alexander papa IIIus, pontificatus sui anno quarto, cum certis cardinalibus et prelatis apulit Magalonam, et stetit ibi trebus diebus, et exta feria dedicavit majus altare in ecclesia Magalone, in honorem apostolorum Petri et Pauli." Arnaud de Verdale, *Catalogus episcoporum Magalonensium,* ed. A. Germain, *Arnaud*

de Verdale, évêque et chroniqueur, Montpellier, 1881, 98; *Gallia Christiana,* VI, 753. (The date is in fact in error, noted by Fabrège, 276, fn. 1, since Easter in 1163 fell instead on March 24). On papal dedications, see also see also R. Crozet, "Etude sur les consécrations pontificales," BM, 104, 1946, 5–46.

15. The Statutes are published in Germain, 1869; and in the *Cartulaire de Maguelone,* Vol. 5, no. 1641, 205–352. See Appendix 11 for an extensive excerpt.

16. On modern repairs, see the archives preserved for Maguelone in Monuments Historiques, Paris.

17. See J. Vallery-Radot, "L'ancienne cathédrale de Maguelone," CA, 108 (Montpellier), 1950, 60–89, esp. plan, 67, which assigns the walls and the machicolations of the nave to two separate (but contemporaneous) phases.

18. Portions of the machicolations were consolidated by Monuments Historiques in 1942 under the supervision of M. Creuzot. While Vallery-Radot separates the walls and machicolations of the northern and western faces into two phases of construction, he accepts the machicolations of the chevet as integral with the eastern fabric. He describes a "sondage profond de 1m50," next to the chevet wall, carried out by H. Lefebvre, architect of Monuments Historiques, at the request of Vallery-Radot. No distinction could be observed by Vallery-Radot beween the foundations of the wall and machicolations. It seems that no corresponding excavation was carried out for the other wall foundations. See J. Vallery-Radot, "L'ancienne cathédrale de Maguelone," CA, 108 (Montpellier), 1950, 60–89, esp. 81–82. No further report seems to exist on the excavations.

19. For the galleries of the "tower of Saint Augustine," see J. Vallery-Radot, "L'ancienne cathédrale de Maguelone," CA, 108 (Montpellier), 1950, 60–89; and Chapter 4, this volume.

20. Augustinian customaries dictate the necessity for canons (who were also consecrated priests) to serve daily Mass. A copy of the customary for nearby Augustinian Saint-Ruf survives as Ms. 716 in the Bibliothèque d'Avignon. This manuscript, an edition of the eleventh century, was reedited for use at Maguelone. See A. Carrier, *Coutumier du XI siècle de l'Ordre de Saint-Ruf en Usage à la cathédrale de Maguelone,* Quebec, 1950, esp. 43–5.

21. The *Chronicon vetus* is preserved at the Archives départementales de l'Hérault, Montpellier, inserted into the *Cartulaire de l'évêché de Maguelone,* Reg. B; fol. 257v. to 259v. It was discovered by A. Germain, and first published in *Chronique inédite de Maguelone,* an extract from *Mémoires de la Société archéologique de Montpellier,* III, Montpellier, 1853, 357–70. Germain republished the Chronicon in 1869 as an appendix to his study (Germain, 1869). It was again reprinted by E. Mabille in DeVic and Vaissete, V, Toulouse, 1875, cols. 55–60. The definitive edition is J. Berthelé, *Chronicon Magalonense vetus,* Montpellier, 1908. Berthelé makes critical comparison of the original twelfth-century Chronicon with the fourteenth-century "corrected" transcription written by Arnaud de Verdale in his *Catalogus episcoporum Magalonensium.* The best edition of Arnaud's text is given by A. Germain as an appendix to his *Arnaud de Verdale, évêque et chroniqueur,* Montpellier, 1881, 481–601.

22. See the *Cartulaire de Maguelone,* Vol. 1, no. 130 (1168), 250–1.

23. B. of Trèves seems not to have been a canon at Maguelone, and there is no mention of him in the abbey's cartulary. A "Bernard of Treviers" appears once in the cartulary of the Guilhems (ed. A. Germain, p. 244) but is listed there in the middle of a listing of lay supporters. For a discussion of the identity of Bertrand and B. of Trèves, see the *Cartulaire de Maguelone,* Vol. 1, 259–60. For a discussion of the lintel, we await Calvin B. Kendall's forthcoming book on inscriptions in southern French buildings.

24. On the date of Jean de Montlaur's death, see the *Cartulaire de Maguelone,* Vol. 1, no. 202, which fixes the date as 2 November 1190. See also Rouquette's discussion, 259–60. The text of the slab is very ambiguous and does not make clear if the last stanza refers to Jean de Montlaur's death or to Bertrand's act of burial.

25. "Anno MCLXIII III idus aprilis, que fuit II feria post Pascha, Alexander papa IIIus, pontificatus sui anno quarto, cum certis car-

dinalibus et prelatis apulit Magalonam, et stetit ibi trebus diebus, et exta feria dedicavit majus altare in ecclesia Magalone, in honorem apostolorum Petri et Pauli." Arnaud de Verdale, *Catalogus episcoporum Magalonensium*, ed. A. Germain, *Arnaud de Verdale, évêque et chroniqueur*, Montpellier, 1881, 98; *Gallia Christiana*, VI, 753. (The date is in fact in error, noted by Fabrèges, 276, fn. 1, since Easter in 1163 fell instead on March 24.) On papal dedications, see also see also R. Crozet, "Etude sur les consécrations pontificales," BM, 104, 1946, 5–46.

26. On the papal visit, see the *Catalogus* (Appendix 8).

27. *Cartulaire de Maguelone*, 7 vols., 1912–25; and J. Rouquette and A. Villemagne, eds., *Bullaire de Maguelone*, 2 vols., 1911.

28. Louis' acts of 1155, 1156, 1161, and 1179 are published in A. Luchaire, *Etude sur les actes de Louis VII*, Paris, 1885, nos. 340, 366, 466, and 771. See also Pacaut, 1964, 84.

29. "Romanae ecclesiae protectione specialiter confovendum suscipimus." Epistolae Urbani Papae II, 14 Dec. 1088, in RHF, XIV, 690; and *Gallia Christiana*, VI, Instrumentum 350–1.

30. On Roman *opus isodomus*, or alternating header-stretcher construction, see J.-P. Adam, *La construction romaine: matériaux et techniques*, Paris, 1989, 117–23.

31. On the portal, see R. de Lasteyrie, *Etudes sur la sculpture française au moyen-âge*, Paris, 1902, 76–7, 130–1; and R. Saint-Jean, "Maguelone," in *Languedoc roman*, 236–7.

32. On the use of Carolingian precedent by the Capetians, see A. Luchaire, *Histoire des institutions monarchiques de la France sous les premiers Capétiens*, Paris, 1871, esp. I, 74; F. Lot, "Origine et signification du mot 'carolingien,'" *Revue historique*, XLVI, 1891, 68–73; R. Folz, *Le souvenir et la légende de Charlemagne dans l'empire germanique médiéval*, Paris, 1950; K.F. Werner, "Die Legitimitat der Kapetinger und die Entstehung der 'reditus regni Francorum ad stirpem Karoli,'" *Die Welt als Geschichte*, XII, 1952, 203ff.; C. van de Kieft, "Deux diplômes faux de Charlemagne pour Saint-Denis au XIIe siècle," *Le Moyen Age*, XIII, 1958, 401ff.; and G. Spiegel, "The *reditus regni ad stirpem*

caroli magni: a new look," *French Historical Studies*, VII, 1971, 145–74.

33. On the early history of Agde, see J. Pichiere, *Histoire d'Agde*, Lyon, 1961.

34. The foundation of the bishopric of Agde is controversial. The *Notitia Gallicarum*, of the fourth century A.D., does not mention Agde in its accounting of the province of Narbonne. The authors of the *Gallia Christiana* list bishop Venuste as the first bishop, with a foundation in 408 A.D. (*Gallia Christiana*, VI, 664–6). However, the first certain documentary attestation of a bishop of Agde comes in 506 A.D., when a council at Agde is called with Sophronius in attendance. By this time at least two churches had been established within the late Roman walls of the city: S. André and S. Martin. It is not until the the late ninth century that the testament of Apollonius (written in 872), attests to a church with dedication to Saint Stephen and to the existence of a group of canons. Testament of Apollonius (872): "via qui discurrit ad ecclesiam S. Stephani."

35. On the excavated apse, see M. Martin, "Mémoire sur la cathédrale d'Agde," published by L. Noguier in a "Rapport sur le concours des mémoires historiques," in *Bulletin de la Société archéologique de Béziers*, 2nd ser., VII, 1873, 152–206; and L. Noguier, "L'église Saint-Etienne d'Agde," *Mélanges publiés à l'occasion du jubilé épiscopal de Msgr. Cabrières*, Paris, 1899. On the Carolingian phase at Agde, see J. Vallery-Radot, "L'ancienne cathédrale Saint-Etienne d'Agde," CA, 108, (Montpellier), 1950, 201–18, who however, mistakes the forged charter of 848 for legitimate.

36. D. Cazes, "Notes sur un chapiteau du cloître de la cathédrale d'Agde," *Etudes sur l'Hérault*, n.s., 4, 1988, 91–2.

37. M. Adgé, "Les marques de tacherons à la cathédrale d'Agde," *Etudes sur Pézénas*, 1967.

38. See, for example, L. Noguier, "L'église de Saint-Etienne d'Agde," *Mélanges publiés à l'occasion du jubilé épiscopale de Mgr. de Cabrières*, Paris, 1899, I, 157.

39. Published plans of this disaxiality, however, vary widely. The plan reproduced here is the result of two campaigns of measurement with steel tapes and theodolite, in 1987 and 1989–90.

40. This opinion is expressed by L. Noguier, "L'église de Saint-Etienne d'Agde," *Mélanges publiés à l'occasion du jubilé episcopal de Mgr. de Cabrières*, Paris, 1899; Dainville, M. de, "Les églises romanes du diocèse de Montpellier," *Monspeliensia*, 2.1 (1936); 2.2 (1937) 177–290; 2.3 (1940), 297–443; and P. de Gorsse, *Monographie de la cathédrale Saint-Etienne d'Agde*, Toulouse, 1922.

41. The south crossing arm has two cubic capitals, both decorated with curious beasts: a four-legged beast and a duck to the east, and the same motives but abraded to the west. The capitals in the north transept are Corinthian, with a double row of leaves with berries. These are probably local copies of the reused capitals of the crossing. The consoles upon which the intermediate transverse arch rests are decorated with human heads and animals.

42. The chronology of fortification of the cathedral has been discussed by R. Foreville, "Les testaments agathois du Xe au XIIIe siècle d'après les cartulaires de l'église d'Agde," *Bulletin philologique et historique du Comité des Travaux Historiques et Scientifiques*, 1961 (1963), 386; and Castaldo, 1970, 69. See also R. Foreville, "Un diocèse languedocien au Moyen-Age: Histoire et documents de l'église d'Agde," *Journal des Savants*, n.s., III, 1971, 187–205; R. Foreville, "Le chapitre cathédrale d'Agde d'après le cartulaire de Saint-Etienne," in *Les évêques, les clercs et le roi (1250–1300)* (*Cahiers de Fanjeaux, VII*), Toulouse, 1972, 285–333; and L. Gigou, "Les possessions des évêques d'Agde des IXe au début XIIIe siècle: étude historique et archéologique des fortifications et des édifices religieux," *Etudes sur Pézénas et sa région*, V, no. 3, 1974, 3–16. The cartulary of the bishopric is preserved in Paris, Bibliothèque Nationale, ms. lat. 9999, in a copy by A. Jourdan dated 1764. This cartulary is signaled by Henri Stein, *Bibliographie générale des cartulaires français*, Paris, 1907 (Kraus reprint, 1967), 4. Two copies survive of the chapter cartulary: the first, a copy by L'abbé de Gohin (1767–90), is conserved in the Bibliothèque de Montpellier, ms. 33. This copy is also cited in Stein, *Bibliographie*, 4. The second, also a copy by de Gohin, is now in the Archives départementales de l'Hérault, ms. G20. Manuscript 33 of the chapter cartulary was partially published by J. Rouquette, *Cartulaire de l'église d'Agde. Cartulaire du chapitre*, Montpellier, 1925; and was more fully published and analyzed by Terrin, 1969.

43. See Appendix 23 for an extensive excerpt. The charter, preserved in the *Cartulaire de l'Evêché* (no. 3) as well as in the *Cartulaire du Chapître* (no. 3), was established as false by A. Levillain, "Le sacre de Charles le Chauve," *Bibliothèque de l'Ecole de Chartes*, LXIV, 1903, 36, no. 3. It is published and discussed by A. Giry, M. Prou, and G. Tessier, *Recueil des actes de Charles II le Chauve*, II, Paris, 1952, 560; as well as by Terrin, 1969, no. 3; and Castaldo, 1970, 64–8, and pièce justificative no. 1.

44. Foreville, "Les testaments agathois," passim; and Castaldo, 1970, 66–8.

45. See, for example, J. Vallery-Radot, "L'ancienne cathédrale Saint-Etienne d'Agde," CA, 108 (Montpellier), 1950, 201–18; and J. Nougaret and A. Burgos, "Saint-Etienne d'Agde," in *Languedoc roman*, 245–52. Historians such as Foreville, "les testaments agathois," 386, and Castaldo, 1970, 69, however, have signaled the possibility of an earlier chronology for the fortifications at Agde.

46. The question of whether testament gifts are "liquid" in the year of donation or in the year of death, has seldom been explored in the scholarship. I continue here the common practice of accepting them as property of the cathedral in the year of donation, but Terrin, 1969, and Foreville ("Les testaments agathois") have recognized that more variance must surely have occurred. It is sometimes the case that the terms *fabrica* and *opus* refer to separate entities, the first to the actual building in progress, and the second to the building fund, not necessarily related to present construction. Although this distinction sometimes obtains in the documentary records of other sites, only the terms *opus* or *operi* are used in the testaments for Agde.

47. Cartulary of the Chapter, no. 9. See Terrin, 1969, 20–1. On donations, see Castaldo, 1970, 9–11, 97–100.

48. See Castaldo, 1970, esp. 69, and 96–100; Forcville, "Les testaments agathois," esp. 386; and Terrin, 1969, passim.

49. On this issue generally, see R. Branner, "'Fabrica, opus' and the Dating of Mediaeval Monuments," *Gesta*, XV, 1976, 27–9.

50. "Ad reparationem altaris S. Stephani et ad chorum perfeciendum mille solidorum melgorinsium . . . et reaedificationem ecclesias S. Stephani." The testament of Ermengaud is published in *Gallia Christiana* VI, Instrumentum, cols. 323–4; and Terrin, 1969, Introduction, lxxxiii–lxxxiv, and is excerpted in Appendix 15 of this volume.

51. I am grateful to Michael Gleason for help in clarifying the terms of Bertrand's debt repayment schemes.

52. "De municipio autem illo quod in eadem (terra) ad utilitatem nostram et regni nostri defensionem constituimus, quia in confinio hostium eis importunum, nobis autem aptum et opportunum erit, praecipimus et confirmamus ut deinceps firmum maneat et sicut abbas ejusdem ecclesiae illud firmum fecerit ita stare et in nullo infirmari permittus." M. de Laurière et al., eds., *Ordonnances des Roys de France de la Troisième Race, recueillies par ordre chronologique*, 21 vols., Paris, 1723–1849, XI, 178. Discussed by C. Coulson, "Seigneurial Fortresses in France in Relation to Public Policy: c. 864–c. 1483," unpublished doctoral dissertation, King's College, London, 1972, 47.

53. See Appendix 30.

54. Louis d'Outremer awarded protection to the abbey of Saint-Pons in a charter of 939. See DeVic and Vaissete, V, 173–85, and *Gallia Christiana*, VI, 223–4.

55. J. Bènes, *Recherches historiques sur Frotard* (Montpellier, 1875).

56. On the history of the abbots of Saint-Pons, and the sequence of donations, see Sahuc, 84–103.

57. Ruinart, *Vita papae Urbani II*, no. 267; cited in Bènes, *Recherches historiques*.

58. Pierre II, who reigned for only a year (1145–6) can have had no real impact.

59. These donations are recorded in the unpublished sixteenth-century abbey inventories, in *Gallia Christiana,* and in papal bulls of confirmation. Among the members of the monastic community at Saint-Pons were: Ramire, who later became king of Aragon; Pierre, who later became abbot of Pampelona; Bérangar, son of the viscount of Narbonne and later the abbot of LaGrassse; Pons, son of Pierre, count of Melgueil and later abbot of Cluny; and Sicard, son of the viscount of Lautrec (see Sahuc, p. 9, fn. 1).

60. Archives municipales, Saint-Pons-de-Thomières.

61. Ibid.

62. My plans (Figs. 52, 58–60) were produced in a series of survey campaigns with steel tapes and theodolite, from 1986 through 1989. No previous plans of the galleries at Saint-Pons have been published. My ground-floor plan differs from previous published plans in its greater attention to the irregularities of the building (which are considerable) and in its registration of features such as the stair vises, which allow us to correlate and to understand the interrelationship of the entire galleried system of the building.

63. M. Durliat, "Saint-Pons-de-Thomières," CA, 108 (Montpellier), 1950, 271–89.

64. Unfortunately, no excavation report exists, and no photographs or drawings record the masonry of these foundations, so that further identification is impossible. In private conversation (Oct. 1989), M. Durliat agreed with my later dating of the excavated apse.

65. A handwritten report by Granier is preserved in the archives of the Direction des Antiquités in Montpellier. I am grateful to Mlle Claire Granier for sharing with me her recollection of her father's observations, to l'Archiprêtre Michel Quatrefages for his notes, and to several local eyewitnesses for their memories of the excavations. The dimensions for the Gothic chevet set in brick in the present parvis are certainly in error in both their dimensions and their polygonal shape.

66. Sahuc, 26–7.

67. On mural passages and galleries in southern buildings, see principally, P. Héliot, "Les coursières et les passages muraux dans les églises fortifiées du Midi de la France, d'Espagne et du Portugal aux XIIIe et XIVe siècles," *Anuario de estudios medievales,* VI, 1969, 187–217; and E. Vernolle, "Passages muraux et escaliers," *Cahiers de civilisation médiévale,* XXXII, 1989, 43–58. See also the Bibliography, Section XII.

68. For an account of the sad archival history of the town and abbey, see Sahuc, 10–14.

69. Published in RHF, tome 16, Paris, 1814, 114, no. 349. M. Durliat was the first to signal the importance of this text to the chronology of construction at Saint-Pons in "Saint-Pons-de-Thomières," CA, 108 (Montpellier), 1950, 271–89.

70. In episcopal sees where there was a very strong lord with whom Louis was not allied, Louis often did not intervene, even when invited to do so by bishop or community. For example, a request for protection, in 1169, from Bishop Artaud of Elne was answered but not acted upon, since Louis evidently did not wish to cross the powerful count of Rousillon. See Chap. 2.

71. Sadly, nothing medieval now remains of this twelfth-century castle that would aid in comparison with the twelfth-century campaigns at Saint-Pons. On La Salvetat, see J. Clerc, *Pierres d'histoire: Ballade historique autour du thème Salvetois*, Ferrières, 1987.

CHAPTER 4

1. See Chap. 2.

2. See, for example, the *Cartulaire de Maguelone*, Vol. 1, no. 70 (1144), 139–43; no. 115 (1163), 228–31; and no. 135 (1168), 260–3.

3. See Chap. 3.

4. "Anno eiusdem Incarnacionis millesimo centesimo sexagesimo VII, manifestum sit, quod de querimoniis et querelis, quas prepositus Magalonensis adversus dominum J(ohannem), episcopum Magalonensem. . . . De cultellis, sic, ut sint in poteste episcopi, ita tamen ut non possit eos alienare; sed habeat eos ad mensam Magalone, et sint salvi Ecclesie. . . . De armigeris vero et cursoribus atque familia sua, sic, ut nullum in camera sua ad mensam introducat" in the *Cartulaire de Maguelone*, Vol. 1, no.135 (1168), 260–3. I am indebted to Fredric Cheyette for drawing my attention to this passage.

5. *Anglo-Saxon Chronicle*, 1070.

6. Rey, 1925, 32–3; DeVic and Vaissete, VIII, col. 1472.

7. See Chap. 2.

8. Sahuc, 51. Guilhem, count of Toulouse witnessed an act at the abbey of Saint-Pons at the altar, and in the presence of the relics of Saint-Pons and other saints. See Devic and Vaissete, V, 648ff. Sources for the feasts of commemoration for these saints can be found in Bibliothèque de Toulouse ms. 64, f. 45; B.N., Paris ms. lat. 12, 733, f. 286 v.

9. The text is reproduced in *Gallia Christiana*, 6, col. 349.

10. See Patrick Geary, *Furta Sacra*, Princeton, 1978, for a careful analysis of the varied motivations behind the "translations" of relics. On Saint-Savin, see R. Favreau, "L'abbaye de Saint-Savin-sur-Gartempe," in *Romains et Barbares entre Loire et Gironde IV-X siècles*, exhibition catalogue, Poitiers, 1989. Geary observes (*Furta Sacra*, 136–9), however, that the destruction of archives during the Norman depredations permitted retrospective rationalizations for relic theft as well as identifications of relic identity. On the holy shroud of Cadouin, see Rey, 1925, 34–5; Catel, *Mémoires de l'histoire de Languedoc*, 1673, 265, 929; On Vénerque, see Rey, 1925, 35–6; E. Roschach, *Foix et Comminges*, 303; de Lahondès, *Bulletin de la Société archéologique du Midi de la France*, 1893, 67.

11. On the archaeology of Maguelone, see above, Chap. 3.

12. This plan is now conserved as part of the "Archives Fabrèges" in the Société archéologique de Montpellier. An annotated copy was published by H. Buriot-Darsiles, *Maguelone, petite île, grand passé*, Montpellier, s.d. (1937). Robert Saint-Jean, then président of the SAM, was the first to publish the original nineteenth-century plan in *Les Etangs à l'Epoque Médiévale*, Montpellier, 1986.

13. See Chap. 3.

14. For a discussion of dedications to Saint Michael, see Chap. 1.

15. If we accept this reconstruction of a southern gallery passage in the thickness of the wall, we must wonder where the passage was intended to lead. It may have connected the "Tower of Saint Augustine" with the tribune and, eventually, to the thirteenth-century west tower block. Unfortunately, both ends of this passsage are so rebuilt as to prevent verification.

16. J.-C.M. Richard, "Maguelone, petit île, grand passé," *Archéologia*, 23 (1968), 50–5.

17. See, for example, J. Rouquette and A. Villemagne, eds., *Cartulaire de Maguelone*, Vol. 5, 1923, no. 1602 (1329); no. 1603 (1329); or no. 1693 (1335).

18. A. Castaldo, *Le consulat médiéval d'Agde*, Paris, 1974, 340.

19. See Chap. 3.

20. Castaldo, 1970, 74–80.

21. On the *consulat*, see esp. A. Dupont, "Les origines des consulats en Languedoc (Xe au

XIIe siècle)," *Ecole antique de Nîmes*, 15, (1934), 85–107; A. Gouron, "Diffusion des consulats méridionaux et expansion du droit romain aux XIIe et XIIIe siècles," *Bibliothèque de l'Ecole des Chartes*, 121 (1963), 26–76; and A. Castaldo, *Le consulat médiéval d'Agde (XIIIe-XIVe siècle)*, Paris, 1974.

22. For a discussion of the military organization of the town, see A. Castaldo, *Consulat*, 1974, 331–69.

23. See A. Castaldo, *Consulat*, 1974, 335, fn. 14.

24. Ibid., 341, fn. 28.

25. Ibid.

26. It is interesting to note that at least one of these *capitaines* was a priest who the consuls complain "is more occupied with things divine than with military strategy." See Castaldo, *Consulat*, 1974, 364 and fn. 81.

27. The "Livre des Libertés et Franchises" of the abbey is preserved in the Archives départementales de Nîmes. It is discussed in Sahuc, II, 11.

CHAPTER 5

1. On twelfth-century architecture of the Midi, see principally, E. Mâle, "L'architecture gothique du Midi de la France," *Revue des deux mondes*, I, 1926, 826–57; R. Rey, *L'art gothique du Midi de la France*, Paris, 1934; V. Allègre, *Art roman dans la région albigeoise*, Toulouse, 1943, 197–8; P. Héliot, "Les débuts de l'architecture gothique dans le Midi de la France, L'Espagne et le Portugal," *Anuario de estudios medievales*, IX, 1972–3, 105–41; Durliat, 1973–4; Paul, 1974; and Paul, 1988. See the Bibliography, Section X.

2. On the use of the transverse arch and of the pointed barrel vault, see H. and E. du Ranquet, "De l'emploi des arc-doubleaux sous les berceaux romans," BM, 98, 1939, 189–214, esp. 200–2, "Eglises à nef éclairée sous berceaux brisés."

3. J. Bony, *French Gothic Architecture of the Twelfth to Thirteenth Centuries*, Berkeley, 1983, 73–6.

4. For a structural discussion of the spans of these buildings, see Paul, 1988, 106–7. Paul suggests that if the passages were positioned at the springing of the vault, then they may have helped to deflect the horizontal thrust of the main vault. In many cases, such as that of Saint-Pons, however, the passages are above and behind the springing and instead lighten the upper walls. In my structural understanding of these buildings, I have profited from discussion with Robert Mark, Vivian Paul, Richard Sundt, and my co-authors in *Architectural Technology up to the Scientific Revolution*, Cambridge, MA: 1993.

5. On the so-called temple of Diana, see R. Peyre, *Nîmes, Arles, Orange*, Paris, 1903, 22; R. Naumann, *Der Quellbezirk von Nîmes*, Berlin and Leipzig, 1937; V. Lasalle, *Nîmes de l'Antiquité à nos jours*, Paris, 1967; and V. Lasalle, "Temple de Diane," in X. Barral i Altet, ed., *Le paysage monumental de la France autour de l'an mil*, Paris, 1987, 417.

6. D.S. Robertson suggests that the vaulting system at Nîmes was designed to reduce the amount of centering necessary for construction. According to his view, the transverse arches would have been constructed with centering but the rest of the vault lifted into place by hoists. R. Peyre disagrees, seeing the vault as an unusual interlocking system of ashlar blocks, all installed at the same time and with centering. On the construction of Roman vaults, see principally, J.-P. Adam, *La construction romaine: matériaux et techniques*, Paris, 1989, Chap. 6; and D.S. Robertson, *Greek and Roman Architecture*, Cambridge, 2nd ed., 1943, Chap. 15.

7. I will develop this topic further in a book entitled *The Afterlife of Antiquity: Roman Architecture in Medieval Provence*.

8. Other masonry vaults, such as the funerary monument of Patara in Lycia (2nd c.?) are, however, known. (See Adam, *La construction romaine*, 1989, Chap. 6.)

9. J. Boube, "Les sarcophages paleochretiens de Martres-Tolosane," *Cahiers archéologiques*, 9 (1957), 34.

10. L. Noguier, "L'église Saint-Etienne d'Agde," *Mélanges publiés à l'occasion du jubilé épiscopal de Msgr. Cabrières*, Paris, 1899; and Fabrège.

11. W. Whitehill, *Spanish Romanesque Architecture*, Oxford, 1941, esp. 13–18; and J. Puig i Cadafalch, *Le Premier Art Roman*, Paris, 1928, esp. 46–8.

12. R. Guild, *The Cathedral d'Aix-en-Provence: Etude Archéologique*, Paris, 1987; and R. Guild, J. Guyon, L. Rivet and M. Vec-

chione, "Saint-Sauveur d'Aix-en-Provence: la cathédral et le baptistère," CA , 143, Pays d'Aix (1985), 37–42.

13. L. Sigal, "Contribution à l'histoire de la cathédrale Saint-Just de Narbonne," *Bulletin de la Commission Archéologique de Narbonne,* xv (1921–3), 12–153; A. Bonnery, "Narbonne (Aude) Cathédrale Saints-Just-et-Pasteur," in X. Barral i Altet, ed., *Le Paysage monumental de la France autour de l'an mil,* Paris, 1987, 456–7.

14. Paul, 1988, 105, fn. 8.

15. V. Allègre, "Lavaur, ancienne cathédrale Saint-Alain," *Dictionnaire des églises de France,* III-A, 1967, 69–71; although G. Ahlsell de Toulza, "La cathédrale Saint-Alain de Lavaur," CA, 143, (1985), 325–44, argues that the thirteenth-century nave does not incorporate earlier fabric.

16. A. Mayeux, *Histoire de Saint-Jean-le-Vieux,* Caen, 1913; J.-A. Brutails, "Rapports sur les fouilles pratiquées dans l'église de Saint-Jean-le-Vieux," *Bulletin de la Société agricole, scientifique et littéraire des Pyrénées-Orientales,* 28 (1887; P. Ponsich, "Saint-Jean-le-Vieux," *Etudes roussillonaises,* 3 (1953); R. Marichal, "Perpignan (Pyrénées-Orientales) Cathédrale Saint-Jean-le-Vieux," in X. Barral i Altet, ed., *Le Paysage monumental de la France autour de l'an mil,* Paris, 1987, 471.

17. M. Durliat, "L'église de Caunes-Minervois," CA, 131, Pays de l'Aude (1973), 44–53; and Durliat (1973–4), 63–132, esp. 79.

18. V.M. Barsch, "The Sculpture and Architecture of Saint-Trophîme, Arles," unpublished Ph.D. dissertation, Northwestern University, 1971, Paul, 1988, 105.

19. A. Bonnery, "Azille (Aude) Saint-Etienne-de-Tersan," in X. Barral i Altet, ed., *Le Paysage monumental de la France autour de l'an mil,* Paris, 1987, 453.

20. Paul, 1974, 29; M. Durliat, "L'église de Saint-Martin de Moissac," BM, 128 (1970), 41–5.

21. J.-L. Biget, "La cathédrale Sainte-Cécile d'Albi. L'architecture," CA, 143 (1985), 20–62.

22. Durliat, 1973–4, 63–132, esp. 80; P. Lablaude, "Saint-Nazaire de Béziers," CA, 108 (1950), Montpellier, 325–36; Y. Esquieu, "L'oeuvre de maître Gervais de Béziers," *Annales de Midi,* 89 (132), 1977, 153–165; C.

Lapeyre, "Béziers (Hérault) Cathédrale Saint-Nazaire," in X. Barral i Altet, ed., *Le Paysage monumental de la France autour de l'an mil,* Paris, 1987, 433.

23. *La chanson de la croisade albigeoise,* ed. and trans. E. Martin-Chabot, I, Paris, 1931, 61.

24. Y. Esquieu, "L'art roman à Béziers," unpublished Thèse de troisième cycle, Université de Toulouse-Le Mirail, 1975.

25. Durliat, 1973–4, 63–132, esp. 80.

26. J. Bousquet, "Saint-Papoul," CA, 131, Pays de l'Aude, (1973), 437–57.

27. F. Journot, "Riols (Hérault) Saint-Aulary," in X. Barral i Altet, ed., *Le Paysage monumental de la France autour de l'an mil,* Paris, 1987, 430.

28. Richard Sundt made this observation for Albi in an unpublished paper delivered at the International Congress on Medieval Studies at Kalamazoo in 1986 entitled, "The Design of Albi Cathedral's Interior Elevation: Evolution and Necessity."

29. The problem of circulation in the upper parts of Romanesque and early Gothic buildings has been traced by Jean Bony, Pierre Héliot, and most recently by Eliane Vergnolle. See esp., J. Bony, "La technique normande du mur épais à l'époque romane," BM, 98 (1939), 153–88; P. Héliot, "Les coursières et les passages muraux dans les églises du Midi de la France, d'Espagne et du Portugal aux XIIIe et XIVe siècles," *Annuario de estudios medievale,* 6 (1969), 187–217; and E. Vergnolle, "Passages muraux et escaliers: premières expériences dans l'architecture du Midi," *Cahiers de civilisation médiévale,* 32 (1989), 43–58. For further sources, see the Bibliography, Section XII.

30. The smaller duns (fortified private houses) and the somewhat larger (and probably later) brochs are found only in Scotland, duns in the west and southwest, and brochs principally in the north. In these areas, they replace the larger Iron Age hillforts of the southern areas of Britain. Begun in c. 200–100 B.C. as defense against raids, they had virtually ceased to be built by A.D. 100. See Charles Kightly, *Strongholds of the Realm,* London, 1979, 14–16; J. Forde-Johnston, *Pre-historic Britain and Ireland,* London, 1976; and *Hillforts of the Iron Age in England and Wales,* Liverpool,

1976; A.H.A. Hogg, *Hill Forts of Britain*, London, 1975; and A.L.F. Rivett, *The Iron Age in Northern Britain*, Edinburgh, 1966.

31. E. Vergnolle, "Passages muraux et escaliers: premières expériences dans l'architecture du Midi," *Cahiers de civilisation médiévale*, 32 (1989), 48, fn. 12.

32. The best treatments of the history of machicolation in the East are P. Barbier, *La France Féodale*, Saint-Brieuc, 1969; and several articles by P. Héliot: "Le Château-Gaillard et les forteresses des XIIe et XIIIe siècles en Europe occidentale," *Château Gaillard*, 1, 1962, 55–75, esp. 64–5, and "Les donjons de Niort et la fortification médiévale," *La Revue du Bas-Poitou et des Provinces de l'Ouest*, 1, 1970, 45–69, esp. 59–60.

33. On portcullises, see Polybius (X.33.8), Livy (XXVII.28) and Vegetius, *Epitoma Rei Militaris*, IV.4. On Roman fortification gates and walls, see S. Johnson, *Late Roman Fortifications*, New Jersey, 1983.

34. K.A.C. Creswell, *Early Muslim Architecture*, 2 vols., Oxford, 1932–40, rpt. New York, 1979, II, 50–91.

35. S. Johnson, *Late Roman Fortifications*, New Jersey, 1983, p. 48.

36. R.W. Edwards, "The Fortifications of Medieval Cilicia," Ph.D. dissertation, University of California at Berkeley, 1983 (University Microfilms International), esp. 64, 82–8.

37. Ibid., 68, fn. 14.

38. On Ukhaidir, see principally, G.L. Bell, *Palace and Mosque at Ukhaidir: A Study in Early Mohammadan Architecture*, Oxford, 1914; K.A.C. Creswell, *Early Muslim Architecture*, 2 vols., Oxford, 1932–40, rpt. New York, 1979 (esp. 50–91); A.J. Jaussen and R. Savignac, *Mission archéologique en Arabie*, Vol. III: *Les châteaux arabes*, Paris, 1922, 116–20; O. Reuther, *Ocheïdir, nach Aufnahmen von Mitgliedern (F. Wetzel and K. Müller) der Babylon-Expedition der Deutschen Orient-Gesellschaft dargestellt*, Leipzig, 1912; and Werner Caskel, "al-Uhaidir" in *Der Islam* 39 (1964), 28–37.

39. On Qasr al-Hayr, see Creswell, *Short History*, 111–23.

40. D. Schlumberger, "Le palais ghaznévide de Lashkari Bazar," *Syria* 39 (1952), and idem, *Lashkari Bazar*, Paris, 1978.

41. The Byzantine walls of Constantinople have arches on the inside face, on the western circuit built by Manuel Comnenus (1143–80) to enclose the Blachernae Palace. Though these arches are similar in visual impact to continuous machicolations, they have no surviving openings and no evidence of any original apertures. Machicolations on the interior of a circuit wall would in any case have had limited utility. The arches most likely supported a crenellated walkway. For the fortification walls of Constantinople, see F. Krischen, *Die Landmauer von Konstantinopel I, Denkmäler antiker Architektur . . .* (Berlin, 1938); B. Meyer-Plath and A.M. Schneider, ibid. II, *Denkmäler . . .* (Berlin, 1943); and C. Foss and D. Winfield, *Byzantine Fortifications: An Introduction* (Pretoria, 1986). Similar supporting arches are used in the Hieron fortress of Anadolu Kavak, probably also built by Manuel Comnenus. The Blachernae Palace has remnants of machicolations on the southern and eastern sides not protected by the ramparts, but these are late additions of the thirteenth century and therefore probably influenced by European fortification design. See C. Foss and D. Winfield, *Byzantine Fortifications*, 1986, esp. 41–52 and 148. The Blachernae machicolations are not supported on arches, but on spoliate corbels inserted into the walls. The castle of Rumeli Hisar also has *machicoulis*, or more properly, portcullis slits above the main entrance gate and above one of the tower entrances. These slits, however, are clearly part of the Seljuk rebuilding of the castle after its siege in 1452. On the Bosphoros fortifications, see S. Toy, *Castles: Their Construction and History*, New York, 1953, 83–9; and S. Toy, "Castles of the Bosporos," *Archaeologia*, 80 (1930).

42. On Krak des Chevaliers, see R. Fedden and J. Thomson, *Crusader Castles*, London, 1957, 84–90; W. Müller-Wiener, *Castles of the Crusaders*, New York, 1966, 59–62; P. Deschamps, *Les Châteaux des Croisés en Terre Sainte*, Vol. I: *Le Krak des Chevaliers*, Paris, 1934, esp. 186–7, 265.

43. On Saone, see R. Fedden and J. Thomson, *Crusader Castles*, London, 1957, 79–84; W. Müller-Wiener, *Castles of the Crusaders*, New York, 1966, 44–5; P. Deschamps, "Le

château de Saone dans la principauté d'Antioche," *Gazette des Beaux-Arts,* II, 1930, 329–64; and P. Deschamps, "Le château de Saone et ses premiers seigneurs," *Syria,* 16, 1935, 73–88.

44. On the gate and portcullis at Saone, see P. Deschamps, "Les entrées des châteaux des Croisés en Syrie et leurs défenses," *Syria,* 13, 1932, esp. 375.

45. On the *ribats* of North Africa, see esp. A. Lezine, *Le ribat de Sousse,* Tunis, 1956.

46. On the Templars' connection with the Peace tax, see esp., Bisson, 1977, 301.

47. On the basilica at Trier, see R. Günter, *Wand, Fenster und Licht in der Trierer Palastaula und in spätantiken Bauten,* Herford, 1968. (Put-log holes between the upper and lower windows, however, suggest that external galleries may originally have broken the exterior elevation.) On San Simpliciano at Milan, see E. Arslan, *Arte Lombarda,* 1961, 149ff.; G. Traversari, *Architettura paleocristiana milanese,* Milan, 1964; and R. Krautheimer, *Early Christian and Byzantine Architecture,* rev. ed., Harmondsworth, 1975, 86–7.

48. On the churches of the Rouergue, see J.-C. Fau, *Rouergue Roman,* 3rd ed., Zodiaque, 1990, 71–2; 351–99; and B. de Gauléjac, "Castelnau-Pégayrolles," CA, 1937, 408–24. See Chap. 1.

49. For a fuller discussion of Lincoln, see Chap. 1, fn. 118.

50. "Juxta castellum turribus fortissimus eminens in loco forti fortem, pulchro pulchrem quae et grata esset Deo servientibus, et, ut pro tempore oportebat invincibilis hostibus." Henry of Huntingdon, *Historia Anglorum,* vi, 41, ed. T. Arnold (Rolls Series, 74, 1879), 212.

51. For a summary of the sources, see R. Gem, "Lincoln Minster: Ecclesia Pulchra, Ecclesia Fortis," in *Medieval Art and Architecture at Lincoln Cathedral,* The British Archaeological Association conference transactions for 1982, Vol. 8, Leeds, 1986, 10.

52. "Ecclesiam vero suam, quae combustione deturpata fuerat, subtili artificio sic reformavit, ut pulchrior quam in ipsa sui novitate compareret." Henry of Huntingdon, *Historia Anglorum,* viii, 23, ed. T. Arnold (Rolls Series, 74, 1879), 278–9.

53. "Civibus ubique lacrymose euilantibus, vel quia suorum cimiterium in castelli sustolle-

batur vallum, vel quia de turri, unde dulces et imbelles audierant tintinabulorum monitus, nunc ballistas erigi." *Gesta Stephani,* ed. T. R. Potter, London, 1955, 72; trans. T. Forester, London, 1853, 220–1.

54. A. Klukas, "The Architectural Implications of the Decreta Lanfranci," *Anglo-Norman Studies,* 6 (1983), 150–3.

55. On the gate at Exeter and other stone fortifications, see D. Renn, *Norman Castles in Britain,* 2nd ed., London, 1973; R. Allen Brown, *English Castles,* 3rd rev. ed., London, 1976, Chaps. 2 and 3; and S. Bonde, "Saxo-Norman Overlap Architecture: Castle and Church Building in Mid-Eleventh-Century England," unpublished Ph.D. dissertation, Harvard University, 1982, 118–57.

56. For the castle and gate at Lincoln, see R. Allen Brown, H.M. Colvin, and A.J. Taylor, *The History of the King's Works, The Middle Ages,* London, 1963, 704–705; and D. Stocker, "Lincoln Castle," *Eleventh Annual Report of Lincoln Archaeological Trust,* 1983, 18–27, results of which are discussed in R. Gem, "Lincoln Minster: Ecclesia Pulchra, Ecclesia Fortis," in *Medieval Art and Architecture at Lincoln Cathedral,* The British Archaeological Association conference transactions for 1982, Vol. 8, Leeds, 1986, 9–27.

57. Henry of Huntingdon, *Historia Anglorum,* vii, 22, ed. T. Arnold (Rolls Series, 74, 1879), 278.

58. On the participation of bishops and abbots at councils, see above, Chap. 3.

59. Mansi, 22, 458–68.

60. Mansi, 22, 465.

61. On Niort, see P. Héliot, "Les donjons de Niort et la fortification médiévale" *Revue du Bas-Poitou et des Provinces de l'Ouest* (1970), no. 1, pp. 45–69; and J. Duvallon and J.M. Rapinat, *Architecture militaire en Poitou: le donjon du château de Niort (Deux-Sèvres)* (Niort, n.d.); J. Bily-Brossard, *Le château de Niort et son donjon* (2nd ed., Niort, 1968).

62. Viollet-le-Duc's reconstruction of machicolations atop Château-Gaillard, is published in his *Dictionnaire,* Vol. 3. All authors writing on Chateau-Gaillard, including Héliot, have accepted this reconstruction. See P. Héliot, "Le Château-Gaillard et les forteresses des XIIe et XIIIe siècles en Europe occidentale," *Château Gaillard,* I, 1964, 53–75.

63. On Vic, see E. Bonnet, *Antiquités et Monu-*

ments, 1905, 448–9; M. Dainville, *Monuments historiques de l'Hérault*, 1933, 93; and *L'enfance des églises du diocèse de Montpellier*, 1935; J. Vallery-Radot, "L'église de Vic-la-Gardiole," CA, 1950, 186–90; H. Eydoux, *Monuments méconnus*, 1979, Chap. 11; *Languedoc Roman*, 1985, 30; and P. Clément, *Eglises romanes oubliées du Bas-Languedoc*, 1985, 325.

64. P. Alaus, l'abbé Cassan and E. Meynial, eds., *Cartulaire des abbayes d'Aniane et de Gellone*, Montpellier, 1898, 31; and *Dictionnaire Topographique de la France. Hérault*, 223–4.

65. J. Rouquette, and A. Villemagne, eds., *Bullaire de Maguelone*, , 1911, Vol. 1, 22; and *Cartulaire de Maguelone*, Vol. 1, no. 108, pp. 210–11, and no. 130, pp. 250–1.

66. My survey was carried out in the fall of 1987, with steel tapes and theodolite. Two plans are preserved in the Archives of Monuments Historiques in Paris: one from the 1920s by Sallez and an undated plan by Nodet, presumably drawn while he was inspector of works during restorations in the 1930s. Neither plan is without problems. Sallez's overregularizes the spaces between the bays and machicolations and results in a plan that is too short. Nodet's, on the other hand, overemphasizes the differences in the easternmost bays, which are separated from the other bays by an irregularly shaped buttress. Nodet incorrectly recorded this as a recessed eastern chancel area.

67. Cartulaire des Guilhems, 1113 (p. 612) and 1121 (pp. 172–3).

68. J. Rouquette and A. Villemagne, eds., *Cartulaire de Maguelone*, I, 1925, no. 70, pp. 139–143.

69. On Montbazin, see A. Burgos and J. Nougaret, "Préliminaires à l'étude de la décoration figurée des églises romanes du Bas-Languedoc," *Mélanges offerts à René Crozet*, Poitiers, 1966, 487–97; P. Clément, *Eglises romanes oubliées du Bas-Languedoc*, 328–30; Montpellier, 1989; *Languedoc Roman*, 35.

70. P. Clément, *Eglises romanes oubliées*, Montpellier, 1989, 312.

71. Ibid., 415.

72. L. Gigou, "Les possessions des évêques d'Agde du IXe au début du XIIIe siècle: étude historique et archéologique des fortifications et des édifices religieux," *Etudes sur Pézénas et sa région*, 5.3 (1974), 3–16.

73. A. Bon, "Celleneuve," CA, 108, 1950, 120–2; P. Clément, *Eglises romanes oubliées*, Montpellier, 1989, 42–4.

74. On the history of Psalmodi, see A. Borg, "Psalmodi," *Gesta*, 10 (1971), 63–70; and W. Stoddard, "Histoire de Psalmodi," in *Les Etangs à l'époque médiévale*, Lattes, 1986, 106–12.

75. On the excavations at Psalmodi, see most recently, "J. Dodds, B.W. Stoddard, W.S. Stoddard, B.K. Young, and K. Carter-Young, "L'ancienne abbaye de Psalmodi (Saint-Laurent d'Aigouze, Gard), Premier bilan des fouilles (1970–88)," *Archéologie médiévale*, 19 (1989), 7–34.

76. In private conversation Jan., 1987, Prof. Whitney Stoddard agreed with my suggestion that Psalmodi may have been fortified in the manner I suggest here.

77. The stonework of the machicolations matches closely with the ashlar of the earlier building, but slight differences in size and workmanship can be noted, and breaks in campaign are visible. J. Boyer, "Les Saintes-Maries-de-la-Mer, travaux et décoration," CA, 134, 1976, 267–316; X. Barral i Altet, "L'église fortifiée des Saintes-Maries-de-la-Mer," CA, 134, 1976, 240–66; and F. Benoit, "Les Saintes-Maries-de-la-Mer," BM, 95, 1936, 164ff.

78. F. Benoit, *Recueil des actes des comtes de Provence*, II, 1925, 461; and "Eglise de Saintes-Maries-de-la-Mer," BM, 95, 1936, 145–80.

79. On the precinct at Béziers, see Y. Esquieu, "L'enceinte canoniale de la cathédrale de Béziers," in *L'église et son environnement*, 40.

80. R. Guild, *The Cathedral d'Aix-en-Provence: Etude Archéologique*, Paris, 1987; and R. Guild, J. Guyon, L. Rivet, and M. Vecchione, "Saint-Sauveur d'Aix-en-Provence: la cathédrale et le baptistère," CA, 143, Pays d'Aix (1985), 17–64, esp. 50–2.

81. On Lagrasse, see principally, M. Durliat and D. Drocourt, "L'abbaye de Lagrasse," CA, 131, 1973, 104–29.

CONCLUSION

1. On machicolation in the north of France, see Jean Mesqui, *Ile de France Gothique: Les demeures seigneuriales*, Vol. 2 (Paris, 1988), esp. 46, and 187–96. On Farcheville, see also

Julia Fritsch, "Essone, Bouville le chateau de Farcheville," BM, 146.1, 1988, 40–1; and H. Delhumeau, "Farcheville: un château 'méridional' en Ile-de-France," BM, 151.1, 1993, 279–92.

2. P. Barbier, *La France féodale,* Saint-Brieuc, 1968, 2 vols., 57, observes that royal castles do not use the technique of *machicoulis sur arcs.*

3. On Benedict XII and the papal palace at Avignon, see G. Mollat, *The Popes at Avignon, 1305–1378,* London, 1963 (trans. of the ninth, rev. French ed., 1949; and L.-H. Labande, *Le Palais des Papes et les Monuments d'Avignon au XIVe siècle,* 2 vols., Marseille and Aix-en-Provence, 1925.

BIBLIOGRAPHY

Manuscript sources have been consulted at the Bibliothèque Nationale, Paris, the Archives départementales de l'Hérault in Montpellier, the Archives Municipales d'Agde, and the Archives Municipales de Saint-Pons-de-Thomières. Many are reproduced in the Appendixes. Plans, drawings, maps, photographs, and other visual sources have been consulted at the Bibliothèque Nationale in Paris and in the Archives des Monuments Historiques in Paris and in Montpellier. Records of archaeological excavation have been consulted in the Direction des Antiquités in Montpellier. The selected bibliography listed below includes, with several exceptions, only published sources.

I. GENERAL BIBLIOGRAPHY

Bisson, Thomas N. *Assemblies and Representation in Languedoc in the Thirteenth Century.* Princeton, 1964.

_____. "The Problem of Feudal Monarchy: Aragon, Catalonia and France." *Speculum,* 53 (1978), 460–78.

_____. "Mediterranean Territorial Power in the Twelfth Century." *Proceedings of the American Philosophical Society,* 123 (1979), 143–50.

_____. *Fiscal Accounts of Catalonia under the Early Count-Kings (1151–1213),* 2 vols. Berkeley, 1984.

_____. *The Medieval Crown of Aragon. A Short History.* Oxford, 1986.

Bonnassie, Pierre. *La catalonia du milieu du Xe à la fin du XIe siècle: Croissance et mutations d'une société,* 2 vols. Toulouse, 1975–6.

Bonnet, Emile. *Antiquités et monuments du département de l'Hérault,* Montpellier. 1907.

_____. *Bibliographie du diocèse de Montpellier.* Montpellier, 1900.

_____. *Répertoire architecturale du département de l'Hérault: périodes wisigothiques, carolingiennes et romanes.* Montpellier, 1938.

Bourin-Derruau, Monique. *Villages Médiévaux en Bas-Languedoc: Genèse d'une Sociabilité (Xe-XIVe siècle),* 2 vols. Paris, 1987.

Bredero, Adrian H. *Cluny et Cîteaux au douzième siècle: L'Histoire d'une controverse monastique.* Amsterdam and Maarssen, 1985.

Castaldo, André. *Histoire des institutions publiques et des faits sociaux.* Paris, 1979.

Chalon, G., dir. *Histoire du diocèse de Montpellier.* Paris, 1976.

Cheyette, Fredric L., ed. *Lordship and Community in Medieval Europe.* New York, 1968.

_____. "The Castles of the Trencavel: A Preliminary Aerial Survey," in *Order and Innovation in the Middle Ages. Essays in Honor of Joseph Strayer.* Princeton, 1979.

_____. "The Origins of European Villages and the First European Expansion." *Journal of Economic History,* 37, no. 1 (1977), 182–206.

Clément, Pierre A., *Les chemins à travers les âges en Cevennes et bas-Languedoc.* Les Presses du Languedoc, 3rd rev. ed., 1989.

_____. *Eglises romanes oubliées du bas-Languedoc.* Les Presses du Languedoc, 1989.

Dainville, F. de. *Cartes anciennes de l'église de France*. Paris, 1956.

Dainville, M. de. "Les églises romanes du diocèse de Montpellier." *Monspeliensia*, 2.1 (1936); 2.2 (1937), 177–290; 2.3 (1940), 297–443.

_____. *L'enfance des églises du diocèse de Montpellier*. Montpellier, 1935.

_____. *Monuments historiques de l'Hérault*. Montpellier, 1933.

DeVic, Dom Claude, and Dom J.J. Vaissete. *Histoire Générale du Languedoc . . .*, new ed., 16 vols. Toulouse, 1872–1904.

Gallia Christiana in Provincias Ecclesiasticas Distributa; In quae Series et Historia Archiepiscoporum et Abbatum Regionum Omnium quas Vetus Gallia. Tomus Sextus: Provincia Narbonensi. Paris, 1739. [Facsimile ed., Paris, 1899]

Hamlin, Frank R. and Abbé André Cabrol. *Les Noms des Lieux du Département de l'Hérault*. Montpellier, 1983.

Inventaire Général des Monuments et des Richesses Artistiques de la France. Répertoire: Languedoc-Roussillon (Paris: Bibliothèque Nationale).

Les Etangs à l'Epoque Médiévale d'Aigues Mortes à Maguelone, Musée Archéologique de Lattes. Catalogue d'exposition 1986. Montpellier, 1986.

Lewis, Archibald R. *Naval Power and Trade in the Mediterranean A.D. 500–1100*. Princeton, 1951.

Lewis, Arthur R. *The Development of Southern French and Catalan Society 718–1058* Austin, 1965.

_____ "The Guillems of Montpellier: A Sociological Approach." *Viator*, 2 (1971), 159–69.

Magnou-Nortier, Elisabeth. *La société laïque et l'église dans la province ecclésiastique de Narbonne*. Toulouse, 1974.

_____. "La terre, la rente et le pouvoir dans les pays de Languedoc pendant le Haut Moyen-Age." *Francia*, 9 (1981), 80–115.

Migne, J.-P., ed. *Patrologiae cursus completus . . . Latinae*, 221 vols. Paris, 1844–64.

Mortet, Victor. *Recueil des textes relatifs à l'histoire de l'architecture et à la condition des architectes en France au moyen âge*, 2 vols. (Vol. 2 with Paul Deschamps), Paris, 1911–29.

Poly, J.-P. *La Provence et la société féodale (879–1166): Contribution à l'étude des structures dites féodales dans le Midi*. Paris, 1976.

Revoil, Henry. *Architecture romane du Midi de la France*, 3 vols. Paris, 1873.

Structures féodales et féodalisme dans l'Occident Méditerranéen (Xe-XIIIe siècles: Bilan et perspectives de recherches). Colloque international, CNRS et L'Ecole Française de Rome, 1978. Collection de L'Ecole Française de Rome, 44, 1980.

Les structures sociales de l'Aquitaine, du Languedoc et de l'Espagne au premier âge féodal. Colloque international, CNRS, Paris, 1969.

Teulet, Alexandre, et al., eds. *Layettes du Trésor des Chartes*, 5 vols. Paris, 1863–1909.

Thomas, Eugène, ed. *Dictionnaire Topographique de la France comprenant les noms de lieu anciens et modernes*. Paris, 1865.

Thomas, Jean-Pierre. *Mémoires historiques sur Montpellier et le département de l'Hérault*. Paris, 1827.

Toubert, P. *Les structures du Latium médiévale: Le Latium méridional et la Sabine du IXe à la fin du XIIe siècle*, 2 vols. Rome, 1973.

II. FORTIFICATION

Coulson, Charles L.H. "Fortresses and Social Responsibility in late Carolingian France." *Zeitschrift für Archäologie des Mittelalters*, 4 (1976), 29–36.

_____. "Rendability and Castellation in Medieval France." *Château Gaillard*, 6 (1973), 59–67.

_____. "Seignorial Fortresses in France in Relation to Public Policy c. 864 – c. 1483." Unpublished Ph.D. dissertation, University of London, 1972.

Finó, J.-F. *Forteresses de la France Médiévale*. Paris, 1977.

Fournier, Gabriel. *Le château dans la France médiévale: Essai de sociologie monumentale*. Paris, 1978.

Héliot, Pierre. "Les château-forts en France du Xe au XIIe siècle à la lumière de travaux récents." *Journal des Savants* (1965), 483–514.

Mesqui, Jean. *Châteaux et enceintes de la France médiévale. De la défense à la résidence*. Paris, 1991.

Miquel, Jacques. *L'architecture militaire dans le Rouerge au moyen-âge et l'organization de la défense*, 2 vols. Rodez, 1981.

Moulis, Adelin. *L'Ariège et ses châteaux féodaux*. Verniolle, 1964.

Pous, A. de. "Notice sur l'évolution de l'archère

dans les châteaux féodaux des Pyrénées méditerranéennes entre le Xe et le XIV siècle." *Gladius*, 4 (1965), 67–85.

———. "L'architecture militaire occitane (IXe–XIVe siècle)." *Bulletin archéologique du Comité des travaux historiques*, n.s. 5 (1969), 41–139.

Richard, J. "Châteaux, châtelains et vassaux en Bourgogne aux XIe et XIIe siècles." *Cahiers de civilisation médiévale*, 3 (1960), 433–47.

Rocolle, Col. *2000 ans de fortification française*. Paris, 1972.

Salch, Charles-Laurent. *Dictionnaire des châteaux et des fortifications du moyen-âge en France*. Strasbourg, n.d. (1980?).

Thompson, M.W. *The Rise of the Castle*, Cambridge. 1991.

Verbruggen, J.F. "Note sur le sens des mots castrum, castellum et quelques autres expressions qui designent des fortifications." *Revue belge de philologie et d'histoire*, 28, nos. 1 and 2 (1956), 147–55.

Viollet-le-Duc, Eugène. *Dictionnaire Raisonné de l'architecture Française du XIe au XVIe siècle*, 10 vols. Paris: Libraries-Imprimeries Réunies, 1854–68. Esp., "Architecture militaire," Vol. 1, 327–452; "Hourd," Vol. 6, 123–141; "Machicoulis," Vol. 6, 196–213.

III. THE FORTIFICATION OF RELIGIOUS ESTABLISHMENTS

Ancien, Bernard. "Les églises du Soissonais et Valois." *Mémoires de la Fédération des Sociétés d'Histoire et d'Archéologie de l'Aisne*, 21 (1975–6), 99–115.

Anghel, Gheorghe. "Typologie des églises fortifiées de Roumanie." *Château Gaillard*, 9–10 (1982), 13–27.

Barbier, Pierre *La France Féodale*, 2 vols. Saint-Brieuc, 1968.

Coulson, Charles. "Hierarchism and Conventual Crenellation: An Essay in the Sociology and Metaphysics of Medieval Fortification." *Medieval Archaeology*, 26 (1982), 69–100.

Durliat, Marcel. "Les crenellages du clocher-porche de Moissac et leur restauration par Viollet-le-Duc." *Annales du Midi*, 78 (1966), 433–47 (cf. also the compte-rendu by F. Salet in *Bulletin monumental*, 125 (1967), 179–82).

Esquieu, Yves. "Système défensif de quartiers canoniaux dans quelques cités épiscopales du Midi." *Actes du 105e Congrès National des Sociétés Savantes: Archéologie* (1980), 331–45.

———. "Quartiers Canoniaux des Cathédrales dans la France Méridionale." Unpublished Thèse pour le doctorat des lettres, Université de Toulouse, 1986.

Fage, M.R. "Les clocher-murs de la France." *Bulletin Monumental*, 80 (1921); 81 (1922).

Goguel, Bertrand. "Les églises fortes-refuges." *Vieilles Maisons Françaises*, 110 (1985), 26–9.

Head, Thomas, and Sharon Farmer. "Monks and their Enemies: A Comparative Approach." *Speculum*, 66 (1991), 764–96.

Hinz, Hermann. "Wehrkirchen und Burgenbau." *Château Gaillard*, 9–10 (1982), 117–44.

———. "Die schwedischen Kirchenkastale auf Gotland." *Château Gaillard*, 9–10 (1982), 433–44.

Johnson, Walter. "The Secular Uses of Church Fabric," in his *Byways in British Archaeology*, Chap. 3. Cambridge, 1912.

Kantorwicz, Ernst. *"Laudes regiae." A study in Liturgical Acclamations and Ruler Worship*. University of California Publications in History, 33. Berkeley, 1946.

Lahondès, J. de. "Les églises fortifiées du pays de Foix et du Couserans." *Bulletin Monumental* (1883).

Lugand, Jacques, Jean Nougaret, and Robert Saint-Jean, with André Burgos. *Languedoc Roman*, 2nd ed. Zodiaque, 1985.

Mann, Janice. "San Pedro at the Castle of Loarre. A Study in the Relation of Cultural Forces to the Design, Decoration and Construction of a Romanesque Church." Ph.D. dissertation, Columbia University, 1991. [UMI, 1992.]

McCormick, Michael. *Eternal Victory: Triumphal Rulership in Late Antiquity, Byzantium and the Early Medieval West*. Cambridge and Paris, 1986.

———. "The Liturgy of War in the Early Middle Ages: Crisis, Litanies and the Carolingian Monarchy." *Viator*, 15 (1984), 1–23.

Meuret, Jean-Paul. *Les Eglises Fortifiées de la Thiérache*, 2nd ed. Vervins, 1977.

Oman, Charles. "Security in English Churches A.D. 100–1548." *Archaeological Journal*, 136 (1979), 90–8.

Ponsich, Pierre. "Les églises fortifiées du Roussillon." *Les cahiers de Saint-Michel de Cuxa*, 17 (1986), 9–12.

Ravegnani, Giorgio. *Castelli e citta' fortificate nel VI secolo*. Quaderni di storia bizantina e slava diretti da A Carile, 1. Ravenna, 1983.

Rey, Raymond. *Les Vieilles Eglises Fortifiées du Midi de la France*. Paris, 1925.

Roger, Robert. "Quelques églises fortifiées de l'Ariège," *Bulletin de la Société ariègeoise des sciences, lettres et arts*, 8 (1902).

Rosenwein, Barbara H. "Feudal War and Monastic Peace: Cluniac Liturgy as Ritual Aggression." *Viator*, 2 (1971), 129–57.

Sheils, W.J., ed. *The Church and War*. Studies in Church History, 20. Oxford, 1983.

Settia, Aldo A. *Castelli e villaggi nell'Iatlia padana: Populamento, potere e sicurezza fra IX e XIII secolo*, Nuovo medioevo, 23. Naples, 1984.

_____. *Chiese, Strade e Fortezze nell'Italia Medievale*. Italia Sacra: Studi e Documenti di Storia Ecclesiastica, 46. Rome, 1991 (collected essays).

_____. "Eglises et fortifications médiévales dans l'Italie du Nord," in *L'église et le château, Xe-XVIIIe siècles*. Bordeaux, 1988, 81–94.

_____. "'Ecclesiam incastellare,' Chiese e castelli nella diocesi di Padova in alcune recenti pubblicazioni," in *Fonti e studi di storia ecclesiastica padovana*, 12 (1981), 47–75.

IV. INCASTELLAMENTO

Bourin, Monique. "Le paysage bâti dans les campagnes bas-languedociennes: Le temps de nos incertitudes," in Xavier Barral i Altet, ed., *Le Paysage monumental de la France autour de l'an mil*. Paris, 1987, 409–14.

Bourin-Derruau, Monique. *Villages Médiévaux en Bas-Languedoc: Genèse d'une Sociabilité (Xe-XIVe siècle)*, 2 vols. Paris, 1987.

Châteaux et peuplement en Europe occidentale du Xe au XIIIe siècle. Premières journées internationales d'histoire 1979. Auch, 1980.

Cheyette, Fredric, and C. Amado. "Organisation du terroir et d'un habitat concentré: Un exemple languedocien." *Habitats fortifiés et organisation de l'espace en Mediterranée médiévale*. Lyon, 1983, 35–44.

Gramain, Monique. "Castrum, structures féodales et peuplement en Biterrois au XIe siècle," in *Structures féodales et féodalisme dans l'Occident Méditerranéen (Xe-XIIIe siècles: Bilan et perspectives de recherches)*. Colloque international, CNRS et L'Ecole Française de Rome, 1978. Collection de L'Ecole Française de Rome, 44, 1980, 119–34.

Settia, Aldo A. "Incastellamento e decastellamento nell'italia padan, X e XI secolo." *Bolletino storico-bibliografico subalpino* (1976), 5–26.

_____. *Castelli e villaggi nell'Italia padana: popolamento, potere e sicurezza fra IX e XII secolo*. Naples, 1984.

Tabacco, Giovanni. *The Struggle for Power in Medieval Italy: Structures of Political Rule*. Cambridge, 1989.

V. HERESY

Berne-Lagarde, P. de. *Bibliographie du catharisme languedocien*. Institut d'études cathares, Collection textes et documents. Toulouse, 1957.

Cathares en Languedoc (Cahiers de Fanjeaux, 3). Toulouse, 1968.

Dossat, Yves. "Le clergé méridional à la veille de la Croisade Albigeoise." *Revue historique et littéraire du Languedoc*, I (1944), 263–78.

Erbstösser, Martin. *Heretics in the Middle Ages*, trans. J. Fraser. Leipzig, 1984.

Griffe, E. *Les débuts de l'aventure de catharisme en Languedoc (1140–90)*. Paris, 1969.

Peters, Edward. *Heresy and Authority in the Middle Ages*. London, 1980.

Moore, R.I. *The Formation of a Persecuting Society: Power and Deviance in Western Europe, 950-1250*. Oxford, 1987.

Strayer, J. *The Albigensian Crusades*, Ann Arbor, 1992, with a new epilogue by C. Lansing.

Thouzellier, C. *Catharisme et Valdéisme en Languedoc à la fin du XIIe et au début du XIIIe siècle*. Paris, 1969.

Wakefield, N.L. *Heresy, Crusade and Inquisition in Southern France, 1100-1250*. London, 1974.

VI. PIRACY AND MERCENARIES

Balleto, Laura. *Mercanti, pirati e corsari nei mari della Corsica (sec. XII)*. Genova, 1978.

_____. *Genova nel Duecento. Uomini nel porto e uomini sul mare*. Genova, 1983.

Castaldo, André. "Le roi, l'évêque et les pirates. A l'origine de l'inaliénabilité du domaine public (Agde, 1332)." *Fédération Historique du Languedoc méditerranéen et du Roussillon* (1970), 179–89.

Cheyette, Fredric. "The Sovereign and the Pirates, 1332." *Speculum*, 45 (1970), 40–68.

Coulet du Gard, René. *La course et la piraterie en Méditerranée*. Paris, n.d. (c. 1980).

Durand, Loup. *Pirates et barbaresques en Méditerranée*. Avignon, 1975.

Géraud, H. "Les routiers au douzième siècle." *Bibliothèque de l'Ecole de Chartes*, 3 (1841–2), 125–47.

Kedar, B.K. *Merchants in Crisis: Genoese and Venetian Men of Affairs and the Fourteenth-Century Depression*. New Haven, 1976.

Ormerod, Henry A. *Piracy in the Ancient World: An essay in Mediterranean History*. Liverpool, 1978.

Panetta, Rinaldo. *Pirati e corsari turchi e barbareschi nel Mare Nostrum*. Milan, n.d. (c. 1981).

Vicaire, M.-H. "'L'affaire de paix et de foi' du Midi de la France," in *Paix de Dieu et guerre sainte en Languedoc au XIIIe siècle* (*Cahiers de Fanjeaux*, 4). Toulouse, 1969, 102–27.

VII. THE PEACE OF GOD

Bisson, Thomas N. "The Organized Peace in Southern France and Catalonia (c. 1140–1233)." *American Historical Review*, 82 (1977), 290–311.

Bonnaud-Delamare, Roger. "La légende des associations de la paix en Rouerge et en Languedoc au début du XIIIe siècle (1170–1229)." *Bulletin philologique et historique, Comité des travaux historiques et scientifiques.* (1938), 47–78.

Cowdrey, H.E.J. "The Peace and the Truce of God in the Eleventh Century." *Past and Present*, 46 (1970), 44–53.

Duby, Georges. "Les laïcs et la paix de Dieu," reprinted in *Hommes et structures du moyen-âge*. Paris, 1973, 227–40.

Erdmann, Carl. *The Origin of the Idea of Crusade*, trans. M.W. Baldwin and W. Goffart, Princeton, 1977. From the original, *Die Entstehung des Kreuzzugsgedankens*, Stuttgart, 1935.

Goetz, Hans-Werner. "Kirchenschutz, Rechtswahrung und Reform: Zu den Zielen und zum Wesen der frühen Gottesfriedensbewegung in Frankreich." *Francia*, 11 (1983), 193–239.

Graboïs, Aryeh. "De la trêve de Dieu à la paix du roi: étude sur les transformations du mouvement de la paix au XIIe siècle," in *Mélanges offerts à René Crozet*, ed. Pierre Gallais et Y-F. Riou, 2 vols. Poitiers, 1966, Vol. 1: 585–96.

Head, Thomas, and R. Landes, eds. *The Peace of God: Social Violence and Religious Response in France around the Year 1000*. Ithaca, 1992.

Hoffmann, Hartmut. *Gottesfriede und Treuge Dei* (Schriften der Monumenta Germaniae Historica, 20). Stuttgart, 1964.

Huberti, Ludwig. *Studien zur Rechtsgeschichte der Gottesfrieden und Landfrieden*. Vol. 1: *Die Friedensordnungen in Frankreich*. Ansbach, 1892.

Kennelly, Dolorosa. "Medieval Towns and the Peace of God." *Medievalia et Humanistica*, 15 (1963), 35–53.

Kluckhohn, August. *Geschichte des Gottesfriedens*. Leipzig, 1857. [Rpt., Aalen, 1966]

Lewis, A.R. "The Formation of Territorial States in Southern France and Catalonia, 1050–1270." *Mélanges Roger Aubenas in Recueil des Mémoires et Travaux publiés par la Société d'Histoire du Droit et des Institutions des Anciens Pays de Droit Ecrit*, 9 (1974), 505–16.

MacKinney, Loren C. "The People and the Peace Movement." *Speculum*, 5 (1930), 181–206.

Molinié, Georges. *L'organisation judiciaire, militaire et financière des associations de la paix. Etude sur la Paix et la Trêve de Dieu dans le Midi et le Centre de la France*. Toulouse, 1912.

Moore, R.I. "Family, Community and Cult on the Eve of the Gregorian Reform." *Transactions of the Royal Historical Society*, 5th ser., 30 (1980), 49–69.

Paix de Dieu et guerre sainte en Languedoc au XIIIe siècle (*Cahiers de Fanjeaux*, 4). Toulouse, 1969.

Semichon, Ernest. *La paix et la trêve de Dieu: Histoire des premiers développements du tiers-état par l'église et les associations*. Paris, 1857. [2nd rev. ed., Paris, 1869]

Töpfer, Bernhard. *Volk und Kirche zur Zeit der beginnenden Gottesfriedensbewegung in Frankreich* (neue Beiträge zur Geschichtswissenschaft, i). Berlin, 1957.

Werner, Karl-Ferdinand. "Observations sur le rôle des évêques dans le mouvement de la paix aux Xe et XIe siècles." *Medievalia Christiana XIe -XIIe siècles: Hommage à Ray-*

monde Foreville, ed. Coloman Viola. Paris, 1989, 155–95.

VIII. CHURCH COUNCILS

Alberigo, J., P-P. Joannou, C. Leonardi, and P. Prodi, eds. *Conciliorum oecumenicorum decreta,* ed. Centro di Documentazione Religiose, Bologna, Fribourg-en-Brisgau, 1963.

Foreville, R. *Latran I, II, III et Latran IV.* Paris, 1965.

Hefele, C.H., and H. Leclerq. *Histoire des conciles d'après les documents originaux.* Paris, 1913.

Jedin, H., ed. *Consiliorum oecumenicorum decreta,* 3rd ed. Bologna, 1973.

Longère, Jean, ed. *Le troisième Consile de Latran (1179): Sa place dans l'histoire.* Communications présentées à la table ronde du CNRS, 1980. Paris, 1982.

Mansi, J.D. *Sacrorum conciliorum nova et amplissima collectio . . . ,* 31 vols. Florence and Venice, 1759–98.

Schroeder, Rev. H.J. *Disciplinary Decrees of the General Councils: Text, Translation, and Commentary.* London, 1937.

IX. LOUIS VII AND THE CAPETIANS

Bruguière, M.B. "Un mythe historique: l'impérialisme capétien dans le Midi de la France aux XII et XIII siècles." *Annales du Midi,* 97, no. 171 (1985), 245–67.

Fawtier, Robert. *The Capetian Kings of France: Monarchy and Nation 987–1328,* trans. Lionel Butler and R.J. Adam, London, 1960.

Hallam, Elizabeth. *Capetian France (987–1328).* London, 1980, esp. Chap. 4.

Halphen, Louis. "Observations sur la chronologie des actes de Louis VII (1137–1180)." *Revue historique* (1911), 55–68.

Hirsch, R. *Studien im Geschichte König Ludwigs VII von Frankreich (1119–1160).* Leipzig, 1892.

Jehel, Georges. *Aigues Mortes: Un port pour un roi. Les Capétiens et la Méditerranée.* Roanne, 1985.

Luchaire, Achille. *Etudes sur les actes de Louis VII.* Paris, 1885.

_____. "Le roi Louis VII et le pape Alexandre III." *Comptes rendues des séances de l'Académie des sciences morales et politiques* (1897), 425–60.

Newman, W.M. *Le domaine royal sous les premiers Capétiens (987–1180).* Paris, 1937.

Pacaut, Marcel. "Louis VII et Alexandre III." *Revue d'histoire de l'Eglise de France,* (1953), 5–45.

_____. *Louis VII et les élections épiscopales dans le royaume de France.* Paris, 1957.

_____. *Louis VII et son royaume.* Paris, 1964.

Recueil des Historiens des Gaules et de la France, tome 16. Paris, 1814 (Letters of Louis VII).

X. ROMANESQUE AND GOTHIC ARCHITECTURE OF THE MIDI

Biget, J.-L. "Recherches sur les financements des cathédrales du Midi au XIIIe siècle," *Cahiers de Fanjeaux,* 9 (1974), 127–64.

Biget, J-L., H. Pradelier, and M. Pradelier-Schlumberger. "L'Art Cistercien dans le Midi Toulousain." *Cahiers de Fanjeaux,* 21 (1986), 312–70.

Durliat, Marcel. "Problèmes posés par l'histoire de l'architecture religieuse en Catalogne du XIe siècle." *Cahiers de Saint Michel de Cuxa,* 3 (1972).

_____. "L'architecture gothique méridionale au XIIIe siècle." *Bulletin de l'école antiquaire de Nîmes* (1973–4), 63–132.

Paul, Vivian. "Le problème de la nef unique," in *La naissance et l'essor du gothique méridional au XIIIe siècle (Cahiers de Fanjeaux, 9).* Toulouse, 1974, 21–53.

_____. "The Beginnings of Gothic Architecture in Languedoc." *Art Bulletin,* 70 (1988), 104–22.

Sundt, Richard A. "The Jacobin Church of Toulouse and the Origin of Its Double-Nave Plan." *Art Bulletin,* 71 (1989), 185–207.

XII. MURAL PASSAGES AND GALLERIES

Bony, Jean. "La technique normande du mur épais à l'époque romane." *Bulletin monumental,* 98 (1939), 153–88.

Héliot, Pierre. "Les antécédents et les débuts des coursières anglo-normands et rhénanes." *Cahiers de civilisation médiévale,* 2 (1959), 429–43.

_____. "La cathédrale de Cefalu . . . et les galleries murales dans les églises romanes du

Midi." *Arte lombarda*, 10 (1965), 19ff. and 11 (1966), 6f.

———. "Les coursières et les passages muraux dans les églises fortifiées du Midi de la France, d'Espagne et du Portugal aux XIIIe et XIVe siècles." *Anuario de estudios medievales*, 6 (1969), 187–217.

———. "Coursières et passages muraux dans les églises gothiques de la Belgique Impériale." *Bulletin de la commission royale des monuments et des sites* (1970–1), 14–44.

Rolland, R. "La technique normande du mur évidé et l'architecture scaldienne." *Revue belge d'archéologie et d'histoire d'art* (1940), 169–88.

Vernolle, Eliane. "Passages muraux et escaliers." *Cahiers de civilisation médiévale* 32, (1989), 43–58.

XIII. MAGUELONE

Berthelé, Joseph. *Chronicon Magalonense vetus.* Montpellier, 1908.

Boucassert, abbé Manlius. *Histoire du siège épiscopal de Maguelone et de Montpellier.* Montpellier, 1876.

Buriot-Darsiles, H. *Maguelone, petit île, grand passé, suivi d'un guide historique.* Montpellier, s.d. (1937).

Carrier, A. *Coutumier du XIe siècle: de l'ordre de Saint-Ruf en usage à la cathédrale de Maguelone.* Etudes et Documents sur L'Ordre de Saint-Ruf, no. 8. Sherbrooke (Canada), 1950.

Eydoux, H.P. *Cités mortes et lieux maudits de France.* Paris, 1959.

Fabre de Morlhon, Jacques, and Paul Lacaze. *Maguelone, La Cathédrale et l'île de Maguelone.* Guidebook, s.d.

Fabrège, Frédéric. *Histoire de Maguelone,* 3 vols. Paris, 1894–1902.

Fliche, Augustin. *Montpellier.* Aris, 1935.

Germain, Alexandre C., ed. *Catalogus episcoporum Magalonensium* (extr. Mémoire de la Société archéologique de Montpellier). Montpellier, 1881.

———. *Chronique de Maguelone* (extr. Mémoire de la Société archéologique de Montpellier). Montpellier, 1853.

———. *Etude historique sur les comtes de Maguelone* (extr. Mémoire de la Société archéologique de Montpellier). Montpellier, 1854.

———. *Maguelone sous ses évêques et ses chanoines. Etude historique et archéologique* (extr. Mémoire de la Société archéologique de Montpellier). Montpellier, 1869.

Hébrard, Chanoine J. *Anciens autels du diocèse de Montpellier.* Montpellier, 1942.

LaJudie, Chanoine M. de. "Une communauté de chanoines sur les bords de la Méditerranée au moyen âge." *L'Université catholique*, n.s. 15 (1890).

Renouvier, Jules. *Monuments de quelques anciens diocèses du Bas-Languedoc, expliquées dans leur histoire et leur architecture.* Montpellier, 1840.

Richard, Jean-Claude M. "Maguelone, petit île, grand passé." *Archéologia*, 23 (1968), 50–5.

Rouquette, J., and A. Villemagne. *Bullaire de Maguelone.* Montpellier, 1911.

———. *Cartulaire de Maguelone,* 7 vols. Montpellier, 1912–24.

Segondy, Chanoine Jean. *Les églises du diocèse de Maguelone.* Unpublished manuscript in the Bibliothèque de Montpellier, s.d.

Suger, (Abbot) *Vie de Louis VI le Gros,* ed. Henri Waquet. Paris, 1929.

Vallery-Radot, Jean. "L'ancienne cathédrale de Maguelone." *Congrès archéologique,* 108 (1950), 60–89.

XIV. AGDE

Adgé, Michel. "Les marques de tacherons du comble de la cathédrale d'Agde." *Etudes sur Pezenas et sa région,* 7, no. 3 (1976), 9–22.

Aris, R. "Agde: ancien port, ancien quai. Notes sur quelques restes antiques et médiévaux." *Etudes sur Pézénas et sa région,* 7.1 (1976), 3–12.

Berthelé, Joseph. *Cartulaires municipaux d'Agde. Inventaire sommaire (série AA).* Montpellier, 1901.

Castaldo, André. "L'église d'Agde. Xe-XIIIe siècle." Travaux et Recherches, série *Sciences Historiques,* 20. Paris, 1970.

———. *Le consulat médiéval d'Agde: seigneurs, villes et pouvoir royal en Languedoc, XIIIe-XIVe siècle.* Paris, 1974.

Cazes, Daniel. "Note sur un chapiteau du cloître de la cathédrale d'Agde conservé au Musée d'Augustins, Toulouse." *Etudes sur l'Hérault,* 4 (1988), 91–2.

Despetis, J. "Nouvelle chronologie des évêques d'Agde." *Mémoires de la Société archéo-*

logique de Montpellier, 2nd ser., 8 (1920), 33–101.

Foreville, Raymonde. "Les testaments agathois du Xe au XIIIe siècle d'après les cartulaires de l'église d'Agde." *Bulletin philologique et historique du Comité des Travaux Historiques et Scientifiques*, 1961 (1963), 357–88.

_____. "Un diocèse languedocien au Moyen-Age: Histoire et documents de l'église d'Agde." *Journal des Savants*, 3 (1971), 187–205 (review of Castaldo).

_____. "Le chapitre de la cathédrale d'Agde d'après le cartulaire de Saint-Etienne." *Cahiers de Fanjeaux*, 7 (1972), 285–333.

Gigou, Laure. "Les possessions des évêques d'Agde du IXe au début du XIIIe siècle: étude historique et archéologique des fortifications et des édifices religieux." *Etudes sur Pézénas et sa région*, 5.3 (1974), 3–16.

Gorsse, Pierre de. *Monographie de la cathédrale Saint-Etienne d'Agde*. Toulouse, 1922.

Jordan, Balthazar. *Histoire de la ville d'Agde*. Montpellier, 1824.

Martin, M. "Mémoire sur la cathédrale d'Agde," published by Louis Noguier in a "Rapport sur le concours des mémoires historiques." *Bulletin de la Société archéologique de Béziers*, 2nd ser., 7 (1873), 152–206.

_____. *Notice archéologique sur l'église Saint-Etienne*. Castre, 1873.

Noguier, Louis. "L'église Saint-Etienne d'Agde." *Mélanges publiés à l'occasion du jubilé épiscopal de Msgr. Cabrières*. Paris, 1899.

Picheire, J. *Histoire d'Agde*. Lyon, 1961. [Rpt. 1978]

Rouquette, J. *Cartulaire de l'église d'Agde. Cartulaire du chapitre*. Montpellier, 1925.

Secondy, Chanoine Jean. *Les Eglises du diocèse d'Agde*. Unpublished typescript and scrapbook in the Bibliothèque de Montpellier. Montpellier, 1954.

Terrin, Odile. *Cartulaire du chapitre d'Agde*. Publication de la Société d'Histoire du Droit et des Institutions des anciens pays de droit écrit, no. 1. Nîmes, 1969.

Vallery-Radot, Jean. "L'ancienne cathédrale Saint-Etienne d'Agde." *Congrès archéologique*, 108 (1950), 201–18.

Vidal, C. *Histoire de la ville d'Agde des origines à nos jours*. Agde, 1938.

XV. SAINT-PONS-DE-THOMIERES

Barthès, Joseph. *Etude critique sur la vie de Saint Pons*, Pt. 1 of Vol. 1. Unpublished ms., 1937, in the Bibliothèque Nationale, Paris.

_____. *Saint-Pons avant la fondation de l'abbaye: Fondation de l'abbaye de Saint-Pons-de-Thomières en 936*, Pts. 2 and 3 of Vol. 1. Unpublished ms., 1938, in the Bibliothèque Nationale, Paris.

_____. *L'abbaye de Saint-Pons-de-Thomières*, Vol. 2 in 2 parts. Unpublished ms., 1941, in the Bibliothèque Nationale, Paris.

Bène, l'abbé. *Recherches historiques sur Frotard, 10e abbé de Saint-Pons-de-Thomières, légat de Saint Grégoire VII*. Montpellier, 1875.

Bousquet, Jacques. "A propos d'un des tympans de Saint-Pons: La place des larrons dans la crucifixion." *Cahiers de Saint Michel de Cuxa*, 8 (1977), 25–54.

Bussis, Leslie. "The Twelfth and Thirteenth Century Sculpture from Saint-Pons-de-Thomières." Ph.D. dissertation, Columbia University, 1990. [UMI, 1993]

Durliat, Marcel. "Saint-Pons-de-Thomières." *Congrès archéologique*, 108 (1950), 271–89.

Giry, abbé Jean. "Aperçu archéologique sur l'ancienne voie Le Pouyol-Saint-Pons." *Parc national du Caroux*, 3 (1961–2), 10–16.

Granier, A., and P. Granier. *Saint-Pons-de-Thomières: La Cathédrale*, Saint-Pons, 1938.

Granier, M. *L'abbaye de Saint-Pons-de-Thomières à l'occasion du millénaire de sa fondation*. Montpellier, 1937.

Griffe, E. "La réforme monastique dans les pays audois." *Annales du Midi* (1963), 457–69.

Lane, Evelyn Stauder. "The Sculpted Capitals of Saint-Pons-de-Thomières." Unpublished seminar paper, Brown University, 1989.

Sahuc, Joseph. *L'art roman à Saint-Pons-de-Thomières*. Montpellier, 1908.

_____. *Dictionnaire topographique et historique de l'arrondissement de Saint-Pons*. Montpellier, 1910.

_____. "Notes sur l'archéologie religieuse dans l'ancien diocèse de Saint-Pons-de-Thomières." *Mélanges Msgr. de Cabrières*, 2 (1899), 379–462.

_____, ed. *Procès-verbal de la visite de l'église-cathédrale de Saint-Pons*, by Pierre-J.-F.

Percin de Montgaillard, évêque de Saint-Pons (1694). Narbonne, 1901.

_____. *Quelques documents inédits sur l'ancien diocèse de Saint-Pons-de-Thomières.* Saint-Pons, 1910.

_____. "Répertoire archéologique du canton de Saint-Pons." *Société languedocienne de géographie* (1896), 56–86.

_____. *Saint-Pons-de-Thomières: Ses Vieux Edifices, Ses Anciennes Institutions.* Montpellier, n.d. (1895). [Rpt., Marseille, 1979]

Segondy, Chanoine Jean. *Les églises du diocèse de Saint-Pons-de-Thomières.* Unpublished manuscript in the Bibliothèque de Montpellier. Montpellier, 1958.

Soupairac, l'Abbé V. *Nouveau Petit dictionnaire géographique et historique du département de l'Hérault: diocèse de Montpellier. Agde, Béziers, Lodève et Saint-Pons-de-Thomières. Arrondissement de Saint-Pons,* 5 vols. Montpellier, 1881.

ILLUSTRATION CREDITS

1. Map of Gallia Narbonensis. *From Gallia Christiana, vol. 6, 1739.*

2. Map of fortification sites, roads, and rivers in Languedoc. *Author. (Mapping of roads adapted from P. Clément,* Les Chemins à travers les âges en Cevennes et bas-Languedoc, *Les Presses du Languedoc, 1989.)*

3. Saint-Pons-de-Thomières, exterior view of the nave, south side. *C. Maines.*

4. (A) Machicolated arches; (B) Machicolation on corbels; (C) Hoarding; and (D) Portcullis. *From E. Viollet-le-Duc,* Dictionnaire Raisonné, *Paris, 1854–68.*

5. Map of major sites mentioned in the text. *Author.*

6. Saint-Allyre, engraved bird's-eye view. *From Dom M. Germain,* Le Monasticon Gallicanum, *ed. M. Peigné-Delacourt, Paris, 1871.*

7. Saint-Nectaire, capital depicting the fortified priory of Saint-Nectaire. *From E. Mâle,* Religious Art in France. *Copyright © 1978, Princeton University Press. Reproduced by permission of Princeton University Press.*

8. Saint-Jean-des-Vignes, Soissons, bird's-eye view. *Louis Barbaran, 1673 (Musée de Soissons).*

9. Wimy, view of west façade. *C. Maines.*

10. Saint Catherine's, Mount Sinai, aerial view. *From G. Forsyth and K. Weitzmann,* The Monastery of St. Catherine at Mount Sinai: The Church and Fortress. *Copyright © 1978, University of Michigan Press. Reproduced by permission of University of Michigan Press.*

11. Gross-Comburg, plan. *Adapted from W. Braunfels.*

12. Tournus, town plan. *Adapted from W. Braunfels.*

13. Avila, Cathedral of San Salvador, east end. *Catherine Wilkinson Zerner.*

14. Durham, plan of cathedral and castle precinct. *Courtesy Durham Tourist Board.*

15. Rochester, plan of cathedral and castle precincts. *The Bridge Warden's map, 1717. From* Archaeologia Cantaniana, xviii, *1896. Copyright © Kent Archaeological Society. Published with the permission of the Society.*

16. Seintein, cemetery church, plan. *After R. Rey.*

17. Lincoln Cathedral, view of west façade. *Author.*

18. Lincoln Cathedral, detail of west façade: machicolated arch in the southwest portal. *Author.*

19. Moissac south porch. *Reproduced with the permission of Editions Zodiaque.*

20. Candes, north porch. *C. Maines.*

21. Saint-Denis, west front. *Author.*

22. Tower of London, plan at gallery level. *Author.*

23. Rudelle, exterior view. *C. Maines.*

24. Vez, castle plan. *After J. Mesqui.*

25. Abou-Gosh, exterior view, and plan. *Reproduced with the permission of Editions Zodiaque.*

26. Cruas, exterior view. *C. Maines.*

27. Narbonne, Cathedral of Saint-Just, exterior view. *Author.*

28. Béziers, Cathedral of Saint-Nazaire, exterior view. *Author.*

29. Albi, Cathedral of Sainte-Cécile, Albi, exterior view. *Author.*

30. Mâcon, Saint-Vincent, porch capital of Saint Michael. *From* Bulletin Monumental, 88, *1929, p. 477. Photograph by D. Loison. Reproduced with the permission of the Société Française d'Archéologie.*

31. Castelnau-Pégayrolles, church of Saint-Michel, exterior view. *From M. Aubert,* Romanesque Cathedrals and Abbeys of France, *Paris: Editions Artaud. English edition, New York: London House and Maxwell, 1966.*

32. Maguelone, aerial view of the church. *Reproduced with the permission of Editions d'Art Yvon.*

33. Maguelone, reconstruction plan of the abbey. (Fabrège plan) *F. Fabrège. Musée de la Société Archéologique de Montpellier. Reproduced with the permission of the Société.*

34. Keyed redrawing of the Fabrège plan. *Author.*

35. Maguelone, phased plan of the church. *Diagonal shading:* Eleventh-century; *Black:* Early twelfth-century; *Outline:* Mid- to late twelfth-century. *Surveyed and drawn by author.*

36. Maguelone, detail of north wall, showing campaign break and gallery opening in vault. *Author.*

37. Maguelone, interior view, showing gallery in south wall. *C. Maines.*

38. Maguelone, interior view to the south, showing archer slits in tribune. *Author.*

39. Maguelone, exterior view from the south, showing upper gallery. *C. Maines.*

40. Maguelone, detail of west portal: Saint Peter. *Author.*

41. Agde, aerial view of cathedral. *Reproduced with the permission of Editions d'Art Larrey.*

42. Agde, plan of town. *Adapted from A. Castaldo.*

43. Agde, plan showing excavated apse and destroyed cloister. *P. de Gorsse, 1920, after M. Martin, 1873.*

44. Agde, exterior view of the church from the southwest. *Author.*

45. Agde, interior view of the church to the east. *Author.*

46. Agde, plan of church. *Surveyed and drawn by author.*

47. Agde, interior view of the church to the west, showing northwest bay with original elevation. *C. Maines.*

48. Saint-Pons-de-Thomières, plan of abbey fortifications. *Société Archéologique de Montpellier. Reproduced with the permission of the Société.*

49. Saint-Pons-de-Thomières, plan of town fortifications. *J. Sahuc, 1900, after plan by François Boudène, 1699.*

50. Saint-Pons-de-Thomières, aerial view from the northeast (eighteenth-century façade is at the east on the site of the destroyed chevet). *Reproduced with the permission of Editions Cap-Théojac/Compa-Carterie.*

51. Saint-Pons-de-Thomières, interior view toward the east. *C. Maines.*

52. Saint-Pons-de-Thomières, phased plan of church. *Black:* Twelfth-century; *Outline:* Fifteenth- and sixteenth-century; *Diagonal shading:* Eighteenth-century. *Surveyed and drawn by author.*

53. Saint-Pons-de-Thomières, interior view of northern bay, showing original elevation. *C. Maines.*

54. Saint-Pons-de-Thomières, exterior view of the nave, north side. *Author.*

55. Saint-Pons-de-Thomières, exterior view of the nave, north side, detail. *Author.*

56. Saint-Pons-de-Thomières, plan of church from 1950 *Congrès archéologique,* showing excavated apse, marked A on the plan. *M. Durliat and J. Pelissier. Reproduced with the permission of M. Durliat.*

57. Saint-Pons-de-Thomières, phased sequence of plans and reconstruction views: (A) Eleventh-century; (B) Twelfth-century; (C) Fifteenth- and sixteenth-century; (D) Eighteenth-century. *Adapted from A. and P. Granier, 1938.*

58. Saint-Pons-de-Thomières: (A) Plan of lower gallery; (B) Plan of upper gallery. *Black:* Twelfth-century; *Outline:* Later fabric. *Surveyed and drawn by author.*

59. Saint-Pons-de-Thomières, section of church. *Surveyed and drawn by author.*

60. Saint-Pons-de-Thomières, reconstruction section. *Surveyed and drawn by author.*

61. Maguelone, interior of the church, nineteenth-century view to the west, showing upper gallery with timber balustrade before reconstruction. *From P. Lacaze, Maguelone, n.d.*

62. Maguelone, plans of (A) tribune and (B) upper levels, showing gallery system. *Surveyed and drawn by author.*

63. Maguelone, exterior view, southwest. *A. Javary, 1861. Courtesy J.-C. M. Richard.*

64. Maguelone, excavation plan of the site. *Courtesy J.-C. M. Richard, excavation director, adapted from plan by F. Siragusa. Surveyed by C. Rouvarel, with corrected church plan by author.*

65. Agde, axonometric section. *Adapted from M. Adgé.*

66. Agde, roof of the church, showing machicolation slots. *C. Maines.*

67. Saint-Pons-de-Thomières, interior view of narthex, showing gallery. *C. Maines.*

68. Saint-Pons-de-Thomières, western passage of lower gallery. *C. Maines.*

69. Saint-Pons-de-Thomières, detail of west façade showing archer slits which open from the lower gallery. *Author.*

70. Saint-Pons-de-Thomières, machicolation, north side (exterior view of slot shown in Fig. 71). *Author.*

71. Saint-Pons-de-Thomières, machicolation, north side (interior view of slot shown in Fig. 70). *C. Maines.*

72. Silvanès, interior view. *Reproduced with the permission of Editions Zodiaque.*

73. Temple of Diana, Nîmes, view. *From R. Naumann,* Der Quellbezirk von Nîmes, *Berlin: Walter de Gruyter, 1937. Reproduced with the permission of the Deutsches Archäologisches Institut.*

74. Temple of Diana, Nîmes, section and plan. *From R. Naumann,* Der Quellbezirk von Nîmes, *Berlin: Walter de Gruyter, 1937. Reproduced with the permission of the Deutsches Archäologisches Institut.*

75. Aix-en-Provence, cathedral plan and section. *After R. Guild, Jr., La Cathédrale d'Aix-en-Provence. Etude Archéologique, Paris: CNRS, 1987. Reproduced with the permission of Rollins Guild, Jr.*

76. Béziers, plan of twelfth-century cathedral of Saint-Nazaire and claustral complex. *Black:* Twelfth-century fabric; *Outline:* Gothic. *Adapted from Y. Esquieu.*

77. Comparative section of aisled and hall church. *Author.*

78. Porta Nigra, Trier, plan at upper story. *After E. Vergnolle.*

79. Distribution map of surviving machicolated monuments. *Author.*

80. Armenian slot machicolation, diagram (arrow indicates passage of projectile). *Author.*

81. Ukhaidir, view of machicolations. *From Creswell,* Early Muslim Architecture, *Oxford: Clarendon Press, 1940.*

82. Ukhaidir, plan, detail. *From Creswell,* Early Muslim Architecture, *Oxford: Clarendon Press, 1940.*

INDEX

The Index covers material in both the main text and the Appendixes. For the Appendixes, reference is given to the English translation rather than to the parallel Latin text, although in most cases the page reference is identical for both. Figures are indicated by the relevant page number followed by "fig." Proper names have been standardized to English (e.g., "Petrus" becomes "Peter"). Where, however, the individual is reasonably well-known in the literature by a French name, I have kept that name (e.g., "Pierre de Melgeuil" rather than "Peter of Melgeuil"). *Sancti Stephani* is thus translated as "Saint Stephen," but the cathedral of Agde remains "Saint-Etienne."